FROM DIVISION
TO UNIFICATION

New Edition

Ian Derbyshire

Chambers

First published by Sandpiper Publishing as a *Sandpiper Compact*, 1985
First edition published by W & R Chambers Ltd, 1987
Reprinted 1988

This edition published 1991 by W & R Chambers Ltd,
43–45 Annandale Street, Edinburgh EH7 4AZ

British Library Cataloguing in Publication Data
A catalogue record for this book is available from the British Library

ISBN 0-550-20751-1

Cover design by James Hutcheson

Typeset by Hewer Text Composition Services, Edinburgh
Printed in England by Clays Ltd, St Ives plc

Contents

List of Tables

Preface

Originally, this *Spotlight* was conceived as a study of West German politics since the mid-1970s, examining, in its first edition, the transition from the Social Democratic Party (SPD) and Free Democratic Party (FDP) federal coalition led by Helmut Schmidt to, following the *Machtwechsel* of 1982–3, governance by a new conservative-liberal alliance led by Helmut Kohl. Attention was directed at the different policy programmes pursued during the late Schmidt and early Kohl eras; at the growing fissures within the SPD and concurrent emergence of the environmentalist Greens; and at the splits within the FDP and between the Christian Democratic Union (CDU) and its Bavarian sister party, the Christian Social Union (CSU), as conflicts emerged over defence and economic policy.

In the light of the dramatic events of 1989–90, the *Spotlight* has, however, been recast, being broadened substantially so as to embrace coverage of political developments in both Germanies, before and after reunification. Particular attention is accorded to the means by which German reunification was achieved in October 1990 and to the political, social and economic consequences of merger and the early problems encountered. A new chapter covering East German politics since 1949 has also been included.

In Part Five, recent economic and social developments in western Germany are examined. These include the changing energy balance, demographic movements, industrial restructuring, the economy's southward shift, and trade unions' estrangement as the 'social market economy' consensus has begun to crumble. Part Six looks at influences on the Federal Republic's external relations.

Figure 1: The Länder of the New Germany

Part One

GERMAN POLITICAL AND CONSTITUTIONAL DEVELOPMENT

Chapter 1

HISTORICAL FOUNDATIONS

From Empire to Weimar Republic

Political unity came late to Germany. In 1815 a large confederation of 39 principalities covered the German empire, with Prussia in the east and Habsburg Austria to the south vying for supremacy. During the 1860s Prussia, guided by its astute Prime Minister, Otto von Bismarck (1815–98), established hegemony over the smaller north German states, but not until 1871 was the polyglot German confederation fully united. A further eventful eight decades were needed before political stability and a liberal democracy was finally established.

One factor behind this laggardly democratic development had been the slow pace of industrial growth in 'late developing' Imperial Germany. There had been small pockets of industrialization before 1850 in the Rhineland and Saxony, but it took political unification, the establishment of the free-trading *Zollverein* and the spread of railways before Germany achieved economic 'take off'. Thus at the time of the 1848 revolution the German middle class was too weak to wrest any significant political concessions, while in the eastern half of the German empire the large semi-feudal *Junker* landlords continued to dominate. The traditional military and landed elite remained in power during the rest of the Imperial period buttressed through a nationalist and statist ideology, popularized by the romantic poets and philosophers, Goethe and Hegel, and through economic and military success. A democracy of types did emerge after 1871 with a bicameral parliament (*Reichstag*) and universal male suffrage, but it was the Prussian Emperor (*Kaiser*) and Prime Minister (*Chancellor*) who continued to wield real, practical power. Germany thus entered the twentieth century with an autocratic and paternalistic political and economic tradition, with the state involved in numerous fields of activity – for example, sickness and old age insurance tariff protection, and technical education.

Military defeat during the First World War finally brought the abdication of the Kaiser and the proclamation of a parliamentary republic – the Weimar Republic. This experiment with democracy was, however, short-lived, being doomed from the beginning, and it was destined to be superseded in 1933 by the autocracy of Adolf Hitler and National Socialism.

The Weimar Republic (1918–33) was encumbered by tremendous economic problems – brought on by postwar territorial losses, crippling reparation charges and the world depression – and by a flawed constitution which created a confused 'dual executive' consisting of a President, who was elected for a seven-year term and who enjoyed significant plebiscitary and emergency powers, and a Chancellor – the intended chief executive officer – who required both the confidence of the lower house and the support of the President. This shared executive form of government was similar in many respects to that later adopted in the contemporary French Fifth Republic (1958–). The key difference was in the electoral system, with the legislators of Weimar Germany being elected by a generous system of proportional representation which promoted the growth of a multitude of narrow splinter parties, each unable to obtain a governing majority, while Fifth Republic France has utilized a two-ballot 'run off' majority system. The Weimar period was thus one of coalition government and political instability, with 15 Chancellors holding office between 1919 and 1933. In the final years of the Weimar Republic, power shifted away from the parties and the Chancellor towards the conservative President, Von Hindenburg (1847–1934), before Hitler's National Socialists, having secured 33% of the popular vote in the November 1932 Reichstag election, gained power in January 1933. They proceeded to eliminate all significant opposition, pushing through an Enabling Act which granted Hitler full dictatorial powers in March 1933.

The 1933–45 Nazi Era and Its Consequences

The rise to power of Adolf Hitler (1889–1945) and the events of 1933–45 have clouded all subsequent judgments of German politics. Many have viewed Nazism as a logical outcome of Germany's historical and economic development, with its weak bourgeoisie and failed revolutions, and the German national psyche, with its tradition of firm, autocratic rule, statism, deference to authority and legendary discipline. In this interpretation, Germans, by nature, prefer direction from above and groupism to individualism and liberal democracy. Others have viewed the rise of Hitler as a chance development resulting from the specific economic circumstances of the early 1930s and his subsequent extreme nationalist and racist policies as unexpected aberrations. What is clear is that both the structural and economic circumstances of inter-war Germany provided, as in contemporary Italy, a fertile ground for fascism. Hitler did attract significant popular support, particularly from the north and Bavarian south of the nation, from Protestants, small towns, the lower middle classes, rural and marginal groups and the unemployed, and his remarkably successful interventionist and autarchic economic policies were a prime factor behind this popularity.

The Nazi regime proved in the end to be self-destructive, its expansionism meeting with increasing external resistance from the winter of 1942 as Soviet troops turned the tide at Stalingrad. The Third Reich finally collapsed in May 1945, following the suicide of Hitler as the Allies advanced upon Berlin, and the large German empire was thereafter dismembered. The eastern, Prussian, half was divided between Poland, the USSR and the newly created Soviet satellite, the German Democratic Republic (GDR). Out of the larger western portion, the Federal Republic of Germany (FRG) was constructed. It was placed under temporary Allied rule between 1945 and 1949, as a new stable democratic system was devised.

Chapter 2

The 1949–90 WEST GERMAN POLITICAL SYSTEM

Constitutional Foundations

The 1949 Grundgesetz

In the postwar Federal Republic rebuilding began first at the provincial or state (*Land*) level, where political parties began operating in the interim period. Then in September 1948 Allied military governors met with provincial leaders and set up a 65-member constituent assembly to draft a new provisional constitution (the Basic Law; *Grundgesetz*), which was ratified by the *Länder* parliaments in May 1949.[1] This, 146 article, provisional document survived to become the constitutional charter for the modern West German state. The chief concern of the architects of this document was to avoid the mistakes of the Weimar constitution and to prevent a revival of totalitarian Nazism. They aimed, first, at strengthening the authority of the Chancellor and the parliamentary parties vis-à-vis the President and the state bureaucracy and armed forces; second, at devolving significant powers to the provincial level; and third, at establishing the supremacy of the law. A unique and unusually successful 'liberal-democratic' political system was created, borrowing from British, American and European precedents.

The Strengthening of the Bundestag and the Chancellor

The powers of the President were drastically reduced in the Federal Republic after 1949. Instead of being directly elected by the public – as in the Weimar period – the President was now appointed, for a maximum of two five-year terms, by a Federal Convention (*Bundesversammlung*) composed of the members of the Bundestag and an equal number from the Länder assemblies. The President was thus destined to become just a party and parliamentary nominee (*see* Table 1) – a ceremonial figurehead, whose powers of intervention

4

were unusually limited.[2] Instead, in the West German state, real power was transferred to the lower house of parliament – the *Bundestag* (Federal Diet or Assembly) – and to the Chancellor (Prime Minister), who, through his political party, commanded a majority in this house.

TABLE 1   THE PRESIDENTS OF WEST GERMANY

	Party	Age on Election	Term in Office
Theodor Heuss	FDP	65	1949–1959
Heinrich Lübke	CDU	64	1959–1969
Gustav Heinemann	SPD	70	1969–1974
Walter Scheel	FDP	55	1974–1979
Karl Carstens	CDU	65	1979–1984
Richard von Weizsäcker	CDU	64	1984–1990

The new Bundestag, located in Bonn, was composed of at least 402 (later 496) full voting deputies[3] elected at regular four-year intervals[4] by a unique and complicated system of 'personalized proportional representation', termed the Additional Member System. Each adult was granted two votes, one – the *Erststimme* on the left side of the ballot paper – for a local constituency seat, the other – the *Zweitstimme* on the right side – for a party list covering his or her Land. Political parties were thus able to win seats both in the constituencies – from which 248 Bundestag members were being returned during the 1980s (being elected on a simple majority basis) – and within the Länder. The size of a party's list vote determined the final number of seats it would be entitled to from each region, with seats already gained at the constituency level being deducted from this proportionate number.

The Bundestag was made the key legislative body in postwar West Germany. It elected and controlled the federal government (i.e. the Chancellor and his cabinet),[5] selected one half of the members of the Federal Constitutional Court, and it supervised the work of the bureaucracy and armed forces. The Chancellor appointed a 16–20-member cabinet, taking account of the demands of party factions and coalition partners, and determined policy with the aid of a large, 450-member, specialist and supervisory private office (*Kanzleramt*), headed by a like-minded cabinet minister. The Bundestag scrutinized legislation through an increasingly vigorous system of 20 functional committees (each staffed by a chairperson and 17–33 members drawn from party *Fraktionen*[6] on a proportionate basis), through the use of a restrained Westminster-style 'question hour' (*Fragestunde*), and through petitions for debates or inquiries. It was, however, only able to remove a Chancellor through a 'constructive vote of no-confidence', whereby a majority of delegates voted not only to reject the incumbent, but also positively in favour of a new Chancellor. This was successfully accomplished on only one occasion, in October 1982.

The actual authority of the Chancellor vis-à-vis his cabinet colleagues and the Bundestag varied with the particular stature and personal qualities of each leader and the strength of his parliamentary party majority. During the period between 1949 and 1963 Konrad Adenauer (leader of the Christian Democratic Union – CDU) dominated West German politics to such an extent that the term 'Chancellor Democracy' was invented – with the Chancellor governing in an unusually dominant, almost authoritarian, fashion and exerting control over his ministers in a manner akin to that of the US President. Subsequently, however, as a consequence of the rise of the Social Democratic Party (SPD) as an alternative governing party, the regularization of coalition government and the increased assertiveness of Bundestag deputies, the Chancellor's authority diminished. The relationship between the Chancellor, the cabinet and elected chamber moved closer to the British prime ministerial model. Between 1974 and 1982, there was a revival in the use of the term 'Chancellor Democracy', as Helmut Schmidt took decisive personal control over key sectors of federal government activity. Schmidt's successor as Chancellor, Helmut Kohl, was, however, somewhat less assertive, leaving greater scope for policy making in the hands of individual, specialist cabinet ministers.[7]

Federalism and Regional Checks

One distinguishing feature of the West German political system was the devolution of significant powers to its constituent regions. Such devolution was a consequence of the early regrowth of local democracy during the interim period between 1946 and 1949 and of a desire to diffuse political power. It also, however, reflected the continuing strength of regionalist culture and sentiment which has resulted from Germany's long tradition of strong state-level government.

Figure 2: West German Länder

West Germany, up to unification, was (exclusive of West Berlin: *see* Appendix D) composed of 10 Länder, which varied substantially in size from the large states of Bavaria and North-Rhine-Westphalia, each with a population in excess of 10 million, to the tiny city-states of Hamburg and Bremen (*see* Figure 2 and Appendix A). Each Land possessed its own miniature government headed by a minister-president and supported by an elected assembly, written constitution, and constitutional court.[8] These Länder parliaments (*Landtage*) had only a few original powers (mainly, *see* Table 2, involving the police, local government, and education), but they, through their own sizeable civil services, were responsible for carrying out the administration of federal matters (excluding defence, foreign policy and currency affairs) within their region.[9] They had thus discretion in implementing federal priorities and they had powers of taxation and a voice in the assignation of revenue. Thus whereas in Great Britain, for example, the local governments were responsible for only a quarter of total government spending and were dependent on the centre for a half of their revenue, in West Germany more than 60% of government spending was carried out by the Länder and bodies below, who received their own sizeable shares of income tax and VAT and only a quarter of their revenue from Bonn. The significant powers held by Länder parliaments meant that state elections were hard-fought (with turnouts in excess of 70% – compared to 40% in Britain – and with contests being seen as important tests of national midterm popularity) and that Länder attracted talented politicians, using the state stage for subsequent entries into the higher levels of federal politics. The power wielded by Länder governments also meant that federal ministers were forced to compromise over programmes and enter into backroom agreements with Länder officials and that many federal policies – for example, economic reflation and the introduction of comprehensive education during the 1970s and privatization and conservative economic liberalism during the 1980s – were substantially thwarted. During the 1980s, the public profile of the minister-presidents of the larger Länder increased, with state leaders emerging as unusually assertive champions for their Land economy, establishing lobbying offices at the European Community headquarters at Strasbourg and Brussels and engaging in personal international diplomacy of their own.

The Länder in addition were granted, under the 1949 Basic Law, a powerful voice at the federal level in Bonn in the second chamber of government, the *Bundesrat* (Federal Council). This upper house consisted of 41 voting delegates sent and instructed by Länder

TABLE 2   LEGISLATIVE COMPETENCES OF THE FEDERATION
AND LÄNDER OF WEST GERMANY

Federation (Bund)	Länder
EXCLUSIVE POWERS	EXCLUSIVE POWERS
Foreign affairs	Cultural affairs (incl. broadcasting)
Defence	Education
Citizenship	Health service
Passports, immigration, etc	Police
Currency matters	Organization of local government
Customs & free movements of goods	
Post and telecommunications	

THE FRAMEWORK CONDITIONS SET BY FEDERATION[1]
Principles of higher education
Hunting & conservation
The press & the film industry
Land distribution & regional planning

CONCURRENT POWERS
Civil & criminal law & sentencing
Registration of births, deaths & marriages
The law of association & assembly
Residence & establishment of aliens
Production & use of nuclear energy

[1] The Länder were required to incorporate the framework conditions in their own legislation.

governments. The four largest regions sent five delegates, the three intermediate Länder, four delegates, and the three smallest Länder, three delegates (see Table 6).[10] This system favoured the small Länder, with Bremen, for example, sending one delegate per 224 000 people, compared to North-Rhine-Westphalia's one delegate per 3.4 million citizens. Delegates were chosen by ruling Länder parties and voted in blocs – opposition parties in regions not being represented. The Bundesrat was given no real powers of initiating legislation but it formed an important constitutional check with three main spheres of influence. First, all legislation which directly related to Länder responsibilities required Bundesrat approval – more than 60% of Bundestag bills fell into this category by the 1980s. Second, a two-thirds majority in the Bundesrat (as well as in the Bundestag) was required for constitutional amendments.[11] Third, on other matters the Bundesrat could suggest amendments to Bundestag legislation, send disputed items to a 'joint conciliation committee' (*Vermittlungsausschuss*) drawn equally from both houses, and could temporarily block bills until a countervailing vote of either 50% or 66% in the Bundestag was passed.[12]

The Bundesrat held plenary sessions for voting on legislation only once a month. The remainder of its work was effected in committees which were staffed by senior Länder civil servants who were allowed to deputize for their Länder ministers and minister-presidents. Despite this complexion, however, the political nature and importance of the Bundesrat increased over time. In particular, during the 1970s, the CDU, enjoying a Bundesrat majority, used the body to block and delay Bundestag legislation passed by the dominant SPD-FDP coalition.[13] In an attempt to place restrictions upon such activities, the Federal Constitutional Court decided in 1974 that new Bundestag legislation which merely amended statutes which had already been passed by the Bundesrat would no longer require further upper house approval. Despite this ruling, however, the indirectly elected Bundesrat remained an influential and controversial body. Such was the continued strength of regional power in a polity that, during the 1980s, West German federal politicians sought its reduction to facilitate policy co-ordination in an increasingly complex modern society. This contrasted with the movement against excessive centralization experienced concurrently in neighbouring Western democracies.

The Rule of Law

A second check and balance was built into the West German political system through the creation of a written constitution (the Basic Law) and the establishment of the Federal Constitutional Court as a policing body.

West Germany, like other continental countries, had inherited a codified legal system, influenced by Roman practice, in which judges acted merely as neutral executers and administrators even during the excesses of the 1933–45 Third Reich. This contrasted with the judge-made and interpreted law of Britain and the United States. The Allied occupying powers were anxious to move closer towards the latter system through granting certain courts the power of judicial review. They thus set up, at Karlsruhe, the Federal Constitutional Court (*Bundesverfassungsgericht*) to act as final arbiter in constitutional questions and as the guarantor of civil liberties.

This court, which was independently financed, was composed of

16 judges, qualified in law and appointed for a 12-year, non-renewable term up to the retirement age of 68 years. Half of these judges were selected by the Bundesrat and half by the Bundestag. They were each nominated by a balanced selection committee and required a two-thirds majority of support – a fair balance of different party representatives was thus ensured, with extremists being excluded by the 66% rule. The Court was responsible for ensuring that Länder rights were upheld, that the correct balance was maintained between federal and Länder interests, that government organs acted constitutionally, and that the individual civil rights set out in Articles 1–19 of the Basic Law – the freedoms of speech, assembly, association, security and choice of employment – were maintained. Opposition politicians in the Bundestag could thus use the body to challenge legislation on the grounds of constitutional legality. The Constitutional Court was held in high regard by the West German public and, although subject to political appointment and less confident and 'activist' than the United States Supreme Court, was not afraid on occasion to controversially overturn federal decisions. Indeed, between 1951 and 1987 it deemed 156 laws to be contrary to the constitution.

Political Stability and Mature Democracy

The checks and balances created by the Basic Law proved remarkably successful in creating a popular and stable democratic system during the decades since 1949. There were only six different Chancellors during the 41 years of the Fourth Reich and two major political parties dominated the parliamentary arena. Although foreign observers constantly sought to uncover the evidence of cracks in West German democracy and anticipated a lurch back towards autocracy, postwar West German politics, in comparison to French, Italian or British, were unusually tranquil and consensual. This fed through to the West German economy which enjoyed four decades of unparalleled growth and prosperity. The creation of a strong 'party-state' controlled by two sensible, modern political parties was the key ingredient during this harmonious era.

The Party State

Germany's political parties had opposed Nazism, before they were themselves outlawed in 1933. They were thus seen as the true bastions of democracy around which the new West German polity should be constructed. The framers of the Basic Law, therefore, gave a special role to the new parties in 'forming the political will of the people'. They thus introduced (from 1959) state financing of parties and extended the authority of parties over the bureaucracy (now staffed at its upper levels by party members), military and judiciary – groups who had been dangerously independent during the Imperial and Weimar periods. Such was to be the all-pervading influence of postwar political parties, with their powerful, well-funded apparatuses, that West Germany came to be termed a 'party-state' (*Parteienstaat*). This state was dominated by two major parties, the CDU and SPD, who, individually or in coalition with minor parties, held political power for 25 and 13 years respectively during the period between 1969 and 1990, and governed together between 1966 and 1969. A third minor party, the Free Democratic Party (FDP) participated in coalition governments with each of these two parties for 34 of these 41 years (*see* Table 3).

TABLE 3   FEDERAL GOVERNMENTS IN WEST GERMANY

	Coalition Parties	*Chancellor*	*Departure*
1949–1963	CDU–CSU, FDP[1]	Adenauer	Resignation
1963–1966	CDU–CSU, FDP	Erhard	Resignation
1966–1969	CDU–CSU, SPD	Kiesinger	Election defeat
1969–1974	SPD, FDP	Brandt	Resignation
1974–1982	SPD, FDP	Schmidt	Bundestag defeat
1982–1990	CDU–CSU, FDP	Kohl	—

[1] Also involved in the coalition between 1949 and 1961 were the DP German Party and, between 1953 and 1957, the BHE expellees party. The FDP left the coalition between 1957 and 1961.

Such party dominance was unusual. During the Imperial and Weimar era Germany had been famed for its weak and diffuse party system. More than a dozen political parties vied for power, with half of these gaining significant electoral support. This profusion of political parties had been a consequence of both the late and uneven economic development of pre-war Germany and of its electoral system.

The economic and social revolution wrought by the Nazi era and the constitutional innovations of 1949 overcame these barriers to political maturity. The Nazi and wartime period first speeded up the pace of industrial development and urbanization and removed traditionalist elites – reducing all groups to the same level and bequeathing a dissevered nation in 1945. This essentially destructive period paradoxically helped modernize the German nation, providing the flattened and, with the loss of East Germany, homogenous base from which the successful Fourth Reich could be constructed anew, and it provided an environment in which new broadly based, non-sectional, 'catch-all' parties could later flourish. Continuing industrialization and urbanization during the postwar decades and the constitutional changes of 1949 reinforced this shift away from diffusion to concentration in the party system. The most significant constitutional innovations were Article 21 Section 2, which granted the Constitutional Court the power to ban extremist anti-democratic political parties (this was used in 1952 against the neo-Nazi SRP, in 1956 against the communist KPD, and in 1989 against *Nationale Sammlung*, or National Gathering), and the changes made in the electoral rules.

During the Weimar period an extreme pure proportional representation system operated in which the country was divided up into 35 giant constituencies and where it was possible for local regionalist parties to win seats with barely 0.2% of the national vote. The framers of the 1949 constitution introduced, by contrast, the 'personalized proportional representation' system built around 248 individual constituencies (with an average of 240000 voters each by the 1980s) and a parallel Länder list. This represented a compromise between the British and American 'first-past-the-post' and the Weimar list systems which became buttressed by the additional rule introduced in 1956 that a party was required to win more than 5% of the federal vote or three constituencies outright in order to qualify for seats. (Between 1953 and 1956 the 5% clause applied only to the Land vote.) This change precipitated the demise during the early 1950s of minor regionally-based parties, such as the Bavarian Party, the right-wing northern Protestant, Lower-Saxony based, German Party and the BHE expellees party; it also propelled the movement towards a three-party state with the CDU and SPD dominating, yet unable to gain a full Bundestag majority, and with the FDP acting as a crucial 'hinge' party and coalition partner. In 1949 these three principal parties gained 72% of the total federal vote, in 1957 90% and in 1976 99% (*see* Table 4). Only from 1978 with the rise of the ecological Green Party as a significant minor party did cracks begin to appear in this established 'two-and-a-half' party system.

TABLE 4   PARTY SHARES OF BUNDESTAG ELECTION VOTES: 1949–87 (% OF ZWEITSTIMMEN LIST VOTE)

	1949	1953	1957	1961	1965	1969
CDU–CSU	31.0	45.2	50.2	45.3	47.6	46.1
SPD	29.1	28.8	31.8	36.2	39.3	42.7
FDP	11.9	9.5	7.7	12.8	9.5	5.8
GREENS	—	—	—	—	—	—
Electoral Turnout	78.5%	85.8%	87.7%	87.7%	86.8%	86.7%
	1972	1976	1980	1983	1987	
CDU–CSU	44.9	48.6	44.5	48.8	44.3	
SPD	45.8	42.6	42.9	38.2	37.0	
FDP	8.4	7.9	10.6	6.9	9.1	
GREENS	—	—	1.5	5.6	8.3	
Electoral Turnout	91.1%	90.7%	88.6%	89.1%	84.4%	

The Christian Democratic Union (CDU)

The CDU dominated West German politics and government during the first two decades of the Fourth Reich and subsequently remained the single most popular political party throughout the postwar era. The roots of the CDU went back to the Catholic Party of the Imperial period (set up to protect Catholic rights) and the Centre Party, which had played a prominent role in the coalitions of the Weimar era. However, the postwar CDU, while still centred around a core of church-going Catholic support (Catholics provided 59% of the party's membership in 1982), became a far broader alliance of both centre-left and centre-right Protestants and Catholics who had resisted National Socialism and who were determined to defend the new postwar liberal democratic and anti-Soviet West German state.

The CDU benefited from the division of Germany – which resulted in the loss of radical Protestant, socialist-orientated areas to the GDR – and was able to firmly establish itself in the large rural, Catholic Länder of southern and western Germany (Bavaria, Rhineland-Palatinate and Baden-Württemberg) and in rural Protestant Schleswig-Holstein and Lower Saxony. With its strong Länder base, the CDU emerged as the largest single federal party in 1949 and came to permanently dominate the Bundesrat. During the 1950s support for the party expanded rapidly as the CDU absorbed minor regional and centre-right parties, gained a further support base in the industrialized Catholic Saar (which was restored to the

Federal Republic in 1957) and successfully presided over the economic and political rejuvenation of the Federal Republic. The CDU integrated West Germany into NATO (1955) and the new European Community (1957), while at home its economics expert, Ludwig Erhard (Minister for Economic Affairs, 1949–63), devised a new economic policy, the 'social market economy' (*Soziale Marktwirtschaft*), which proved to be the ruling philosophy for the successful postwar West German state. Under this formula, free-market forces were encouraged and income inequalities tolerated, while the government was left to 'steer' the economy in a socially responsible fashion – reconciling the interests of capital and labour, guarding against the formation of dangerous monopolies and providing the infra-structure of a modern welfare state. This policy proved to be a great success and helped to win over to the CDU new blue- and white-collar secular groups, converting it into a broad-church *Volkspartei* (People's Party), with, by the 1970s, 35% of its support being drawn from the industrial workforce.

With such an electoral combination, the CDU was able to gain near majorities in the Bundestag between 1949 and 1966, governing with the support of the liberal FDP, and to control the majority of Länder and hence the Bundesrat. The hold of the CDU began to weaken, however, during the mid-1960s. Its rival for political power, the SPD, came to terms with contemporary conditions, changing its policies accordingly, while also offering attractive new initiatives, most notably *Ostpolitik*. At the same time, the CDU faced increasing internal problems. It had become too tied to the personally popular Adenauer and failed to strengthen its organization to give its leader greater control over its powerful Länder chiefs. Thus the CDU's subsequent chairmen – Ludwig Erhard (1966), Kurt Kiesinger (1966–70), Rainer Barzel (1970–3) and Helmut Kohl (1973–) – found it increasingly difficult to control what became a decentralized and faction-riven party (highlighted by the machinations of its right-wing Catholic offshoot in Bavaria, the Christian Social Union (CSU), led, until 1988, by Franz-Josef Strauss). Support for the CDU remained solid during the 1960s and early 1970s at between 45–48% of the electorate, but the SPD's vote increased significantly from 30% to almost 45% during the corresponding period, forcing coalition government in 1966, before the SPD, in combination with the FDP, eventually took over as the governing party in 1969. This left the CDU with only its Länder bases and Bundesrat majority to attempt to block unpalatable reforms.

The Social Democratic Party (SPD)

The SPD replaced the CDU as the party of government in 1969 and remained in power for the next 13 years. This party boasted a venerable political history dating back to the Bismarckian era (having been founded in 1875 at Gotha), with its early support being derived from industrial areas in response to a programme with strong Marxist leanings. On the eve of the First World War, the SPD had one million members and it became the major political party during the Weimar period, forming governments in 1919–20 and 1928–30. The policy stance of the SPD became more moderate during the 1920s, following the 1917 breakaway of the extremist USPD wing (later KPD) and the crushing of the Spartakus revolution in 1919. The SPD maintained a leadership in exile during the Nazi era and expected to sweep the election in 1949, but they were weakened by the loss of many bastions of support in East Germany and by the populist shift in the CDU programme. The party thus remained excluded from federal government until 1966. It did, however, control the state parliaments in the industrialized Länder of Hamburg, Hesse, Bremen and the Rhine-Ruhr belt of North-Rhine-Westphalia.

During the early postwar years the SPD, led by Kurt Schumacher (1949–52) and Erich Ollenhauer (1952–61), pursued a political programme radically opposed to that of the CDU and refused to engage in coalitions. They pressed for economic planning and nationalization and opposed European integration and re-armament. It became clear, however, after the 1957 Bundestag election, when Konrad Adenauer gained an absolute majority of the votes, that a radical change in policies would be required if the SPD was to break out of its '30% ghetto' and attract sufficient white-collar and middle-class support to form a future government. A campaign for reform was thus instigated by key figures within the SPD – Willy Brandt (the new mayor of West Berlin), Herbert Wehner (later the party's parliamentary Fraktion leader), Karl Schiller (its economic expert) and Helmut Schmidt. Their aim was to modernize the party and bring it into line with the changed circumstances of the postwar era of economic growth, political integration and changing social structures – with the increase in personal mobility, the expansion in the white-collar service sector, the decline in traditional class-based and religious allegiances, and the 'embourgeoisement' of the population. This campaign bore fruit at the party conference in Bad Godesberg in 1959, when a fundamental re-definition of Social Democracy was approved – disavowing the party's traditional Marxist connections, class orientation and anti-clericalism, and accepting the new 'social market economy' and membership of NATO and the EC. The SPD thus moved very close to the programme of the CDU, though showing a greater concern for social equality and a greater willingness to intervene and manage the economy.

With the adoption of this programme and the election of the charismatic Willy Brandt as chancellor-candidate in 1961 and party chairman in 1964, support for the SPD steadily increased during the 1960s. The party first tasted power in 1966, when, after the FDP had withdrawn support from the existing administration, the SPD joined forces with the CDU in a 'Grand Coalition' between 1966 and 1969. This provided an opportunity for the SPD to prove itself responsible and effective custodian of office, and the opportunity was grasped, with the SPD's economics minister, Karl Schiller, proving particularly adept at rescuing West Germany from the economic recession of 1966. This bore dividends in 1969, when a significant advance in the party's electoral support was recorded.

The SPD became the ruling party in the Bundestag between 1969 and 1982 (being led first by Willy Brandt between 1969 and 1974 and then by the pragmatic Helmut Schmidt between 1974 and 1982), partly as a result of this broadening in its electoral appeal and of contemporary demographic movements (the rise in the proportion of younger voters and male voters – a traditionally more radical psephological group), but also as a result of the changing coalition tactics of West Germany's third principal party, the FDP. Although the SPD's share of the Bundestag vote rose to above 40% during the elections between 1969 and 1976, only in 1972 did its total vote exceed that of the CDU (*see* Table 4). It was the additional 6–10% of electoral support provided by the FDP which allowed the SPD to put together governing majorities.

The Free Democratic Party (FDP)

The FDP, the heir of the ill-fated German liberal tradition, emerged as the crucial 'pivot' party around which the Federal Republic coalition system rotated. The party constantly held the balance of power and despite receiving only 10% or less of the popular vote, it captured over 20% of ministerial portfolios during the Fourth Reich and acted as a significant moderating force. Prior to 1966 the FDP, though ostensibly a liberal and non-sectarian party, allied itself with the conservative CDU: between 1969 and 1982 it formed regular pacts with the SPD, threatening to permanently squeeze the CDU out of federal power. Two factors explained this switch in allegiance – the moderation in the SPD policy programme following Bad Godesberg, and the progressivist shift in the FDP's stance, following the election of Walter Scheel as party chairman in 1968. The FDP had during the 1950s been dominated by marginal farming groups and by small town conservatives. However, during the mid-1960s its more radical wings, centred in Baden-Württemberg in the south-west and in Hamburg and Bremen, gained a stronger voice as the party increasingly orientated itself towards white-collar groups. The party, also attracted by Willy Brandt's espousal of conciliatory *Ostpolitik* and seeking to avoid absorption by the CDU, thus abandoned its pact with the CDU in 1966 and formed a new partnership with the SPD in 1969. In return the FDP was granted four significant ministries (foreign affairs, interior, agriculture and, after 1974, economics) in a cabinet of 13. In addition, the party's leader Walter Scheel was made federal President in 1974 and his successor Hans-Dietrich Genscher was appointed foreign minister and Vice Chancellor.

Political Maturity and Consensus Politics

West German politics became distinguished by a remarkable degree of political stability, with two major parties dominating, but with, as a result of its electoral system, coalition governments – invariably involving the FDP – having been the rule. The two principal parties, while retaining specific core areas of support (the CDU – church-going Catholics, rural groups, South Germans and the elderly: the SPD – industrial workers, urban areas and the young) and while still differing in philosophy and policy orientation, converged to an unusual degree. They competed strongly to win the fickle allegiance of the well-educated, often white-collar, modern 'classless' voter, the support of whom became crucial in the quest for political power. West Germany thus became a mature democracy with peaceful and increasingly regular alternations in governments and with a high degree of popular participation – Bundestag election turnouts averaging 84–91% compared to 70–75% in Britain.

West German political parties became geared to an unusual extent towards the acquisition and retention of this power, rather than ideological squabbles. Principled opposition was rare; instead coalition pacts were made in advance and, once in government, the Chancellor remained in office for his four-year term – scandals and unusual crises aside – unable, as for example in Britain – to seek an advantageous early dissolution. The absence of mid-term Bundestag by-elections (vacant seats being filled by unsuccessful candidates next on the party list), and the fact that an unusually high proportion of West German politicians were civil servants by background and that ministers were skilled, specialist technocrats, added to the administrative, rather than adversarial nature of the Federal Republic's politics – a form of politics concerned with utilizing rather than arguing over the acquisition of power.[14] Such a corporatist, consensual approach to politics was evident, above all, in the economic field with the co-operative, 'social-market' *Konzertierte Aktion* strategy of the government and the trade-union and managerial interest groups enshrined in the 1967 'Stability Law', which was to be an important factor behind the postwar West German 'economic miracle'.

Paradoxically, it was Germany's past history of fragile, insecure political democracy, coupled with the destruction of traditional power bases wrought by the Nazi Third Reich and the Second World War, which proved advantageous in the construction of a successful liberal democratic system during the postwar era. A new constitution and political system was framed afresh, learning from past mistakes and from the experience of other democracies. Checks and balances were built into a constitution which divided power between the centre and the regions, forcing compromise and co-operation between Bonn and the constituent states. New modern 'catch all' *Volksparteien* were to develop largely free from the class and interest group ties which encumbered political parties in neighbouring European countries and were to be led by responsible, moderate-minded leaders. From this base, a successful consensual and corporatist economic and political system emerged, with integration into the European Community solidifying and underpinning this democratic stability. However, despite these achievements, not all groups were satisfied with the 'Fourth and Richest Reich'. For a number of citizens there remained a lack of roots, ideals, purpose and radicalism in the Fourth Reich. Such feelings were reflected in the intermittent campaigns for German reunification, in the 1970s urban terrorist movement and in the 1980s rise of the ecologist Green Party. Even more serious problems were presented by the economic recession and new 'cold war' of the 1980s, which seriously undermined West Germany's post-1959

19

political consensus, creating widening divisions over defence and economic strategies between the CDU–CSU and the SPD.

However, the most profound challenge to the political system of the postwar Federal Republic was issued at the close of the 1980s by the onset of a 'new detente' between East and West and a deepening reform movement that was instituted in the USSR by Mikhail Gorbachev. By means of a cascading 'ripple effect', entailing, first, the flight from East Germany, Poland and USSR to the Federal Republic of tens of thousands of ethnic German refugees and then, eventually, a mass exodus from the GDR, leading to effective collapse of its economic and political structures, a unified New Germany was dramatically forged. Later, in Chapters 7–8, the process by which this union, or, more accurately, takeover of the GDR by the Federal Republic, was secured will be analysed. First, however, in the following chapter, the political bequest provided by the GDR and the impact that reunification has had upon the political structures of the Federal Republic, as now constituted, are detailed and assessed.

Chapter 3
THE POLITICAL SYSTEM OF THE NEW UNITED GERMANY

The GDR Inheritance: A Centralized Façade Democracy

Until the 'counter-revolution' of October–November 1989, the German Democratic Republic, had upheld a conventional Marxist-Leninist regime. As elsewhere in the Socialist Bloc, there had been two parallel channels of political authority: the state and the Communist Party.

The State Channel of Government

Lying at the heart of the state structure of authority was the national legislative assembly, or *Volkskammer* (People's Chamber), a unicameral body, officially described in the 1968 constitution (as amended in 1974) as the 'supreme organ of state power'. It was composed of 500 deputies, directly elected for five-year terms, from 1971, by universal adult suffrage from 'block vote' lists presented in multi-member constituencies. Unlike, however, the Federal Republic's Bundestag, which averaged 60 plenary sessions each year, the Volkskammer met in full session very infrequently: only two to four times, each for a day, annually. Indeed, its deputies were part-time 'amateurs', receiving only travel expenses and loss of earnings compensation when required to be absent from work on official business. Thus, rather than being a true law-making and debating institution, the Volkskammer served instead as a formal forum for the unanimous ratification of decisions taken and bills and treaties conceived by bodies and individuals elsewhere. In short, it was a 'rubber-stamping' assembly, an *Akklamationsorgan*.

The more significant components of state authority were the committees or commissions of the Volkskammer, the Council of State (*Staatsrat*) and the Council of Ministers (*Ministerrat*).

The Volkskammer's functional committees, which numbered 15 during the 1980s, were responsible for examining the drafts of proposed legislation and investigating the implementation of laws. They could call in outside experts and ministers and public administrators to provide specialist and inside information.

The Council of State, a 29-member grouping 'elected' by the Volkskammer to serve as its permanent collective organ between sessions, was, initially, from its formation in 1960, a most influential body. Indeed, for more than a decade it functioned, in effect, as a 'substitute parliament', having the authority to issue decrees, to examine the constitutionality of laws and to direct the work of the Volkskammer's committees. However, in 1972, when the new Honecker administration became concerned to curb the authority of the Council's chairman, Walter Ulbricht, who had recently been ousted as Communist Party leader, it was to lose these powers. Thereafter, the Staatsrat was allowed only to pass 'resolutions'. However, it remained influential in relation to military and diplomatic matters, with the authority to appoint members of the National Defence Council and organize the country's defence, as well as representing the GDR in foreign relations. Headed from 1976 by Erich Honecker, the Communist Party leader, the Staatsrat's authority waxed somewhat during the 1980s.

However, from the early 1970s onwards, it was the Council of Ministers that was the most important locus of authority within the GDR's state system. Explicity referred to, under Article 76 of the constitution, as the nation's government (*Regierung*), it comprised between 40 and 50 members, including a chairman who (*see* Table 5) was viewed as the equivalent of a Western Prime Minister, though he was usually required to operate in a more collective environment. The chairman and fellow members of the Ministerrat, who were, in the main, either ministerial heads of state departments or chairmen of government agencies/commissions, were formally 'elected' by the Volkskammer for five-year terms, the chairman being drawn from the largest party group. Together they had charge of the nation's day-to-day executive government, the co-ordination of the work of ministries and the preparation of legislation. A smaller 12-member Presidium operated within the Ministerrat as its influential 'inner cabinet'.

TABLE 5   THE POLITICAL LEADERS OF THE GDR

Communist Party Leader[1]	Prime Minister[2]	Head of State[3]
Wilhelm Pieck (to 1950)	Otto Grotewohl (1949–64)	Wilhelm Pieck (1949–60)
Walter Ulbricht (1950–71)	Willi Stoph (1964–73)	Walter Ulbricht (1960–73)
Erich Honecker (1971–89)	Horst Sindermann (1973–6)	Willi Stoph (1973–6)
Egon Krenz (1989)	Willi Stoph (1976–89)	Erich Honecker (1976–89)
Dr Gregor Gysi (1989–90)	Hans Modrow (1989–90)	Egon Krenz (1989)
	Lothar De Maizière (1990)	Dr Manfred Gerlach (1989–90)
		Sabine Bergmann-Pohl (1990)

[1] Chairman of SED to 1950, general-secretary 1950–3 and 1976–90, first secretary 1953–76, chairman of PDS 1990.
[2] Chairman of the Council of Ministers.
[3] State President to 1960, chairman of Council of State 1960–90, president of Volkskammer 1990.

The 'Democratic Centralist' Hegemony of the SED

On the surface, the institutions of the state channel of government possessed considerable authority. However, their powers could not be exercised independently. This was a consequence, first, of the overarching authority asserted by the Communist Party (Socialist Unity Party: SED) and, second, of the fact that, at all levels, members of state bodies were not elected in an openly democratic, pluralist manner.

The SED's political predominance was made explicit in the opening two articles of the constitution, under which it was accorded a 'guiding', that is leading, role. It exercised this in two ways. First, its party committees and bureaux, which (*see* Chapter 7) functioned at all political levels, were assigned the task of overseeing and, effectively, directing the work of analogous state organizations. Second, and more directly, SED members were 'elected' to state assemblies and, through the *nomenklatura* system of reserved appointments, installed at the head of state agencies. However, it is true to say, not all assembly deputies were card-carrying SED members. This was because, instead of standing alone, the SED contested elections as part of a united-front organization, the National Front of the GDR, which included four allied 'satellite parties' and four 'mass organizations' to whom seat quotas were assigned. As a consequence, the SED *Fraktion* (group) within the Volkskammer comprised only 127 deputies during the 1980s, equivalent to a quarter of the chamber's total strength. However, a

Communist Party majority was ensured by the fact that a further 30% of deputies, drawn from the four 'mass organizations', were also members of the SED. Furthermore, within the institutions where real power actually resided, SED domination was much more pronounced. For example, the SED membership proportion within the Ministerrat and Staatsrat stood at around two-thirds, while the key posts of chairmen of these bodies were always held by a leading communist.

This still left a sizeable fraction of non-SED representatives within all state bodies, amounting to as much as 45% in the case of the Volkskammer. These members did not, however, act in an unpredictable, autonomous manner, breathing vitality into the political system. This was because of, first, the absence of genuine party pluralism and, second, the character of the electoral process in the GDR.

True pluralism was lacking since, as is later noted in Chapter 7, the four permitted 'allied parties', the Christian Democratic Union, the Democratic Peasants' Party, the Liberal Democratic Party and the National Democratic Party, were controlled, neutered organizations. Their memberships were constantly vetted by the State Security Agency, a 'clearing' from whom was required for those appointed to any positions of potential influence. In addition, the parties themselves were required to acknowledge the paramountcy of the SED and to pledge, in their statutes, a determination to work under the SED's guidance for the continued development of a socialist society.

Similarly, the electoral system failed to provide a measure of real choice and accountability. First, this arose because while, on paper, there was a requirement that the candidate lists that were presented needed to secure at least a 50% share of the vote, this was nullified, in practice, because only one 'party', the National Front, actually proffered aspirants. Second, voters were potentially afforded the opportunity to use their powers of discrimination since candidate lists usually contained more names than the seats available. However, social pressure ensured that few actually exercised this right. This was because in order to delete the names of unappealing nominees an elector was required to enter a special cubicle, drawing attention to him or herself. With little to be gained from such principled action and much to be lost, in terms of possible victimization and stigmatization as a troublesome critic of the regime, very few, or less than 0.1% of voters, failed to thoroughly endorse the official slate of candidates.

For these reasons the GDR polity was suffused at all levels by SED influence. Moreover, it was an influence, or more accurately mastery, that was itself to be concentrated within the upper reaches of the ruling party. This occurred because the SED, as well as state organs, under the terms of Article 47 of the constitution, operated in accordance with the key Leninist tenet of 'democratic centralism', the principle that subordinate organizations were compelled to comply in a disciplined, unquestioning manner with the decisions made and orders emanating from organs situated immediately above. As a consequence, in marked contrast to the Federal Republic, where subsidiarity, or the devolution of state functions to the lowest level of government at the first instance, was the governing creed, political and, through the central planning process, economic power was unusually concentrated in the GDR. It resided ultimately within the SED's Politburo, a small, *circa* 20-member executive cabinet, headed by the party's general-secretary. Orders emanating from this apical body were subsequently sent downwards via a chain of command running through both the party and state hierarchies. The checks and balances of authority and the parcellization of sovereignty, so prominent a feature of the Federal Republic, a polity variously dubbed the 'semi-sovereign state' and the 'state without a centre', were visibly absent. Below the Volkskammer, a comprehensive grid of assemblies or councils (*Räte*) functioned at the regional (*Bezirk*), urban (*Stadtkreis*) and rural (*Landkreis*) district and urban (*Stadtgemeinde*) and rural (*Landgemeinde*) municipality/commune levels. These could in no way, however, be compared to the *Landtage, Bürgerschafte, Kreise* and *Gemeinden* of the FRG since they lacked genuine autonomy.

The Political Institutions and Culture of the New Enlarged Federal Republic

A 'Fast-Track' Path to Reunification

When reunification of the two Germanies was mooted during the spring and summer months of 1990, two courses were available for achieving the goal.

The first, and the one favoured in Bonn by the opposition SPD, was by means of Article 146 of the FRG's Basic Law, involving negotiation of a new pan-German constitution. This would have entailed a genuine fusion of the two polities, with possibly a few advanced elements of the GDR's constitution, for example, social, and especially female, rights, being incorporated within a new Basic Law and with some rationalization of Länder boundaries, involving the merger of several of the smaller western states. However, such changes promised to be both time-consuming and contentious.

The second option was by means of Article 23, under the terms of which the GDR's Volkskammer, having reconstituted the eastern Länder, would vote for its own dissolution and for accession to the Federal Republic under the terms of the Grundgesetz. This constituted the 'fast-track' course to reunification and was one which had been earlier employed, in 1957, by the Saarland, which had previously been under French occupation. It was a path advocated by Bonn's ruling CDU-CSU-FDP coalition and was earnestly pursued by the post-communist government that was swept to power in the GDR following the free multi-party elections of March 1990. Preceded by the monetary union of the two states, which began on 1 July 1990, it was brought about, first, by the Volkskammer voting on 22 July 1990 to re-establish on 14 October 1990 the five Länder of East Germany, Brandenburg, Mecklenburg-West, Pomerania, Saxony, Saxony-Anhalt and Thuringia, which had been abolished by the SED regime in 1952. A month later, on 31 August 1990, a detailed, 900-page state treaty, setting out a timetable for and the precise details of reunification, was signed by the two German governments. This was followed, on 12 September 1990, by the Treaty of Final Settlement on Germany, which, ratified by the 'four powers' (Britain, France, the USA and the USSR) who, since 1945, had retained formal mastery over Berlin, accorded external blessing upon the reunification process. With no internal or external obstacles remaining, the two Germanies eventually became one on 3 October 1990 after the Volkskammer had voted on the previous day by the necessary two-thirds majority to dissolve itself so as to allow the eastern territories to amalgamate with the Federal Republic. As a temporary expedient, 144 former Volkskammer deputies were delegated to sit in the FRG's Bundestag as 'interim observers', pending the holding of all-German elections, the first since November 1932, on 2 December 1990. This election was duly held, marking the successful end point of the complex reunification operation. More accurately, however, the process had been one of takeover of East Germany by its larger western sibling. The Federal Republic had consumed the GDR.

The New Reunified Germany: The Federal Republic 'Writ Large'

The clearest evidence that absorption of East Germany, rather than true fusion, had occurred was, apart from such matters as national flags and anthems, the FRG's being retained, the limited extent to which the constitutional and party political system of the Federal Republic, as earlier described in Chapter 2, was to undergo substantial change.

Thus the federation's central institutions, the Bundestag, Bundesrat and Federal Constitutional Court, remained in place. Only in details of their sizes and future location were the first two, along with the Bundesbank[1], to be altered.

The Bundestag was enlarged from the existing 496 full-voting members to 662, 128 deputies being added for the five reconstituted eastern Länder, the so-called *Beigetretene Teile Deutschlands* (BGTD: 'newly adhered parts of Germany'), 28 for the newly merged Land of Berlin and 10 additional seats accorded to the western Länder. This gave the eastern territories, including Berlin, 23% of the Bundestag's seats, a proportion in line with its share of the all-German population. In the case of the Bundesrat, each of the five BGTD, comprising as they did (*see* Appendix A) individual populations ranging between 2 and 5 million, was assigned four seats. So also was Berlin. If not compensated for, this would have left the six new eastern Länder with a 37% share of Bundesrat mandates and nearly five times as many seats as the almost equally populous western Land of North-Rhine-Westphalia. On the grounds of equity, it was thus decided to amend Article 51 of the Basic Law so as to increase the Bundesrat representation of the four largest western Länder, with populations in excess of 7 million, from five to six seats. This led to the Bundesrat being increased in size from 41 full-voting members to 69 (*see* Table 6).

Swayed both by historical associations and the desire to make a symbolic gesture, as well as by popular pressure exerted by easterners (*Ossis*) who demanded that federal legislators become more intimately aware of the economic and social plight of their region, on 21 June 1991 the Bundestag decided, by the narrow margin of 337 votes to 320, to move from Bonn to the Reichstag in Berlin, the city which, under the terms of the 31 August 1990 Political Unification Treaty, had already been declared Germany's new official capital. This transfer, which would also involve the relocation of the federal government (*Bundesregierung*), was to be

**TABLE 6 BUNDESRAT SEATS HELD BY THE LÄNDER OF
THE NEW GERMANY**

Former West German Länder	Seats in new Bundesrat	Bundesrat (Old)	Former East German Länder	Seats in New Bundesrat
Baden-Wurttemberg	6	(5)	Brandenburg	4
Bavaria	6	(5)	Mecklenburg-Western Pomerania	4
Bremen	3	(3)	Saxony	4
Hamburg	3	(3)	Saxony-Anhalt	4
Hesse	4	(4)	Thuringia	4
Lower Saxony	6	(5)	TOTAL	20
North-Rhine-Westphalia	6	(5)		
Rhineland-Palatinate	4	(4)	Berlin	4[1]
Saarland	3	(3)		
Schleswig-Holstein	4	(4)		
TOTAL	45	(41)		

[1] West Berlin had four non-voting seats in the old West German Bundesrat.

effected in stages and to be completed within 12 years. It was anticipated that it would cost something in the region of DM 50 billion and would lead to the economic ruin of Bonn, a relatively small Rhineland city with a population of 300 000, of whom 100 000 were employed in federal government service, and where a new federal legislative chamber (*Bundeshaus*) was already in an advanced state of construction. A fortnight later, on 5 July 1991, Bonn had the consolation of hearing that the Bundesrat voted to defer a decision on transfer for at least two years. It seemed almost certain, however, that, in the course of time, it would follow the lower house and federal government to Berlin.

At the Länder level and below, replicas of western Germany's political, judicial, administrative, educational and penal institutions were immediately established in eastern Germany, in October 1990, replacing the existing, still substantially communist, structures. During the initial stages, thousands of civil servants and professionals were imported into the BGTD, attracted by tax perks and promotion incentives. At the same time, a major training and 're-education' programme was instituted for those eastern administrators, jurists, police officers and teachers whose services were retained.

The changes wrought upon the Federal Republic's party structure by reunification were, perhaps more surprisingly, restricted. The first all-German general election of December 1990 confirmed in power Chancellor Kohl's CDU-CSU-FDP coalition with an increased majority. The CDU's Richard von Weizsäcker had earlier, on 23 May 1989 (*see* Table 7), also been re-elected (unopposed) as the Federal Republic's President. Meanwhile, the SPD, with a slightly increased number of seats after December 1990, remained the chief opposition party.

TABLE 7 THE POLITICAL LEADERS OF THE NEW GERMANY

President	Dr Richard von Weizsäcker (CDU)	Re-elected May 1989
Chancellor	Dr Helmut Kohl (CDU)	From October 1990

However, one new minor party was added to the federal political spectrum by reunification, the Party of Democratic Socialism (PDS), the reformed and partially liberalized version of the former communist SED. In the December 1990 federal election it secured 17 Bundestag seats, benefiting from the temporary amendment to the FRG's electoral law. Exceptionally for this one poll, the 5% support cut-off rule for representation applied to the two, eastern and western, portions of the new Germany rather than to the Bund as a whole. However, the PDS's federal presence seemed certain to be transitory, it being likely to fall well short of the 5% federal hurdle in future Bundestag contests. Its prospects of enduring as a minor party force within the Landtage and municipal assemblies of eastern Germany were much better. However, the announcement at the June 1991 PDS congress that, over the course of the preceding 18 months, 90% of its members had resigned, leaving the party with an exceptionally top-heavy age structure – almost half of its remaining members were aged 60 or over – did not bode well for the PDS's longer-term fortunes.

The four established major and minor parties that had operated in the Federal Republic before reunification, the CDU, FDP, SPD and Greens, were each affected to varying degrees by the establishment of new branch structures and the infusion of new members, as they extended their operations into the eastern Länder, carrying out mergers with sibling parties based there.[2]

The East and West German CDUs formally united on 1 October 1990 at a congress held in Hamburg. After Helmut Kohl's election as chairman of the amalgamated party and Volker Rühe its general-secretary, the western German wing of the movement was clearly predominant. However, as a consolation, the eastern arm secured three out of the 10 seats on the party executive's enlarged presidium and Lothar de Maizière, the GDR CDU's former leader, served as the Federal Party's deputy chairman, until his embittered resignation in September 1991. The merger initially brought into the party something in the region of 130000 new members, drawn both from the former East German CDU, which had formally broken with its past as an SED 'satellite party' in December 1989 and had swept aside many of its local and national leaders, and from the Democratic Peasants' Party, which had fused with the CDU earlier in 1990. These new members were predominantly Protestant, materially poorer than their western associates, and strong supporters of generous welfare provision. Their accession thus strengthened the federal party's so-called left wing, represented by such liberals as Kurt Biedenkopf who was to become minister-president of the eastern Land of Saxony. Biedenkopf's election to this position was an all too typical example of the 'helicoptering in' of adroit western German politicians to take charge of the BGTD's fledgling party machine. This occurred because eastern Germany's indigenous politicians lacked experience of fighting truly competitive election campaigns and were also peculiarly vulnerable to electorally damaging charges of former collaboration with the reviled SED regime.

In terms of the infusion of new members, the FDP was affected by reunification to an even greater extent than the CDU. Indeed, when, on 11 August 1989 at a special congress held in Hanover, the West German FDP amalgamated with the East German League of Free Democrats, a body comprising the restructured Liberal Democratic Party and the GDR FDP, established November 1989, to form the new FDP-Liberals, two-thirds of the amalgamated party's combined membership of 206000 was drawn from the BGTD, the majority of whom were 'social liberals'. Nevertheless, it was the western FDP's leader Count Otto Lambsdorff who was elected the merged party's new chairman and three out of the five deputy leadership positions also went to West Germans.

Of all western Germany's established political parties, the SPD appeared, from an historical perspective, potentially, to have the most to gain from reunification. This was because during the Weimar democracy era it had polled strongly in the industrialized regions of eastern Germany, especially in Saxony and Thuringia's leading cities. However, during the intervening period the forced merger of the SPD with the German Communist Party to form the SED in 1946 had led to the total destruction of the SPD's eastern party machine and when, in October 1989, an independent Social Democratic Party was eventually re-founded within the GDR, it proved very difficult for its leaders and members to emancipate themselves fully in the electorate's minds from this protracted alliance. Indeed, the first leader of this new eastern party, Ibrahim Böhme, was forced to step down in April 1990 after widely publicized allegations, subsequently shown to be baseless, that he had formerly worked as a Stasi informer. For these reasons, when a formal merger was eventually effected with the West German SPD, at a special congress held in West Berlin on 27–28 September 1990, the eastern SPD was able to bring into the new party barely 30000 members. This led to its being swamped by a 9:1 margin by its western 'comrades', who also, not surprisingly, dominated its leadership councils.

Unlike western Germany's other significant federation-wide parties, the Greens decided not to merge with their eastern sisters prior to the December 1990 all-German poll. This was partly a consequence of the party's innate preference for maintaining a decentralized organizational structure, but also of the fact that the eastern Greens, who had emerged in November 1989, were fighting this contest in affiliation with Alliance '90, an intelligentsia-led coalition of citizens' rights groupings. Damaged perhaps by this disunion and certainly impaired by the unpopular position that they chose to adopt on the issue of reunification, the western Greens failed to secure representation in the new all-German Bundestag, admittedly by a narrow margin. However, the eastern Greens, helped by their alliance with the popular local citizens' movements, captured two seats. This persuaded the two wings of the party to merge formally, the day after the Bundestag contest.

The Political Cultures of the New Germany: Set to Fuse or Collide?

Though initially apparently impotent, and dominated, indeed almost colonized, by *Wessi* ('westerner') politicians, in the longer term the Federal Republic's six new eastern Länder will undoubtedly exert a progressive influence on both the manner in which the German polity operates and the outlook and values of its leaders and political parties.

First, the decision-making process, already tortuous in the pre-unification FRG, will undoubtedly become more complicated. Representatives from 16, rather than 10, Länder will now haggle within the Bundesrat and the fault-lines for coalition-building within this council, and also on the political stages of the Länder, are likely to be shifted. In the long term, this may serve to exacerbate the diffusion of authority within the Federal Republic, weakening the centre in relative terms. In the shorter term, however, as was the case in 1930s 'New Deal' America, the pressing need for economic reconstruction within the eastern Länder and their own shortage of local financial resources may, perhaps, temporarily result in the federal government realizing a more interventionist role, at least within the BGTD. Furthermore, internationally, the federal government's relative standing and influence is undoubtedly set to be augmented by reunification's economic and geo-political consequences. Overnight, from 3 October 1990, the Chancellor has been transformed into the leader of a nation which, with a population of almost 80 million and a GDP of $1300 billion, in 1990, is indisputably Europe's economic king. In addition, with a frontier shifted several hundred kilometres eastwards, the FRG now finds itself strategically positioned as a commercial and diplomatic 'bridge' between East and West.

Second, throughout the 1990s the domestic party political agenda seems set to be dominated by issues directly or indirectly associated with the problems encountered in reconstructing and integrating, socially and economically, the new eastern Länder. Pre-eminent will be financial, economic and environmental concerns. Another contentious topic will be harmonization of the two regions' abortion laws, with it having been decided, under the terms of the August 1990 Political Unification Treaty, to allow eastern Germany's existing, and comparatively liberal, abortion regime to continue for a two-year transitional period.

Third, as already suggested, it seems likely that the ideological balance within two of the key component parties' of the governing coalition, the CDU and FDP, will be gradually tilted somewhat leftwards, in a 'social liberal' direction, as these parties' new recruits from the east begin to exert increasing influence within their policy making councils.

Many of the longer-term political consequences of reunification appear likely to be benign. However, in the short term considerable anxieties surround the possible repercussions of what remains an untested endeavour, the assimilation of 17 million people brought up for more than a generation in a state-directed, monist political and economic environment into a new, unfamiliar society governed by the contrasting individualist and competitive principles of liberal democratic capitalism. During the immediate aftermath of reunification, easterners, indeed, endured a severe 'psychological shock' as they were abruptly exposed to this alien political and socio-economic culture. Furthermore, this trauma was exacerbated during 1991 by a steep climb in the level of unemployment within the BGTD, as the region's economy hit rock bottom. Without an historically rooted sense of party identification and with a recently acquired disposition to 'take to the streets' to publicize their political and material demands directly, Ossis, in these difficult economic circumstances, became prey to the superficial attractions of populist extremists, particularly of the right, who offered simple, instant solutions. Evidence of this was furnished by the disturbing rise of racial xenophobia in the BGTD during 1991, fuelled by Ossi resentment of their perceived second-class, economic and political, status within the new Germany. The fact that easterners had their own Länder institutions did help, to some extent, to lighten this sense of disorientation. Nevertheless, during the demanding period of reconstruction and integration that lay ahead, the famed political stability of the Federal Republic seemed set to be presented with its most exacting challenge.

A more extended examination of the difficulties confronted during the early stages of this reconstruction process is provided later in Chapter 9. First, however, in Part Two, political developments in the pre-unification FRG are described and analysed.

Part Two

THE FEDERAL REPUBLIC: 1969–90

Chapter 4

THE BRANDT-SCHMIDT ERA: 1969–82

SPD-FDP Dominance – CDU Re-appraisal: 1969–76

The Brandt-Schmidt Reform Coalitions

The SPD-FDP coalition replaced the CDU in 1969 and continued in office for a further 13 years. This *Machtwechsel* (change of power) ushered in a new and more reformist era in which Chancellor Brandt declared his willingness to 'risk more democracy', improve social justice and encourage greater participation in the political arena. The voting age was lowered to 18 (in 1972), industrial co-determination (*Mitbestimmung*) was introduced, the educational system was re-formed and expanded, and welfare spending on the young, elderly and handicapped was increased significantly. In the economic sphere, there was now greater state involvement in medium- and short-term planning and a more concerted use of fiscal policy in a neo-Keynesian fashion. In foreign affairs, improved relations with the East were encouraged through *Ostpolitik*. During this period the SPD was led by a strong, united and experienced team centred around the troika of party chairman Willy Brandt, parliamentary floor leader Herbert Wehner and, from May 1974, the popular, skilled and highly respected Chancellor Helmut Schmidt. The image presented and marketed was one of sensible, pragmatic, responsible reformism led by a new generation of postwar politicians.

These policies and this approach reaped rich electoral dividends for the SPD during the early 1970s, as the party matched the changing social tenor of the times. New educated white-collar groups, some of whom had been involved in the APO (Extra-Parliamentary) student movement of 1966–9, were now attracted to the SPD, in addition to its more traditional blue-collar and middle-class constituency. This was reflected by the increase in SPD party membership from 710000 in 1965 to a postwar peak of 1022000 in 1976 and by its electoral performance in the 1972 Bundestag contest, when it became the largest national-level single party for the first time ever. The relationship between the SPD and FDP coalition partners was also placed on a more formal and legitimate footing during this period with the introduction of the 'new rules' of 1972. From this date on, coalition preferences and pacts were to be made openly before the date of the election, with both parties pledging to maintain the arrangement throughout the ensuing legislative term. Greater solidity was thus given to the governments of these years and the door was left open for split, tactical voting – in which constituency votes would be given to the SPD and list votes to the FDP – in the Bundestag elections of 1972–80, to the benefit of the coalition ticket. In such circumstances, despite predictions of its imminent demise, the FDP continued to surmount the 5% electoral hurdle and acted as a moderating check upon more extreme elements within the SPD.

The Remodelling of the CDU

The CDU, by contrast, was driven into the federal wilderness during the 1970s. It retained, however, considerable electoral support and continued to dominate the majority of Länder and the Bundesrat, and was thus able to exert pressure to indirectly influence SPD policy programmes. This checked any tendencies there may have been towards the party's disintegration. Instead, the CDU used these years in exile to carry out fundamental party reorganization and to reformulate and redefine its policy approach and public image.

During the 1950s and early 1960s, under Konrad Adenauer and Ludwig Erhard, the CDU had presented the appearance of a loose confederation of regional chiefs coming together every four years to choose and support an agreed chancellor-candidate. The central organization of the party had been limited and ineffectual, thus regional cleavages rapidly emerged once out of office. Recognizing these weaknesses, the CDU's chairmen of the early 1970s, Rainer

Barzel (1970–3) and Helmut Kohl (1973–), and its general-secretary, Kurt Biedenkopf, set about strengthening the central party apparatus (a new headquarters, the Konrad Adenauer House, being constructed at Bonn), establishing new 'wings' to attract targeted support and improving inter-Länder integration. This remodelling programme met with considerable success, CDU membership increasing dramatically from only 300 000 in 1970 to 696 000 in 1980 (membership of the Bavarian CSU increased during the same period from 93 000 to 175 000), and established in place a potentially more efficient structure for mobilizing the party's federal vote in future Bundestag elections. Second, the policy stance of the CDU was redeveloped under the leadership of the moderate-minded Helmut Kohl. The party thus now came to terms with Willy Brandt's Ostpolitik detente and shifted to the centre in its economic and domestic policy approach, though continuing to favour greater fiscal probity than the neo-Keynesian SPD. This did not add up to a transformation of Bad Godesberg proportions, but the changes remained substantial and served to make the CDU more attractive to the floating 'middle ground' centrist voter, as well as opening the door once more to an alliance with the FDP, which would be crucial if the party was to recover federal power once again.

CDU Abortive Recovery: 1976–9

The October 1976 Federal Election

The tide of public opinion moved away from the ruling SPD during the mid-1970s as economic problems mounted and as the impetus fizzled out of Ostpolitik detente. The West German economy, following five years of robust recovery from the 1966–7 recession, spluttered during the mid-1970s as a result of the quadrupling of world oil prices by OPEC in 1973–4. The resulting slowdown in world economic growth pushed unemployment in the heavily export-orientated West German economy to over one million and created public spending and inflationary pressures as the cost of the social welfare programmes of the early 1970s continued to increase.

Chancellor Schmidt dealt with these problems more successfully than other Western leaders, but the onset of recession still brought benefits to the CDU-CSU in the October 1976 Bundestag election. Led by Helmut Kohl, the successful minister-president of the Rhineland-Palatinate, and campaigning under the slogans of 'Freedom in place of Socialism' and 'Less power for the State', the CDU reversed the electoral trend of the preceding decade. Support for the SPD declined for the first time since 1953 (the SPD losing a million votes to its rivals) and the CDU recaptured its pre-eminence as the largest single federal party once more, with the SPD-FDP's Bundestag majority being sliced from 46 to a mere 10 seats (*see* Table 8). The CDU-CSU gained an absolute majority (54%) of direct mandates for the first time since 1965 and captured 48.6% of 'list votes', its second best ever result. Indeed, with a single-ballot, 'first-past-the-post' British- or American-style electoral system it would have gained a large and comfortable parliamentary majority. However, despite being narrowly excluded from office once more by the West German PR list system, the CDU-CSU seemed destined to grasp full control in 1980, if economic conditions deteriorated further.

TABLE 8   THE OCTOBER 1976 FRG BUNDESTAG ELECTION[1]
(TURNOUT 90.7%)

Party	Zweitstimmen Votes ('000)	Share of Total Vote (%)	Seats
SPD	16,099	42.6	214
CDU	14,367	38.0	190
CSU	4,027	10.6	53
FDP	2,995	7.9	39
DKP	118	0.3	0
NPD	123	0.3	0
KBW[2]	20	0.1	0
Others	72	0.2	0
TOTAL	37,821	100.0	496

[1]Excluding West Berlin.
[2]The Communist League of West Germany (a Maoist organization which was disbanded in 1980).

The Post-Election Factional Feud within the CDU-CSU

The CDU-CSU failed, however, to capitalize on this situation. Instead, it fell prey to serious internal divisions during the three years following the October 1976 Bundestag election. Helmut Kohl left Land politics immediately after the federal election and moved to Bonn to become CDU-CSU Bundestag Fraktion leader in an effort to gain greater experience on the federal stage. Kohl, however, encountered increasing criticism and damaging opposition from Franz-Josef Strauss, the experienced and energetic leader of the CSU sister party, who possessed a firm political base in the large, strongly Catholic state of Bavaria.[1] The clash between Kohl and Strauss precipitated the most serious internal crisis in the CDU-CSU coalition since 1950.

Strauss and the CSU were, in policy terms, far to the right of the larger CDU. They were strongly committed to individualism and liberal free-market economics and in foreign affairs were firmly Atlanticist and anti-communist – opposing one-sided detente. Strauss thus wished to move the CDU away from the consensual moderation preached by Helmut Kohl back towards the conservatism of Konrad Adenauer, adding to this a dash of Germanic and Bavarian nationalism and his own aggressive and confrontational personality. He had contested for the CDU-CSU chancellor candidacy in 1976, but had been defeated by Helmut Kohl. He vowed thereafter to plot his downfall and to replace Kohl as CDU-CSU chancellor-candidate in 1980.

Strauss's criticisms of Kohl's allegedly weak and ineffective leadership intensified after the 1976 federal election, and at a meeting held at Wildrab-Kreuth in November 1976 the CSU delegation voted to end its 26-year-old agreement to form a common voting caucus (*Fraktionsgemeinschaft*) with the CDU in the Bundestag. This threatened to precipitate a full schism between the CDU and CSU, with the CDU contesting seats in Bavaria and the CSU setting itself up as a federal-wide fourth party. The CSU, however, aware of the electoral perils of such a policy, pulled itself back from the brink in December 1976, renewing its parliamentary agreement in return for a number of concessions which gave the CSU Bundestag group greater freedom of action. Relations between the sister parties remained, however, strained.

Following the October 1978 Land election, Franz-Josef Strauss resigned his Bundestag seat and left Bonn to become minister-president of Bavaria. He continued, however, to criticize Kohl's federal leadership and pushed himself forward once again as chancellor-candidate. Strauss gained the support of conservative CDU leaders from the southern and central states of Baden-Württemberg and Hesse. Northern liberals (*'Nordlichter'*) and moderates (including Kohl) within the CDU sought to foil Strauss's challenge by promoting the candidacy of the popular minister-president of Lower Saxony, Ernst Albrecht, as a compromise 'unity candidate'. They acted too late, however, and in July 1979 Franz-Josef Strauss was elected as the joint CDU-CSU chancellor-candidate for the October 1980 federal election. This choice was to prove disastrous for the Christian Democrats.

The Ascendancy of Realpolitik: Schmidt in Power, 1976–80

The SPD by contrast, following a lull in its electoral fortunes during the mid-1970s, gained in strength during the late 1970s as a result of the increasing popularity of its leader Helmut Schmidt. Schmidt, born in December 1918, the son of a middle-class Hamburg schoolmaster, had distinguished himself as a Lieutenant and battery commander in the *Wehrmacht* (the German Third Reich army) on the Russian front during the Second World War, being awarded an Iron Cross. Unlike Adenauer or Brandt, Schmidt had not been an active opponent of Nazism, serving instead as a loyal and apolitical defender and servant of the nation. However, during his period as a prisoner of war between April and August 1945 he began to reflect on the Nazi experience and gained a new political awareness and concern for social justice. After the war, Schmidt took a degree in economics at Hamburg University, studying under the supervision of Karl Schiller, joined the radical Social Democratic Student Movement (SDS) and SPD, and began work in the Hamburg city economics and transport department. He moved to Bonn in 1953, serving as an SPD Bundestag 'list delegate', and gained an early reputation as a left-wing socialist who favoured pacifism and greater nationalization. By the time of the SPD's November 1959 Bad Godesberg conference, however, he had reformulated his views, emerging as a moderate, centrist 'social democrat'. Schmidt returned to his native Hamburg in 1961 to take up the position of minister of internal affairs and established a national reputation for himself as a result of his decisive handling of a serious flood crisis in February 1962. Benefiting from this experience, he was promoted to the post of SPD shadow defence minister in the Bundestag in 1965 and was appointed party 'floor leader' during the 1966–9 'Grand Coalition'.

Schmidt gained the reputation during his first 20 years in public service as both a hard-working and efficient administrator, with a fine grasp of details and broader strategy, and as a tough, caustic and persuasive debater. His two fields of particular expertise were defence strategy (writing the well-received books *Defence or Reprisal* and *The Balance of Power* in 1961 and 1971) and economic management. During the 1969–74 Brandt administration, Schmidt thus successively headed the key federal defence (1969–72) and finance (1972–4) ministries. He was also appointed SPD Deputy Chairman in 1968. This was a clear indication that Schmidt was being groomed by Brandt for future party and national leadership. His accession to the Chancellorship in May 1974, following Brandt's resignation over the Guillaume spy scandal, however, came earlier than either leader had expected.

In contrast to the unpredictable, romantic and visionary Brandt, Schmidt was a pragmatic, non-ideological politician concerned with practical solutions – *Realpolitik* – rather than with theory. By the early 1970s he was situated on the moderate, *Kanalarbeiter* ('channel workers') right wing of the SPD and enjoyed extensive personal contacts with industrialists and senior figures from all sides of the West German political spectrum. He ascended to the Chancellorship as the most well-prepared and technically accomplished of postwar West German leaders and further strengthened his authority by gathering together a large and high-powered team of personal Chancellery advisers – Hans Jürgen Wischnewski (party liaison officer and political troubleshooter); Klaus Bölling (government spokesman); Manfred Schüler (head of the Chancellery, 1974–80); Manfred Lahnstein (head of the Chancellery, 1980–2); Horst Schulmann (in charge of the economics department); and Jorgen Ruhfus and Otto der Gablentz (foreign policy advisers). These aides briefed the voracious new Chancellor on all major policy initiatives and engaged in exhausting brain-storming discussions before an agreed policy was hammered out which Schmidt would then proceed to persuasively 'sell' to his ministerial colleagues.

TABLE 9   THE SCHMIDT ADMINISTRATION CABINET OF FEBRUARY 1978[1]

Helmut Schmidt	SPD	Federal Chancellor
Hans-Dietrich Genscher	FDP	Vice-Chancellor & Foreign Affairs
Dr Otto Graf Lambsdorff	FDP	Economic Affairs
Prof. Werner Maihofer	FDP	Interior
Hans Matthöfer	SPD	Finance
Dr Hans-Jöchen Vogel	SPD	Justice
Dr Hans Apel	SPD	Defence
Josef Ertl	FDP	Food, Agriculture & Forestry
Dr Herbert Ehrenberg	SPD	Labour & Social Affairs
Kurt Gscheidle	SPD	Transport, Posts & Telecommunications
Dr Dieter Haack	SPD	Housing & Town Planning
Egon Franke	SPD	Inter-German Affairs
Dr Jürgen Schmude	SPD	Education & Science
Dr Volker Hauff	SPD	Research & Technology
Rainer Offergeld	SPD	Economic Co-operation
Frau Antje Huber	SPD	Youth, Family & Health Affairs

[1] The Schmidt cabinets of 1974–82 were unusually young, with an average age of below 50, containing a new generation of postwar technocrats.

Although constrained by the realities of coalition government (*see* Table 9) and by the federal system, Chancellor Schmidt was able to make a firm imprint upon the direction taken by the government during the years between 1974 and 1980. He pressed for a balanced defence policy between East and West, which involved a European willingness to pursue arms modernization as a means of persuading the Soviet Union to agree to a levelling down of arms capacity; he was instrumental in the establishment of the European Monetary System (EMS) in 1979 to insulate Europe against fluctuations in the value of the American dollar; he pushed forward with the nuclear energy programme following the oil crisis of 1973–4; and, with the aid of his likeminded finance ministers, Hans Apel (1974–8), Hans Matthöfer (1978–82) and Manfred Lahnstein (1982–3), ensured that a tight, neo-monetarist fiscal policy was pursued, while at the same time being willing to countenance small doses of reflation when essential. Helmut Schmidt thus developed the reputation for being a capable and sensible economic manager, the nation's 'managing director', and he succeeded in increasing West Germany's influence abroad, playing a prominent role within the European Community and at the newly instituted World Economic Summits.

It was, however, the terrorist crisis of 1977 which, in particular, boosted the national standing of Schmidt, gaining him the nickname of the 'Iron Chancellor'. First, on 5 September 1977, Hans-Martin Schleyer, the leader of the West German Employers Association (BDA), was kidnapped by the Red Army Faction who demanded the release of 11 jailed terrorists, including their imprisoned former leader Andreas Baader. Then, on 13 October, a Lufthansa airliner, en route between Majorca and Frankfurt and with 86 passengers on board, was hijacked by PLO and West German terrorists who called upon the West German government to meet the demands of the Red Army Faction. Two years earlier, in February 1975, the Schmidt government had given in and released five terrorists following the kidnapping of the CDU party leader in West Berlin, Peter Lorenz. The released terrorists subsequently returned to West Germany and committed further acts of murder. Chancellor Schmidt thus determined in 1977 not to concede to the terrorists' demands and instead sought a covert military solution. On the evening of 17 October a crack squad of West German anti-terrorist troops boarded the Lufthansa airliner at Mogadishu (in Somalia), stunned the hijackers and successfully freed the hostages. Hanns-Martin Schleyer was murdered in retaliation on the next day in Mulhouse, but

Schmidt's actions succeeded in breaking the back of the terrorist menace – precipitating the suicide of three prominent terrorist leaders held at Stammheim jail, including Andreas Baader. Schmidt's strategy at Mogadishu had been high-risk – the Chancellor later stated that if the scheme had failed he would have tendered his resignation to the Bundestag on 18 October – but, with its success, the Chancellor, termed the 'Hero of Mogadishu', enjoyed a wave of unprecedented popularity which was to remain throughout his period in office.

The Closing Years of the Schmidt Era: 1980–2

The October 1980 Federal Election

Strains were beginning to grow within the SPD and between the SPD and FDP coalition partners on economic and defence issues during the closing years of the 1970s. However, Chancellor Schmidt, aided by the firm support of the SPD and FDP floor leaders, Herbert Wehner and Wolfgang Mischnick, managed to retain unity and push through a series of controversial policies – a tough new anti-terrorism law, adherence to the November 1979 decision by NATO to deploy medium-range American nuclear missiles in Europe from 1983, and the expansion of West Germany's nuclear energy programme. Chancellor Schmidt and his economics and finance ministers continued to pursue a tight monetary policy, keeping inflation under firm control, before agreeing to some pump-priming after the Bonn 'Western Summit' in June 1978 to produce a mild pre-election boom and a dent in the unemployment total. The 61-year-old Helmut Schmidt thus contested the October 1980 Bundestag election as a popular statesmanlike figure with a reputation for decision, judgment and integrity. He was opposed by the 65-year-old Franz-Josef Strauss, a flamboyant and radical regionalist leader, revered in Bavaria but feared elsewhere – particularly in the liberal and predominantly Protestant north.

The public divisions within the CDU-CSU and the machinations of Strauss between 1976 and 1979 reflected unfavourably on the opposition party grouping during the run up to the October 1980 Bundestag election. During the six preceding state elections the CDU lost support and the SPD gained ground – increasing their vote by more than 3% in Rhineland-Palatinate (March 1979), Saarland (April 1980) and North-Rhine-Westphalia (May 1980).

The SPD-FDP victory in the October 1978 Hesse election was of particular importance – defeat here would have given the CDU-CSU a two-thirds majority in the Bundesrat and thus an effective veto over all future federal legislation in the absence of a similar countervailing SPD-FDP two-thirds majority in the Bundestag.

The 'Strauss factor' operated against the CDU-CSU alliance in October 1980, with opinion polls registering a 2:1 popular preference for Schmidt over Strauss and with one in seven of supporters of the CDU favouring Schmidt rather than Strauss as the nation's future Chancellor. The election campaign itself was dull, reworking the old issues of Ostpolitik and political extremism. Helmut Schmidt, with the Soviet invasion of Afghanistan in December 1979, the Iran-Iraq Gulf war and contemporary unrest in Poland capturing public attention, made foreign policy the central electoral issue. He visited Moscow in the summer of 1980 and, utilizing the campaign slogan 'Security for the Eighties', projected himself as a responsible statesman seeking to maintain cordial international relations in a deteriorating global situation. He stressed the value of detente and Ostpolitik in reducing East-West tensions and denounced the Russophobe Strauss as a threat to peace and as too unpredictable to be entrusted with control over West Germany's foreign affairs. It was indeed over the issue of Strauss himself that the typically lengthy and personalized West German election campaign ignited – left-wing groups, who branded Strauss a 'neo-fascist', violently disrupted his public meetings; while Catholic bishops controversially circulated a pastoral letter to their congregations on 21 September which pledged support for Strauss and warned against the dangers of an escalation in public debt if the SPD-FDP coalition was re-elected.

Strauss attempted to moderate his foreign policy stance and subdue his dramatic oratory in an effort to soften his popular image. In addition, he gathered together a balanced shadow-cabinet team which included representatives from all the regional and ideological wings of the CDU and CSU – although Helmut Kohl remained excluded. In the end, however, Strauss's forceful personality, his defence posture, his free-market, anti-union economic strategy and his close relationship with Catholic and Bavarian nationalism scared off key sections of the electorate from voting for the CDU – particularly blue-collar workers and northern Protestants. Thus the CDU-CSU suffered a humbling and significant defeat on 5 October 1980, its share of the federal vote falling by 4.1% to only 44.5%. This enabled the SPD-FDP coalition to restore its Bundestag majority to

45 seats (*see* Table 10). In Lower Saxony and Schleswig-Holstein in the north, the CDU vote fell even further, by 5.9% and 5.2% respectively (*see* Table 11). The CDU-CSU alliance still remained, however, the largest single party in the Bundestag after the October 1980 election – the improvements in its organization prevented a more crushing defeat.

TABLE 10   THE OCTOBER 1980 FRG BUNDESTAG ELECTION[1] (TURNOUT 88.6%)[1]

Party	Zweitstimmen Votes ('000)	Share of Total Vote (%)	Seats
SPD	16,262	42.9	218[2]
CDU	12,992	34.2	174
CSU	3,908	10.3	52
FDP	4,031	10.6[3]	53
Greens	568	1.5	0
DKP	72	0.2	0
NPD	68	0.2	0
Others	41	0.1	0
TOTAL	37,942	100.0	497[4]

[1] Excluding West Berlin.

[2] This includes one 'overhang' seat in Schleswig-Holstein.

[3] The FDP gained only 7.2% of constituency (Erststimmen) votes.

[4] 120 of CDU-CSU and 128 of SPD seats were Erststimmen, won directly at the constituency level. All the FDP's seats, as usual, were Zweitstimmen 'list' seats.

TABLE 11   LÄNDER DISTRIBUTION OF BUNDESTAG (ZWEITSTIMMEN) VOTES IN 1980

	SPD		CDU[1]		FDP	
Land	1980 (%)	(1976) (%)	1980 (%)	(1976) (%)	1980 (%)	(1976) (%)
Bremen	52.5	(54.0)	28.7	(32.5)	15.0	(11.8)
Hamburg	51.7	(52.6)	31.2	(35.8)	14.1	(10.2)
N. Rhine-Westphalia	46.8	(46.9)	40.6	(44.5)	10.9	(7.8)
Schleswig-Holstein	46.7	(46.4)	38.9	(44.1)	12.7	(8.8)
Saarland	48.3	(46.1)	42.3	(46.2)	7.8	(6.6)
Lower Saxony	46.9	(45.7)	39.8	(45.7)	11.3	(7.9)
Hesse	46.4	(45.7)	40.6	(44.8)	10.6	(8.5)
Rhineland-Palatinate	42.8	(41.7)	45.6	(49.9)	9.8	(7.6)
Baden-Württemberg	37.2	(36.6)	48.5	(53.3)	12.0	(9.1)
Bavaria	32.7	(32.8)	57.6	(60.0)	7.8	(6.2)
National Average	42.9	(42.6)	44.5	(48.6)	10.6	(7.9)

[1]CSU in Bavaria

The SPD's share of the federal vote remained almost constant at 42.9%, displaying a wide divergence between the personal popularity of the Chancellor – who enjoyed a national 'approval rating' of more than 70% – and that of his party and giving further evidence of the stagnation in SPD support which had been apparent since the mid-1970s. It was the liberal FDP who benefited most from the Strauss and Schmidt 'factors'.

The FDP had for long been the recipient of the disgruntled 'floating voter' who opposed extremism in either of the two major parties, particularly at federal elections. The party had also attracted in new groups of white-collar voters, business executives and managers during the 1970s as it adopted a more attractive and reformist policy stance of 'social liberalism'. However, its performance in Länder elections between 1976 and 1980 had been most erratic – falling below 5% in Hamburg and Lower Saxony in June 1978, holding on at 6% in Bavaria and Hesse in October 1978, improving on its previous poll in Rhineland-Palatinate and West Berlin in March 1979, before then falling below 5% again at North Rhine-Westphalia in May 1980. During these Länder elections the FDP vote had been squeezed by the new force of the environmentalist Greens. However, in the October 1980 federal election voting became more polarized and the FDP once again gained the support of many moderate minded 'floating voters', particularly former CDU electors frightened by the candidature of Franz-Josef Strauss. To these voters were added the split tactical 'list votes' cast by right-of-centre SPD supporters who, following Helmut Schmidt's injunctions, voted to maintain a steadying influence over the future government. With this diverse base of new support, the FDP's share of the federal vote rose from 7.9% to 10.6% – its highest level since 1961 – and its Bundestag seat representation increased from 39 to 53 (see Table 10).

The Significance of 1980?

(a) **The Discredited Radical Option** – The candidature of the controversial Franz-Josef Strauss has obscured interpretations of the 1980 federal election result. It remains debatable whether, with the popularity enjoyed by Chancellor Schmidt and the temporary economic recovery he had engineered, a different CDU leader could have made a substantial enough breakthrough to gain a governing majority. Indeed only once in its history, in 1957, had the CDU

TABLE 12   THE SOCIAL COMPOSITION OF PARTY SUPPORT IN 1980

Social Category	CDU-CSU (%)	SPD (%)	FDP (%)	% of Population in such a Category
18–24-Year-Olds	9	12	12	11
25–29-Year-Olds	7	10	4	9
30–59-Year-Olds	54	56	63	55
Over 60s	30	23	22	16
Men	46	46	43	45
Women	54	54	57	55
Towns of less than 5000	22	11	17	16
Cities of over 100000	31	41	48	37
Trade Unionists	23	41	24	32
Catholics	59	38	43	46
Protestants	39	55	50	48
Regular Church-goers	36	9	20	20
Unskilled Workers	11	11	5	11
Skilled Workers	23	33	18	27
Salaried Workers	34	37	37	35
Managers/Officials	7	6	10	7
Professional/Self-Employed	15	7	19	11
Farmers/Landowners	4	—	4	2

gained more than 50% of the national vote and no ruling government had been voted out of office in the Fourth Reich – the 1966 and 1969 changes in administrations resulting instead from shifts in the alignment of coalitions. What is clear, however, is that the SPD-FDP era was nearing its close between 1976 and 1980, with the CDU-CSU's internecine disputes during this period and the candidature of Strauss serving merely to prolong its life for a further two years. Second, Strauss's stand for the Chancellorship and his subsequent failure discredited at last the much vaunted radical-conservative route to power and forced the party to return to the middle course set out in 1976 by Helmut Kohl. The authority of Strauss was significantly diminished, while that of Kohl, who had acted with propriety and loyalty during the upheavals of 1979–80, was considerably strengthened. The days of a rapprochement between the CDU and FDP were thus paradoxically brought closer by the failed candidature of Strauss.

  (b) **The Re-Emergence of Minor Parties** – While the verdict of the 1980 Bundestag election was equivocal for West Germany's two principal parties, it was much clearer in signalling a revival among the minor parties. The improvement in FDP fortunes was only one example of this revival. An even more significant development was the rise to prominence of the amorphous new environmentalist group, the Green Party. Such a re-emergence of smaller parties was brought about by the uncertainty surrounding West German politics as the country prepared for another *Machtwechsel* and also by the growing popular antipathy towards the larger parties, which had become remote and tainted by corruption scandals, and by a mounting desire for more effective participation in a new style of politics.

The earliest indications of this new public mood were the multitude of 'Citizens' Initiatives Groups' (*Bürgerinitiativen*) which sprang up in West Germany during the later 1960s, campaigning locally for nurseries and children's playgrounds and protesting against environmental pollution and transport policies. They represented an advance upon the more self-centred, 'opting-out' (*Ohne-mich Bewegung*) student protest groups of the mid-1960s and they involved young, well-educated, usually urban-based, white-collar and professional groups (particularly teachers), who were concerned above all with the quality of life rather than with material consumerism. By 1973 2 million West Germans were involved with such 'citizen lobbies', a number which exceeded the total membership of the major political parties (1.8 million). By 1981 the number had climbed to 5 million, attached to 1500 citizens' initiatives. Such organizations proved attractive, in addition, for the style of politics which they offered, a style which was more direct and participatory than that of the increasingly distant and bureaucratic 'systems parties'. This growing interest in both political issues and direct participation, which was reflected in the opinion polls and electoral campaigns of the later 1970s, contrasted starkly with the West German people's deliberate withdrawal from political debate during the 1950s.

These citizen groups remained, however, intensely localized, transient and narrowly-focused bodies during the early 1970s. It was the 1973–4 energy crisis which triggered off a wider movement basing itself around the environment issue. The energy crisis brought into focus West Germany's critical dependence upon imported energy and the future limits to economic growth. Chancellor Schmidt reacted by sanctioning a major expansion in the FRG's nuclear power programme, utilizing the fast breeder reactor. This encouraged the formation of a series of regionally based action groups in Baden-Württemberg and Schleswig-Holstein between 1974 and 1976 to protest against planned new power stations at

Wyhl, near Freiburg, and Brokdorf respectively. Earlier, in 1972, local environmentalist groups had decided to band together in a national coalition termed the Federal League of Citizen Groups for the Protection of the Environment (*Bundesverband Bürgerinitiativen Umweltschutz*: BBU). It remained little known before the mid-1970s, but from it the Green Party (*Die Grünen*) was to emerge in January 1980. This group, termed the 'Green Alternative Lists' (GAL), contested the Hamburg and Lower Saxony Länder elections in June 1978, gaining 4.5% and 3.9% of the vote respectively (18% in one Lower Saxony constituency – Gorleben – where a nuclear fuel reprocessing plant was planned), and they won 3.2% of the federal vote in the June 1979 contest for the European Parliament. They made an even more significant breakthrough in the October 1979 Bremen city-state and March 1980 Baden-Württemberg Länder contests, when they exceeded the 5% limit and gained their first seats in state parliaments.

The performance of the Greens in the October 1980 Bundestag election was disappointing, the party only mustering 1.5% of the national vote after its support had been squeezed during a polarized campaign. The party also suffered during this election from the emergence in public of stark divisions within its ranks between conservative, agrarian ecologists and ultra-leftist radicals. The latter grouping, which included a number of former communists, gained ascendancy in the party during 1980 and forced through a strongly left-wing, anti-NATO and anti-growth, manifesto programme. This led to a large number of resignations of conservative members, including the popular author and former CDU Bundestag deputy, Herbert Gruhl (who was the founder and leader of the autonomous *Grüne Aktion Zukunft* – GAZ) and the Greens' centrist chairman, August Haussleiter, who stepped down at the June 1980 Dortmund pre-election conference to be replaced by Dieter Burgmann.[2] The party recovered from this split and temporary setback, however, and gained significantly in strength between 1980 and 1983.

During these years the party's organization improved and the issues for which it campaigned – defence and the environment – moved to the centre of the national stage as the SPD-FDP government pressed, following the 1979–80 oil price hike, for energy conservation and as a broad debate opened up within the NATO countries over the proposed stationing of new medium-range nuclear missiles. The Greens during this period became increasingly radical. They established new campaigns for the introduction of lead-free petrol and emission controls to check acid rain and pressed for a halting of the nuclear energy programme. In the sphere of defence, the party developed a distinctive unilateralist programme which opposed the deployment of Cruise and Pershing-II missiles in Western Europe, which called for the disbandment of NATO and the Warsaw Pact, which opposed enlistment in the *Bundeswehr* (territorial army), and which sought the creation of a neutral demilitarized zone throughout Europe. The party's economic programme also continued its leftward lurch, which had first become apparent at the March 1980 Saarbrücken conference when the party's rank and file had voted for greater state control over large corporations, the introduction of a 35-hour working week and the unlimited right to strike. This led to fears that the Greens were turning red.

The Greens remained, however, an amorphous body, drawing together a wide amalgam of diverse groups – pacifists, alternatives, feminists, environmentalists, squatters, Maoists and the young unemployed – including disenchanted former supporters of the ruling coalition. After the federal poll of October 1980, the party made further advances in Länder elections – gaining representation in West Berlin (May 1981 – 7.2%), Lower Saxony (June 1982 – 6.5%), Hamburg (June 1982 – 7.7%: December 1982 – 6.8%) and Hesse (September 1982 – 8%) – and in council elections, holding over 1000 council seats by March 1982. In addition, the Greens organized huge demonstrations in cities and at military sites in opposition to the installation of nuclear missiles – one such demonstration at Bonn on 10 October 1981 was attended by 300 000 people – and the construction of nuclear power stations – 100 000 protestors gathering at Hanover in Lower Saxony to demonstrate against the Gorleben reprocessing project in March 1979 and 80 000 people marching on Brokdorf in Schleswig-Holstein in February 1981.

The rise of the Greens was facilitated by the West German electoral system. Proportional representation gave the Greens seats in local areas where it was able to muster support from radical rural and white-collar groups – Baden-Württemberg, the 'cradle of the ecological movement', was a classic example.[3] This created a publicity platform for further successes. In addition, the 1967 Party Law (*Parteiengesetz*) granted state finance (to help reimburse campaign expenses) to parties receiving more than 0.5% of the federal vote – this brought in DM 2 million to the Greens following the 1980 election.[4] The Greens themselves added a new dimension to West German politics by questioning many of the assumptions of the existing system. They proved unwilling at first to enter into coalitions at the Länder level, often asking intolerable prices for their support; they campaigned strongly for local issues – opposing, for example, the construction of an additional runway at Frankfurt airport or extensions to Hamburg port; and they pressed for a new form of rank-and-file, anti-personality politics – establishing a collective executive leadership, alternating their elected *Landtage* delegates every two years and opposing increases in deputies' salaries. This was a challenge to the main parties and affected, in particular, the left-of-centre SPD and FDP. Support was drawn away from these two parties during the years between 1980 and 1983, with adverse electoral consequences. For the SPD the challenge of the Greens exacerbated internal tensions already evident between its right and left wings, before accommodation was later attempted on a green-tinged programme.

The Disintegration of the SPD-FDP Coalition: 1981–2

Divisions over Economic and Defence Policy

Despite gaining an impressive electoral victory in October 1980, cracks rapidly appeared in the 11-year SPD-FDP coalition during the spring of 1981. Economic and defence policies remained the critical issues. The SPD had always possessed a radical urban and university educated 'youth' wing (the *Jungsocialisten* or *Jusos*, which was open to members under the age of 35), many of whom looked back upon Bad Godesberg as a betrayal of the party's Marxist principles, others of whom looked forward to a new form of participatory and decentralized socialism. This wing, which included many who had been radicalized as supporters of the APO student movement in 1968 before later joining the SPD, moved higher up within the party's ranks during the early 1980s and became increasingly alienated from the leadership of the moderate and pragmatic Helmut Schmidt – some leaving Bonn to construct a new and more radical form of socialism at the Länder level (particularly in Hamburg, Hesse, the Saarland, Schleswig-Holstein and Baden-Württemberg). The SPD's radical wing, like the Greens, favoured unilateralism, opposed nuclear power and were ambivalent to West Germany's continued membership of NATO. In addition, they favoured greater state control over the economy, including a thoroughgoing programme of nationalization. The strength of the SPD's left wing within the Bundestag – a grouping which was termed the Leverkusen Circle (after the Ruhr town where they first met) – increased from around 30 to over 50 deputies (out of 218) following the October 1980 federal election. At the SPD's June 1980 pre-election conference at Essen, they accounted for a similar proportion, around 20% of the conference delegates, forcing fudged compromises over nuclear issues.

These internal divisions were temporarily masked by the 1978–80 economic recovery and by the need to close ranks for the October 1980 federal election. However, with the sudden downturn in the West German economy between 1980 and 1982 a wide cleavage opened within the party. The economic indicators began to move sharply against the government during the winter of 1980, as both prices and unemployment raced upwards. By December 1981 unemployment had reached 1.7 million and by the winter of 1982 the figure exceeded 2 million. Chancellor Schmidt responded to this deteriorating situation by introducing tight deflationary budgets in the autumns of 1980 and 1981 in which state borrowing was pegged back, with children's allowances and public sector wages being reduced, while defence spending (in accordance with 1979 NATO pledges) was allowed to increase in real terms.

The Chancellor was driven on in this direction by his FDP coalition colleagues, who, following their electoral success in October 1980, sought to exert an even greater influence over federal policy and who now favoured a shift away from neo-Keynesianism towards freer-market liberalism. Schmidt himself, however, also believed in the need to maintain firm control over welfare spending programmes and to keep in check public spending as a proportion of GNP so as not to overburden and choke off the wealth-creating industrial sector through mounting tax liabilities. This led to jibes by SPD leftwingers that Schmidt was the 'best CDU Chancellor we have ever had'. The rightward shift in SPD economic policies persuaded some on the left that a coalition split and a period in opposition might be preferable to continuation in government and that it would enable the party to regenerate with a more socialist policy programme. Conflicts with Chancellor Schmidt, who was now being seen as a traitor to party principles, over defence and environmental issues added weight to this view.

During 1981, support for the SPD rapidly dwindled as the party took the blame for the contemporary recession and as its internal divisions widened. By October 1981, although Helmut Schmidt remained the most popular politician in the country, the opinion poll rating of his party had slumped to barely 33% – its lowest level since the Guillaume spy scandal of April–May 1974. Eight months earlier, in February 1981, the SPD's deputy chairman, Hans-Jürgen Wischnewski, declared that the party was in a worse shape than at any time since 1945. In Schmidt's native city-state of Hamburg, the SPD's leftist mayor, Hans-Ulrich Klose, refused to co-operate over the Brokdorf nuclear power station project, resigning in June 1981, while in the Bundestag, on 27 January 1981, 24 SPD rebels, led by Manfred Coppik and Karl-Heinz Hansen, broke the traditional strict discipline of West Germany's parliamentary *Fraktionen* by voting against increases in the defence budget and arms sales to Saudi Arabia.[5]

This setback was followed in May 1981 by a stunning defeat in the Land election in West Berlin, a city which the SPD-FDP coalition had held almost continuously since 1949 and where the SPD's vote fell to only 38.4%. Recent city government corruption scandals, housing shortages and social unrest contributed to this result, but West Berlin, the flashpoint for Ostpolitik and detente, was viewed as a barometer of the nation and the May 1981 result was taken as an indication that the public had lost faith in the ruling coalition. This interpretation was supported by the collapse of the party's vote in the March 1982 elections in Lower Saxony. Matters were compounded for Chancellor Schmidt during this period by a deterioration in his own personal health – a pacemaker being fitted to his heart in October 1981 – and by major changes within the Chancellery team which deprived him of the advice of Wischnewski, Bölling and Schüler.

During the spring of 1982 there was a temporary upturn in the fortunes of the SPD. The party's Munich conference in April 1982 agreed once more, following a resignation threat by Schmidt, to delay and fudge the issue of acceptance of Cruise and Pershing-II missiles until the close of the US-USSR Geneva arms control talks, while in February 1982 a major new DM 12.5 billion jobs creation programme, which was to be funded by increases in VAT and wealth taxes, was passed by the Bundestag following the Chancellor's successful and unprecedented call of a vote of confidence in his administration. This was followed by a major cabinet reshuffle on 27 April 1982 – which involved the induction of Manfred Lahnstein (44) as minister of finance, Heinz Westphal (57) as labour and social affairs minister and Frau Anke Fuchs (44) as youth, family and health minister; and the return of Hans-Jürgen Wischnewski as minister of state in the Chancellery and Klaus Bölling as chief government spokesman – aimed at giving new impetus to the ruling coalition. Unfortunately for the Chancellor, however, the administration's rebirth proved to be short-lived, with his FDP coalition colleagues refusing during the summer of 1982 to sanction tax increases to pay for the SPD's proposed public investment programme. The divisions between the coalition partners widened and the popularity of the SPD dipped once more. At the June 1982 Hamburg city-state election the SPD's share of the vote slumped by 9% to 42.8%, leaving the CDU as the major party, but the SPD as a minority government dependent upon unpredictable support from the Greens. With the Hesse state elections forthcoming in September, Helmut Schmidt was faced with the almost certain probability that the CDU-CSU would at last achieve a two-thirds majority in the Bundesrat and a majority on the Bundestag-Bundesrat Joint Conciliation Committee and would thus be in a position to block his federal programmes.[6]

The FDP and CDU Move Closer Together

The FDP was similarly adversely affected by the declining popularity of the Schmidt government. Its votes fell significantly in West Berlin in May 1981, and in the Lower Saxony and Hamburg contests of March and June 1982 it dropped sharply below the earlier federal election level. During the years between 1969 and 1980 the FDP had been in full accordance with the SPD on foreign policy and Ostpolitik and on domestic and human rights issues. They had, however, as free-market liberals by inclination, only been lukewarm supporters of the SPD's economic policies. From the summer of 1981 the FDP leader, Hans-Dietrich Genscher, concerned with the party's electoral future, began to talk openly about an approaching *Wende* (turning point) and secret negotiations commenced between the FDP and CDU at the Land and federal level. The FDP had temporarily joined with the CDU as coalition partners in Lower Saxony between 1976 and 1978 and had continued to operate with the CDU in the Saarland since 1977, when they came to the unique agreement that the state's three votes in the Bundesrat would not be employed in a manner which would harm the federal SPD-FDP coalition. In February 1981 a number of FDP delegates temporarily rebelled against the party leadership in West Berlin and precipitated the resignation of the SPD mayor Dietrich Stobbe. It was, however, the decision of the FDP Land party conference in Hesse on 17 June 1982 to form a coalition pact with the CDU for the forthcoming elections in September, which, when ratified by the federal FDP's national presidium by a 15:3 margin, was the first clear indication that a full split with the SPD was imminent.

The CDU had, meanwhile, been quietly rebuilding under the leadership of Helmut Kohl after the turmoil of 1979–80. They performed well in the Lower Saxony and Hamburg polls of mid-1982, and in the West Berlin election of May 1981 they finally captured control (with the 'toleration' of the FDP), following years of patient nursing by their popular leader, Richard Von Weizsäcker. The decisive moment for the party came on 9 September 1982, when the FDP's federal economics minister, Count Otto Graf Lambsdorff, presented a memorandum to Chancellor Schmidt calling for major cuts in welfare spending to provide a sound base for economic recovery. This plea for what Schmidt termed the 'elbowing society' conflicted sharply with SPD philosophy and was taken to be a statement of grounds for a divorce which only awaited the final sanction from the forthcoming FDP conference due to be held in November 1982. Chancellor Schmidt decided therefore to act first and he challenged the opposition to attempt to topple the government through employing Article 67 of the Basic Law, the 'constructive vote of no confidence', and, if successful, to seek an early election to gain a full mandate from the people.

The Constitutional Crisis of September–October 1982

The 'constructive vote of no confidence' was introduced into the Basic Law in an effort to give greater stability to governments, so as to prevent the formation of the temporary, negative majorities to unseat an incumbent government which had been so commonplace in the Weimar period. This constitutional innovation had worked well during the Fourth Reich. Only once, in April 1972, when the CDU-CSU, led by Rainer Barzel, tried to unseat Willy Brandt's precarious coalition, had this procedure been initiated and on that occasion it had been unsuccessful – failing by two votes.

Thus in September 1982 Helmut Kohl, the CDU leader, initially recoiled from taking this risky course, and called instead for Chancellor Schmidt to resign. Helmut Schmidt refused and attempted instead to engineer a dissolution through requesting a confidence vote in which the SPD would abstain and the opposition would vote against. This move failed, however, with the opposition, not wishing to leave Schmidt fighting the election as the incumbent

Chancellor, refusing to co-operate. It did, nevertheless, persuade the FDP to finally leave the coalition and begin negotiating with the CDU on 17 September 1982. Helmut Schmidt soldiered on for another two weeks at the head of a minority SPD government, taking over the FDP leader's foreign ministry portfolio, before Helmut Kohl called for and won a 'constructive vote of no confidence' motion – polling 256 votes, compared to 235 against and four abstentions. Kohl was sworn in as Chancellor on 1 October 1982 and declared his wish to hold a federal election at an early date.

The employment by the CDU of the 'constructive vote of no confidence' was legitimate under Article 67 of the constitution. The action of the FDP *Fraktion* was, however, most controversial. In October 1980 they had campaigned with the SPD as part of a four-year coalition pact. This they deserted after barely two years, establishing a new administration with the opposition party. Helmut Schmidt was thus justified when he called in September 1982 for a new Bundestag election to give a genuine mandate to this change in government.

The problem, however, for both Schmidt and Kohl, was the lack of provision for midterm elections under the FRG constitution. Elections outside the four-year term were discouraged and had to be engineered by a Chancellor calling for and failing to win, through deliberate abstentions, a vote of confidence (Article 68). This Willy Brandt obtained in September 1972 and Helmut Kohl on 17 December 1982. The Federal President, Karl Carstens (a CDU delegate between 1972 and 1979), although first entertaining reservations concerning the constitutional legality of the move, assented to this orchestrated vote in January 1983, arguing that an early election had been the desire of all four parties and that the formation of a long-term government would have been unlikely without dissolving the Bundestag. This interpretation was supported by the Federal Constitutional Court by a 6:2 margin on 16 February 1983, after the issue had been referred to it by four Bundestag deputies (two FDP, one SPD and one CDU). Kohl's tactics remained, nevertheless, controversial. In September 1972 when Chancellor Brandt called for such a vote he had already lost his Bundestag majority through the defection of disaffected deputies. In December 1982, by contrast, Chancellor Kohl possessed a sound and substantial majority. The events of September–December 1982 served to highlight the rigidity of the West German constitution and the controversy which could be provoked by departures from its written principles.

Chapter 5

THE CONSERVATIVE WENDE: KOHL'S FIRST TERM

The March 1983 Federal Election

Pre-Election Party Developments

During the months immediately following the October 1982 *Machtwechsel* the West German public reacted against the machinations in Bonn and became disillusioned in particular with the FDP, which had reneged on its October 1980 electoral pledge and then proceeded to block Helmut Schmidt's call for an immediate fresh election in the winter of 1982. The FDP, with opinion polls recording only 2.3% national support, feared that an early election would result in their annihilation. Some CDU-CSU rightwingers, including Franz-Josef Strauss, looked forward to such a prospect and pressed for an early poll, but Helmut Kohl – anxious to maintain a liberal element within the coalition – agreed upon a delay until March 1983.

This opportunistic delay alienated voters from both the CDU and the FDP in the Länder elections in Hesse (September 1982), Bavaria (October 1982) and Hamburg (December 1982) and provoked a wave of sympathy for Helmut Schmidt and the SPD. It also contributed towards a rise in support for the 'anti-system' party, the Greens. (See the Länder electoral tables in Appendix B.) The FDP was reduced in all these contests to between 2.2% and 3.5% of the total vote, with a consequent loss of representation in the Hesse and Bavaria *Landtage*. The CDU, in turn, failed to wrest Hamburg and Hesse from the SPD and thus did not gain its expected two-thirds majority in the Bundesrat upper chamber.

Sharp internal divisions opened up within the FDP during the months between the September 1982 change of government and the March 1983 Bundestag election. The party, like the SPD, possessed an increasingly vociferous liberal anti-nuclear wing – the Young

Democrats (*Jungdemokraten* or *Judos*) – which had been prominent at the June 1981 Cologne conference, when 30% of the delegates opposed the executive's endorsement of NATO's Pershing-II missile deployment decision. This dissent extended within the parliamentary party, with 18 of the FDP's 53 deputies voting for Chancellor Schmidt and two abstaining during the historic 1 October 1982 'confidence vote'. On 4 October 1982, the FDP leadership agreed to an interim coalition programme with the CDU-CSU which included cuts in welfare spending and an enhancement of VAT to finance new investment, and which enabled Hans-Dietrich Genscher, Otto Lambsdorff and Josef Ertl to remain in office as foreign, economics and agriculture ministers. However, radical 'social liberal' deputies, who were firm believers in the party's 1971 progressive Freiburg Theses and who comprised a third of the FDP's Bundestag *Fraktion*, felt betrayed by this sudden switch in allegiance and made visible their opposition. In October 1982 the interior minister, Gerhart Baum (a former chairman of the Judos), resigned from the government, while the party's general-secretary, Günter Verheugen, went a step further and left the party to join the SPD. Five other FDP deputies abandoned the party in November 1982 – two joining the SPD.

This opposition continued at the FDP party conference held in West Berlin on 5–6 November 1982, as old cleavages last visible at the time of the breakaways of 1956 and 1969 re-emerged. This time, however, breakaways occurred on the left. Hans-Dietrich Genscher captured only 57% of the votes cast in the conference's leadership election, his lowest ever total, and, in retaliation, the party's right wing decided to dissolve the rebellious Young Democrat section of the party. This persuaded 1500 defiant radical Free Democrats to hold a conference in Bochum on 27–28 November 1982 at which a new liberal democratic party was suddenly launched. This new body did not establish itself as a credible new political force, but it did increase tensions within the party and serve to persuade further waverers to leave – FDP party membership declining from 86 000 to 80 000 during the last three months of 1982. The FDP thus entered the campaign for the March 1983 Bundestag election as a deeply divided and unpopular party. Its quiet, businesslike leader, Hans-Dietrich Genscher, was an electoral asset in October 1980: in March 1983 he was a liability.

The SPD, by contrast, enjoyed a wave of popular sympathy in the immediate wake of the October 1982 constitutional crisis – the SPD being viewed as the party which had sought to give the electors a voice in the change of federal government, but which had been blocked by the FDP and CDU. However, the SPD was unable to build upon this initial public goodwill, as it failed to decide on a clear sense of direction in the wake of the *Machtwechsel*. On 26 October 1982 its leader and Chancellor for the previous eight years, the 63-year-old Helmut Schmidt, announced that he would not stand again. This decision was ostensibly taken on the grounds of health. Schmidt was also, however, tired of the internal feuds and back-biting within the SPD and felt unable to work in the future with either the CDU, FDP, or the Greens as a possible coalition partner after the election.

Schmidt was replaced as SPD chancellor-candidate by the 56-year-old Hans-Jöchen Vogel, a former minister of justice and mayor of Munich, who formed a competent, but colourless, substitute.[1] Power within the party now shifted back towards its idealistic 69-year-old veteran chairman, Willy Brandt. He dreamed of forming a new leftward coalition which would embrace peace campaigners, anti-Genscher Free Democrats, 'alternatives' and Greens, campaigning on a green-tinged programme renouncing Cruise and Pershing-II missiles and nuclear power. Hans-Jöchen Vogel, although drawn from the conservative *Kanalarbeiter* wing of the party, had sympathy with this 'broad church' view, but did not decisively come out in its favour. The SPD thus entered the March 1983 election in an uncertain mood. Its membership rolls were stagnating and its policy stance remained vague and fudged.

The CDU, by contrast, entered the March 1983 election campaign in a strong, confident and bullish mood. It was beginning to recover from the public's disapproval of its machinations during the autumn of 1982, party membership had increased to over 700 000, and its leader, the 53-year-old Helmut Kohl, had used the months since October 1982 to establish himself as a respected statesman on the domestic and international stage.

Elections Issues and the Campaign

The Bundestag election of March 1983 was fought around the dual issues of defence – the imminent installation of Pershing-II missiles – and the economy. The campaign, though lacking the sharp contrast in personalities evident in October 1980, became one of the most ideologically polarized in postwar West Germany, with the two main parties, the SPD and the CDU, offering policy prescriptions which varied to an unusual degree.

Defence – The SPD, while not rejecting the stationing of Pershing-II missiles if absolutely necessary, stressed the 'twin-track' aspects of the November 1979 NATO agreement – the commitment on the part of the United States to enter into serious arms-control talks with the Soviet Union, with Cruise and Pershing-II installation existing only as a final option. Hans-Jöchen Vogel, Willy Brandt, Egon Bahr (the SPD's defence spokesman) and even Helmut Schmidt were not, however, convinced that the American President, Ronald Reagan, had made a genuine effort to reach an arms-control agreement or to respond to Soviet concessions made in January 1983. The SPD thus sought greater exertion the part of the US and USSR to reach a compromise solution and withheld its final decision on deployment until the outcome of the Geneva arms talks was known. The CDU and FDP, while also hoping for progress at Geneva, were by contrast more willing to give unconditional support to their American allies and to accept deployment in the winter of 1983. They accused the SPD of lacking full commitment to NATO and of being influenced by the Soviet Union, whose foreign minister, Andrei Gromyko, had published an article in *Pravda* (the organ of the Soviet Communist Party) calling for all European countries to resist NATO's re-armament initiative 'as an indication of political maturity'.

The Economy – The economic programme presented by the SPD to the West German electorate in March 1983 also differed significantly from that presented by the ruling CDU-FDP coalition. The SPD campaigned for an increase in the level of taxes on high income earners to provide funds for state 'job creation' investment; for a shorter working week; for the extension of workers' participation in industry; and for a reform of the EC's Common Agricultural Policy, so as to reduce food stockpiles and price levels. The ruling coalition advocated, in contrast, a reduction in the level of the government's budget deficit through the enforcement of economies in the social services and by reducing industrial subsidies; the promotion of private enterprise and investment; a lowering of tax levels; and the continued progress of the nuclear energy programme. Chancellor Kohl campaigned under the optimistic, forward-looking slogan 'Vote for the Upturn' and spoke of a new mood in the country which favoured reduced government interference and a turnaround (*Wende*) in broader economic and moral values. His programme was strongly supported by business interest groups who threatened to launch an 'investment strike' if the SPD was elected to power.

The campaign was typically scurrilous, being filled with daily 'scandals' unearthed by an inquisitive and sensationalist West German press, the right-wing, mass-circulation *Bild Zeitung* even accusing the SPD leader, Hans-Jöchen Vogel, of having been the 'extended arm of Goebbels' in enforcing loyalty to Hitler when he had served as a Hitler Youth leader during the Second World War. Defence was, however, the key issue in the March 1983 election.[2] The country was deeply divided over this issue, but on balance felt more secure with the CDU-CSU's pro-NATO stance.

The Election Outcome

The defence issue, coupled with greater confidence in the party's economic programme and a general desire for change following more than a decade of social democracy, propelled the CDU-CSU towards a landslide victory, the allied parties gaining their second largest ever share of the national vote, 48.8%, and gaining 2 million more votes than in October 1980 (*see* Table 13). The most notable feature of this victory was the major advance made by the CDU in the moderate and Protestant Länder of northern Germany, as the centrist Kohl, in contrast to Strauss in October 1980, proved appealing to northern electors, who were faced on this occasion by a southern-based SPD leader. This advance gave a more even geographical spread to CDU-CSU support in March 1983, significantly reducing the traditional Main river electoral divide.[3]

TABLE 13   THE MARCH 1983 FRG BUNDESTAG ELECTION[1]
(TURNOUT 89.1%)

Party	Zweitstimmen Votes ('000)	Share of Total Vote (%)	Seats
SPD	14,866	38.2	193[1]
CDU	14,857	38.2	191
CSU	4,140	10.6	53
FDP	2,706	6.9[2]	34
Greens	2,165	5.6	27
DKP	66	0.2	0
NPD	91	0.2	0
Others	47	0.1	0
TOTAL	38,938	100.0	498[3]

[1] Excludes West Berlin.
[2] These include two 'overhang seats' in Bremen and Hamburg.
[3] The FDP gained only 2.8% of Erststimmen votes.
[4] The CDU-CSU captured 180 direct Erststimmen constituency seats, the SPD 68.

The SPD, deprived of the 'Schmidt factor', which polls had suggested had brought the party an extra 5% of support in the previous election,[4] and burdened by the disappointing economic record of its final years in power, managed to capture only 38.2% of the national vote – its most disappointing showing since 1961. It retained much of its traditional working-class, skilled and unskilled workers, support, but suffered a haemorrhage among middle-class and white-collar electors (*see* Table 14), losing more than a million such votes to both the CDU-CSU and the Greens.

TABLE 14   THE SOCIAL COMPOSITION OF PARTY SUPPORT IN MARCH 1983

Social Category	CDU-CSU (%)	SPD (%)	FDP (%)	Greens (%)	% of Population in such a Category
18–24-Year-Olds	11	12	11	49	13
25–29-Year-Olds	6	9	7	20	8
30–59-Year-Olds	53	54	58	25	53
Over 60s	31	24	25	5	27
Men	45	48	47	44	46
Women	55	52	53	56	54
Towns of less than 5000	19	12	16	9	16
Cities of over 100 000	29	42	35	51	35
Trade Unionists	14	27	12	19	19
Catholics	58	32	42	37	46
Protestants	39	60	53	45	49
Regular Church-goers	32	12	19	8	23
School Leaving Age 16–19 Years	36	27	46	76	34
Skilled/Unskilled Workers	33	48	25	18	39
Salaried Employees	51	46	58	74	50
Professional, Self-Employed	11	5	14	8	8
Farmers/Landowners	5	1	3	0	3

It was, however, the FDP who, as expected, fared worst, capturing only 6.9% of the national vote and losing a third of its 1980 support (1.3 million votes). The FDP managed nevertheless – with the help of CDU 'ticket-splitting' – to surmount the 5% electoral hurdle and continued to hold (with 34 seats) the balance of power in the Bundestag. However, in the Länder elections in Rhineland-Palatinate and Schleswig-Holstein in March 1983 the FDP vote slumped to 3.5% and 2.2% – below the threshold for Landtag representation. Thus by April 1983 the FDP held seats in only five Länder assemblies – Baden-Württemberg, Bremen, Lower Saxony, Saarland and West Berlin – six years before they had been represented in all Landtage.

The FDP, although still holding the balance at the centre, could only barely maintain its claim to be West Germany's third party after the March 1983 Bundestag election and the concurrent Länder polls. The Greens now closely challenged the FDP, holding seats in five Landtage (Baden-Württemberg, Bremen, West Berlin, Hamburg and Lower Saxony) and capturing 5.6% of the national vote in the federal election. They became the first new party since 1957 to gain seats in the Bundestag and to break the monopoly of the three 'system parties'. With defence being such a prominent issue in the March 1983 election campaign, the Greens had been able to break out of their threatened regional ghetto and gain recognition as a national party, drawing votes away from both the SPD and FDP and capturing 23% of the votes cast by young first-time electors. At one stage during the campaign, with support for the Greens exceeding 6% and with the FDP promising to fall below the 5% threshold, the possibility briefly emerged of the Greens holding the balance of power. The 'Green vote' was, however, squeezed during the closing weeks of the campaign and the FDP was saved. The Greens had nevertheless arrived on the federal stage. It remained to be seen, however, whether the party's presence would be permanent and whether the Greens would develop from being a single issue 'peace party' into a more broadly-based and challenging new force in West German politics.

The CDU-CSU-FDP Coalition in Power: 1983–7

Assembling a Cabinet Team

Helmut Kohl was relieved that the FDP had managed to surmount the 5% electoral hurdle and continued to hold the balance of power in the Bundestag after March 1983. It provided for Chancellor Kohl, as for his predecessor Helmut Schmidt, a useful counterweight to the governing party's more extreme wing – in this case Franz-Josef Strauss's CSU – enabling Kohl to pursue a centre-right policy programme.

Helmut Kohl assembled a cabinet of 17 which included three members of the FDP – holding three of the six 'classic ministries' (foreign, defence, economics, finance, interior and justice) – and five members of the CSU (*see* Table 15). The FDP lost the interior ministry to the CSU rightwinger Friedrich Zimmermann in the October 1982 transfer of power (gaining the justice ministry in compensation). It was now also, as a result of the contraction in its parliamentary strength, deprived of the agricultural ministry, which had been held by the controversial pro-farmer Bavarian, Josef Ertl (58), since 1969. The FDP still, however, retained a strong voice in the decision-making process. The CSU captured the important interior (home office) ministry and the agricultural and transport portfolios – enabling the party to uphold the interests of the small farmers and car and aircraft industries of Bavaria. However, the party's ambitious leader, Franz-Josef Strauss, who had openly sought the office of foreign secretary (held since 1974 by the FDP leader Hans-Dietrich Genscher) and had turned down the offer of a minor ministry, remained outside Bonn, continuing as minister-premier of Bavaria. Strauss was to criticize the Kohl administration from the wings, obstruct its policies through his influential position in the Bundesrat, and embarrass the government with his frequent overseas visits as an unofficial and self-appointed foreign minister.

Chancellor Kohl's cabinet contained a mixture of moderates (including Stoltenberg and Geissler) and conservatives and, although promising during the election campaign a significant turn towards the right, the policy programme of his new government did not differ markedly from that pursued by Helmut Schmidt. Ostpolitik remained in place under the continued direction of Hans-Dietrich Genscher (56) – although the new administration remained more firmly committed to the US relationship and to the November 1979 NATO arms modernization programme. In economic affairs, change was gradual and progressive, with strong emphasis now being given towards reducing the budget deficit (through welfare economies) and, later on, towards 'new conservative' liberalization, deregulation and privatization. The most sudden and significant change was at the interior ministry, where, with Friedrich Zimmermann replacing the 'social liberal' Gerhart Baum, policy shifted sharply to the right and sanction was now given to the introduction of computerized identity cards, stricter immigration controls and a tough new law on demonstrations. There were, secondly, major changes at the top of West Germany's politicized federal civil service – as had previously occurred immediately following the 1969 Machtwechsel – among the ranks of the *Beamten* under-secretaries and the ministerial directors (*Staatssekretäre*). Chancellor Kohl, in addition, brought into the Chancellery his own team of personal advisers and secretaries – these included his foreign-policy adviser Horst Teltschik (a Sudetenland refugee keen on improving ties with Eastern Europe), his chief-of-staff Waldemar Schreckenberger (an old school friend), his communications director Eduard Ackermann, his loyal secretary Frau Juliane Weber, and Philipp Jenninger (who handled relations with East Germany).

TABLE 15   THE KOHL ADMINISTRATION CABINET OF MARCH 1983

Dr Helmut Kohl	CDU	Federal Chancellor
Hans-Dietrich Genscher	FDP	Vice-Chancellor & Foreign Affairs
Dr Manfred Wörner	CDU	Defence
Dr Otto Graf Lambsdorff	FDP	Economic Affairs
Dr Gerhard Stoltenberg	CDU	Finance
Dr Friedrich Zimmermann	CSU	Interior
Hans Engelhard	FDP	Justice
Ignaz Kiechle	CSU	Agriculture
Dr Werner Dollinger	CSU	Transport
Dr Norbert Blüm	CDU	Labour & Social Affairs
Frau Dr Dorothée Wilms	CDU	Education
Heiner Geissler	CDU	Youth, Family & Health Affairs
Dr Oscar Schneider	CSU	Housing Construction
Heinrich Windelen	CDU	Inter-German Affairs
Dr Jürgen Warnke	CSU	Economic Co-operation
Dr Christian Schwarz-Schilling	CDU	Posts & Telecommunications
Dr Heinz Riesenhuber	CDU	Research & Technology

Leadership Style: The Detached Chancellor

Despite this pool of personal advisers, Helmut Kohl rapidly developed the reputation of being a detached and cautious Chancellor, in contrast to the sharp-minded and decisive Helmut Schmidt who had taken a keen personal interest in economic management, foreign affairs and a number of other policy programmes, for example the nuclear-energy programme. Helmut Kohl, by contrast, took a more detached view of his office. He presided over the cabinet in a manner akin to that of a chairman of a board of directors, delegating great authority to his ministers, who were allowed to get on with their jobs, while being assured that they could rely on the loyal support of the Chancellor during periods of personal crisis. Such crises afflicted the Kohl administration with an unusual frequency during the first three years of its life, as first the Kiessling and then the Flick and Tiedge scandals rocked the government and led to the resignations of key cabinet ministers.

One factor which explained this change in Chancellorship style was the personality and natural inclinations of Kohl himself. The new Chancellor, who had gradually worked his way up the CDU state ladder in Rhineland-Palatinate during the 1960s[5] before being elected federal party chairman in 1973, was by temperament more of a party politician than an administrator or strategic thinker. As Chancellor, therefore, he was to devote far more time to the crucial, but often mundane, affairs of backroom and town-hall party politics, building up alliances and firm support bases for himself and his legislative programme across the Länder, than his predecessor Helmut Schmidt, who delegated such activities to his party lieutenants, Willy Brandt and Herbert Wehner, and concentrated instead on administrative problem-solving and international states-manship. The second crucial factor, however, was the unusually diverse and unstable nature of the new CDU-CSU-FDP governing coalition. Chancellor Kohl had to seek to maintain a working relationship with two troublesome coalition partners – one, the FDP, which found itself being torn apart by scandals and divisions: the other, the CSU, led by the unpredictable Franz-Josef Strauss. A series of periodic co-ordinating meetings were arranged in order to quietly settle such intra-coalition differences behind closed doors and to co-ordinate broad policy strategies. Much, however, was left to the discretion of individual ministers.

The Early Policy Record: 1983–4

During 1983, despite the continuing economic recession (with unemployment now exceeding 2 million), Chancellor Kohl and the CDU-CSU-FDP coalition continued to profit from the defence issue. The 'year of the missiles', 1983 was to be distinguished by a rising tide of popular protest which culminated in huge demonstra-tions in Bonn, Hamburg and Stuttgart on 22 October as the anti-nuclear lobby sought to prevent the stationing of Pershing-II missiles.[6] The Pershing-II issue seriously divided the opposition SPD, who finally came out against deployment at their November 1983 conference. The CDU-CSU-FDP coalition, by contrast, adopted a consistent line in support of the United States and deployment, which remained the majority view in the country. By November 1983, with the Pershing-II deployment vote in the Bundestag won, Chancellor Kohl (dubbed the 'Rocket Chancellor' by opposition leader Hans-Jöchen Vogel) and the CDU stood well ahead of the opposition parties in the national opinion polls. As an added bonus for the Chancellor, his bitter rival Franz-Josef Strauss was distracted by internal disputes within the Bavarian CSU as the CSU deputies Franz Handlos and Eberhard Voigt established a small breakaway party – the Republican Party – in opposition to Strauss's personalized style of leadership.[7]

Chancellor Kohl's position of dominance did not, however, last for long. From November 1983, two unfortunate scandals rocked the new administration – the 'Kiessling affair' and the Flick corruption case.

The Kiessling Affair – This controversy, although producing a barrage of adverse publicity for the Chancellor, was of only short-term consequence for the government. It had its roots in defence minister Manfred Wörner's dismissal of the deputy NATO commander, General Gunther Kiessling, on 31 December 1983 as a result of a series of counter-intelligence reports which had suggested that Kiessling was a homosexual who posed a serious security risk. Subsequent press and Bundestag investigations showed, however, these reports to be grossly inaccurate and that Kiessling may well have been 'framed' by officers opposed to his policy stance. A fierce political row developed, with the SPD opposition demanding that Kiessling be reinstated and that Wörner should resign as a matter of honour. Helmut Kohl rejected those demands and remained fiercely loyal to Wörner, his close and longstanding foreign and defence policy adviser, fearing that, if Wörner left the cabinet, Franz-Josef Strauss would make a bid to gain the defence portfolio. Kohl thus eventually settled upon a fudged, compromise solution in which General Kiessling was reinstated and publicly exonerated, before retiring early with full military honours in April 1984, while Manfred Wörner was retained at the defence ministry. This was not, however, a popular decision and Kohl's uncertain handling of this crisis cast grave doubts over the leadership qualities of the new Chancellor.

This crisis was soon, however, overshadowed by the broader and far more serious 'Flick scandal' which concerned the financing of political parties and which tarnished the reputation of both the FDP and the CDU and which even impugned the integrity of the Chancellor himself.

Party Finance and the Flick Scandal – In the modern Federal Republic state, an attempt has been made to give political parties independence from the unhealthy pressures exerted by business and labour interest groups. Generous state financial support totalling more than DM 132 million (in 1980) was thus granted, through the subsidy of DM 3.5 per federal vote and DM 1.5 for each vote gained in a Land election contest.[8] State finance did not, however, go all the way towards rendering parties independent of outside interests. State finance has provided only a third of party revenue, the rest has had to be raised, as in other countries, from members and outside donors. The SPD, which pioneered the modern party form, relies overwhelmingly upon the collection of party membership dues:[9] for the FDP, CDU and CSU it is business firms which provide much of party funds (31%, 13% and 29% respectively in 1984). These donations have, however, led the parties into controversial and murky waters. Donor companies have sought to keep their contributions secret, while the political parties have looked for tax exemption on such 'gifts'. Such wishes ran up, however, against the 1967 Party Law (amended in 1981), which required the source of all large donations to be declared and which only granted tax immunity to contributions of less than DM 1800. To circumvent these inconvenient regulations, the political parties, most prominently the FDP and CDU, thus established secretive 'front organizations' claiming charitable status.

A blind eye was initially turned to these illicit operations, but in the later 1970s it was decided that a thorough reform of the Party Law should be effected to remove the need for such clandestine activities by finally granting tax immunity to large company donations. As part of this 'cleaning-up' process, a series of investigations were made into the hundreds of existing cases of alleged tax evasion and it was during such enquiries in 1981 that a large tangled web of suspicious dealings involving the huge Flick industrial corporation and key figures within the FDP, SPD and CDU was uncovered. Month by month, new revelations were leaked to the German public by the crusading weekly *Der Spiegel*, building up what became known as the 'Flick scandal' into a West German 'Watergate' which tarnished the reputation of key figures within the ruling coalition, including the Chancellor himself.

The first damaging exposure occurred in March 1982, when it was revealed that the FDP's federal economics minister, Dr Otto Lambsdorff, and his predecessor, Dr Hans Friderichs, had granted the Flick corporation tax exemptions worth DM 0.8 million in connection with the company's DM 2 billion sale of its 29% stake in Daimler-Benz in return for a donation of DM 0.5 million to the straitened FDP's party coffers. Throughout 1983, *Der Spiegel* leaked further details concerning these dealings. Helmut Kohl at first reacted to this gathering scandal by attempting in January 1984 to push through a bill which would grant tax deductions of 50% to political contributions up to specified limits.[10] He went further in May 1984 and tried to extend an amnesty to those involved in past political-fund tax evasions. However, such was the wave of criticism from the opposition SPD and Green parties and from the West German media that Kohl was forced eventually to abandon the latter bill.

During 1984 the Flick affair ticked away like a time-bomb under the governing coalition, before it finally exploded during the summer and autumn. First, Otto Lambsdorff was forced to resign in June 1984 when a date for his trial was finally set. Then, on 25 October 1984, Rainer Barzel, the former CDU chairman who was currently Bundestag president (speaker), stepped down after it was revealed that between 1973 and 1979 he had secretly accepted DM 1.7 million from the Flick company on behalf of his party.[11] Two weeks later, in November 1984, the scandal directly touched Helmut Kohl, who admitted before a Bundestag investigating committee that he had received DM 140000 from Flick on behalf of the CDU when serving as minister-president of the Rhineland-Palatinate during the mid-1970s. Kohl stated, however, that these contributions had been purely political, with no conditions attached, and he denied knowledge of any deliberate tax evasion by his Land party's 'charitable research foundation'.

Chancellor Kohl's apparently candid testimony temporarily took the heat out of a 'scandal' which had been blown up out of all proportion by the West German media: it remaining unclear, for example, whether any substantive political favours had been granted in return for Flick's donations. The 'Flick scandal' had nevertheless served to seriously undermine public respect for the major 'system parties' and to encourage popular cynicism. It particularly harmed the FDP and it lowered the standing of Helmut Kohl, whose indecision during this long-running crisis led to him being termed the 'Do-Nothing Chancellor' by *Der Spiegel*. Only the anti-establishment Greens profited from these proceedings.

Mounting Troubles for the 'Do-Nothing Chancellor': 1984–6

Ructions within the Coalition

Tainted by the 'Flick scandal' and faced with still high levels of unemployment and only fragile economic recovery, support for the CDU declined substantially during 1984 and 1985. In the old industrial Länder of Hesse, Saarland and North-Rhine-Westphalia, which bore the brunt of the contemporary recession, the CDU vote collapsed during the state elections of this period. The party's defeat in Saarland (March 1985) – control of which reverted back to the SPD – was of particular significance. It meant that Franz-Josef Strauss, with his five Bavarian seats, now held the balance of power in the Bundesrat.[12] The right-wing CSU's voice within the federal coalition was thus considerably strengthened. This occurred just at the time when influential figures within the CDU, including its general-secretary and campaign manager for the 1987 Bundestag election, Heiner Geissler, were seeking to move the party back towards a more centrist and interventionist policy course, so that the crucial support of blue-collar workers could be regained.

In April 1983, the newly elected CDU-CSU-FDP coalition had looked set for more than a decade in office, dominating both the Bundestag and the Bundesrat. Less than two years later the future of the party and Chancellor Kohl appeared far less certain. Criticism from the Chancellor's coalition partners and from the conservative Springer[13] press (*Die Welt* and *Bild Zeitung*) mounted, calling for more decisive leadership and for conflicting policy changes. In August 1985, the trial of Otto Lambsdorff, Hans Friderichs and Eberhard von Brauchitsch (a former general-manager of the Flick corporation) began. It re-opened the old wounds of the 'Flick scandal' and, set to last more than a year, would keep the issue in the public's mind all the way up to the January 1987 federal election. On top of all these problems came the Tiedge spy scandal of August-September 1985, which directly affected both the interior minister, Friedrich Zimmermann, and the new FDP leader and federal economics minister, Martin Bangemann.

The Tiedge Spy Scandal

This spy scandal was the latest in a long-running series which afflicted West Germany from 1949. It was, however, one of the most serious. West Germany, with its open-door attitude towards its eastern neighbour, its lingering desire for reunification and its concern for open-government and the protection of civil rights against state interference, had been a fertile ground for Eastern bloc spies. Markus Wolf, the talented East German spy chief who finally retired in 1987, was alleged to have established a network of 30 000 agents in the Federal Republic, many of whom found employment as secretaries working in government departments in Bonn. The West German security forces established the Office for the Protection of the Constitution (*Bundesamt für Verfassungsschutz* – BFV) as a counter-intelligence agency in an attempt to break into and uncover this spy network and it was Hans-Joachim Tiedge who headed a key section of this organization during the early 1980s.

Tiedge, a 19-stone alcoholic, faced increasing personal problems after his wife died mysteriously in July 1982 and amassed debts in excess of £60 000. On 19 August 1985 he defected to East Germany as a means of escaping these problems. He brought with him vital intelligence information and agency lists, but, more importantly, his defection led to the unearthing of an extensive network of spies within key government departments, including Sonja Luneberg, who had worked as a secretary for the FDP, serving Martin Bangemann (the new FDP leader and economics minister) for 12 years; Margarete Höke, who had worked as a secretary to successive federal Presidents for 21 years; and Herta-Astrid Willner, who had worked within the Chancellery in a department dealing with domestic security and nuclear power.

The Tiedge scandal precipitated calls by the SPD for the resignation of the interior minister, Friedrich Zimmermann, since in 1974 and 1978 Willy Brandt and the SPD defence minister, Georg Leber, had resigned as a matter of honour when the East German spies Günter Guillaume and Renate Lutze had been unmasked. However, Zimmermann refused to tender his resignation. Instead, Heribert Hellenberoich, the former head of the BFV and the new chief of the BND (*Bundesnachrichtendienst*) foreign espionage service, who had been aware of Tiedge's personal problems for several months but had not informed Zimmermann, was sacked on 28 August 1985. The ability of Friedrich Zimmermann to remain in office despite this scandal was another example of the authority and independence of individual ministers when drawn from coalition party partners in the West German system of government. Zimmermann, who only two months previously had openly criticized Kohl for his weak leadership and had forced a controversially tough law and order package on the government, was no personal friend of the Chancellor. He could, however, count on the firm support of Franz-Josef Strauss and his CSU colleagues who, with 53 seats, held the balance of power in Bundestag and who played a key role in the Bundesrat. Zimmermann, like foreign minister Genscher, was secure in his post until the next Machtwechsel.

A One-Term Chancellorship?

By the autumn of 1985, however, the next Machtwechsel appeared unusually imminent. Chancellor Kohl, despite his cheerful, unruffled exterior, had emerged as the least popular West German Chancellor for more than two decades and it was becoming seriously questioned whether he would be chosen to lead his party into the 1987 federal election. Opinion polls showed that only 12% of those asked preferred Helmut Kohl as Chancellor to other names suggested, for example his liberal-minded finance minister, Gerhard Stoltenberg, or Lothar Späth, the successful and innovative minister-president of Baden-Württemberg, and that only 31% of the West German public believed that Kohl was doing a good job as Chancellor.

Things failed to improve for the Chancellor during the spring of 1986 as his involvement in the 'Flick scandal' was re-examined by the public prosecutor after the Green Party's MDB, Otto Schily, filed a legal suit claiming that Kohl had lied to the Land and Bundestag investigating committees in November 1984. Matters were further compounded for the CDU-CSU-FDP coalition by the continued revelations of the Lambsdorff trial;[14] by the irruption of a corruption scandal in West Berlin which forced the resignation in April 1986 of the CDU deputy mayor and two local ministers (including one from the FDP); by intra-coalition wrangles over foreign and domestic policy; and by the alienation of trade unionists, as a result of proposed new labour legislation, and of farmers, who felt that the government had not been giving them enough financial support. Then, on 26 April 1986, 800 miles east of Bonn, occurred the devastating nuclear accident at the Chernobyl nuclear power station in the Soviet Union which shocked the West German people, radically re-arranged the political agenda and boded ill for the pro-nuclear CDU. The CDU, not surprisingly in such circumstances, polled poorly in local elections in Schleswig-Holstein in March 1986 and figures showed that it had lost 12000 members during the previous year. Its prospects in the general election, due ten months hence, thus appeared to be in doubt. The party still held a plurality of support over the SPD, but its overall success in January 1987 would very much depend upon the relative performances of the two minority parties which might hold the balance of power – the FDP and the Greens.

Intra-Coalition and Opposition Party Developments: 1983–7

The FDP: Policy Shifts and Public Disfavour

The FDP emerged from the March 1983 federal election weakened and divided. However, during the following months the party consolidated around a more conservative policy programme which stressed economic 'laissez faire' liberalism – involving deregulation, intensified market competition, privatization, and a thinned-down public sector – rather than 'social liberalism', as the North-Rhine-Westphalia, Lower Saxony and Hesse based wing of the party gained ideological ascendancy. The FDP sought now to win over the young, mobile professional voter to add to its traditional clientele of the self-employed and the marginal farmer. Such FDP ideas formed an important input into the economic programme of the CDU-CSU-FDP coalition. However, attempts to build up support for this 'new liberalism' were dashed by the 'Flick scandal', which directly affected the programme's chief architect, Otto Lambsdorff.

The standing of the party, already lowered by its political deceptions during September–October 1982, plunged once more with this new crisis. At first the party did not fare too badly. It lost its voice in the Bremen assembly following fresh elections in September 1983, but regained, with the aid of CDU 'ticket-splitting', its representation in the Hesse Landtag. However, in the June 1984 European Parliament elections, when only one vote – for a regional party list – was available, the party fared disastrously. It fell below the 5% electoral hurdle and thus failed to obtain a voice in the European Parliament to which the party was so passionately committed.

This disastrous result finally persuaded the increasingly unpopular Hans-Dietrich Genscher to announce his resignation as party leader after February 1985 – Genscher would still continue, however, as foreign minister, ensuring the continuance of Ostpolitik detente. He was replaced by Martin Bangemann, a former Euro-

MP and the new economics minister, who stood on the free-market wing of the party. This change of leadership failed, however, to heal the divisions within the party: during Bangemann's inaugural address to the party's February 1985 Saarbrücken conference one quarter of the delegates left while he was speaking. Nevertheless, there was evidence of a limited revival in party fortunes under the new leadership during 1985 – the party returning creditable performances in the Länder elections in West Berlin, the Saarland and North-Rhine-Westphalia – before the 'Tiedge scandal' and the opening of the Lambsdorff trial in August 1985 threatened to damage the party once again. Nevertheless, the much-trumpeted demise of the balance-holding FDP had failed to materialize.

Tensions and differences did, however, grow within the ruling coalition, particularly between the FDP and CSU during 1985–6. These two parties, while united in their support for a radical, deregulatory 'liberal' approach to economic affairs, found themselves at odds over foreign policy – particularly over the issues of Ostpolitik, West Germany's involvement in work on the American 'Star Wars' project and the imposition of sanctions against South Africa[15] – and over the new anti-libertarian law and order measures introduced at home. In May 1986, the coalition was further strained when FDP rank-and-file delegates, influenced by Chernobyl, revolted against the party leadership and supported a series of anti-nuclear motions at the party's pre-election conference at Hanover in direct opposition to government policy.[16] Despite these differences, however, the coalition held together during 1986, being helped by the consensual bridge-building work of the moderate, cross-class CDU and its leader Helmut Kohl, and by a realization among senior figures within the FDP that, at present, there remained no alternative but to remain members of the incumbent administration.

The Greens: The Pains of Political Maturity

The Greens continued to make electoral advances in the years following the March 1983 federal election. Their most spectacular successes were in Baden-Württemberg (March 1984) and West Berlin (March 1985) – two areas with a distinctive radical tradition – where they gained 8.0% and 10.6% of the poll, and in the June 1984 elections to the European Parliament, when they captured 8% of the national vote. By 1984, with seats in six Länder, the Greens had moved ahead of the FDP as West Germany's third party.

During 1983, the heated national debate over the stationing of Pershing-II missiles and the demonstrations of the 'hot autumn' – which involved more than 900 000 at Hamburg, Bonn, Stuttgart and West Berlin – gave the party a high national profile. However, once these missiles had been deployed the peace movement lost momentum, although the proposed deployment of Cruise missiles at Hasselbach in 1986 provided another target to campaign against.

Instead, it was the environmental issues of nuclear power and acid rain which gained increasing importance for the party from 1984. On these issues, the Greens had considerable success in persuading the CDU-CSU-FDP government – concerned with the destruction of forests in its southern German heartland – to take decisive action. Restrictions were now placed upon sulphur-dioxide discharges from coal-fired power stations, incentives were granted to purchasers of vehicles with catalytic converters (which reduce exhaust emissions) and legislation was passed for the introduction of lead-free petrol by 1989. During this same period, both CDU and SDP administrations within the Länder were also goaded into delaying the execution of projected nuclear-power programmes by the activities of the Green movement.

However, while the Greens were able to influence the policy debate on environmental issues, as a party they became divided over which political direction to adopt – one of collaboration or one of confrontation with the existing 'system parties'. The Greens presented themselves to the electorate as an informal, broad-church, anti-establishment and anti-elitist 'new party'. The entry of its representatives into the Landtage and Bundestag served to shock the existing 'system parties'. Green deputies were young (average age 40 years), an unusually high proportion (more than 40%) were female and they dressed informally in jerseys, jeans and T-shirts. They acted as mandated delegates to their rank-and-file membership; they stepped down in mid-term in favour of understudies on the party list, in accordance with the party's unique 'rotation principle'; and they drew only a quarter of their official salary (ploughing back the remainder into the party treasury).

However, differences gradually developed between elected Green delegates and the rank-and-file over whether to persist with this informal strategy or whether to weld the party into a more efficient, streamlined and 'professional' movement. Key figures within the party's leadership, including Otto Schily (a former defence lawyer to the Baader-Meinhof terrorist gang), General Gert Bastian (a former member of the CDU) and Joschka Fischer (a former *Sponti* student activist during the 1960s who was now the Greens' Bundestag floor leader), favoured the adoption of a more pragmatic and responsible stance of working within the existing political institutions and of engaging in coalitions with the major parties at state level to achieve particular goals. They became termed the *Realos*. In contrast, many of the younger rank-and-file membership, the so-called *Fundis*, disagreed, viewing such an approach as a betrayal of the Greens' 'anti-party' principles. They firmly opposed entering into coalitions with the 'system parties', preferring an antagonistic nuisance-making role, and pressed hard for continuance of the 'rotation principle'.[17]

The 'Fundis' dominated the Greens' national executive committee and gained initial support from the party's charismatic leader, Petra Kelly, who was situated on the centre left of the party. At its November 1982 conference at Hagen (Westphalia), the 'Fundis' easily won a motion to maintain the principle of a rotating leadership – Rainer Trampert (a Hamburg trade unionist and an ally of the 'Fundis') replacing Petra Kelly as national chairperson. In March 1984, the 'rotation principle' was re-affirmed when it was decided to replace six of the Greens' most prominent Bundestag deputies – including Schily (who had gained wide attention for his work on the Flick investigation committee), Kelly, Fischer, Bastian and its anti-nuclear campaigner, Roland Vogt – with a sextumvirate of obscure female 'shadow-deputies' (three teachers, one lecturer, one professor and one nurse). Kelly and Vogt, however, objected to this principle, arguing that it wasted accumulated experience. They pressed instead for deputies to be allowed to continue in office so long as 70% of their Land branch voted in their favour. Such divisions over the 'rotation principle' caused the first major split in the party when General Bastian left the Fraktion in frustration with the amateurish ineptitude of the party's organization, retaining his Bundestag seat as an independent. A compromise of sorts was eventually arrived at, with 23 new deputies entering the Bundestag for the new session in March 1985, but with the party's principal leaders, Kelly, Vogt and Schily, retaining their seats.[18] The 'Fundis' had, nevertheless, won the major portion of their rotation argument.

At the Länder level, the Greens had to decide what position to adopt when they found themselves holding the balance of power. This occurred in Hamburg between June and December 1982 and in Hesse from September 1982.

In Hamburg, the June 1982 election gave the incumbent SPD government only 55 seats compared with the CDU's 56, and left them dependent on the Greens (with nine seats) for support. The SPD leader, Klaus Von Dohnanyi, attempted to reach a 'toleration agreement' with the Greens, but the Greens demanded in return the abandonment of the city's nuclear-energy programme and the scrapping of planned extensions to Hamburg port. This the SPD could not accept. They thus stumbled on until December 1982, before winning an absolute majority of seats in a new election.

In Hesse the September 1982 elections also resulted in a 'hung Landtag', with the Greens' nine deputies holding the balance of power, and 'toleration' negotiations broke down once more when the SPD refused to accede to the Greens' demands to halt plans to expand Frankfurt airport. A new election was called in September 1983, but, in contrast to Hamburg, no decisive result was obtained: the Greens continuing to hold the balance of power following the new contest. Pressure now mounted on the Greens to act responsibly and form a coalition with the SPD in the interests of political stability. The Greens' actions in Hesse were thus viewed with great interest as indicative of their likely attitude to a possible 'red-green' coalition with the SPD at the federal level if the January 1987 Bundestag election produced a hung parliament.

In June 1984 the centre-right SPD minister-president of Hesse, Holger Börner, following lengthy negotiations, eventually came to a 'toleration agreement' with the Greens at the cost of a number of environmental and budgetary concessions – the SPD agreeing to limit the construction of new motorways, restrict the dumping of chemical waste and stop building new nuclear power stations: the Greens (led by the 'Realo' Karl Kerschgens) assenting in return to tolerate the operation of existing nuclear plants and to lift their opposition to a new runway at Frankfurt airport. However, this loose alliance lasted barely six months before 'Fundis', accusing Kerschgens of a sell-out, withdrew their support in November 1984 after the SPD had failed to cancel plans for two nuclear power stations.

Holger Börner made a renewed attempt to form a coalition in June 1985 when he offered the Greens' Joschka Fischer the state ministry for the environment and energy – although ultimate control of nuclear energy policy was to be wielded by the SPD economics minister – if the Land party would agree in return to ensure the passage of the state budgets between 1985 and 1987. The Greens remained divided over whether to opt for coalition or to reject collaboration – their 22 June conference at Hagen passing an equivocal resolution – but, following weeks of tortuous negotiations,

Kerschgens finally agreed to the arrangement in September 1985. A month later, on 27 October 1985, the pact was approved by a two-thirds majority at a special Land conference at Neu-Isenberg and on 12 December 1985 Joschka Fischer (37), wearing jeans and tennis shoes, was sworn in as environment minister in Wiesbaden, becoming the first Green to hold state office in West Germany.[19] Fischer's appointment, which sent tremors through the Hesse financial and industrial community, was seen as a possible precursor to a coalition at the federal level with the SPD in 1987. However, the majority of Greens still remained bitterly opposed to such collaboration and at the party's annual national conference in Offenburg in December 1985 the 'Fundis' remained dominant at executive committee level.

By the autumn of 1985, however, the Green movement appeared to have passed its peak. Party membership was stagnant at 40000 and the Greens' electoral popularity was on the wane: in the North-Rhine-Westphalia state election of May 1985 it gained only 4.6% support (compared to 8.6% in local elections there in October 1984) and in Saarland two months earlier it polled only 2.5%. The anti-growth economic policies of the party failed, in particular, to attract blue-collar workers in these industrial states. The Green Party was also being forced to clarify its ambiguous position on a wide range of issues and present a coherent national programme. This created internal dissent as a number of the variegated interests within the party were disappointed with the direction chosen. The issue of coalition with the SPD was the most fundamental question.

The Greens also now found its appeal with younger voters, who had been attracted by its freshness and nuisance-making value, declining, as the public began to grow tired of the party's organized chaos, and it found that many of the defence and environmental issues for which it had campaigned were now being adopted by the major 'system parties', which took on a greener hue during the early 1980s. Within the CDU, for example, Lothar Späth, the minister-president of Baden-Württemberg, pursued a dynamic anti-pollution programme and even in conservative Bavaria the CSU, prompted by anxious local farmers, showed a genuine concern for the condition of the state's decaying forests. It was, however, the SPD which came out against the installation of Pershing-II missiles in November 1983 and which was now being driven forward by a group of new environmentally conscious state leaders – the most prominent being the eco-socialist Oskar Lafontaine, leader in the Saarland – which was making the strongest inroads into the Green vote. The Greens had certainly tapped a new section of the electorate attracted by the fresh style of politics it offered and by its alternative political and economic vision. However, this segment remained small. The survival of the party in the Bundestag after 1987 began, from the autumn of 1985, to appear doubtful.

In the spring of 1986, however, the Greens, who had been engaged in a determined series of demonstrations at the sites of the proposed Brokdorf and Wackersdorf nuclear power and reprocessing plants and at the Hasselbach Cruise missile base, were suddenly revivified by the numbing nuclear catastrophe at Chernobyl. This accident, which led to the contamination of 1000 sq kms of Russian farmland and to momentary panic in the Federal Republic as a radioactive cloud swept overhead, stunned the West German people and suddenly transformed the political agenda. The popular concern was even greater than that aroused by the construction of the Berlin Wall in August 1961. Not surprisingly, therefore, national support for the Greens suddenly surged from a level of 6% to more than 8%, with the protest rallies called by the party at Wackersdorf and Brokdorf in June and July 1986 being unusually well attended. Chernobyl, however, had a second and less salutary impact on the Green movement, radicalizing it to a dangerous degree. This was seen most visibly at the Wackersdorf and Brokdorf demonstrations, which grew increasingly violent, reaching riot proportions in Hamburg on 8 June 1986. It was, also, most evident at the special pre-election conference called by the national party at Hanover on 16–19 May at which, with the 'Fundis' in the ascendant, a hardline party programme was adopted calling for the immediate cessation of nuclear-power generation, withdrawal from NATO, removal of Pershing-II and Cruise missiles and the disbandment of West Germany's border guards, army and intelligence forces.[20] Such radicalization pushed the Greens further beyond the bounds of conventional West German politics and placed new, and seemingly insurmountable obstacles, in the way of a future 'red-green' federal coalition with the SPD.

The SPD: Which Road Back to Power?

The SPD remained divided throughout 1983 by the debate over the stationing of Pershing-II missiles. Helmut Schmidt and the centre right saw the need to accept these missiles to show solidarity with West Germany's NATO allies. However, the party's influential chairman, Willy Brandt, came out against deployment – speaking at the huge Bonn peace rally on 22 October – and was supported by the bulk of party activists at a special conference in Cologne on 18 November 1983, when the party voted by 383 to 14 (with three abstentions) against acceptance. This historic decision represented the first major breach in the all-party defence consensus in West Germany since 1959.

The decision established the SPD as a clear centre-left party, with Willy Brandt its controlling figure supported by a left-dominated executive committee. Helmut Schmidt, who had spoken against the 18 November decision, announced shortly afterwards that he would not be standing for the Bundestag in the next federal election or for any leading party post. (In May 1984 he resigned as one of the party's two deputy chairmen to be replaced by Hans-Jöchen Vogel.) Herbert Werner, the stern 77-year-old Bundestag floor leader – a passionate left-wing supporter of detente and reunification – had also stepped down a year earlier to be similarly replaced in his post by Hans-Jöchen Vogel. Control of the SPD thus now passed to a new generation of leaders – under the guardianship of Willy Brandt – as the party sought a new sense of direction.

The party remained unclear as to what this direction should be during 1983 and 1984. The SPD drifted leftward in its defence stance, though still remaining committed to NATO, and became more environmentally conscious, as it toyed with the idea of a 'red-green' majority seeking coalition with the increasingly popular Green Party. At the state level, however, individual party leaders pursued differing programmes – centre right (in West Berlin under the former defence minister, Hans Apel), centre (in Hamburg, Hesse, Bremen and North-Rhine-Westphalia), radical left (in the Saarland under the anti-NATO Oskar Lafontaine, in Baden-Württemberg under Erhard Eppler and in Schleswig-Holstein under Björn Engholm) – with varying degrees of success. The SPD's policy position was thus kept necessarily vague during these years.

At home, however, the CDU-CSU-FDP coalition's failure to reduce unemployment, particularly in the older industrialized north, presented an issue around which the party could unite and attract wider electoral support. The SDP pushed for an expansionary and interventionist economic strategy and picked up increasing support from blue-collar groups for this programme. This was first apparent in the Bremen and Hesse elections of September 1983 and in the Munich municipality election of March 1984 (when the SPD won the mayorship for the first time since 1972–8). During 1984 the party benefited from the 'Flick scandal' and by the spring of

1985 the advance of the SPD was spectacular. It regained control of the Saarland, ending more than a decade of CDU rule, and captured a record 52% of the poll in North-Rhine-Westphalia, the key barometer region in West Germany which contained almost a third of the total electorate.[21]

In their victor in North-Rhine-Westphalia, the 54-year-old Johannes Rau, the SPD had appeared to have finally found the vote-winning personality which they had missed since the departure of Helmut Schmidt. Rau, the devout son of a Protestant pastor who was married to an attractive 29-year-old wife, and had a small family, proved to be a popular and engaging centrist leader very much in the mould of Helmut Schmidt – down to his love for wearing a 'student cap' during election campaigns.[22] He had already acted as a party deputy chairman since April 1982 and in September 1985 Rau agreed to stand as chancellor-candidate in January 1987 if endorsed by the SPD conference in Nuremberg in August 1986. Rau was duly endorsed, replacing the uninspiring stop-gap Hans-Jöchen Vogel, who remained nevertheless as the party's Bundestag leader. During the autumn of 1985 and spring of 1986 Rau made a strong impression on the West German public and engaged in well-publicized visits to Moscow, Paris, London and Washington. He still remained politically 'raw', being prone to making policy gaffes, but his warm, optimistic and intuitive manner enabled him to open up a 10-point lead over Chancellor Kohl in opinion polls during the spring of 1986.

Rau's accession to the leadership also strengthened the party's right wing in the intra-party policy battle. Leftwingers still pressed for the adoption of a radical defence programme – some, for example Lafontaine, favouring complete withdrawal from NATO and the immediate removal of Cruise and Pershing-II missiles; others, including Brandt and Bahr, seeking to give new emphasis to Ostpolitik with the ultimate aim of creating a neutralized, nuclear-free Central Europe[23] – for a curb on nuclear-power generation and for the formation of a 'red-green' federal alliance. They were forced to give way, however, to Johannes Rau, who sought to regain the political middle-ground through the pursuit of a compromise, centrist programme of firm attachment to NATO, the 'freezing' of Cruise and Pershing-II missile deployment, opposition to the 'Star Wars' project, the phased reduction of nuclear power and the re-emphasis of traditional 'bread and butter' economic and 'social justice' issues, but which rejected the possibility of a future federal coalition with the Greens.

Chapter 6

CONSOLIDATING THE WENDE: THE 1987 FEDERAL ELECTION AND START OF KOHL'S SECOND TERM

Party Politics on the Eve of the 1987 Federal Election

The Ruling Coalition's Fortunes Revive

During the spring of 1986, faced with the 'Rau Factor', Chernobyl and the perjury allegations against Chancellor Kohl, victory for the CDU-CSU-FDP alliance in the January 1987 federal election appeared very much in doubt. The ruling coalition also faced the real prospect of defeat in the Land election in Lower Saxony in June 1986 and the loss of its Bundesrat majority. This defeat was, however, averted as the fortunes of the CDU-CSU-FDP coalition were dramatically revived by the events of the summer and autumn of 1986.

First, on 21 and 30 May 1986, the Koblenz and Bonn public prosecutors terminated their investigations into the 'Kohl perjury case' and exonerated the Chancellor fully of all charges of deception.[1] This boost to the ruling coalition was supported, secondly, by strong signs of improvement in the West German economy, which now began to boast a zero rate of inflation and a buoyant level of industrial growth which was at last making some dent on the unemployment total. This provided the opportunity for the government to introduce major tax cuts and to raise farm subsidies (in May 1986) by DM 500 million in an attempt to win back the support of previously alienated middle-class and agricultural groups. A third, and more surprising, boost to the government's fortunes was provided by the Chernobyl disaster. Chernobyl initially lost the government considerable support, but slowly the Kohl administration began to profit from the clear stance it took on the divisive issue of nuclear power. The government made clear its commitment to nuclear safety by calling for a new series of safety checks on the country's reactors and establishing a new environment ministry in June 1986.[2] It refused, however, to countenance a retreat from nuclear power, viewing it as essential to the maintenance of the nation's industrial pre-eminence. This stance reflected the views of many non-committed voters who were concerned with the growing radicalism and violence of the anti-nuclear movement. It proved sufficient for the CDU to narrowly retain, with FDP support, control over the Lower Saxony assembly after the crucial elections of 15 June 1986.

The result in Lower Saxony (*see* Appendix B), despite a significant 6% fall in the CDU vote and a reduction in the CDU-FDP's overall majority from 11 seats to a bare majority of one, came as an immense relief to the ruling coalition. It ended speculation concerning the replacement of Helmut Kohl (56) as the CDU chancellor-candidate for January 1987 and it gave a boost to Martin Bangemann's leadership of the FDP. The poll result came as the greatest blow to the Greens, whose share of the vote rose by only 0.6%. The voters in this bench-mark state clearly became alarmed by the mounting extremism of the ecological party and decided instead to support the SPD, whose local leader, Gerhard Schröder (42), promised radicalism but refused to countenance a 'red-green' coalition. The SPD thus won over many of Lower Saxony's floating voters and raised its share of the state poll by an impressive 5.6%.

Chancellor-candidate Johannes Rau declared himself buoyed by the Lower Saxony result, which he hoped would give a 'good following wind' for the January 1987 federal contest in which the SPD sought to achieve an unprecedented outright electoral majority. Rau was also cheered by the outcome of the party's national conference held at Nuremberg in August 1986 at which he gained warm and unified backing from the party's elder statesmen and acceptance of a radical, but fudged, centre-left manifesto policy programme. In its motion on defence, the conference pledged West Germany's continued support for its alliance with the United States, while at the same time calling for the withdrawal of both American and Soviet medium-range nuclear weapons from Europe (the 'zero option') and an end to West German participation in the 'Star Wars' project. On the issue of nuclear power, the party pledged itself to halt the construction of all new plants, but sought, not the immediate closure, but rather the phasing-out over a 10-year timespan of stations already operating, and a gradual switch towards a new conservation and coal-based energy strategy.

Finally, on the domestic issues of unemployment and social justice, on which Rau himself placed overriding emphasis during his 90-minute keynote address, the party promised, if elected to power, to introduce a major new job-investment programme, which would be financed by tax surcharges on high-wage earners; to continue the move towards a shorter working week; to cut the taxes of lower- and middle-income earners; to improve the opportunities for women; and to reduce social divisions within the country: Rau declaring his intention to govern as a 'Chancellor of all the citizens'.

A Scandal Rocks the Left

Despite the success of Nuremberg, the SPD's repeated assertions that, with a further push, it could achieve a single-party majority within the Bundestag grew increasingly fanciful as 1986 progressed. The opinion-poll rating of Chancellor Kohl steadily improved as a consequence of his exculpation from the 'Flick scandal' in May and the continuing growth in the West German economy, while the rating for Johannes Rau began to dip as political commentators and senior party colleagues, most prominently Klaus Bölling, began to question his lack of federal administrative experience and to examine closely and critically his Land record and imprecise policy prescriptions. Matters worsened for the SPD from September 1986 with news of the collapse of the huge, trade union linked, *Neue Heimat* (New Home) low-cost housing syndicate amid allegations of gross mismanagement and financial irregularities.[3] Although not itself directly involved in the running of the Neue Heimat concern, the failure of what had been seen as one of the shining lights of the 1970s, Brandt-Schmidt era, *Gemeinwirtschaft* (social economy) approach to economic and social affairs seriously disillusioned SPD supporters, particularly blue-collar voters. This was reflected in the 12 October 1986 Bavaria state election, where the SPD vote, despite energetic leadership by Land chairman, Karl Heinz Hiersmann, fell by 4.4% and the party recorded its worst ever result since 1949. A month later, on 9 November 1986, the SPD polled even more disastrously in its traditional stronghold of Hamburg. In the northern city state, which was the headquarters for Neue Heimat, the SPD's vote declined by almost 10% as the party was beaten into second place by the CDU and forced to form a temporary minority administration with the Greens and CDU 'toleration'.

In both elections one of the most notable features of the polls was the low turnout – in Bavaria only 70.3% of the Land electorate voted compared with 78% in 1982, in Hamburg only 77.2% compared with 84% in 1982[4] – as many blue-collar, core SPD supporters, stayed at home. The other significant feature was the sharp rise in support for the Green Party, which entered the *Landtag*, with a 7.5% vote, for the first time in traditionally conservative Bavaria and which, fielding an all-female Land list and campaigning for the immediate closure of all nuclear power stations, significantly increased its strength in the Hamburg *Bürgerschaft* (city parliament), capturing 10.4% of the vote. The party benefited from public concern over a major accident at the Sandoz chemical factory in Basel (Switzerland) on 1 November 1986, which resulted in the widespread and lasting pollution of the Rhine river, and from local opposition to the Wackersdorf (Bavaria) and Brokdorf (near Hamburg) projects. It also profited from splits within the ranks of the SPD, as more radical elements, critical of the centrist Rau's fudged policy programme and his continued refusal to countenance a 'red-green' coalition, transferred support to the ecologist party.

The dismal showing of the SPD in Hamburg produced consternation and disarray in party ranks, with its chief spokesman Wolfgang Clement tendering his resignation and senior colleagues publicly voicing recognition that victory in January 1987 was no longer possible. Indeed, with the national opinion-poll rating of the SPD having fallen from a level of 44% to one of 35–38% since the autumn of 1985, party chairman Willy Brandt declared that a figure of 43% for the party in January 1987 would be a 'good result'. Chancellor-candidate Johannes Rau soldiered on out of a sense of duty, but victory for the right-coalition had become certain as the election campaign entered its final straight in December 1986 and January 1987.

The January 1987 Federal Election

Strauss's Pre-Election Power Play Backfires

By the winter of 1986 polls showed the right-coalition to hold a level of national support of between 52–54%. This could be attributed largely to improved material circumstances, with opinion polls showing that four-fifths of the electorate felt satisfied with the economic situation, though there was concern over the still high level of unemployment (*see* Table 16). However, the crucial question for the coalition's members was how support would be distributed among the individual parties in January 1987. As in 1983, the debate revolved around two issues: first, whether the FDP would once more surmount the 5% federal hurdle; and second, if it did, whether the CDU-CSU *Fraktion* would still be able to secure a majority of Bundestag seats on its own. Again, as in 1983, it was CSU leader Franz-Josef Strauss who took the lead in encouraging this intra-coalition debate.

TABLE 16   THE FIVE LEADING ISSUES FOR VOTERS IN THE 1987 FEDERAL ELECTION

(Ranking in 1983 election is displayed in brackets)[1]

1	Unemployment (1)
2	Environmental Protection (5)
3	Pensions (2)
4	Disarmament (–)
5	Price Stability (4)

[1] In 1983 the third-ranking issue was 'reducing government borrowing'. It ranked seventh in importance in 1987.

The 71-year-old Strauss viewed January 1987 as possibly his last chance of returning to the federal stage as a leading minister, setting his sights on replacing the FDP's Hans-Dietrich Genscher as Vice-Chancellor and foreign minister or, as a second option, taking over from Manfred Wörner as defence minister. He thus began a campaign during the autumn of 1986 which was aimed at discrediting Genscher, by personally interfering in the conduct of foreign affairs and calling into question what he saw as the latter's one-sided policy of *Ostpolitik* detente and his lukewarm support for the United States. In August 1986, as part of this strategy, Strauss precipitated a diplomatic crisis with neighbouring Austria by brusquely replying to the Austrian President Kurt Waldheim's request for the Bavarian Land government to reconsider the Wackersdorf nuclear reprocessing plant project. The crisis had to be resolved by a shuttle-trip by Genscher to Salzburg to smooth ruffled Austrian feathers. Then in September 1986, in an interview with *Welt am Sonntag*, Strauss fiercely criticized Genscher's conduct of foreign affairs and, in particular, his attempt to play mediator between the two superpowers which the Bavarian minister-president likened to 'little Fritz running after the regimental band with his rattle'.

Strauss's actions drew concern from Helmut Kohl and led to the Chancellor's adoption of a more hawkish and conservative image and policy line during the closing months of 1986 in an effort to outflank his right-wing ally. Thus during October 1986 Kohl cautioned the Reagan administration, at that time engaged in arms-control negotiations with the Soviet Union in Reykjavik, not to suddenly remove medium-range nuclear missiles from Europe and made plain West Germany's backing of the American 'Star Wars' programme. The Chancellor, in addition, during the autumn of 1986 continued to resist calls for the imposition of economic sanctions against South Africa; took a firm stance against international terrorism; and employed lax and controversial language in October 1986 and later in January 1987 when he likened the Soviet leader Mikhail Gorbachev's public relations skills to those of 'Goebbels' and declared that East Germany held 2000 political prisoners in 'jails and concentration camps'. More importantly, Helmut Kohl, as the first Chancellor to have lived all his adult life in the democratic Fourth Reich, sought during his campaign speeches between October 1986 and January 1987 to lay to rest the country's Nazi legacy and to give sanction to the espousal of a new, responsible, forward-looking national feeling and pride. This theme was given particular emphasis at the CDU's national conference at Mainz on 6–8 October 1986 and at a major pre-election rally at Dortmund in January 1987, when the Chancellor declared that 'Love of fatherland (*Vaterland*) is a virtue that becomes every people, the Germans as well.'

The rightward shift in the CDU-CSU approach to foreign policy was paralleled at home. The two parties' joint manifesto, entitled 'Manifesto for the Future', placed emphasis upon continuing technological modernization to maintain West Germany as a 'world leader'; on further deregulation, privatization and tax reductions; and on a firmer approach to law and order and immigration control. This hardening of policy and rhetoric worked to the FDP's advantage, resulting in a rallying of support to the liberal party, which was once more viewed as a vital 'corrective' within the coalition by a public supportive of Hans-Dietrich Genscher's vision of beginning a new 'second phase' of Ostpolitik and detente. Thus, as the election campaign entered its closing weeks the poll rating of the FDP increased markedly and when votes were finally cast on 25 January 1987 the Houdini-like third party comfortably surmounted the 5% barrier and recorded its second best national result since 1965, capturing 9.1% of the federal total (*see* Table 17) as 'ticket-splitting' reached a postwar high of 16% of all votes cast.

TABLE 17   THE JANUARY 1987 FRG BUNDESTAG ELECTION[1]
            (TURNOUT 84.4%)

Party	Zweitstimmen Votes ('000)	Share of Total Vote (%)	Seats
CDU-CSU	16,923	44.3	223
SPD	14,134	37.0	186
FDP	3,476	9.1	46
Greens	3,171	8.3	42
NPD	229	0.6	—
Others[2]	267	0.7	
TOTAL	38,200	100.0	497[3]

[1] Excludes West Berlin.

[2] Ten smaller parties captured votes. These included the Ecological Democrat Party OÜDP) and Women's Party, which captured 0.3% and 0.2% of the federal vote respectively.

[3] The CDU-CSU captured 169 direct Erststimmen constituency seats, the SPD 79.

The CDU-CSU, by contrast, despite polls showing its national rating at 49% during December 1986, found its vote severely squeezed during the final weeks of the campaign, and recorded its lowest share of a Bundestag election poll since 1949. The party's share of the national vote fell by 4.5% and its total number of votes captured by more than 2 million. Surveys showed that a net 800 000 CDU-CSU voters, particularly those in the south-west and central Rhine regions, switched support to the FDP; 400 000, concentrated in the industrialized north, to the SPD; and more than 100 000 of its votes were drawn away by the extreme-right NPD, whose share of the national vote tripled to 0.6% (the NPD's best national performance since 1972). A further 750 000 former supporters of the conservative alliance chose to stay at home, as the overall electoral turnout slumped to 84.4%, the lowest level since 1949.

The rightward shift in the CDU-CSU stance on foreign policy and domestic economic issues was the principal factor explaining the alliance's loss of votes to the FDP and SPD respectively. The large-scale abstentions and abnormally low voter turnout was ascribed by psephologists to bitterly cold weather conditions, January 1987 having been the first national election held during winter in the Federal Republic, and to a general lack of interest in what proved to be a dull and predictable campaign, with victory for the incumbent coalition appearing to be certain months in advance. The Kohl team, aware of the dangers of a loss of support as a result of such abstentions, campaigned hard during the closing weeks of the election contest, spending heavily on a media-blitz of advertisements. However, the CDU-CSU's slogans of '*Weiter so Deutschland*' ('More of the same, Germany') and '*Zukunft*' ('The Future') proved tepid and uninspiring.

Vote Shifts on the Left

The SPD was even more concerned and disappointed with its national performance in January 1987 than the conservative CDU-CSU, although its overall share of the federal vote fell by only 1.2% and its total number of votes captured by 730 000. The party, while gaining some net support from the CDU and holding firm in Lower Saxony, the Saarland and North-Rhine-Westphalia, where its locally based chancellor-candidate proved to be a popular figure, lost votes on the centre-right to the FDP and suffered a further haemorrhage of support (estimated at 650 000 votes) on the left and among young first-time voters to the ecologist Greens.[5] The party thus achieved its lowest share of the national poll since 1961 (the first election following its renovation at Bad Godesberg). The result could, however, have been far worse for the SPD. At the end of December 1986, a major survey poll by the Allensbach Institute showed the party's national rating standing at the humiliating level of only 32.4%. Support, however, rallied towards chancellor-candidate Rau, who fought a spirited and well-mannered campaign, during the closing weeks of the contest.

The most striking performance in January 1987 was, however, the continued rise in the fortunes of the ecologist Green Party. Following a typically unorthodox and largely non-political campaign, termed 'Winter Magic', consisting of music festivals, poetry recitals and demonstrations at nuclear power stations and weapons sites, the ecologist party succeeded in easily surmounting the 5% electoral hurdle, raising its share of the federal poll by a third (or by one million votes) to a level of 8.3%. The party drew in considerable support from the 3.6 million new first-time voters and from disillusioned former SPD voters. It made advances, however, all across the country, raising its share of the vote in rural Bavaria, for example, by 7.6%. This, taken in conjunction with the fact that it held seats in seven Landtage, meant that the Greens had truly established themselves as a national party and as a permanent fixture in what had become a quadripolar (two major and two minor) West German party political system. In addition, the entry of the Greens' deputies into the Bundestag, 57% (i.e. 25) of whom were females, significantly altered the complexion of the lower chamber, doubling the proportion of women in the Bundestag to 81 (16%) and placing women's issues to the forefront of the national agenda.[6]

Kohl's Second Term: The Opening Phase, 1987–9

The New Kohl Administration: Continuity or Change?

Chancellor Kohl, despite his rhetorical gestures to the party's right wing, had contested the January 1987 federal election as a man proud and content with the achievements of 1983–7 and who promised no stark policy changes. He pledged instead, under the slogan 'More of the Same', to maintain a steady hand on the tiller and to continue his programme of modernizing and streamlining the economy and maintaining West Germany as a loyal pillar in the Atlantic alliance. The strong showing for the FDP helped ensure that Kohl's programme of economic liberalization, involving the removal of industrial subsidies and support, privatization, further tax reductions and an overhaul of the welfare system, would continue. It secondly ensured, however, that any thoughts that CDU-CSU rightwingers may have had of abandoning West Germany's Ostpolitik brokerage role between East and West and moving towards a more narrowly partisan alignment with the United States would need to be jettisoned. The electorate had rejected calls for a fundamental change in foreign policy and had voted instead in favour of Hans-Dietrich Genscher remaining as foreign minister to pursue his 'second phase of detente'.

Coalition negotiations to decide upon a new cabinet team and common policy programme commenced between representatives of the CDU, CSU and FDP immediately the election was over. During these talks, intense bickering and back-stabbing rapidly developed between CDU and CSU leaders over who was to blame for their recent loss in national support and although Franz-Josef Strauss ruefully accepted Hans-Dietrich Genscher's re-appointment as foreign minister, he made clear his party's continued opposition to Genscher's policy approach and warned that if necessary the CSU might 'drop out (from the coalition) and only tolerate a CDU-FDP government'.[7]

In the more general coalition negotiations, however, following its advances in January 1987, it was the balance-holding FDP which held the upper hand and which clearly stamped its identity over the final agreed programme. First, it forced significant modifications in and liberalization of the proposed new CSU-inspired laws for fighting terrorism and curbing violent demonstrations. Second, it gained a further cabinet portfolio, that of education (*see* Table 18), from the CDU.[8] Third, and most importantly, the FDP succeeded, after three weeks of intense bargaining, in adding to the new legislative programme a radical new DM 44 billion tax reform package designed at reducing the top rate of income tax from 56% to 53%, cutting corporation tax from 56% to 50% and lowering the bottom level of income tax from 22% to 19%.

TABLE 18   THE KOHL ADMINISTRATION CABINET OF MARCH 1987

Dr Helmut Kohl	CDU	Federal Chancellor
Hans-Dietrich Genscher	FDP	Vice-Chancellor & Foreign Affairs
Dr Manfred Wörner	CDU	Defence
Dr Martin Bangemann	FDP	Economic Affairs
Dr Gerhard Stoltenberg	CDU	Finance
Dr Friedrich Zimmermann	CSU	Interior
Dr Wolfgang Schäuble	CDU	Head of the Chancellery
Hans Engelhard	FDP	Justice
Dr Norbert Blüm	CDU	Labour & Social Affairs
Ignaz Kiechle	CSU	Agriculture
Jürgen Möllemann[1]	FDP	Education
Walter Wallmann	CDU	Environment
Frau Dr Dorothée Wilms[2]	CDU	Inner-German Affairs
Dr Jürgen Warnke[2]	CSU	Transport
Hans Klein[1]	CSU	Economic Co-operation
Dr Christian Schwarz-Schilling	CDU	Posts & Telecommunications
Dr Heinz Riesenhuber	CDU	Research & Technology
Frau Dr Rita Süssmuth	CDU	Youth, Family & Health Affairs
Dr Oscar Schneider	CSU	Regional Planning, Construction & Urban Development

[1] New appointment.
[2] Changed responsibility.

The changes to the interior ministry's proposed reforms were bitterly opposed by the CSU, while the plan to reduce taxation on higher income earners was strongly criticized by the CDU's trade unionist and blue-collar wing led by labour minister Norbert Blüm and party general-secretary Heiner Geissler. Thus, when the coalition programme was finally presented to the Bundestag on 11 March 1987, 16 members of the ruling coalition failed to vote in favour of the Chancellor, who received a total of 253 secret-ballot Bundestag votes, only four more than the minimum number required. This, following the decline in CDU support in January 1987, represented a further blow to the diminished prestige of Chancellor Kohl and suggested that the coalition would experience an uncomfortable and unpredictable second term in office.

Wrangles within the Coalition over Defence Strategy: January–August 1987

In Hesse on 5 April 1987, in what was to be the first Land election to be held after the January 1987 federal contest, the CDU polled strongly. The election had been precipitated by the resignation on 10 February of the SPD's minister-president Holger Börner (56) after having been presented with an unacceptable ultimatum from his Green Party coalition partner to refuse permission for the local Alkem plutonium-processing plant, at Hanau near Frankfurt, to continue manufacturing fuel for nuclear power stations. Börner subsequently retired as Land leader, for health reasons, and was replaced as interim minister-president by Hans Krollmann. Differences were swiftly resolved between the Land SPD and Greens. However, with both the local and federal SPD temporarily in a state of disarray, the CDU, led in the Land by the popular Walter Wallmann (54), was able to draw electoral benefit. Adding 2.7% to it 1983 poll showing, it succeeded in bringing to an end SPD-Greens' control of the Landtag by securing a slim seat majority in coalition with the FDP and in strengthening the CDU-CSU position within the Bundesrat, holding 27 seats, one short of the 'decisive 28', to the SPD's 14. For the first time ever, the SPD had lost control of 'Red Hesse'. Immediately, Walter Wallmann resigned as federal environment minister to become Hesse's new minister-president. His replacement in Bonn was Dr Klaus Töpfer, formerly environment and health minister in Rhineland-Palatinate.

This post-election strengthening of the CDU's position proved, however, to be short-lived. A month later, on 17 May 1987, in Länder contests held in Rhineland-Palatinate and Hamburg, the latter having been called in the hope of resolving the 'hung Bürgerschaft' that had existed since November 1986, the Christian Democrats suffered a clear loss of support. This was greatest, 6.4% since 1983, and most humiliating in Chancellor Kohl's Rhineland-

Palatinate fiefdom. Here the ruling party lost the absolute majority of both votes and seats it had held since 1971 and was forced into a coalition with the FDP, who, polling strongly, regained representation in the Landtag. However, even more worrying for the CDU's federal future, was the result in Hamburg. Here, as a result of both a strengthening of the SPD's and FDP's position, the latter similarly regaining Bürgerschaft representation, the first SPD-FDP Land coalition since the collapse of the Schmidt administration in 1982 was formed in August 1987. This led to mounting fears within CDU ranks that this accommodation might be a precursor to an imminent change of partners in Bonn.

The reason for this anxiety and for the disappointing Länder performances of the CDU in May 1987 was the appearance of a serious rift within the Bonn coalition over foreign policy. This resulted from the unexpected acceptance by the reformist Soviet leader Mikhail Gorbachev, in the spring of 1987, of the so-called 'double zero' option for disarmament, under whose terms all nuclear missiles with a range of between 500 and 5000 kilometres, including the 27 ageing Pershing 1A missiles maintained by the *Bundeswehr*, would be removed from Europe. Both the SPD and FDP warmly backed this plan, foreign minister Genscher arguing in justification that even after 'double zero' NATO would be left with sufficient long-range, airborne and tactical nuclear weapons to deter a possible conventional and chemical forces attack on Western Europe by the Warsaw Pact. However, conservatives within the CSU and CDU disagreed with this analysis, maintaining that assent to this proposed scheme would leave West Germany unacceptably vulnerable. On 15 May 1987, on the eve of the Rhineland-Palatinate and Hamburg polls, Chancellor Kohl, seeking to reconcile the seemingly irreconcilable, issued a nine-point policy statement. In it he intimated that, while anxious for disarmament, the CDU could not accept it at any price. This ambiguous, vacillating line irritated an electorate which overwhelmingly supported the policy approach advocated by the SPD and by Hans-Dietrich Genscher. Indeed, national opinion polls showed Genscher, benefiting from the stance he adopted on this issue, emerging as the nation's most popular politician and a 'Genscher bonus' was transferred to the FDP which now enjoyed a national support rating of 10% or more.

Immediately after the two Länder polls of May 1987, Chancellor Kohl attempted to extricate himself from his quandary by unveiling a personal 'triple zero' disarmament scheme, which would also embrace very short-range and tactical nuclear weapons. However, it was ill conceived and attracted little support. Instead, as the summer of 1987 progressed, the Chancellor was forced, both by domestic and international pressure, to come round to the viewpoint of Gorbachev and Genscher, announcing on 26 August 1987 in a keynote Bundestag address that West Germany would support the proposed US-Soviet Intermediate Nuclear Forces (INF) treaty, which was subsequently to be signed in Washington in December 1987, and, when implemented, would destroy its Pershing IAs. This decision enraged the Chancellor's right flank, particularly the CSU, which had pressed for retention of the Pershing IAs as bargaining chips to be used in further negotiations.

Länder Scandals and the Continuing Slide in CDU Support: September 1987–May 1988

Chancellor Kohl's summer 'S-turn' over defence strategy failed, however, to check the slide in both the government's and CDU's popularity as the autumn of 1987 approached. Instead, in the 13 September 1987 Länder elections held in Schleswig-Holstein, a traditional CDU stronghold, and in Bremen, support for the Christian Democrats slumped spectacularly, by 6.4%, over 1983, and 9.9% respectively. One of the principal gainers was the FDP whose vote share rose by 3% and 5.4% respectively. This enabled the party, buoyed by its 'Genscher bonus', to regain representation in the respective assemblies and meant that the FDP now had seats in all 11 Landtage and Bürgerschafte except Bavaria. In Bremen, the Greens also polled strongly, adding 4.8% to their 1983 vote share, as, more surprisingly, did the far-right, in the form of the German People's Union/List D (DVU), an extremist body set up in March 1987 in Munich by Gerhard Frey (54), the wealthy publisher of the neo-Nazi *National Zeitung* newspaper. This party was an offshoot of a DVU established in the early 1970s, subsequently classified by the Federal Office for the Protection of the Constitution as 'extreme right wing'. Contesting Bremen in alliance with the NPD, it captured 3.4% of the votes and one seat in the Bürgerschaft, as well as two seats on the Bremerhaven city council. Farmers, disgruntled about the Bonn government's recent support for agricultural-subsidy cutbacks proposed by the EC, and those recently made unemployed especially deserted the CDU in these Länder polls.

As well as the loss of such special interest support, the CDU was harmed by heightened quarrelling among the coalition partners, both in Bonn and outside, over foreign and domestic policies. Divisions were especially strong over five issues: first, the social balance and financing of the proposed federal tax reforms; second, law and order strategy; third, the deregulation of the post and telecommunications system; fourth, plans to contain escalating health-service costs and to revamp the pensions and *Finanzausgleich* systems; and fifth, the pace and scope of EC integration.

On 10 October 1987, one month after the Bremen and Schleswig-Holstein polls, a tax-reform package, dubbed eulogistically the 'tax reform of the century', was provisionally agreed. However, containing as it did pledges to impose from 1989 a 10% withholding tax on savings and investments, to raise, also in 1989, consumer taxes, to modify regional allowances and employer tax subsidies, and to reduce company tax perquisites, it remained subject to sniping as it passed through the Bundestag. It was also criticized by CDU Länder leaders outside and, on balance, failed to attract public favour.

Differences over law and order strategy also broadened as CSU and CDU rightwingers, the latter termed the *Stahlhelm* ('steel helmet') faction, and CDU and FDP moderates drew conflicting lessons from the Länder poll results. The former grouping, dissatisfied with what they saw as the feebleness of the post-1982 *Wende* and fearing possible future outflanking by the rise on the right of a new competing force, pressed for the administration to adopt a firmer line and exhibit a clearer sense of direction. In the forthright words of Franz-Josef Strauss, the Chancellor was entreated to establish a 'clear political timetable' for action on such matters as the control of political demonstrations,[9] the tightening of political-asylum rules and mandatory testing for AIDS. In contrast, the latter, led by CDU general-secretary Heiner Geissler, and Norbert Blüm, the federal labour minister who had recently been elected CDU leader in North-Rhine-Westphalia, advocated movement towards the 'middle ground' as a means of attracting back voters, especially the young,[10] who had recently 'defected' to the FDP and SPD.

This intra-party and intra-coalition debate over political-electoral strategy continued throughout 1987–9. However, more immediately troubling were events in Schleswig-Holstein where, even before polling had closed in September 1987, a serious political scandal was brought to light. Disclosed to *Der Spiegel* by former CDU press aide Reiner Pfeiffer, it entailed allegations that during the Land election campaign the ruling party's fast-rising minister-president, Dr Uwe Barschel (43), had apparently sanctioned the phone-tapping and surveillance of his SPD centre-left opponent Björn Engholm, as well as the fabrication of compromising evidence. Immediately dubbed 'Waterkantgate' by the popular press, the publicizing of this '*Schmutzige Tricks*' scandal led to Barschel's resignation on 25 September 1987, although he continued to protest his innocence. A week later, on 11 October, Barschel was found dead in mysterious circumstances in a bathtub at an hotel in Geneva. The coroner's report and a subsequent Swiss inquest concluded that he had committed suicide by taking an overdose of drugs and tranquilizers. His family claimed, however, that he had been murdered. The next day, he had been due to face a parliamentary commission of inquiry in the Land capital, Kiel.

Locally, the 'Barschel affair' proved deeply damaging to the CDU. Already, after the September 1987 election, the party had lost the absolute majority it had held in the Landtag since 1971 and had been replaced by the SPD as the largest single party. Immediately after the poll a new CDU-FDP coalition government was formed, but it was dependent for its success on the 'toleration' of Karl-Otto Meyer, deputy for the tiny Danish-speaking minority orientated South Schleswig Electoral Union (SSW), who effectively held the balance of power. However, as the 'Barschel affair' unfolded, the FDP suspended its co-operation. A fresh election was thus called in 1988, being held on 8 May. In it the CDU vote slumped a further 9.3% to only 33.3% and the FDP vote fell by 0.8%, depriving the party of Landtag representation, while, in contrast, the poll share of the SPD, led by the hugely popular, Björn Engholm (48), soared to 54.8%, breaking the CDU's 38-year long hold over the state.

In tandem with a 'state casino scandal' in Lower Saxony that forced the resignation of the Land interior minister Wilfried Hasselmann (64) in October 1988 and almost led to the toppling of the CDU Land administration in a confidence vote, the 'Barschel affair' did much, in the short term, to tarnish the national reputation of the CDU and, in turn, further lower the public-support rating enjoyed by the Bonn coalition. Occurring in the Land in which Dr Gerhard Stoltenberg was CDU chairman, until, in April 1989, he was persuaded by events to resign, its damaging effect was to distract the attention of the federal finance minister.

'Fire on the Right': June 1988–March 1989

Evidence of discontent with Helmut Kohl's leadership of both the CDU and the Bonn coalition was clearly visible at and before the CDU's annual congress held at Wiesbaden on 13–15 June 1988. Indeed, on the eve of the congress younger CDU members, characterized by the media as 'forward thinkers', drew up an anonymous memorandum which, published in the Sunday tabloid *Bild am Sonntag*, speculated that the party was in danger of losing the next federal election if the Chancellor remained at its helm. Nationally, the opposition SPD was neck and neck with the CDU-CSU in voting-intention opinion polls, being accorded a 40% national-support rating (*see* Table 19). Moreover, following its success in Schleswig-Holstein, it had succeeded in trimming the CDU-CSU's Bundesrat majority to only three seats: 23 to 18. Meanwhile, membership of the CDU was declining and even in Rhineland-Palatinate, Kohl's influence was apparently waning. This was demonstrated by the deposition, in November–December 1988, of his friend and ally Bernhard Vogel as CDU Land chairman and minister-president.

TABLE 19   PARTY NATIONAL OPINION POLL RATINGS DURING 1988–9

	CDU-CSU (%)	FDP (%)	SPD (%)	Greens (%)	Republicans (%)
Feb 1988	40	12	40	8	—
Aug 1988	40	9	43	7	—
Feb 1989	38	9	41	8	4
Apr 1989	34	5	43	9	7

There were some areas of improvement for the Chancellor as 1988 progressed. Foremost was the economy. During 1987 its performance had been sluggish, unemployment rising to 2.3 million in December 1987. However, as, in the wake of the October 1987 'Wall Street' stockmarket crash, a concerted attempt began to be made to reflate the European and American economies, West Germany started to benefit from an international investment boom. Also rapidly improving were West Germany's external relations, particularly with Eastern Europe. This was highlighted by the East German leader Erich Honecker officially visiting the FRG for the first time in September 1987 and, his 'Goebbels' comments by now forgotten, Chancellor Kohl visiting Moscow a year later and President Gorbachev Bonn in June 1989. Earlier, in December 1987, Franz-Josef Strauss, as Bavaria's 'head of state', had flown privately to Moscow to hold extended talks with Mikhail Gorbachev. So impressed and captivated by the Soviet leader was Strauss that he pronounced publicly that the Kremlin's reforms were genuine and that no longer should the West 'be afraid of [the] offensive, aggressive intentions of the Soviet Union'. This dramatic 'conversion' of a one-time arch Russophobe helped to bring a greater consensus to Bonn's approach to disarmament and East-West issues.

However, the result of elections held in West Berlin on 29 January 1989, followed by local elections in Hesse in March 1989, precipitated renewed panic within CDU-CSU ranks. In West Berlin Eberhard Diepgen's CDU-FDP coalition lost its governing majority, with support for the CDU falling 8.6% from its 1985 level and with the FDP, whose vote share fell by 4.6%, failing to gain representation in the city's House of Representatives. Both the SPD and Greens/Alternative List made advances. However, the most dramatic success in West Berlin was attained by the far right Republicans. Contesting the city for the first time, the party, led locally by Bernard Andres (37), a policeman with a disquieting toothbrush moustache, captured 7.5% of the vote and 11 seats. This entitled it to two non-voting seats in the Bundestag following the December 1990 general election. Many of the 120 000 votes cast for the party were drawn either from the working-class districts of Neuköln and Wedding or from younger, ill-educated elements within the lower middle class. Two months later, in the Hesse local elections, this voting pattern was replicated. Control of Frankfurt's *Abgeordnetenhaus* (parliament) was wrested from the CDU by the SPD and Greens who, as in West Berlin in March 1989, established a 'red-green' coalition. At the same time, the extremist NPD captured 6.6% of the vote, their best result for two decades, and seven seats. The Republicans put up candidates in only a few wards, but in places achieved a vote share as great as 10.5%.

The far right's surge during January and March 1989 came as a profound shock to West Germany's political establishment. Some viewed the trend as marking a watershed in the FRG's political development, which, by siphoning support away from the CDU-CSU, threatened to erode the incumbent coalition's support base and lead to a transfer of power in December 1990 to the SPD, possibly with the 'toleration' of the Greens. This was because the alternative, an alliance between the 'conventional right', FDP and pariah extreme right had been ruled out of the question. Others viewed the development as a temporary hiccup. Nevertheless, the Republicans' ascent was to be continued into the early summer of 1989, when, fighting on an anti-EC platform and with overall turnout low, the party managed to secure 7.1% of the national vote in the 18 June elections to the European Parliament (*see* Table 20).

TABLE 20   THE JUNE 1989 EUROPEAN PARLIAMENT ELECTION IN THE FRG (TURNOUT 62%)

Party	Share of Vote (%)	(1984 Result)	Number of Seats	(1984 Result)
CDU-CSU	37.8	(46.0)	32	(41)
SPD	37.3	(37.4)	31	(33)
Greens	8.4	(8.2)	8	(7)
Republicans	7.1	(-)	6	(-)
FDP	5.6	(4.8)	4	(0)
Others	3.8	(3.6)	0	(0)

A retrospective examination of the far right's rise between 1987 and 1989 does point to the existence of a number of unique, short-term factors which seemed likely to make it something of a 'flash' phenomenon. However, somewhat longer-term elements were also apparent. Indeed, the far right's 'surge' can be traced back at least to the mid-1980s.

The earliest electoral indication was the Republicans' strong showing in the Bavarian Land election of October 1986. This was followed during 1987–8 by the surprising performances of the Republicans, DVU and NPD, as well as right-of-centre Independent Electors' Associations (FWG), basing their campaigns on local issues, in Länder and municipal contests. The ability of these minor parties to attract between 2% and 3% of the vote in these polls could, first, be attributed to the temporary disaffection of farmers and the self-employed, formerly solid supporters of the CDU-CSU and FDP. Second, it reflected the West German electorate's growing volatility as the secular trend towards voter polarization between the two main right-of-centre and left-of-centre party blocs that had been apparent between 1959 and 1976 progressively gave way to one of fission. Initially such splintering was concentrated on the left, as the ascendant Greens siphoned away support from the SPD. From 1986, however, it had, apparently, spread to the right. Indicative of this party political fission was the January 1987 federal election, in which, at 81.3%, the share of the national vote commanded by the CDU-CSU and SPD stood at its lowest level since 1953. In the June 1989 Euro-election the two major parties' combined share slipped further to 75.1%. Indeed, both individually fell below the 40% mark for the first time ever in a national contest within the FRG.

In addition to the above factors, several more general international and domestic developments cohered to provide a context favourable for the far right's advance.

The relevant international element was the almost concurrent ascent of the extreme right elsewhere in Western Europe. The most notable and dramatic such case occurred in France. There, seizing on the issues of immigration, rising crime and high rates of unemployment, Jean-Marie Le Pen's National Front captured 10% of the national vote in the 1984 and 1986 elections to the European and French parliaments and secured assembly representation. Such success had a spillover and bandwagon effect, helped, as the 1980s progressed, by the closening of cross-national links between the leadership and rank-and-file extreme-right groups. Distressing evidence of the latter was presented on the suicide death in August 1987, in Berlin's Spandau prison, of the Nazi leadership's last survivor, Rudolf Hess, at the age of 93. Though initially buried secretly at an unknown location, in March 1988 his corpse was later transferred to Hess's family cemetery in the Bavarian village of Wunsiedel, which was to become a symbolic, wreath-laying focal point and centre of 'pilgrimage' for adherents to the developing West German and pan-European ultra-right movement.

An additional contributory domestic influence was the recent onset, associated with generational changes and the nation's delayed 'coming of age', of a broad debate within the West German media and universities over how contemporary citizens should approach and interpret the 'German past'. Aspects of this debate were touched on by Chancellor Kohl during his 1987 federal election campaign speeches on 'national pride' and 'love of father-land'. More popularly, growing interest in the recent past had begun to be generated by the highly acclaimed television serial *Heimat* ('Homeland'), which, movingly, depicted the mixed cross-generational experiences of ordinary small-town Germans from before the Third Reich to the present day. It was, however, within West Germany's intellectual community where controversy was being most visibly generated as a 'new historical revisionism' began to be promoted by several prominent scholars, most notably

Andreas Hillgruber and Ernst Nolte. In monographs published during 1986–7 and in journal and newspaper articles, they controversially propounded the view that, while obviously abhorrent, the Nazi era should not be treated as uniquely evil. Indeed, Nolte argued, in his study *The European Civil War, 1917–1945* (1987), that Stalin's resort to mass terror and brutal purges was equally, if not more, execrable and both provided a model and, through its threat of communist expansionism, helped to promote such Nazi atrocities as the 'Final Solution'. Furthermore, in these and other works the case was presented for placing the relatively brief Nazi era in its proper historical and comparative perspective. In particular, it was felt that it should not be allowed to fully overshadow other 'brighter' and more favourable chapters in the history of a nation which Nolte viewed as having frequently stood out as a 'middle state' buttress of freedom within Europe.

Clearly influenced by the 'new thinking' emanating from the 'great historians' dispute' (*Historikerstreit*), Dr Philipp Jenninger (56), president (speaker) of the Bundestag and a close ally of Chancellor Kohl, in an address on the 50th anniversary of the infamous *Reichskristallnacht* (9–10 November 1938) anti-Jewish pogrom, attempted to explain frankly to the West German public how Hitler had been able to rise to power and secure the collusion of many ordinary Germans in his crimes. In particular, he emphasized the specific socio-economic circumstances of the period, as well as Hitler's renowned talent for mass psychology and the apparent political and economic achievements of 1933–8. Unfortunately for Jenninger, the speech, delivered in a clumsy and pedantic manner, was misinterpreted, wrongly, as an apologia for Nazism and its persecution of the Jewish community. During the address, around 50 deputies from the SPD, Greens and FDP walked out of the federal assembly in disgust. A day later, on 11 November 1988, with the public uproar showing no sign of abating, Jenninger, whose own Catholic parents had been harassed for their opposition to the Nazis, was forced to resign as speaker.

Such changes in the *Zeitgeist*, though, as the response to Jenninger's speech revealed, being by no means universally shared, provided a potential seedbed in which the new extremism could begin to grow. However, in seeking to explain why, specifically, between 1988 and 1989 the far right proved able to advance so swiftly, emphasis must be given to two additional, unexpected events.

The first, and pre-eminent, was the rapid post-1985 influx into the FRG of refugees, both 'ethnic Germans' from Eastern Europe, the by-product of the 'new detente', and asylum-seekers from the troubled and impoverished 'South'. The sharp rise that took place during 1986 and 1988–9 among the latter immigrant category (*Asylanten*) is showed in Table 21. Far more dramatic, however, was the post-1986 inrush of *Aussiedler* 'moving out' of Eastern Europe, especially Poland and the USSR, as East-West political and economic relations thawed dramatically. The inflow of *Übersiedler*, 'moving over' from East Germany, was, initially, more gradual. However, from the summer of 1989 it was to turn into an unstoppable torrent (*see* Chapter 7).

TABLE 21   IMMIGRATION INTO WEST GERMANY: 1980–9 (BY CATEGORY)

Period	Übersiedler (From GDR) ('000s)	Aussiedler (Ethnic German Immigrants from USSR and Eastern Europe) ('000s)	Asylanten (Non-German Asylum-Seekers) ('000s)	Grand Total
1980–4 (Av.)	20	47	50	117
1985	23	40	75	138
1986	26	43	100	169
1987	20	80	57	157
1988	40	204	103	347
1989	344	376	122	842

The immigration of East European 'ethnic Germans' was, during 1986–8, broadly welcomed at first and helped, in the process, to create within the FRG a growing sense of 'Germanness', a feeling of shared history and culture. However, as the numbers increased during 1988–9, the difficulties of integration mounted. Already, by the autumn of 1988 the three principal Aussiedler reception camps, Friedland in Lower Saxony, Unna-Massen in North-Rhine-Westphalia and Nuremberg in Bavaria, were seriously overcrowded and the Länder and local authorities were beginning to complain of shortages of affordable accommodation and training facilities for those moved on, as well as the burden that was being placed on their welfare budgets. Meanwhile, public-opinion polls shifted, registering, as early as September 1987, a clear majority (58%) in favour of the federal government taking firm measures to staunch the inflow. Resentment of the financial and accommodation privileges that were being afforded to these 'returning Germans' and to the potential competition that they presented in the job and housing markets, at a time of high unemployment and rising rents, was especially acute in the poorer wards of such larger cities as West Berlin and Frankfurt, which already had sizeable immigrant communities, supra-10% in the case of West Berlin. In response to this disquiet, in August 1988 the Bonn government announced a two-year DM 2.3 billion investment package, entailing the construction of temporary Aussiedler homes, as well as skill-training and German-language instruction centres. This belated programme was, however, to be soon swamped by the massive refugee influx of 1989.

The minor parties of the far right took full advantage of the *Überfremdung* (too many foreigners) concern of growing numbers of West Germans that had been sparked off first by the findings of the 1987 census, showing the FRG-born population in decline and the foreign-born proportion rising sharply, and then by the refugee influx of 1987–9. Campaigning on a simplistic *'Ausländer raus'* ('foreigners out') slogan, they drew support away from both the outer flank of the CDU-CSU, as well as from marginal groups who had formerly voted for the SPD. Indeed, an analysis of the June 1989 Euro-election suggested that while 750 000 Republican Party voters were former CDU-CSU supporters, at least 150 000 had been redirected from the SPD camp.

However, as well as the immigration issue, a second unexpected event provided the extreme right with a 'window of opportunity' for rapid advance. This event was the death on 3 October 1988, from a massive circulatory collapse during a hunting expedition, of Franz-Josef Strauss, the so-called 'uncrowned king' of Bavaria. Though by now in his early 70s, Strauss had remained, until his sudden death, a formidably active figure and, moreover, despite his conversion to 'detente', a continuing thorn in Chancellor Kohl's side. Indeed, so great had his influence remained that in June 1988 he had been able to force the inclusion in the Bonn government's tax reform bill of an embarrassing and controversial clause which granted tax exemption on aviation fuel to amateur pilots, whose number included Strauss. A fierce nationalist and rousing, populist orator with strong views on law and order, Strauss had, since 1982, established himself as the 'conservative counterweight' in the federal coalition. In the process, he had channelled into the CSU and CDU support originating from beyond the centre right. On his death a vacuum was immediately created on the conventional right, presenting a potential opportunity for the leaders of the extreme right. The chance was to be seized by the Republicans' leader, Franz Schönhuber (66), a one-time colleague of Strauss's. Schönhuber, who had left the CSU in 1983 in disgust when the Bavarian leader helped arrange a $483 million loan for communist East Germany, was endowed with both charisma and an oratorical prowess which had been derived from his earlier experience as host of a popular Bavarian television talk-show. He was to utilize these gifts during 1989–90, as he embarked upon a bid to become the acknowledged leader of the fast-rising far right.

Kohl Responds: March–October 1989

In the immediate wake of the electoral shocks of January and March 1989, a bandwagon appeared to be growing for the extreme right. The combined membership of the Republicans, NPD and DVU had climbed by mid-1989 to around 40000, a figure which was almost double the 1987 level. In addition, funds were pouring in, both from the new members attracted and from the state, the Republicans alone deriving DM 16 million of state subventions as reward for their performance in the June 1989 Euro-election. Meanwhile, as support for the ultra right grew, political and racial friction was heightened in West Germany's leading cities, clashes between far-right and far-left ('*Nazis raus*') groups becoming increasingly commonplace. With four contests due in the Länder in 1990, including one in the Republicans' Bavarian homeland, where they had garnered 15% of the vote in June 1989, further progress for the extreme right was anticipated.

The advance of the far right and the concomitant erosion of support for the CDU in seven successive Länder contests between May 1987 and January 1989 set alarm bells ringing within the governing party. Despite a vigorous economic upturn being under-way and a dramatic improvement in West Germany's relations with its eastern neighbour and the USSR, leading to an enhanced sense of national security, no electoral bonus had yet been transmitted either to Chancellor Kohl or to the parties of Bonn's black-yellow coalition. Instead, in the early months of 1989, with a federal election due at the end of 1990, the combined opinion-poll rating of the CDU-CSU standing, at around 38%, at its lowest level for decades and CDU deputies showing signs of revolt in the Bundestag, notably, on 15 March, over a child-benefit package agreed with the FDP, speculation began to mount that, at the party's September 1989 Bremen conference, a move might be made to secure a new leader and, in the process, chancellor-candidate for December 1990. The possible candidate most frequently mentioned was Dr Lothar Späth (51). Premier of the nation's most prosperous and successful state, Baden-Württemberg, Späth, largely through distancing himself from Bonn's recent initiatives, had succeeded in the Land election of March 1988 in confining the party's vote loss to less than 3%. This had left him as the sole CDU minister-president able to rule without the support of a coalition partner.

However, this crisis situation brought to the fore the fighting qualities and political skills, particularly party political, of Chancellor Kohl, a politician who throughout his career had been consistently underrated by opponents and political commentators, and who had frequently been written off prematurely. Much criticized for 'flabby' and indecisive leadership, Kohl, between April and September 1989, acted decisively to shore up national support for the ruling coalition and, striking with what a former aide termed his concealed 'killer instinct', at the same time secured his own position of dominance within his CDU party. It was a counterthrust which had been carefully planned by the Chancellor during his Easter break at his favourite retreat in the Austrian Alps.

First, in a wide-ranging policy speech delivered to the Bundestag on 27 April 1989, Kohl announced the reversal of a series of unpopular recent decisions. These included, first, the imposition of a 10% withholding tax on investment earnings. Since coming into force in January 1989, it had led to an outflow of funds abroad and was thus now immediately abolished. Second, a plan to extend the period of military conscription from 15 to 18 months, due to come into force in June 1989 but fiercely opposed by the FDP, was summarily postponed. Third, in an effort to take the heat out of the immigration issue, the Chancellor announced that Aussiedler would be encouraged, in future, to remain in their own countries. In addition, in March 1989, visa requirements were imposed for visitors from Turkey and Yugoslavia. Fourth, with the clear intention of attracting support from centre-left progressives, schemes designed to encourage the use of catalytic converters on small cars and to improve the position of women (through family benefit changes) were also unveiled in Kohl's April 1989 'declaration' and, despite American and British misgivings, it was announced that a decision on modernization of the short-range Lance nuclear missile launchers stationed on FRG soil would be shelved until 1992, at least.

This volley of executive decisions exhibited to the full Chancellor Kohl's pragmatic and realistic approach to political affairs, as well as his willingness to recognize past errors. They also showed a desire on the part of the CDU to continue as a *Volkspartei*, with initiatives being designed both to draw in support from right and left, as well, with respect to the Lance decision, to mollify Hans-Dietrich Genscher and the FDP.

As a means of underpinning the change of direction that the March–April 1989 policy initiatives were designed to signal, as well as, hopefully, improving the ruling coalition's image, Chancellor Kohl also effected a major reshuffle of the federal cabinet on 13 April 1989. The heads of three of the leading ministries, Defence, Finance and Interior, were changed and there was also a facelift in five more minor portfolios (*see* Table 22). Overall, in what constituted a slight rightward shift in the ideological balance within the cabinet, the conservative CSU gained one additional seat, as the post of government spokesman was now accorded cabinet rank.

TABLE 22   THE KOHL ADMINISTRATION CABINET OF APRIL 1989[1]

Dr Helmut Kohl	CDU	Federal Chancellor
Hans-Dietrich Genscher	FDP	Vice-Chancellor & Foreign Affairs
Dr Gerhard Stoltenberg[2]	CDU	Defence
Helmut Haussmann	FDP	Economic Affairs
Dr Theodor Waigel[3]	CSU	Finance
Dr Wolfgang Schäuble[2]	CDU	Interior
Rudolf Seiters[3]	CDU	Head of the Chancellery
Hans Engelhard	FDP	Justice
Dr Norbert Blüm	CDU	Labour & Social Affairs
Ignaz Kiechle	CSU	Agriculture
Jürgen Möllemann	FDP	Education
Dr Klaus Töpfer	CDU	Environment
Frau Dr Dorothée Wilms	CDU	Inner-German Affairs
Dr Friedrich Zimmermann[2]	CSU	Transport
Dr Jürgen Warnke[2]	CSU	Economic Co-operation
Dr Christian Schwarz-Schilling	CDU	Posts & Telecommunications
Dr Heinz Riesenhuber	CDU	Research & Technology
Frau Ursula Lehr	CDU	Women, Youth, Family Affairs & Health
Frau Gerda Hasselfeldt[3]	CSU	Regional Planning, Construction & Urban Development
Hans Klein[2]	CSU	Special Tasks & Government Spokesman

[1] Earlier, in November 1988, Ursula-Maria Lehr (58), formerly director of the Institute of Geriatric Research at Heidelberg University, had entered the cabinet, replacing Dr Rita Süssmuth (51), the country's most popular politician, who had succeeded Philipp Jenninger as Bundestag president. In the same reshuffle, Helmut Haussmann (45), the FDP's secretary-general, took over from Martin Bangemann (54) as economy minister, after his party colleague and leader had resigned to assume charge of the EC Commission's internal market and industry portfolio.
[2] Altered portfolio.
[3] New appointment.

The most striking move was the replacement at defence, by Gerhard Stoltenberg, of Dr Rupert Scholz (51), who had held charge of this key ministry for barely 11 months. As a former professor of law and senator for justice in the West Berlin government, Dr Scholz had been a controversial choice to succeed Dr Manfred Wörner, when the latter resigned in May 1988 to become the new secretary-general of NATO. Indeed, not only did Scholz lack experience in defence matters, he had not even done military service. In addition, he had been a CDU member for only five years. At the time, Scholz's appointment was interpreted as a move by Chancellor Kohl to strengthen his hand, vis-à-vis Hans-Dietrich Genscher, in the strategic sphere by installing his 'own man' and one, moreover, who, with a hawkish outlook, was attractive to the CDU's right wing and to the CSU. However, Scholz's 11-month period in charge at defence was an unhappy one. He exhibited a lack of tact in his relations with his department's professionals and, through continuing to support outspokenly modernization of NATO's short-range nuclear weapons, had ended up at odds both with the foreign minister and the Chancellor.

His successor, Gerhard Stoltenberg, was almost equally inexperienced in military affairs. The reason for his transfer was political. As a consequence of his ineffective presentation of the administration's tax reform package, Stoltenberg had simply become an electoral liability as head of the finance ministry. As his successor, Chancellor Kohl selected Theo Waigel (49), who had succeeded Franz-Josef Strauss as CSU chairman in October 1988. A lawyer by background, the new finance minister was an affable, clear-speaking and astute conservative politician who had the benefit, moreover, of a good television manner.

The three other significant changes occasioned by this reshuffle were: the replacement of the abrasive Friedrich Zimmermann (63) at the interior ministry by the highly regarded former head of the chancellery, Wolfgang Schäuble (46); the dismissal of the unpopular Friedhelm Ost (46) as government spokesman and his substitution by Hans Klein (57), a personable former development-aid minister and journalist; and the induction, as building minister, of the CSU's Gerda Hasselfeldt (38), thus bringing the number of women in the federal cabinet to a record figure of three.

Initially, Chancellor Kohl had also sought to utilize the opportunity of the April 1989 reshuffle to bring to heel one of his most serious intra-party critics, Heiner Geissler, by offering him a cabinet post in return for his agreeing to step down as CDU general-secretary. Geissler rejected this suggestion. Four months later, however, on 21 August 1989 he was to find himself ruthlessly dismissed. Geissler (59), who counted among his allies the influential figures of Lothar Späth and Bundestag president Rita Süssmuth, threatened a fight back at the CDU's 11–13 September 1989 Bremen congress. However, this threatened 'day of reckoning' failed to materialize. Instead, Geissler's sacking after 12 years as party general-secretary was confirmed. He was replaced by Volker Rühe (46), a former deputy leader of the CDU's Bundestag Fraktion and security expert who, somewhat to the right of Geissler, was a pragmatic ally of Chancellor Kohl. In addition, Lothar Späth surprisingly failed to secure re-election to the party praesidium, while Kohl himself was re-elected CDU chairman unopposed, with 77% of the delegates' votes. Although this vote share was the lowest ever achieved by Kohl in his 16 years as party leader, the events of August–September 1989 served to highlight the decisive behind-the-scenes influence that the Chancellor continued to wield within the CDU. Renowned for both the breadth and warmth of his personal relationships with officials within the CDU at Land and federal level, Kohl drew upon these contacts to decisively rout his chief opponents and secure his own position.

The Opposition Parties During 1987–9

The SPD: Progressive Advance under a New United Leadership

While January 1987 had produced acrimony within the ruling coalition as its members fought amongst themselves over the spoils of office, for the SPD it represented a depressing realization that former Fraktion leader Herbert Wehner's prediction in October 1982 that the party, once out of power, would face more than a decade in the wilderness before the next *Machtwechsel* appeared increasingly prophetic and realistic. Wehner had believed that the SPD would need to maintain itself as a moderate, respectable *'seriös'* opposition party within the Bundestag during these wilderness years, making itself ready to accommodate the FDP once the latter 'hinge party' decided to switch coalition partners again. The dramatic rise in support for the Greens on the SPD's left flank since Wehner's 1982 prognosis had served, however, to significantly modify the calculations of senior party strategists and to open up a major intra-party debate over the most propitious route forward during the months following January 1987.

The lead in this debate was assumed by party leftwingers, a group which during the 1986–7 Bundestag campaign had been privately critical of the Rau centrist majority strategy and thus had failed to give the SPD's chancellor-candidate wholehearted support. Within hours of the announcement of the federal result, Oskar Lafontaine made public, in a national press conference, his personal conviction that Rau's ruling-out of the possibility of a 'red-green' coalition following the 1987 election had been a 'fatal mistake'. This view was reiterated by fellow leftwingers at the SPD executive's post-election conclave at Bonn on 26 January 1987. The position of the left was further strengthened at this meeting when the weary and dispirited Johannes Rau announced that he intended to return to North-Rhine-Westphalia and concentrate on his duties as minister-president. He stated that he would remain as one of the party's two federal deputy chairmen, but had no desire to seek future nomination as party chairman when Willy Brandt retired. During 1986, Brandt had declared his intention of stepping down as SPD chairman when the next leadership elections took place in 1988. In fact, however, Brandt's tenure continued barely two months after the January 1987 election before he was forced to resign prematurely on 23 March 1987 as a result of mounting criticism of a number of his recent leadership decisions. In particular, there was uproar within the party over Brandt's attempt to appoint Frau Dr Margarita Mathiopoulos (31), a young, inexperienced Greek journalist with CDU leanings and who was a personal friend of his wife, as the party's new national spokesperson, replacing Günter Verheugen.[11]

The retirement of Brandt, after 23 years at the party's helm, and the departure of Rau from the federal stage left the door open for a new generation of younger and more radical politicians to capture control of the SPD executive machinery. In fact, however, the left, with Lafontaine having overplayed his hand during January–February 1987, proved unable to immediately secure the party's chairmanship. Instead, Hans Jöchen-Vogel (61), a pragmatic centrist who had efficiently led the SPD's Bundestagfraktion since 1983, was elected unopposed to this position at a special congress held in Bonn on 14 June 1987. Moreover, another tough-minded centrist, Frau Anke Fuchs (50), a former health minister who had a background in the trade union movement, was elected, at the same time, as party manager, replacing the ineffectual Peter Glotz. The left, however, did secure, in this June change-around of personnel, the party treasuryship (Hans Ulrich Klose), while its leading star, the dynamic and controversial Oskar Lafontaine (43), the so-called 'Ayatollah of the Saarland', was elected to replace Vogel as a party deputy chairman and clear heir-apparent. Lafontaine's elevation to second-ranking position within the SPD hierarchy was a reflection of the continuing leftward shift that had taken place within the party's ranks since the later 1970s. At the August 1986 Nuremberg conference, for example, political commentators noted that an 80% majority existed for centre-left policy positions, while, almost without exception, all the new members elected to the SPD's 42-member national executive were drawn from what had come to be termed the 'new left'.[12]

The January–March 1987 intra-party quarrels and turmoils were punished by the electorate in the Hesse Land poll. In this contest, a 6% slump was recorded in the party's vote share and control was lost over one of the left's core Länder, as well as four important Bundesrat seats. With the initial cause of the Hesse debacle being the breakdown of the Land's 14-month-old SPD-Greens coalition as a result of intransigence on the part of the environmentalist party, it also caused an intensification of the intra-SPD debate over the likely efficacy of a future red-green coalition in Bonn for which the party's Lafontaine wing continued to press.

The setback of Hesse was, however, to prove to be an isolated reverse for the SPD during 1987–9. True, in three (Rhineland-Palatinate, Bremen and Baden-Württemberg) of the subsequent seven Länder polls which were held between May 1987 and January 1989 the party's vote share did fall very slightly. However, in the other four contests encouraging advances were achieved. Indeed, control was secured over two additional Länder, Schleswig-Holstein and West Berlin (in alliance with the Alternative List/Greens), while a new SPD-FDP alliance was formed in Hamburg. This brought, by March 1989, the number of the FRG's 11 Länder ruled by the SPD to 6 and its share of the 41 voting seats in the Bundesrat to 18. Furthermore, with an opinion poll rating at this time of between 40% and 43%, the SPD had established itself as the nation's most popular party, enjoying a lead over the CDU-CSU combined of around 3%.

One of the chief reasons for the upturn in SPD fortunes between 1987 and 1989 was the strong leadership that was being provided by Hans-Jöchen Vogel. In contrast to the indulgent and ambiguous

Brandt, Vogel, noted as a workaholic and disciplinarian who was nicknamed 'the Headmaster', brought order and a clearer sense of purpose to a party that had formerly been drifting somewhat aimlessly and, in the process, had been losing members, 8000 between 1985 and 1987, and voter support. In addition, as a consensus-seeking, integrative leader, Vogel did much to bring the SPD's previously warring wings much closer together. He was helped in this task by the fast-improving international environment, which served to convert many former 'hawks' within the party into disarmament-supporting 'doves'. Additionally, he was aided by the fact that a number of former party radicals became more moderate in outlook, shifting progressively towards the SPD's centre-left mainstream. One such example was the new minister-president of Schleswig-Holstein, Björn Engholm. The most prominent, however, was Oskar Lafontaine who, once dubbed 'Red Oskar', caused uproar among the SPD's trade-union supporters when, in March 1989, he publicly advocated that, as a means of tackling the huge unemployment problem, those already employed ('insiders') should accept more flexible labour hours, including working more at weekends, and should adopt a shorter working week, but with a proportionate pay cut. Such a programme of 'economic realism' would, Lafontaine believed, helped generate employment, in a job-sharing fashion, for so-called 'outsiders' (the unemployed and part-time workers). The proposal was condemned by the leaders of the IG Metall, OTV (public service) and IG Chemie trade unions. However, it was supported within the party by the veteran figures of Brandt and Schiller, as well as such representatives of the 'new left' as Engholm, Klose and Gerhard Schröder, SPD leader in Lower Saxony.

The SPD's new-found unity, which contrasted sharply with the divisions manifest among the partners of the Bonn coalition, was clearly exhibited by the almost unanimous approval that was accorded to the party's preliminary platform for the December 1990 federal election, the Berlin Programme, by the delegates attending its 18–20 December 1989 congress. This policy programme combined radicalism in the external sphere, where it called for the creation of nuclear-free zones and an end to the deployment of US and Soviet troops in Europe, with a new-found, almost 'neo-liberalism', in its approach to economic matters, advocating the promotion of entrepreneurial activity and a gradual reduction in the length of the working week to 30 hours as a job-creation measure. In addition, the platform committed the party to granting high priority to protection and improvement of the environment and to impro-ving and strengthening workers' and women's rights. To show that it was serious in achieving progression on the latter issue, and also to respond to the challenge that had been presented here by the Greens, the party had earlier, at its August–September 1988 Münster congress, passed a series of far-reaching rule changes to put its own house in order. These included the establishment of fixed minimum quotas for the representation of women in party posts, beginning immediately at a third and rising to 40% by 1994. As a consequence, a new deputy-chair was created, being filled by Herta Däubler-Gmelin (47). It was similarly pledged that immediately, commencing with the June 1989 Euro-elections, one-third and by 1998 40% of SPD Bundestag, state and local deputies would be female. At the time these changes were made only 16% of SPD MDBs, 17% of Landtage and Bürgerschafte deputies and 25% of its overall membership were female. (The corresponding CDU-CSU proportions were 8%, 10% and 20%.)

However, despite the SPD's renewed cohesion, founded at its centre upon the reconciled controlling duumvirate of Vogel, in charge of organization, and Lafontaine, a telegenic prospective chancellor-candidate, its chances of success in the upcoming federal contest still appeared somewhat remote. This was because no obvious minor partner existed upon which a majority coalition could be built.

During much of 1988, with the CDU-CSU and FDP divided over defence matters and with a SPD-FDP alliance having been formed in Hamburg, speculation began to mount that a *Gezeitenwechsel*, ('change of tide') and of coalition partners in Bonn, was imminent. This talk was, however, dampened by the election, on 8 October 1988, of Count Otto Graf Lambsdorff (61) as the FDP's new leader.[13] As the chief architect of his party's September 1982 break with the SPD and further to the right on economic matters than his predecessor Martin Bangemann, Lambsdorff's elevation, despite his outspoken and abrasive personal qualities, appeared likely to lead to a forging of closer CDU-CSU-FDP links, especially since it coincided with the departure of the destabilizing figure of Franz-Josef Strauss.

The Greens remained the alternative potential federal partner for the SPD. During 1987–8 divisions within the former party appeared to render impracticable such an alliance. However, from the spring of 1989, with red-green city government coalitions being formed in West Berlin and Frankfurt, speculation concerning the possible future formation of a SPD-Green coalition in Bonn was rekindled. Toleration of the notion had spread to the party's centre, with Hans-Jöchen Vogel no longer categorically ruling out the possibility. Much appeared to depend upon how long and how well national support for the SPD continued to hold up and also whether or not the Greens could heal their internal divisions and transform themselves into a responsible movement and reliable prospective coalition partner.

The Greens: The 'Fundi' versus 'Realo' Feud for Party Control

In the immediate wake of the January 1987 federal election, buoyed by its impressive poll performance, confidence soared among the Greens, especially among the party's *Fundi* wing, which began to gain ascendancy. As a reflection of this, there was a clear hardening in attitude towards the terms that the party would demand for entering coalition governments, with Rainer Trampert, one of the Greens' national leaders, declaring in February 1987 that the party would hold back from pacts with the SPD until the latter had thoroughly 'renewed themselves'. He added confidently, 'We are firmly in the saddle.' In the same month, the SPD-Green Hesse coalition in February 1987 foundered as a consequence of such obduracy.

A further indication of this changed mood within the party was the significant shift in the balance of power that now occurred within the party's controlling councils. First, the radical Hamburg 'eco-socialist', Thomas Ebermann (35), was elected in place of the *Realo* Otto Schily as one of the Greens' six Bundestag executive-committee members. Then in early May 1987, at the party's annual federal congress, held at Duisburg, the 'Fundis' strengthened their grip over the party's national executive, capturing eight of its 11 seats, an advance of two. Moreover, all three of the new 'spokes-people for the year' were 'Fundis': Fräulein Jutta Ditfurth (35), Rainer Trampert and Lukas Beckmann.

With the party's 'Fundi' wing ascendant, a controversial campaign was launched in the late spring of 1987 designed to disrupt operations connected with the country's census; the Greens argued that this *Volkszahlung* (people count) was an intolerable intrusion of privacy and that any data gathered would be misused. As a consequence of this stance, the Greens' party headquarters was raided by police on 25 April 1987 and leaflets bearing the slogan,

'Only sheep let themselves be counted', were confiscated. A measure of public support for the Greens' stand was, however, manifested in large anti-census rallies in West Berlin and Hamburg and by the boycotting of the 1 June count by a significant minority, despite the threat of liability to fines of up to DM 10000.

In the Länder elections of 1987 the Greens, despite the party's evident internal divisions, performed respectably, achieving not inconsiderable advances in Rhineland-Palatinate (where it secured Landtag representation), Hesse and Bremen and only sustaining one reverse, in Hamburg, where a 'Fundi'-dominated list had been presented. As a consequence, by the year's end the Greens held representation in all but three, North-Rhine-Westphalia, Saarland and Schleswig-Holstein, of the nation's 11 state assemblies. However, the following year, 1988, was one of deepening turmoil for the party.

An initial tumult had been caused at the close of 1987 by the murder, at Frankfurt airport on 2 November, of two policemen by hooded *Chaoten* who had attached themselves to an environmentalist demonstration. This prompted the party's Bundestagfraktion, which was dominated by 'Realos' and effectively led by Otto Schily, to secure, on 8 December 1987, passage of a resolution which defined the Greens as a 'non-violent, eco-pacifist, radical democratic reform party' and repudiated links of any kind with groups which advocated the use of force. However, immediately, this initiative was condemned as 'presumptuous' by non-parliamentary 'Fundis'.

An even more fundamental challenge was presented to the party by the fact that one of its key campaigning planks, its call for nuclear disarmament, was increasingly fading as a party political issue. This arose from the accelerating moves towards demilitarization that were being taken by the two global superpowers, commencing with the December 1987 INF accord, and which had gained the support of all the significant parties within the FRG. In other areas also, environmental protection and women's rights, both the Bonn coalition and oppposition SPD were beginning to steal the Greens' clothes. Green issues had clearly moved to the forefront of the national agenda; however, little of the electoral benefit was now accruing to the Greens. Indeed, in both of the Länder contests held during 1988, in Baden-Württemberg and Schleswig-Holstein, the Greens' vote actually declined.

The Greens' fortunes hit rock bottom in early December 1988 when a special conference had to be suddenly convened as a result of the unearthing of a scandal concerning the allegedly irregular handling of the party's funds by its 'Fundi'-dominated national executive. A confidence motion was called by the 'Realos' in combination with the so-called 'Neutralos', an independent, centrist faction led by Frau Antje Vollmer, and went against the executive, by 214 votes to 186. As a consequence, the 11-member national executive was forced to resign and was replaced on 11 December by an interim, 'Realo'-dominated, five-member commissariat.

In retrospect, however, the humiliation of the 'Fundis' at the Karlsruhe special conference marked an important turning point in the Greens' development. A month later, the party's Alternative List allies polled strongly in West Berlin, and in March 1989, with the 'Realos' now ascendant, they were persuaded to moderate their demands and enter into an alliance with the SPD, led by Walter Momper (44), to assume charge of a city government that was to contain the first-ever female majority in the FRG. A similar red-green coalition was formed in Frankfurt and concurrently, at the party's annual congress, held in Duisburg between 3–5 March 1989, the 'Fundis' were decisively marginalized. A new moderate five-strong national executive was elected and, in addition, a vote was taken in favour of seizing, what was described by party strategist Hans-Christian Ströbele as, the 'chance of the century' to form, if possible, a federal coalition with the SPD after December 1990. These moves were reflective of a new mood for unity and integration that had begun to sweep though the party. Also enjoying success in its campaigns to secure closure of the Brokdorf nuclear plant and the shelving of plans to build a nuclear reprocessing plant at Wackersdorf, clearly the fortunes of the Greens were, by the summer of 1989, on the rise again. However, this 'second coming' was abruptly checked from the autumn of 1989 by unexpected developments beyond the Elbe which, as 1990 progressed, were to transform dramatically both political priorities within the FRG and the relative standings of individual parties and their leaders. These developments are examined in Part Three, commencing, in Chapter 7, with a tracing of their essential roots, as the postwar political history of the 'Other Germany', the GDR, is briefly analysed and the heady events of the summer and autumn of 1989 described.

Part Three

TOWARDS THE NEW GERMANY

Chapter 7

THE OTHER GERMANY: THE RISE AND FALL OF THE GDR'S SED REGIME, 1949–89

The Model Socialist State: The GDR 1949–76

As a direct Cold War riposte to the Western Allies' backing for the formation of the Federal Republic, 16 days earlier, the German Democratic Republic (GDR) was fashioned on 7 October 1949 from the Soviet zone of occupation (SBZ) that had been established east of the river Elbe after the *Wehrmacht*'s surrender in May 1945. It comprised a much-reduced eastern, substantially Prussian, segment of the Third Reich, centred around Berlin, with raw material-rich Silesia, agriculturally fertile Pomerania and, in the far northeast, abutting the Baltic, the area of East Prussia, which included the city port of Königsberg (Kaliningrad), ceded to Poland and the USSR under the terms of the August 1945 Potsdam Accord. Following that accord, their large ethnic German populations had been swiftly and systematically expelled. Extending for just over 108 000 square kilometres between the rivers Elbe and Oder-Neisse and embracing a population of around 16–17 million, the state comprised less than half the area and below a third of the people of the neighbouring FRG. An artificial creation, it remained officially unrecognized outside the socialist camp until 1969. What is more, as late as March 1952, when the creation of a neutral unified Germany was proposed by Stalin, even the commitment of its Soviet overlords to its separate existence remained in doubt. In addition, with its leading cities, Berlin, Dresden, Leipzig and Magdeburg, having been subjected to ferocious Allied bombing raids and military assaults between 1939 and 1945 and, thereafter, gutted by heavy Soviet war reparation demands, the territory had lost a huge share of its industrial capacity and infrastructure, far more than had the FRG, which was to soon receive a much-needed infusion of Marshall Aid.

Despite these unpromising origins, the new GDR state, benefiting, it was widely assumed, from its inheritance of the Prussian virtues of diligence, respect for law and fealty to the established order, was to swiftly acquire a reputation as the most politically stable, loyal and successful, in economic terms, of the Soviet Union's East European 'satellites'. Indeed, just as the new FRG became characterized as the paradigm modern liberal-democratic capitalist state, so the GDR was viewed as the model socialist polity. Its communist leaders, of whom there were but two between 1950 and 1989, Walter Ulbricht (1950–71) and Erich Honecker (1971–89), adhered faithfully to the changing party line set by Moscow, at least until the onset of the Gorbachev era. Moreover, domestically, though shaken early on by the popular uprising of 17 June 1953, an insurrection which had to be suppressed with the assistance of Soviet troops at the cost of between 25 and 100 lives, the authorities kept a firm lid on dissident activity. Occupying a key frontline position, the state played contented host to 380 000 Red Army soldiers and, until the implementation of the 1987 US-Soviet INF accord, Soviet medium-range nuclear missiles, in addition to contributing a fifth of a million troops to the Warsaw Pact, which it had joined in May 1955. Moreover, such was the new nation's apparent economic success that, by the mid-1980s, it claimed Europe's ninth highest national output and was ranked among the world's dozen foremost industrial powers. Furthermore, its per capita living standards and health and welfare services were the most advanced in the communist world.

Instruments of Political and Social Control

The dominant force within this East German state, accorded a 'leading role' by the constitutions of 1968 and 1974, was the Socialist Unity Party (*Sozialistische Einheitspartei Deutschlands*: SED). A Marxist-Leninist body, it had been formed in April 1946 by the Soviet-coerced merger of the German Communist Party (KPD) with the Social Democratic Party (SPD), a much more popular and firmly rooted, especially in well-industrialized Saxony and Thuringia, left-wing force. Like its Eastern bloc counterparts, this new hybrid party became organized pyramidically on the revolutionary cadre model of the Communist Party of the Soviet Union (CPSU). At its base, it encompassed, by the 1980s, almost 80000 small 'primary party organizations'. These were located in factories, collective farms and other workplaces and contained an average of 30 members. Above, there rested a hierarchy of small-town/village (*Ort*), district (*Kreis*), region (*Bezirk*) and national party committees, with secretariats and first secretaries, each being 'elected' by regular congresses and being charged with the authority to oversee the work of parallel state bodies (*see* Chapter 3). In accordance with the key Leninist governing principle of 'democratic centralism', the policy decisions and personnel choices of each of these party units were vetted, and in effect determined, by the level immediately above. This meant that ultimate authority within the GDR resided with the SED's three apical bodies: first, and pre-eminently, with the *circa* 20-member Politburo (*Politbüro*) and its administrative adjunct, the Secretariat (*Sekretariat*), both permanent organs which, together, had charge of formulating and determining policies, supervising cadre selection and executing day-to-day party business, with a general-secretary in charge of proceedings; second, with the *circa* 160-member Central Committee (*Zentralkomitee*), which met privately at least twice a year (and usually four times) and had the authority of 'electing' the Politburo, Secretariat and SED general-secretary; and, third, the National Congress (*Parteitag*), which, comprising several thousand delegates 'elected' at regional conferences, convened quinquennially and, in turn, 'elected' the Central Committee to act on its behalf between congresses. Ultimate authority within the SED was wielded by an inner core of disciplined, obedient, party-trained full-time functionaries, the *Apparat*, of whom 2000, working in 40 departments, were based at the Central Committee's East Berlin headquarters. Its leading representatives also filled key state posts.

From the outset, in accordance with Moscow's strategy of encouraging the establishment of ostensibly popular 'united fronts' across Europe, four allied 'fellow travelling' parties, the Democratic Peasants' (or Farmers') Party (*Demokratische Bauernpartei Deutschlands*: DBD), the Christian Democratic Union (CDU), the Liberal Democratic Party (*Liberaldemokratische Partei Deutschlands*: LDPD) and the National Democratic Party (*Nationaldemokratische Partei Deutschlands*: NDPD), were also permitted to operate in the five

Länder, later (from July 1952) 14 *Bezirke* (regions), of East Germany. They joined with the SED in the National Front of the GDR, an umbrella organization which contested elections as a single bloc, with quotas of seats in state assemblies being guaranteed for each constituent party. However, although designed to broaden support and to integrate into the regime potentially hostile rural, bourgeois, professional and Christian interests, in practice they were subservient, satellite organizations, operating effectively as, what has been described as, '"transmission belts" for SED policies'.

With a membership of around 2.3 million during the mid-1980s, equivalent to 14% of the GDR total population and more than 18% of its adult inhabitants, the SED claimed the third highest 'party:people density' ratio in the communist world. It was only fractionally behind North Korea and Romania, each with membership 15% of the population total. The *nomenklatura*, or system of appointments, ensured that key posts in all areas of public life, the media, diplomatic service, local government and state industries, were reserved for approved party members, who were the country's new privileged elite. This led to the extension of the tentacles of party control throughout the nation, vertically and horizontally. Millions more GDR citizens were also indirectly incorporated within the regime through their association with bodies participating in the SED-led National Front. They included the 470000 members of the four recognized 'allied parties', the 2.3 million enrolled with Free German Youth (*Freie Deutsche Jugend*: FDJ), a wing of the SED specifically designed for young persons aged between 14 and 25 years; the 1.6 million who belonged to the Democratic Women's League of Germany (*Demokratischer Frauenbund Deutschlands*: DFB) and to the League of Culture (*Kulturbund*: KB); and the 9.6 million workers affiliated to the Confederation of Free German Trade Unions (*Freier Deutscher Gewerkschaftsbund*: FDGB).

As well as attempting to integrate its citizens through membership of approved mass organizations, the SED regime, conscious that it was a Soviet imposition bereft of popular legitimacy and accountability – all GDR elections were non-competitive, single-list affairs – also resorted to methods of 'socialization' and ideological tutelage-indoctrination. These were variously effected for the nation's youth by the education system, which sought to inculcate GDR patriotism and love of the Soviet Union. Additionally it was sought through membership of the Young Pioneers and FDJ movements and, then from 1962 and 1978 respectively, by compulsory military service, lasting 18 months, and obligatory military training in schools for 15- and 16-year-olds. For the adult population, wide-ranging controls over the media and nation's culture were imposed, entailing censorship and propagandizing, and also surveillance by the secret police and the concealed threat of the use of terror. The secret police were controlled by the infamous *Stasi*, or ministry for state security (*Staatssicherheit*). Between 1957 and 1989, under the command of the ultra-vigilant General Erich Mielke (1907–), it grew to become the most active and influential state secret police force within Eastern Europe, with the exception of that of Ceaucescu's in Romania. Functioning as 'the shield and the sword' of the SED, at its height the Stasi employed 85000 full-time operatives. It maintained a network of between half and one million part-time, often personally compromised, informers and house-block super-visors, and had eyes and ears everywhere. It monitored domestic and international phone calls, intercepted mail and eventually amassed, in its East Berlin central headquarters, 170 kilometres of files. These included detailed reports on 6 million suspected 'subversives' residing within and outside the GDR.

The Ulbricht Era: Political Developments in the GDR, 1949–71

During the later 1940s and the 1950s, a programme of 'Sovietiza-tion' and 'Denazification' was instituted within the GDR under the, initially, neo-Stalinist leadership of Walter Ulbricht (1893–1973). Ulbricht was a veteran of the *Spartakusbund* and subsequent wartime exile in Moscow, who served as SED first secretary/general-secretary from 1950. The programme involved the estab-lishment, under the terms of the October 1949 constitution, of a new one-party political system; a reliable new National People's Army, staffed almost exclusively by officers who were committed members of the SED; a fundamental re-organization of the judicial and educational systems on 'non-bourgeois' lines, with new young, 'ideologically correct' personnel appointed to replace purged teachers and judges; and a concerted attack on the strength and autonomy of the Christian Churches. In the economic sphere, financial institutions, utilities and industries were progressively nationalized, a central-planning apparatus was set up and large-scale *Junker* agricultural landholdings expropriated. In 1951 the central planners inaugurated a Five Year Plan which, despite the GDR's meagre resource endowment, put a Stalinist emphasis on heavy industrialization. By 1960 the old Junker landholdings were converted into new agricultural collectives and, after its entry into Comecom in 1950, the country became increasingly closely integrated commercially with its fellow East European socialist states.

However, these 'Sovietizing' initiatives provoked visible opposition within the GDR. The most explicit indicators of this discontent were a general strike, involving a third of a million construction and industrial workers, and a wave of mass pro-democracy and pro-unification demonstrations which engulfed the nation on 17–18 June 1953. These uprisings, which affected more than 270 localities, were largely fomented by food shortages caused by the regime's campaign against private farming and by the forthright opposition of the blue-collar labour force to the government's recently passed 'higher work norm' laws. These laws, which were subsequently annulled, required more work for the same level of pay. The unrest was also stimulated by the death, three months earlier, of the Soviet dictator Josef Stalin and the opportunity that seemed to be presented by the vacuum produced by the ensuing power struggle in Moscow and by uncertainty in East Berlin. On 9 June, for example, the SED executive had raised hopes of more fundamental change by announcing the launching of a more liberal 'New Course'. More implicit, but just as telling, evidence of popular dissatisfaction was the huge westward exodus of young adults through the so-called 'Berlin hole'. Between August 1949 and August 1961, when this exit route was finally closed by the erection of the heavily fortified and closely guarded Berlin Wall, described by the regime as its 'anti-fascist protective barrier', at least 2.7 million, or 15% of the population, left for the Federal Republic. Well over half who 'deserted' were under the age of 25. This contributed to a chronic labour shortage within the GDR.

The SED high command initially reacted to these indications of internal malaise by instituting a succession of purges of 'revisionist' party members, particularly former Social Democrats, who were considered unreliable. For example, justice minister Max Fechner (1892–1973) was dismissed in July 1953 and expelled from the SED. In addition, a number of the leaders of the four allied 'bourgeois' parties were eliminated. At the same time, the SED leaders set about constructing new, more reliable, instruments of coercion, including the rapid development of the Stasi. In a more enlightened manner, they also authorized, from 1963, the launching of a series of economic reforms which, taken together, became known as the 'New Economic System'. These entailed a greater resort to material incentives, an initial decentralization of managerial authority, reform of the price system, a new-found concern for plant profitability and, finally, a change of emphasis from heavy industries towards consumer goods' production. These initiatives, combined with the stabilization of the labour supply after the construction of the Berlin Wall, stimulated the industrial sector. Indeed, official figures suggested that manufacturing output rose annually by 5% per annum during the 1960s and early 1970s. Per capita national income also advanced at a similar rate, ownership of such consumer durables as washing machines, fridges and televisions spreading swiftly. All this helped to ease social tensions and earn the SED a greater measure of popular support and respect.

The Early Honecker Era: 1971–6

In May 1971, the ageing Walter Ulbricht, who, during his later years, had become increasingly unpredictable and independent in his policies, finally lost the confidence of the SED's Soviet masters. At the Central Committee's 16th plenum, he was persuaded to retire as SED general-secretary, and was replaced by Erich Honecker. Honecker was the party's specialist on security matters and had been directly responsible for the construction of the Berlin Wall. Ulbricht continued as chairman of both the SED and State Council until his death in August 1973. However, both were to become largely ceremonial positions.

Erich Honecker, the party's new supremo, was, in contrast to the forceful and vigorous-looking Ulbricht, who sported a Lenin-style goatee beard, a somewhat frail, bespectacled, colourless figure. Born across the Elbe, in the Saarland, in 1912, he was a coalminer's son who had joined the communists' Young Pioneers movement as early as 1922. Graduating to the KPD in 1929, he spent a decade during the Nazi era of 1935 and 1945 in prison for his 'subversive' opposition to the regime. After the war, he spent a further decade as chairman of the communists new FDJ youth movement, before, in his mid-forties, being finally made a full member of both the SED Politburo and Secretariat, in 1958, and placed in charge of the defence and security services. In this position, he impressed the Russians by his cautious pragmatism and almost obsequious loyalty. In particular, he caught the eye of the rising Leonid Brezhnev, head of the CPSU between 1964 and 1982.

Initially, Honecker was to share effective authority within the GDR with Willi Stoph (1914–), the country's Prime Minister since

September 1964 and, before that, an interior and defence minister. But within a few years, utilizing his command of the party machine and his patronage authority to promote like-minded associates, he succeeded in establishing himself unquestionably as the polity's truly dominant force.

In the economic sphere, the new Honecker regime was characterized by continuing flexibility and adaptation. Most notable was the creation of more than 150 new, substantially autonomous, concentrated industrial enterprises, termed *Kombinate*, from 1980. The new regime was also distinguished by a deepening concern for social welfare. A major housebuilding programme was launched, though still insufficient to keep up with burgeoning demand, and improvements were made to the material position of pensioners. The Honecker era also witnessed unprecedented cultural liberalization until November 1976, when the expatriation from the FRG of the controversial East German poet and singer Wolf Biermann and the placing under house arrest of the regime's Marxist critic Professor Robert Havemann signified the onset of a new 'freeze'. It also saw a growing toleration towards the Christian Churches. This culminated, after Honecker's landmark, 6 March 1978, meeting with representatives of the League of Evangelical Churches in the GDR, in the allocation of increased time on radio and television to Church affairs and the sanctioning of the construction of new churches in Dresden, Jena and Leipzig.

The cultural and religious 'thaw' of the early and mid-1970s was largely the result of international pressures, in particular the onset of detente between the USSR and USA, which reached its apogee on 1 August 1975 with the signing of the Helsinki Final Act. An even more direct by-product of this East-West detente was (*see* Part Six) the rapprochement occurring between the two Germanies. This was formally signified by the 21 December 1972 Basic Treaty governing relations between the two states. This document entailed the FRG's de facto recognition of the GDR's separate existence. As a consequence of this and concurrent treaties, the GDR's diplomatic isolation was at last ended. On 18 September 1973 the country, together with the Federal Republic, entered the United Nations and by 1976 had secured official recognition by 121 states, an almost five-fold advance on the corresponding 1970 total. At the same time, the GDR's financial, commercial and human contacts with the West began to burgeon. This helped to boost domestic living standards.

A Model Under Strain: The GDR between 1976 and 1989

Honecker's 'Middle Phase': The Era of Abgrenzung, 1976–85

In retrospect, the early 1970s stand out as a golden era in the GDR's political-economic development. It was now, a recognized member of the international community, active overseas as a sponsor of insurgency movements in Black Africa, increasingly successful on the sporting stage at the Munich (1972) and Montreal (1976) Olympics, the home for a newly thriving literature and arts and enjoyed an official standard of per capita income fast approaching that of the UK. This young socialist state, with a vigorous leadership at its helm, had, it appeared, decisively come of age. Subsequently, however, except in the sporting sphere, there was little progression. Instead, problems increasingly accrued for an SED command that was finding itself buffeted by debilitating domestic and external economic and political developments.

The most intractable problem was economic. By the mid-1970s, after a decade and a half of commendable advances, the GDR economy, metaphorically, suddenly hit a brick wall as far as its per capita levels of production and income were concerned. At the same time, its level of foreign indebtedness grew to a worrying extent, its total Western debt reaching \$710 per capita during 1984, compared to a Comecon average of \$230. Increasing imports of capital and consumer goods from the West failed to be balanced by commensurate exports. There were a number of explanations for this state of affairs. First, the gradual exhaustion of the country's already limited raw materials base, with, for example, the GDR's last coal being mined in 1977, even though it continued to produce lignite. Second, the worsening of its terms of trade because of the sudden rise in world energy prices following the OPEC hikes of 1973–4 and 1979–80. Third, the onset of recession in many of the capitalist economies, especially between 1980 and 1983. Fourth, the mounting industrial competition in international markets by the NICs of South-East Asia. Fifth, the widening of the technological gap between the GDR and the capitalist West. Finally, the unsuitability of the rigid framework of central planning for production of the new range of light and high-technology products which were now in increasing global demand. The resulting stagnation in GDR living standards was to have profound consequences, leading to mounting popular dissatisfaction with the SED regime, as well as a loss of self-confidence among the party's rank and file and apparatchiks.

Moreover, public disenchantment was deepened by the obvious comparisons between East and West. As a consequence of growing direct and indirect contacts with the FRG, through cross border exchange visits of *Wessis* and East German pensioners, telephone conversations and FRG television transmissions, awareness of the disparity in real living standards and political freedoms began to spread. A new corrosive feeling of 'relative deprivation' began to emerge and critical comparisons between the relative merits of the respective 'real socialist' and liberal capitalist states were increasingly made.

Alarmed at what it saw as the destabilizing and polluting nature of the growing contacts with the so-called *Klassenfeinde* (class enemies) of the FRG, the SED leadership took firm action in October 1980. By suddenly raising, to DM 25, the minimum daily amount of 'hard currency' which foreign tourists were required to convert into Ostmarks, it succeeded in bringing about, within a year, a 40% reduction, to two million, in the number of visits from the Federal Republic. This initiative formed part of a much broader strategy of ideological *Abgrenzung* (delimitation), instituted by the Honecker regime as the 1970s progressed. It entailed a direct counter-attack against the West German notion of *Ostpolitik*, which sought to strengthen the sense of *Zusammengehörigkeitsgefühl*, or belonging together. It did this by placing emphasis on the two Germanies' historical and current socio-economic differences, suggesting officially that, while the eastern territory had always been characterized by a progressive working-class culture and the western by that of a ruling exploiter class, since 1945 the two states had moved irreversibly apart. As part of this strategy, the names of bodies carrying the word 'German' were altered to 'GDR/DDR' and the constitution revised in 1974 to similarly delete all references to Germany and include the explicit provision that the 'Democratic Republic' would remain 'forever and irrevocably . . . united with the USSR'. Even the international registration letters for East German vehicles were altered from the 'D' for *Deutschland* to the 'DDR'.

This policy was made possible and encouraged by a concurrent change in the external climate as, in the wake of the Soviet invasion of Afghanistan, in December 1979, the imposition of martial law in Poland, in December 1981, and the election, in November 1980, in the United States of the right-wing Republican Party President Ronald Reagan, detente suddenly gave way to a new cold war era. Visibly shaken by the near overthrow of the socialist regime in neighbouring Poland by the Solidarity free trade union movement, during 1980–1, East Germany's SED leadership retreated into its shell and congealed around an increasingly hardline and conservative domestic policy stance. A new 'freeze' engulfed the cultural sphere, with the launch, in November 1976, of the first of a wave of dissident crackdowns and the tightening, in June 1979, of the penal code. Increased penalties were imposed for 'agitation against the state and the establishment of illegal contacts, (and) public vilification'. Church-state relations also became more and more strained, particularly since the former had begun to show signs of seeking to establish itself as a patron and protector of emerging new environmental, peace and civil rights movements. Increasingly paranoid, the regime reverted to policies of coercion and repression, perfecting, in the process, its surveillance state (*Überwachungsstaat*).

Honeckerism under Challenge from Without: 1985–9

During the closing years of the Brezhnev general-secretaryship and throughout the ensuing administrations of Yuri Andropov (1982–4) and Konstantin Chernenko (1984–5) relations between the GDR and the Soviet Union became unusually close. The Honecker regime found itself regularly lauded for its ideological purity and loyalty, demonstrated perhaps most clearly in 1984 when the GDR joined the USSR in boycotting the Los Angeles Olympics. Moreover, the East German economy, based on its substantially autonomous *Kombinate*, despite a slackening during the 1980s of the annual growth rate of 'Net Material Product', the socialist equivalent of GDP, to an official 4%, but more probable 2%, still remained Comecon's most successful. It was presented as a model of 'developed socialism' that the USSR should attempt to replicate.

This state of affairs soon changed after March 1985 with the accession to Kremlin power of Mikhail Gorbachev, the new Soviet leader, committed to radical, liberalizing and decentralizing, political and economic reform. Increasingly, Moscow exerted pressure on the ageing SED leadership to 'change its ways' and 'move with the times', and to join its fellow socialist states of Eastern Europe in a thoroughgoing overhaul of its political and economic structures. These entreaties were, however, resisted by an East Berlin government apprehensive of the likely adverse domestic consequences. A tense cooling-off ensued, eventually to be broken, in October 1989, by the Soviet-sponsored ousting of Honecker soon after the celebration of the GDR's 40th anniversary. This incident revived memories

125

of May 1971, but this time the outcome was very different. There was no smooth succession. Instead, within a matter of weeks, confronted both by popular insurrection and mass desertion across the frontier, the SED regime, which had hitherto seemed almost set in stone, imploded at an astonishing pace. Indeed, the socialist state failed to reach its 41st birthday.

This sequence of events, described and analysed in more detail in the following section, would have appeared inconceivable to any observer of the East German political scene during the mid-1980s. Then, the Honecker regime appeared impregnably entrenched, with the forces of dissident opposition, although beginning to grow, very much scattered and still largely ineffective. Honecker, himself, had been unanimously re-elected general-secretary of the SED in April 1986 by the party's 11th congress. A substantially unchanged, experienced Politburo was also returned. It had an average age, of full members, of 64, and contained eight septuagenarians, all of whom had joined the KPD or SPD during the period between 1925 and 1931 and had spent the Nazi period either in detention or in exile. Each was a committed communist who had endured tremendous hardship and made great personal sacrifices early on in life. All continued to feel proud of the achievements of 'their GDR', though, they conceded, minor adjustments were now required in the economic sphere. Thus, in the new Five Year Plan, covering the years 1986–90, emphasis was given to developing the 'key technologies' of micro-electronics, automation, robotics, nuclear energy and biotechnology, as well as enhancing efficiency in resource use and improving product quality and design. In general terms, however, the SED's high command remained convinced that the country had been set on the correct course, Honecker asserting contentedly in his report to congress:

> Looking back over the past five years, we can say with all due modesty that despite all manner of disruptive manoeuvres on the part of imperialism, the cause of socialism has made further progress in the German Democratic Republic . . . While it has not yet reached a state of perfection, we have made good headway.

Seventeen months later, on 7–11 September 1987, Honecker, clearly enjoying a politician's 'Indian summer', at last achieved one of his life's remaining goals, that of being invited to the Federal Republic to pay an inaugural 'working visit' as the GDR's head of state. This trip, which technically fell short of an 'official visit', had been made possible by a renewed 'thawing' of East-West relations. The early 1980s' cold war, which had bred friction between the two Germanies, forcing them, reluctantly, to accept the respective deployment of Soviet and American intermediate-range nuclear missiles on their soils, gave way to a new era of ever-deepening detente. In addition, it reflected some weakening of the GDR's strategy of *Abgrenzung* as, under mounting financial pressure to secure FRG credits, East Berlin began to allow human contacts between the two peoples to increase once again, East-West travel restrictions being relaxed considerably from 1986. As an additional pre-visit concession to the West German government, the GDR regime announced, in mid-July 1987, a general amnesty for prisoners, excluding war criminals, convicted Nazis, spies and murderers, and the abolition of the country's, rarely used, death penalty. However, this represented only a temporary political liberalization. Soon after the Honecker visit, the Stasi were once more at work rounding-up alleged dissidents.

While the SED regime was attempting, between 1985 and 1989, to pursue this 'business as usual' strategy, assenting to only limited adjustments, dictated by economic exigency, far-reaching reforms were being instituted in the Soviet Union by Mikhail Gorbachev under the three slogans of *perestroika* ('economic restructuring'), *glasnost* ('openness') and *demokratizatsiya* ('democratization'). Appalled by the economic inefficiency and stagnation in both the USSR and other Comecon states since the mid-1970s and by the alienation of their citizens, especially the young, Gorbachev was determined to breathe new life into the political economies of Eastern Europe. His methods were to promote, in the economic arena, greater managerial autonomy and recourse to market mechanisms and, in the cultural and political spheres, a new spirit of unfettered debate and, within socialist bounds, competition. The ideas of the Soviet leader were constantly evolving and, as the decade progressed, became increasingly radical, or, in Western terminology, liberal.

The socialist leaderships in Hungary and Poland promptly followed, and in some cases pre-empted, the Gorbachev lead. In February 1989 the Central Committee of the Hungarian Socialist Workers' (Communist) Party accepted the need for multi-party democracy and sanctioned the passing of a new Law on Associations, enabling opposition groups to operate legitimately. Already in Hungary producer prices had been deregulated and a stock market established. In Poland, in April 1989, following two months of round-table discussions with leaders of the Solidarity free trade union movement and the Roman Catholic Church, the ruling Polish United Workers' (Communist) Party concluded an historic agreement which conceded the right to strike, relegalized Solidarity and established a timetable for semi-free parliamentary elections.

In contrast, in the GDR, as in Czechoslovakia, Bulgaria and Romania, Moscow's 'new thinking' was received coldly. Indeed, for hardliners within the SED command, it was considered simply irrelevant. Kurt Hager, the party's ideology chief, expressed this view perhaps most bluntly when, in an interview with the West German magazine *Stern* on 10 April 1987, once pressed on the issue, he asked rhetorically, 'If your neighbour repapered his house, would you also feel obliged to repaper yours?' Consistently, between 1987 and 1989, the SED's leaders resisted Moscow's entreaties for the GDR to join the USSR, Bulgaria, Czechoslovkia, Hungary and Poland in switching to multi-candidate elections for its local and central government institutions. Similarly, they refused to move away from central planning and embrace 'market socialism'. Nor would they countenance more than the most limited cultural *glasnost*. Indeed, so decided were their views that, on occasions, the custodians of the SED's 'correct socialism' resorted to the unprecedented artifice of excising reform passages from the publicly reported versions of Mikhail Gorbachev's speeches. In November 1988 they went even further, actually ordering the banning of the distribution of the Soviet news digest *Sputnik* and the screening of five Russian films. These works, as a consequence of their revisionist reinterpretations of the Stalin and Brezhnev eras, stood accused of 'distorting history'.

The Façade is Shattered: The Sudden Death of GDR Socialism, May–December 1989

The Collapse of World Communism during 1989–91: The Search for Explanations

Within the space of six short months, between May and November 1989, the SED regime, seemingly solidly entrenched, was incredibly toppled and in a most public manner forced, before the world's watching television eyes, to negotiate hurriedly a transfer of power to its pluralist opponents, as a prelude to the GDR's dissolution. This popular 'counter-revolution from below', which occurred at a dazzling speed and which was to encounter surprisingly limited resistance from the incumbent 'old guard', was totally unexpected. However, almost as if the central prop had been removed from the base of a fragile house of cards, it was to inspire immediately a series of 'people power', anti-communist rebellions across Central Europe. These were to prove so successful that, by the spring of 1991, the yoke of socialist one-party rule had been shed from Berlin to Tirana, while the Soviet Union itself, the world's last great land empire, was in an advanced state of disintegration. Europe's postwar political order had been annulled.

Why did this dramatic 'collapse of communism' occur? For decades to come, historians will be engrossed with this question. As the available perspective lengthens and as a body of detailed research is accumulated, a conclusive answer, or at least an accepted consensus, may eventually be reached. In contrast, less than two years after the giddying events, any snap interpretation offered is liable to be partial. Nevertheless, so fundamental is the question that it must be addressed and below two preliminary explanations, one exogenous and one endogenous, are presented.

The first, entailing both causative and permissive elements, revolves around the socialist reform programme that was progressively adopted by the Soviet leader, Mikhail Gorbachev, during 1988–9, and imitated by his 'reform communist' admirers in Hungary and Poland, and the external repercussions of this 'new thinking'. In particular, two radical departures stand out. The first was Gorbachev's public conversion, at the June 1988 special All-Union CPSU conference, to the concept of a 'socialist pluralist' democracy founded on electoral competition and the sanctioning of candidate choice for the March–April 1989 Congress of the USSR People's Deputies parliamentary election. The second was the CPSU leader's historic acceptance that the peoples of the Soviet 'satellite states' should be permitted to choose their own destinies. Playfully labelled by the media the 'Sinatra, do it their own way, creed', it replaced the prevailing 'Brezhnev doctrine' which, used initially in 1968 to justify the invasion of Czechoslovakia, had laid before the Soviet Union the duty of directly intervening to maintain 'correct' socialism in countries within its sphere of influence. Gorbachev's tolerant new precept, which arose both from a Soviet desire to cut back on its burdensome global military commitments and to gain full re-admission into the world diplomatic and economic community, was first given substance in February 1989 when, after more than nine years of deployment, the Red Army was, at last, unilaterally withdrawn from Afghanistan. Five months later, on 8 July 1989, the new liberal doctrine was made explicit when, in the communiqué issued at the conclusion of the Warsaw Treaty Organization's annual summit, it was conceded that:

> There are no universal models of socialism. The construction of a new society is a creative process and is achieved in each country in harmony with its traditions, specific conditions and demands. No country has the right to dictate events in another country, to assume the position of judge or arbiter.

This new stance was underscored definitively in the same month, in a keynote address to the Council of Europe, when Gorbachev pronounced that:

> Social and political orders of one country or another changed in the past and may change in the future as well. However, that is exclusively the affair of the peoples themselves. It is their choice. Any interference in internal affairs of whatever kind, any attempts to limit the sovereignty of states, both of friends and allies, no matter whose, is impermissible.

These sentiments were duly upheld on 24 August 1989 when, following sweeping success in free multi-party elections, the Catholic journalist and Solidarity adviser, Tadeusz Mazowiecki, was elected by Poland's *Sejm* (parliament) to become the first non-communist Prime Minister in the history of the Soviet bloc.

The second explanation for communism's ready demise during 1989–91 centres on the internal weaknesses of the East-Central European satellite regimes. Their people's disenchantment with the status quo, the parallel detachment of the Communist Party rulers, and the crucial lack of resolve to fight to defend their ways of life, all this was to be demonstrated by the governing elites once the buttress of the Soviet 'military guarantee' had been withdrawn.

The public's alienation was the root cause, even in the supposedly successful GDR. It was founded substantially on the failure of the socialist systems to provide the range and quality of consumer goods and welfare amenities that were available in the capitalist West. Indeed, the gap between the two systems progressively widened. Within intelligentsia and Church circles, disenchantment was engendered additionally by a desire for the popular accountability of governments and their servants and for greater freedom of expression. Also, throughout Central Europe, where the communist regimes, unlike those of South-Eastern Europe, Russia, China, Cuba and South-East Asia, had been imposed by the Red Army and were seen in the public mind as staffed by Soviet lackeys, there was a common nationalist resentment. As a consequence, when the genie of socialist reform, that is political liberalization, was released during 1989–90, the communist regimes found it impossible to retain reliable control over the process and move to a new equilibrium. Instead, under popular pressure, there was a succession of unplanned-for concessions and departures, resulting in in the juggernaut of reform being rammed through its intended barriers.

The isolation of Central Europe's Communist Party elites was created in part, the gerontocratic GDR standing out as the best example, by the existence of a generation gap between governors and governed, and between the ruling party's upper- and middle-lower ranks. In addition, it arose directly from the communists' top-down, 'democratic centralist', unaccountable style of rule. In such a system, power eventually became concentrated in the hands of a self-selected few, who were served by sycophantic, truth-distorting cronies and enjoyed the privileges of luxury countryside villas (*dachas*), chauffeured Volvo limousines and access to special health complexes and elite shops. Inevitably, they became divorced from the realities of everyday living.

More surprising was the unwillingness of East-Central Europe's ruling communist elites to use their accumulated power of coercion to crush the unarmed revolts of their peoples when finally challenged during 1989–91. Such force was to be used ruthlessly in communist China on 3–4 June 1989 to overwhelm a massive, six-week-long pro-democracy insurrection which, incidentally, through the television transmission of its scenes, was to play some part in energizing the subject peoples of East-Central Europe. However, China's veteran Communist Party leaders, having fought their way to power through a protracted succession of civil and liberation wars, possessed an inner self-confidence, viewing themselves as their nation's legitimate rulers. Moreover, they could count on large-scale rural support. In contrast, the 'dummy' Communist Party leaders of East-Central Europe lacked such assurance. Only briefly, during December 1989, in Romania, a unique militarized state dubbed the 'Paraguay of the communist world', was there a determined rearguard stand. This was partly because the old-guard leaders were so beguiled by their own rhetoric of 'socialist progress' that they were simply paralysed when popular disaffection became widespread. More crucially, however, when the moments of truth did finally arrive, they felt unable to rely on the loyalty of their army, police and even party middling and lower ranks, dominated, as they were, by cynical, 'fair-weather socialist' careerists.

The explanations presented above may be broadly applied to each of East-Central Europe's 1989–91 anti-socialist 'counter-revolutions'. Additionally, however, within each individual country a number of more specific, unique 'trigger' or 'catalyst' factors can also be identified. In East Germany there were two such 'triggers', which, once activated, set in motion the SED regime's rapid unravelling. The first was the successive, destabilizing decisions taken by Hungary's 'reform communist' government in early May and September 1989 to, first, dismantle the country's barbed-wire frontier fence with the West and, then subsequently, allow tens of thousands of East Germans to cross unimpeded. The second was the state visit paid to East Berlin by Mikhail Gorbachev on the GDR's 40th anniversary during which criticisms were made of the Honecker regime which were were to have far-reaching popular and intra-party repercussions. In the two following sub-sections each of these episodes is examined in greater detail.

'Voting With Their Feet': The Hungarian Exodus of May–September 1989

Throughout its life, East Germany was encumbered by an ever-present reality which confronted no other of the USSR's East European satellite regimes. Its entire population enjoyed the automatic right of citizenship in the territory of its western neighbour, the other Germany across the Elbe. This fact initially prompted inter-German competition for the minds, hearts and stomachs of each republic's people. However, the socialist regime of the GDR was, in practice, ill equipped for this fight and was forced eventually to concede defeat, on 17 August 1961, when the giant monstrosity of the Berlin Wall was hastily erected to encage the citizens of the so-called 'Democratic Republic'. Standing as an embarrassing, ever-present monument to GDR socialism's failings, it nevertheless served its demographic purpose. Backed by strict travel restrictions, it staunched the outflow of people from the GDR to such an extent that from its construction until the mid-1980s only half a million were to leave the country permanently, either as registered refugees, predominantly defectors, or as pensioners given permission to depart. This was the equivalent to just two years of the annual efflux between 1949 and 1961.

The plugging of the 'Berlin hole' helped, during the 1960s and 1970s, to stabilize the East German demographic and economic situation. By the early mid-1980s, the annual East-West outmigration of Übersiedler had settled down to a steady level of around 20–25000 (*see* Table 21), sufficient to provide a 'safety valve' for the discharge of disenchanted mischief-makers and of the burdensome old, without sapping the nation of its prime stock. This stable situation was brought to a sudden end during the summer and autumn of 1989 as a result of decisions taken by the new 'reform socialist' administration that, represented by the troika of Rezso Nyers, Imre Pozsgay and Miklos Nemeth, had recently gained ascendancy in Hungary. A new, though circuitous, 'exit hole' opened, precipitating an exodus crisis that, eventually, was to dwarf that of 1960–1, and the political repercussions of which were to be momentous.

This crisis's extended fuse was ignited on 2 May 1989 in Budapest, 700 kilometres from East Berlin, by the Hungarian government's taking an historic first step towards the dismantling of the Iron Curtain that, for more than four decades, had estranged East from West. Anxious to improve diplomatic and commercial relations with Western Europe, they ordered the country's 260–kilometre-long, electronically guarded, barbed-wire border fence with Austria to be torn down gradually. Over time, a porous exit route from the Eastern bloc to the West became available. As the summer progressed, increasing numbers of East Germans, ostensibly on holiday at Hungary's lakeside resorts, lacking valid exit visas, illegally slipped across this unsealed frontier. As a consequence, the monthly Übersiedler exodus level, which (*see* Figure 3) had averaged several thousand during the first half of the 1989, climbed steeply to almost 20000 during August. The overwhelming majority of those who were choosing to leave were adults aged between 20 and 40 years, in the productive prime of their working lives. Many of them were well-qualified, highly motivated professionals. Their ready abandonment of their homes, material possessions and positions of responsibility in return for the hope of a better, freer and more affluent life in the FRG represented a telling vote of no-confidence in the Honecker regime.

Clearly embarrassed, and also concerned at the adverse impact that this loss of key personnel was beginning to have on its essential services, particularly medical, the East German government put pressure on Budapest to tighten its border security controls. During July 1989 this had a temporary impact. However, the rush to forsake the GDR had acquired such a momentum that during August 1989

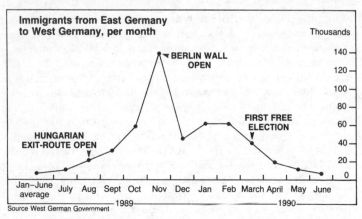

Figure 3: Monthly Emigration from East to West Germany: 1989–90

two additional 'exit routes' emerged: the West German embassies in Warsaw and Prague. Soon these were to become thronged with thousands of refuge-demanding Ossis.

However, what transformed this growing exodus into an apparently unstoppable flood was a critical decision taken by the Hungarian administration on 10 September to 'suspend' its 1969 bilateral agreement with the GDR, requiring it to send back automatically those of its citizens who lacked valid travel documents. This move, which effectively meant that Hungary would no longer stand in the way of those East Germans who were seeking 'economic exile' in the West, arose, ostensibly, from Budapest's desire to uphold the United Nations' convention on refugees and also from its exasperation with East Berlin's failure to check the influx of its citizens into Hungary by cancelling visa-free travel to neighbouring Czechoslovakia. It was also influenced by background pressure exerted by West German interests. A coincidence or not, on 13 September 1989 it was announced that a massive DM 500 million loan from West German banks to help Hungary's export industry had been agreed.

As Figure 3 shows, the outflow of people from the GDR to the Federal Republic, described popularly as 'the Great Escape', increased at a more than exponential rate in the immediate wake of 10 September. Indeed, by the month's end, at least 24 000 East Germans had fled across the Hungary-Austria 'green border'. They were subsequently to move on (*see* Figure 4) to tent-city refugee camps hurriedly established in Bavaria, adjacent to the West German-Austrian border. Between 30 September and 5 October a further 15 000 Ossis who had taken 'asylum' in the FRG's Czech and Polish embassies were transported, with official sanction, to West Germany on bolted, so-called 'freedom trains'. The GDR government had acceded to this 'unique humanitarian act' as a goodwill gesture on the eve of the state's 40th anniversary.

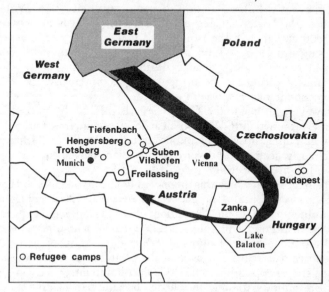

Figure 4: The Hungarian Exodus Route: May–October 1989

On 3 October 1989 the East Berlin government at last took action to try to plug the gaping 'Hungarian hole', by announcing that visa and passport-free travel from the GDR to all neighbouring states was to be temporarily suspended. However, this move had come too late. The mass outmigration of August and September 1989 had already begun to destabilize dangerously the SED-polity, as well as have repercussions on the West German political scene. The exodus was to continue (as Figure 3 shows) at a high level between October 1989 and March 1990, as, under popular pressure, first, on 1 November, the GDR-Czechoslovakia frontier was fully re-opened and, then, most dramatically, on 8–9 November, the Berlin Wall was breached. This relentless westward drift of people, totalling almost 400 000, was to be a continual background influence and pressure on the GDR's political actors as they wrestled to control a fast-deteriorating situation.

135

The Gorbachev Visit and Ousting of Honecker: The Events of October 1989

The visit of Mikhail Gorbachev to East Berlin on 6–7 October 1989, to attend the GDR's 40th birthday celebrations, stands out as the second event to inflame an already combustible situation. Within hours of the Soviet leader's departure, large crowds of between 5–10000 gathered in the capital and in Dresden, chanting pro-democracy slogans. Within a fortnight, Erich Honecker finally stepped down as SED leader. Within a month, a new state government, pledged to the introduction of comprehensive political and economic reforms, was in place.

However, although the Gorbachev visit certainly marked an abrupt caesura in the GDR's political development, it was preceded by a gathering upswell of public agitation as East Germany's customarily feeble and fissured opposition movements at last showed signs of cohering.

The fulcrum on which this union was to be founded was the East German Evangelical Church. With an unofficial membership amounting to 45% of the population, it was the one significant and popular institution within the GDR that had been allowed to retain a substantial measure of autonomy. During the course of the 1980s, as concern over rearmament grew, the Church, which had already voiced strong opposition to the 1978 decision to introduce compulsory pre-military training in schools, became particularly closely associated with the unofficial peace movement. Especially prominent was the East Berlin pastor, Rainer Eppelmann. Having already been jailed for eight months during the early 1960s for refusing to do military service, in February 1982 he was to be taken into custody for two days after publishing, with the prominent Marxist dissident scientist Professor Robert Havemann (1910–82), a 'Berlin Appeal' in which a call was made for the withdrawal of 'all occupation troops from Germany'. Environmentalist pressure groups, campaigning against pollution in Saxony and Thuringia, were also later taken under the Church's wing. So, most controversially, were civil rights activists. In the process, Church-state relations, having enjoyed a rapprochement during the 1970s, became progressively strained. In particular, the Church became outraged by the growing censorship of its publications and, more specifically, by the November 1987 police raid of the Zionskirche's unofficial environmental library. In turn, the SED was angry about the special services that the Church held in support of the release of detained agitators and the sanctuary it provided to dissidents.

Inspired by developments in the Soviet Union, Hungary, Poland and, until June, China, this Church-centred movement in favour of political reform gathered steam as the spring and summer months of 1989 progressed.

The first notable flashpoint proved to be the nationwide communal elections, held on 7 May. In Leipzig, with its appalling problems of pollution and its university-furnished intelligentsia, the opposition movement had, under the patronage of pastor Friedrich Magirius, put down its deepest roots. Almost 1000 people demonstrated in favour of democratic, multi-candidate elections on the evening of the poll. Soon afterwards, when the results were announced there was uproar. An official turnout of 98.77% was claimed, 98.85% of the votes being cast for the National Front candidate slate. This verdict was immediately rejected by Church representatives who had observed the counting process in many cities. Flagrant ballot-rigging was alleged. This served to further undermine the credibility of and respect for the SED-regime.

The state's actions on 7 May 1989 provided an early impetus to the pro-democratization movement. In East Berlin, it led directly to protest demonstrations in the main Alexanderplatz on 6 September and in Leipzig, from 4 September, to weekly rallies of increasing size, after the Monday evening 'peace service' prayer meetings held in the Nikolaikirche by pastor Magirius. During the same month, on 9 September, an umbrella organization, *Neues Forum* (New Forum), was unofficially established by three intellectuals, Professor Jens Reich, a molecular biologist, Bärbel Bohley, an artist, and Rolf Heinrich. Althought it accepted the SED's 'leading role', it campaigned for democratic reforms, justice and environmental issues. It was denied official recognition, but by late October 1989 a petition supporting its founding had attracted more than 100000 signatures, including those of some reformist SED members.

The growth of this reform movement occurred at a time of unusual political paralysis in East Berlin, a temporary leadership vacuum having been created by the incapacitation of the ailing Erich Honecker. Taken ill in early July, and having undergone a gall-bladder operation in late August, the ruling party's leader was laid up through most of September. As a result, the regime's response to the popular challenges presented during September 1989 were uncertain, veering between a crude and antagonizing

137

resort to police repression and mass arrests to a more measured, 'softly-softly' approach.

Honecker resumed full charge of the party and state machines on 25 September 1989, but by this time the popular protest had gained immeasurable strength. On the evening of Monday 2 October the largest demonstration within the GDR since the 1953 uprising took place in Leipzig, subsequently to be dubbed the 'cradle of the 1989 revolution'. It involved 20 000 people, who, in preparation for the imminent Gorbachev visit, enthusiastically chanted 'Gorby, Gorby' and 'liberty, equality, fraternity' as they attempted to force their way into the city's Karl Marx Square. Their march was forcibly broken up by the police, using water cannons, as in Dresden. Four months earlier, between 15–18 May, the Soviet leader had been in Beijing at a time of political turmoil and his visit provoked such an intensification of the popular protest movement that the Communist Party leader, Zhao Ziyang, in this case a reformer, was toppled by his agitated conservative colleagues. Gorbachev arrived in East Berlin on 6 October at a time of similar gathering political unrest and, with a refugee crisis, of mounting socio-economic chaos. As in Beijing, the Kremlin leader was regarded by the onlooking masses as an icon of reform and hope, the torchbearer for a new era of 'enlightened socialism'. Likewise, his visit was to have dramatic repercussions.

The Honecker regime did its best to play down the significance of the Gorbachev visit, extending to its guest-of-honour a muted reception. Indeed, his schedule was kept deliberately secret and television coverage restricted to a bare minimum. As a consequence, the crowds waiting to greet the Gorbachevs were, unsurprisingly, small. For his part, the Soviet leader, in his public speeches, refrained from criticizing his host directly. Nevertheless, it was made clear, in leaks by Soviet press officers, that in his private meetings with Honecker and his senior party comrades there had been a frank exchange of views. Indeed, Gorbachev was later quoted as having warned the East German leader, in relation to the reform process, 'Those who delay are punished by life itself.' To this Honecker, allegedly, retorted, 'Those who are declared dead usually live a long time,' before proceeding to reel off, in a mechanical fashion, the list of the GDR's supposed achievements during his stewardship. So implacably opposed was Honecker to Gorbachev's 'reform socialist' prescriptions that, in a subsequent private meeting with close colleagues, he declared, with prescience, 'everything will collapse if we give an inch'.

Insider reports, most notably provided by Horst Sindermann, then the country's third-ranking politician, have suggested that during his 7 October meeting with the SED Politburo Gorbachev intimated that he believed the general-secretary's 'health' to be too poor for him to continue much longer at the nation's helm. This heavy hint was to fall on receptive ears. So dismayed were many of Honecker's Politburo colleagues at his blinkered and irascible response to the Soviet leader's criticisms that they determined that he should be persuaded to stand down promptly. Splits began to appear in the party's leading councils, as hardliner and reformist factions now emerged, the SED leaders from Leipzig and Dresden standing out as the most prominent members of the latter wing. Meanwhile, on the streets outside, the popular protest movement was gaining in strength as, across the nation, within hours of Gorbachev's departure anti-government protest rallies were mounted, most spectacularly in East Berlin, Dresden, Leipzig, Halle, Potsdam and Karl Marx Stadt. The police and internal security forces were, initially, deployed in a brutal manner, breaking up the demonstrations with tear gas and water cannons and resorting to hundreds of arrests. However, on the evening of Monday 9 October, the authorities' will suddenly weakened. Perhaps benumbed by the large-scale and synchronous character of the gathering unrest, and perhaps under orders from their Soviet overlords to relent, a march by 70 000 people in Leipzig was allowed to go unchecked.[1] The truckloads of *Kampfgruppe* (people's militia) that had been assembled, primed with live ammunition and protected with riot gear, were not deployed. There was to be no 'Chinese solution'. Rejecting the path of confrontation, the city's SED mayor accepted the need for dialogue. A day earlier in Dresden, an identical decision had been made.

From 8 October onwards it was clear that the reformist faction within the SED leadership was in the ascendant. Reflecting this, the state-media blackout on the unrest was partially lifted and protestors who had been arrested in earlier demonstrations were now released. Despite these moves, the urban rallies continued to grow in size, an estimated 120 000 attending the weekly parade through Leipzig on 16 October. Clearly, more drastic changes were required and these were effected on 18 October, at an extraordinary 9th Plenum of the SED's 163–member Central Committee. By now a clearly broken figure, Erich Honecker reluctantly resigned as party leader and head of the State Council, citing 'health reasons'. At the same time, Günter Mittag (63), who had been in charge of directing the GDR economy almost without interruption since 1962 and had served as acting head of state during Honecker's incapacitation during August and September 1989, and Joachim Herrmann (61), the party's media and propaganda secretary, were removed from the Politburo and their secretaryships.[2] Selected to replace Honecker at the party and state helm was Egon Krenz, who at 52 was the 'baby' of the Politburo.

The 'Gentle Revolution' of November–December 1989

The new SED supremo, Egon Krenz, came into office with the reputation of being a hardline, sycophantic protégé of the ousted Honecker, the *Kronprinz* (crown prince). The son of a Kolberg tailor, he had joined the Communist Party in 1955 and, after briefly training and working as a teacher and spending three years at the Communist Party school in Moscow, had spent almost three decades as a full-time apparatchik. His career path had been remarkably similar to that of his patron, Honecker. Until 1983, he had been head of the FDJ youth movement and, since 1981, party secretary for security matters, in effective charge of the feared Stasi and with direct responsibility for the 'managing' of the 7 May 1989 municipal polls.

Less than a month before his elevation to the SED general-secretaryship, Krenz was publicly shown travelling to China to acclaim the bloody quelling of the Beijing pro-democracy movement. Now, however, assuming power at a critical juncture, he attempted to present a more reasonable and attractive public image. His face seemed to be locked permanently into a convivial grin, as he sought to present a new policy programme that would both bridge the ideological and generational divide within the ruling SED and win the regime an acceptable measure of popular support. Proclaiming, in Gorbachev vein, in his first public statement, 'We have to recognize the sign of the times and react accordingly, otherwise life will punish us,' he declared that he was anxious to 'open dialogue' within the nation and embark on a *Wende* (change of course). The reforms he appeared to envisage were limited and closely controlled, with the SED's 'leading party' dominance upheld and the full weight of law to be employed against those who 'abused social democracy'.

Unsurprisingly, the East German public were unconvinced as to the sincerity of this promised Wende. Throughout the closing weeks of October and the opening week in November they continued to 'vote with their feet', absconding, via Hungary, to the Federal Republic in their tens of thousands. Leaving behind an ill-staffed, fast-collapsing economic structure, through the so-called 'suction effect', they encouraged further refugee waves, as increasing burdens were progressively imposed on those remaining. Demonstrations continued to grow in size, an estimated 300 000 attending the weekly Leipzig protests on the 23 and 30 October and 6 November and more than half a million at a 4 November rally in East Berlin. Always disciplined and peaceful and invariably held outside working hours, these rallies embraced insistent demands for the holding of free elections and the dismantling of the Berlin Wall. They also involved the raising of posters, woundingly characterizing the new party leader as, variously, the devil, 'Krenz Xiao Ping' and, arising from his physical appearance, the wolf in Little Red Riding Hood. Even within the established political order cracks began to appear. For example, in Dresden the SED's reform-minded leader and its mayor, Dr Hans Modrow (61) and Wolfgang Berghofer (46) respectively, gave physical support to the reform movement, actually marching alongside the demonstrators and calling for the government's resignation. Similarly, within the Volkskammer the four one-time 'satellite parties' within the National Front gradually became more self-assertive, 52 deputies, predominantly drawn from the Liberal Democratic Party, actually declining to support Krenz's appointment as State Council chairman when, on 24 October, it was formally put to the vote.

Indeed, rather than retaining control of the reform process, as October 1989 progressed, Egon Krenz found himself being pushed remorselessly onwards by events, and forced to make a series of ever more radical concessions in a desperate, but ultimately abortive, attempt to 'buy time' and stabilize what had become a hopelessly frenetic situation.

The first such move was made on 1 November when, immediately on Krenz's return from a whistle-stop visit to Moscow, it was announced that Harry Tisch (62), the influential FDGB trade union chief, had been removed from the SED Politburo, and Margot Honecker (62), the wife of the deposed Erich, dismissed from the position of education minister that she had held since 1963. On the same day, restrictions on travel to Czechoslovakia were lifted and on 7–8 November the entire cabinet, including Prime Minister Willi Stoph (75), and the SED Politburo tendered their resignations. When both bodies were reconstituted, it was apparent that the services of more than a dozen veteran hardliners, including General

Erich Mielke (82), the minister of state security since 1957, Kurt Hager (77), Tisch and Stoph, had been dispensed with. They were replaced by a mixture of conservatives, pragmatists and reformers, most notably Hans Modrow (61), who was both inducted into the new, much smaller Politburo and selected to become Stoph's successor as Prime Minister.

The new Krenz-Modrow administration made a last concerted effort to check the political and economic slide within the GDR and salvage some measure of continued significant influence for the SED by embarking, during November and early December 1989, upon a far-reaching reform strategy, built around five key initiatives and programmes.

First, almost immediately on 8 November, it was announced that the New Forum opposition movement would at last be considered legal and that subsequently, in November, the formation of new parties, including the Greens, Free Democrats, Democratic Awakening and the Social Democrats, would be tolerated.

Second, the position of the non-communist 'allied parties' within the national bloc was greatly enhanced, their members being accorded 10, as against the former four of the 28 portfolios in the new slimmed-down cabinet, presented to the Volkskammer on 17 November by Prime Minister Modrow.

Third, to satisfy the public's desire for retribution, it was announced that unpopular prominent members of the old regime, including Honecker, Mittag, Stoph and Tisch, would be dismissed immediately from the Volkskammer and later, in early December, they were arrested and charged with abuse of office and expelled from the SED.[3] Meanwhile, on 22 November, a committee was established by the Volkskammer to investigate the growing allegations of corruption and misuse of power.

Fourth, a radical and comprehensive 'action programme' was approved by the SED Central Committee on 10 November, entailing approval for the rapid establishment of a genuine, multi-party parliamentary democracy, founded on the rule of law and free electoral competition; the democratization of the SED's internal structures and removal of privileges; a thorough reform of the educational and legal systems; and the transition to a 'socialist market economy', in which priority would be given to consumer goods production. This programme was duly adopted by the new Modrow government and given immediate substance when, on 1 December, the Volkskammer voted almost unanimously to amend Article One of the constitution, so as to remove the SED's guaranteed 'leading role'.

Fifth, and most dramatic of all, it was suddenly announced, on the afternoon of 8 November, by East Berlin's Communist Party boss Günter Schabowski (60), that on the following day all foreign travel restrictions would be lifted and East Germans would at last be free to cross their country's borders, including movement through the Berlin Wall. As midnight approached in East and West Berlin, huge, euphoric crowds of adults and children gathered on each side of the reviled barrier which, since its construction in August 1961 had served as a death trap for more than 70 failed escapees. On the stroke of the appointed hour there was a tumultous surge from either direction as the Berlin Wall was either passed through or scaled and easterners and westerners commingled joyfully in a Hogmanay spirit, chanting deliriously, 'The Wall is gone!' These vast, party-like scenes continued for days as endless streams of Ossis, crammed into tiny, chugging, gas-belching two-stroke Trabants, headed for West Berlin and other frontier crossing points.

East Germany's borders had been opened on 9 November 1989 in a desperate, last-ditch effort to avert the nation's demographic melt-down. It was hoped that if travel restrictions were abolished permanent outmigration would decrease. People would leave but, having savoured their new freedom and exhausted their meagre hard-currency resources, would soon return home. As Figure 3 shows, this prognosis was to be substantially correct. By the end of November 1989 it was estimated that well over half of the GDR's population had chosen to undertake cross-border excursions, yet, as Figure 3 shows, the emigration rate had sharply fallen. Nevertheless, between December 1989 and March 1900 the monthly levels of exodus remained higher than before October 1989. Accordingly, the labour-supply situation continued to deteriorate.

However, while the immediate collapse of the SED regime had been forestalled by the 9 November travel-liberalization gamble, any chances of attaining a new equilibrium were swiftly destroyed by accumulating revelations of an astonishing degree of brazen corruption among the outgoing ranks of the party old guard and apparatchik elite. In an interim report, issued on 1 December, the Volkskammer's committee of inquiry presented a damning picture of the former Honecker Politburo living the lives of almost feudal robber barons or Mafia dons. They had resided in opulent mansions, in an off-limits lakeside compound at Wandlitz, north of Berlin. Provided with weekend hunting lodges and sanatoria; they had been accorded exclusive access to Western luxuries and had engaged in illegal foreign-currency transactions and had embezzled state industrial funds; and plush houses had been built at state expense for their children, and let at peppercorn rents. Honecker himself, formerly regarded as an austere, sincere communist, had, it emerged, even been provided with his own Baltic island, while General Mielke had had football matches rigged so that his favourite team, Dynamo Berlin, would be consistently successful.

This shameful evidence, along with concurrent press exposés of Stasi cruelties, removed what lingering popular respect there may have been for the SED regime and credibility for the leadership of Egon Krenz. The public outrage was ventilated in large demonstrations in early December, during which there were chants, 'The people say no to the SED,' and in several cities Stasi offices were stormed and occupied to prevent incriminating evidence from being destroyed. So untenable had the situation become for the ruling party that on 3 December, five days before an emergency congress was due, the entire SED Politburo and Central Committee, including its general-secretary of just 47 days, resigned. Three days later, bowing to the inevitable, Krenz also stepped down as head of state and as chairman of the National Defence Council.[4] He was replaced, in an interim capacity, by Dr Manfred Gerlach (61), the leader of the Liberal Democratic Party.

Racked by deep internal divisions and recriminations and debilitated by a flood of mass resignations, the SED was now in a chaotic condition. In a desperate effort to revive the party's collapsed fortunes, it was decided, at a special 8–9 December congress, to adopt the new name SED-PDS (Party of Democratic Socialism) and to elect as leader, now designated chairman rather than general-secretary, Dr Gregor Gysi (41). This bespectacled, young Jewish lawyer from Berlin, having gained a reputation for his defence of a number of prominent dissidents, had 'clean hands'. Chosen to work alongside Gysi as deputy chairmen was a troika of reformers: Hans Modrow, Wolfgang Berghofer and Wolfgang Pohl, party leader in Magdeburg.

These changes were made with a clear eye to enhancing the party's performance in free, multi-party elections which, it was agreed, at a 7 December Round Table conference of National Front, Church and opposition representatives, would be held in May 1990. The SED-PDS seemed certain, nevertheless, to suffer a crushing defeat. The existing regime had passed the point of no return. It was discredited and, along with it, was the concept of a continuing, separate German Democratic Republic. Instead, progressively at rallies, commencing in Leipzig on 20 November, banners were displayed declaring, 'One Nation, One Fatherland', accompanied, from early December, by the resounding chant, '*Wir sind ein Volk!*' The issue of reunification had been vaulted to the head of the political agenda. In the months that followed it was to achieve an unstoppable momentum.

Chapter 8

'WIR SIND EIN VOLK!':
THE ACHIEVEMENT OF REUNIFICATION DURING 1990

'From a Whisper to a Scream': The Clamour for Reunification

The 'German Question' between 1952 and 1989: A Dormant Issue

For more than three decades, ever since Adenauer and the Western powers' rejection of Stalin's March–April 1952 proposals for the creation of a new, reunited, neutral Germany, the debate about reunification (*Wiedervereinigung*), or as West Germans preferred to put it, the 'coming together', of the two Germanies had been left to simmer quietly on the political 'back-burner'.

Within East Germany's ruling circles, the notion was rejected absolutely. Indeed, Erich Honecker was quoted as maintaining that a union of the two socialist and capitalist states was as feasible 'as combining fire and water'. The GDR's political backers, the Soviet Union, concurred fully, believing, as did the majority of its Western foes, that Germany's 1945 division, by establishing an effective balance of power at the European core, served as a source of Continental stability. Thus when, during 1987–8, President Gorbachev floated the visionary concept of a 'common European home', he was to repeatedly make it clear that this did not mean that state borders should be tampered with. He appeared to concur with the celebrated pronouncement of an eminent Frenchman: 'I love Germany so much that I rejoice there are two of them.'

Within the Federal Republic popular support for the idea of reunification remained consistently high between the 1950s and 1980s. At least two-thirds told public opinion pollsters that they wanted reunification and during the later 1980s, as West-East travel restrictions were eased, creating a growing sense of shared identity, the proportion climbed to four-fifths. However, conscious of international realities, as late as 1987, fewer than a tenth of West Germans actually believed that reunification would be possible by the century's end. Inevitably, in his October 1988 visit to Moscow, Chancellor Kohl raised the 'German Question', but he had little expectation of a dramatic response. A converted adherent to the strategy of *Ostpolitik* (*see* Part Six), he was resigned to the process of political, economic and social 'convergence' of the two German states remaining protracted.

The 'German Question' from November 1989: A Transformed Public Mood

The dramatic collapse of the SED regime and the unexpected dismantling of the Berlin Wall during October–November 1989 abruptly changed these settled judgments. Inside the Federal Republic, the proportion of people who believed that reunification could be achieved during the 1990s soared to nearly 50% by mid-November as a new spirit of optimism swept through the republic. Sensing the gathering popular mood with prescience and moving with an unusual display of decisiveness, Chancellor Kohl declared, on 10 November, in a public address in front of the Schöneberg city hall in West Berlin: 'We are and will remain one nation, and we belong together. Step by step, we must find the way to our common future.' Just over a fortnight later, on 28 November, the Chancellor presented to the Bundestag a 10-point plan for German confederation, which, it was anticipated, could be achieved in three stages. First, there would be a fundamental revision of the East German constitution and the holding of free, multi-party elections, with, in the interim, the Federal Republic providing emergency financial and food aid. Second, once these elections had been concluded successfully, there would be the establishment of new 'Confederative Structures', including a joint government committee and inter-departmental liaison in the economic, scientific, cultural and environmental spheres by means of joint commissions. Third, and finally, a new, fully fledged 'federal state system in Germany' would be constructed.

These confederation proposals were rejected outright by East Germany's struggling SED administration, Egon Krenz asserting, orthodoxly and categorically, that: 'The question [of reunification] is not on the table. Socialism and capitalism have never existed together on German soil.' Initially, moreover, Krenz's stance appeared to enjoy a considerable measure of public support within the GDR. The fledgling left-of-centre opposition grouped under the New Forum umbrella, fearful of domination by the 'capitalist FRG' in a newly merged state, campaigned instead for the transformation of East Germany into a humane, social-democratic model republic. Indeed, during the Leipzig rallies of October and early November 1989 there were to be insistent chants of 'We want to stay.'

However, from mid-November 1989, the East German popular mood suddenly changed. Now, having, as a result of day-trip excursions to the FRG, been fully exposed to the material riches of the West and, with the disclosures of the cynical venality of their former rulers, become thoroughly disillusioned with the SED state and all that it stood for, three new cries were increasingly heard during street demonstrations in East Berlin, Dresden and Leipzig: 'One fatherland!', '*Deutschland, Deuthschland!*', and, instead of 'We are THE people!' ('*Wir sind das Volk!*'), 'We are ONE people!' ('*Wir sind ein Volk!*'). Nevertheless, East German public opinion remained much more divided than that in the West, chants of 'Nazis out' being commonly raised to answer the calls for reunification. However, as the weeks progressed and as the political and economic situation continued to deteriorate, an overwhelming consensus developed, arguing that swift union with the rich and stable Federal Republic was the only sensible solution.

Influenced by this public temper, on 1 February 1990, the interim GDR administration of Hans Modrow, which during December 1989 had only contemplated at most *Vertragsgemeinschaft* (contractual community), at last came round to accept the notion of full reunification. It was, however, to attach one crucial proviso to it: the New Germany would need to be neutral. This proposal, which brought back memories of March–April 1952, was made immediately after a visit by Hans Modrow to Moscow. It was clearly reflective of prevailing thinking within the USSR and, as such, served to remind Bonn of reunification's sensitive external dimension. On 2–3 December 1989, at a 'saltwater summit' with the US President George Bush in Malta harbour, the Kremlin leader, Mikhail Gorbachev, made it plain that the Soviet Union had no intention of taking direct action to attempt to reverse the recent sequence of events in East Berlin. Indeed, subsequently, on 11–12 February 1990, in a meeting with Chancellor Kohl and FRG foreign minister Genscher, he declared, in what constituted a definitive endorsement of his own 'Sinatra doctrine', that 'the unity of the German people must be decided by the Germans themselves'. Nevertheless, though apparently agreeable to German reunification in principle, throughout the spring and early summer of 1990, Gorbachev 'played tough' over its terms, seeking to extract as much advantage as possible for the Soviet Union from the negotiations that were underway.

By the spring of 1990 the reunification of the two Germanies, which just six months earlier had appeared to be still very much a distant dream, had become assured. Following free elections, a new non-communist government, fully committed to its achievement, had been brought into power in the GDR. The only unresolved questions now remaining concerned its timing, its terms and the stages by which it was to be secured. An outline of possible phases had been sketched by Chancellor Kohl in his 28 November 1989 10-point, three-step, plan. The reality, however, was that pressure of circumstances, in particular the accelerating pace of economic disintegration within the GDR, necessitated a constant revision and successive compression of its schedules. Conceived initially as a 'loose union', which might be achieved over a timespan of anything between three to 10 years, as the economic gap between the Germanies was narrowed, Kohl's concept of 'confederation' was supplanted, as 1990 progressed, by plans for prompt, full-scale merger. In effect, it was transformed into a political and economic takeover of East Germany by the Federal Republic and, astonishingly, this process was completed before the year's end. The aphorism, 'Where there's a will, there's a way,' had indubitably been confirmed.

The remainder of this chapter describes the process by which this brisk absorption (*Anschluss*) of the GDR by the FRG, almost a 'shotgun marriage', was attained. Political developments in both Germanies, during a year when the issue of *Wiedervereinigung* dominated the national agenda, are examined, with an analysis of the all-German general election of 2 December 1990. First, however, attention is focused on events within East Germany, as the 'Democratic Republic', having rejected one-party socialism, prepared itself for the holding of the first, and what were to be the only, truly free and open national elections in its 40-year history.

East Germany's Democratic Transition: January– March 1990

The Political and Economic Situation in Early 1990

The enforced resignation from party and state positions of Egon Krenz on 3–6 December 1989 marked the end of the SED's attempt to hold on to power in East Germany through a rearguard strategy of 'controlled reform'. Instead, with the SED-PDS completely discredited by corruption scandals and losing members at a weekly rate of more than 50000, it was left to Hans Modrow, the so-called 'Gorbachev of the GDR', the nation's most popular, liberal and abstemious 'reform communist' politician, to manage the transition to a genuinely pluralist democracy as harmoniously and smoothly as possible.

Modrow's first two months in office were particularly testing. He faced a persistently deteriorating economic and financial situation, as the outflow of emigrants, now averaging 2000 per day and taking with them precious hard currency, continued, and as the neighbouring West German government was reluctant to provide unconditional, medium-term aid to shore up an illegitimate administration. Political tensions were also high. On the streets there were increasing verbal and physical clashes over reunification and the flying of the East German flag. On 15 January 1990, in what was the first truly violent incident in East Germany's bloodless 'quiet revolution', tens of thousands of demonstrators stormed and ransacked the Stasi's central headquarters in East Berlin. The power struggle between the old elite and the new political forces was clearly not yet over.

Anxious to promote reconciliation, Prime Minister Modrow fell back on the Round Table process. Under the adept chairmanship of the theologian Dr Wolfgang Ullmann, representatives from the SED-PDS, four former allied 'bloc parties', the Churches and nine opposition groups met 10 times during December 1989 and January 1990. Agreement was reached that work should begin on the preparation of a new liberal-democratic constitution, to be subsequently ratified by a referendum. In addition, it was announced, at the 15 January 1990 Round Table gathering, that the hated Stasi, officially disbanded by Modrow on 14 December 1989, but then, influenced by fears aroused by a recent wave of neo-Nazi attacks, replaced immediately by a congruous body termed the Office for the Protection of the Constitution, would be dissolved by 25 January 1990. Similar Round Tables, usually designated 'citizens' committees', operated, with surprising success, at the municipal level. They replaced expired SED-PDS-dominated local-government machines.

With the disintegration of the SED-PDS gathering pace and the economy increasingly damaged by absenteeism and lightning strikes, at the ninth Round Table meeting, on 22 January 1990,

Prime Minister Modrow appealed to the opposition to set aside their differences and join in a new transitional Grand Coalition government of 'national responsibility'. Given the grievous nature of the country's problems, the opposition was naturally reluctant. Eventually, however, on 28 January, they assented and on 5 February the eight opposition party leaders, including pastor Rainer Eppelmann from Democratic Awakening, the physicist Sebastian Pflugbeil from New Forum and Dr Wolfgang Ullmann from Democracy Now, were sworn into office as new ministers without portfolio, with the brief to 'shadow' the normal ministers. For the first time in the GDR's history a government had been formed in which communists were in a minority. This was, however, very much an interim administration since, on 29 January 1990, compelled by the pressure of events, the Volkskammer voted to bring forward to 18 March the national elections that had been pencilled in for 6 May.

Voting for Reunification: The GDR General Election of March 1990

The collapse of the SED regime during October–November 1989 had been followed swiftly by the formation of a number of new political 'associations' and parties. Concurrently, the former 'allied parties' within the SED-led National Front had also reasserted their independence and thoroughly reconstituted themselves, purging their former, 'collaborationist' leaders. Clearly, a new democratic political culture was in the process of formation. It was being constructed, however, in a state in which only a tiny proportion of the adult population had tasted democratic-pluralist political freedoms. A state in which, as a natural consequence, rooted, party-defined ideological allegiances were lacking. A state in which, although formerly television observers of the West German electoral scene, none had direct familiarity with the techniques and influences of competitive political campaigning. Undoubtedly, February–March 1990 was to be a novel learning experience for the East German public.

Indicative of the rootlessness of the East German 'virgin electorate', an unusually large number of parties, totalling 23, participated in the 18 March 1990 national election. They were competing for 400 seats in a new, slimmed-down, four-year Volkskammer. Under the terms of new regulations, which were agreed finally on 20 February, this contest was to be decided on the basis of a party list system of pure proportional representation, each elector being given just one vote. For this purpose, the country was divided into 15 regional constituencies, comprising the Bezirke, plus East Berlin. However, the first count of the completed ballots was to be made on a national basis and, unlike in the FRG, there was to be no cut-off support 'hurdle' that minor parties were required to surmount. This meant that a party securing as little as a 0.25% share of the national poll would be guaranteed a seat. They would also receive five Marks in state subvention for each individual vote won.

During the closing months of 1989 the most clearly ascendant political force within the GDR was New Forum. At its first authorized rally, held in Leipzig on 18 November 1989, there had been an attendance of 50000 and by the end of 1989 it was able to claim more than 200000 signed-up supporters. Akin in some respects to West Germany's Greens, this new movement eschewed the establishment of a formal party structure. Instead, it presented itself as an amorphous discussion and campaigning forum for a broad range of progressive elements, including artists, writers, civil right's activists, environmentalists, 'peaceniks', radical clerics and iconoclastic scientists. As well as championing a 'new style', it proposed a new substance of politics. Termed the 'Third Way', between communism and capitalism, it envisaged the blending of free-market economics with socialist democracy within the framework of a sovereign, second German state.

Given time to evolve, New Forum may well have transformed itself into a valuable and influential political force within a new, democratic East German republic. In reality, however, as the opening months of 1990 progressed, it found itself shunted aside into the 'political sidings' as East German party politics were consumed by the reunification issue and as, with the March elections approaching, a premium was placed on having an efficient, professionalized organization. Already clearly hampered by its anarchic, amateurish structure and lack of a single, charismatic, unifying leader, what proved most electorally damaging for New Forum was the stance it adopted on the compelling question of reunification. Fighting in March 1990 in alliance with two citizens' groups, Democracy Now (a Christian-Marxist body which had been set up on 12 September 1989) and Initiative for Human Rights, as part of the Electoral Pact '90 (*Wahlbündnis '90*) joint list, it advocated only gradual reunification within the future context of a demilitarized Europe. Clearly out of touch with the popular mood on this issue, the quixotic, New Forum-dominated Electoral Pact

'90 coalition attracted less than 3% of the national vote on 18 March. Most of its support came from university towns.

Instead, during January and February 1990, the party that was riding high in public-opinion polls, and which had become the clear favourite to secure victory in the forthcoming Volkskammer contest, was the Social Democratic Party of Germany, the SPD. Although only refounded relatively recently, on 7 October 1989, on the initiative of Steffen Reiche and Ibrahim Böhme, the SPD was shown by an opinion poll taken in Leipzig, and published on 6 February 1990, to enjoy a support rating of as much as 59%. In comparison, the PDS communists had a rating of 12%, the Christian Democratic Union (CDU), 11%, and New Forum, 4%. Formerly strong in eastern Germany in the pre-SED era, the SPD's advocacy of a social market-economy programme, which would protect the disadvantaged, was particularly attractive to the new GDR electorate. In addition, the party enjoyed the fraternal support of its powerful West Germany sibling. Indeed, Willy Brandt, hugely popular in the GDR, was elected the party's honorary chair at a national electoral congress held at Leipzig on 22–25 February 1990 and, along with other leading figures from the 'western SPD', made appearances and speeches at election rallies during February and March 1990. Moreover, vital modern campaigning equipment, including fax machines, computers and phone banks, was donated by its enthusiastic western supporters.

Nonetheless, three potential chinks were always evident within the SPD's election fighting armour. The first was the party's, until recent, full absorption within the SPD. For example, its ebullient chairman, Ibrahim Böhme (45), an historian from Leipzig of Jewish descent, had been an SED member for 15 years, eventually resigning in 1976 as a mark of opposition to the Honecker regime's persecution of intellectuals. Many of the SPD's new members, assuredly, had 'clean hands', being either political neophytes or recruits from the Protestant Church opposition. However, a not insignificant portion were recent, tardy defectors from the SED. The second, and related, weakness was the possibility that, after 40 unsuccessful years as a socialist republic, East Germany's electorate might choose to embark on a complete change of course and, in the process, reject the SPD's promises of a humane and successful new social democracy. The third deficiency was the SPD's somewhat hesitant espousal of reunification. At its 12–14 January 1990 national delegate conference, the party did, eventually, explicitly make reunification, the creation of 'a united Germany . . . with the consent of our neighbours', one of its fundamental policy goals. However, anxious to cushion the harsh economic and social realities of reunification, the approach it advocated was gradualist. It would commence with the setting up of a joint parliamentary commission, in April 1990, followed by monetary union, by 1 July 1990. Thereafter, a completely new all-German constitution would be framed by a joint German Unity Council, based at the Reichstag in Berlin and chaired by Willy Brandt. When this process had been completed, this compact was to be presented to each of the Germanies' parliaments for ratification. All this formed the Article 146 'slow lane' route to reunion.

During February and March 1990, each of these defects was to be exploited fully by the SPD's chief electoral rival, the Alliance for Germany (*Allianz für Deutschland:* AFD). A coalition of right-of-centre forces, the principal element within the AFD was the East German CDU. Formerly a member of the SED-led National Front, since 10 November 1989, when Lothar de Maizière (49) was elected to replace Gerald Götting (66) as its chairman, the CDU had set about reconstituting and rehabilitating itself as a genuinely Christian democratic pluralist party, committed to a market economy. It had expelled thousands of its former officials and members, though many 'old guard' adherents remained with its Volkskammer Fraktion. Also within the Alliance was the German Social Union (*Deutsche Sozialchristliche Union: DSU*), a right-wing body established on 20 January 1990 with the Leipzig parson Hans-Wilhelm Ebeling (56) as its chairman and which had informal ties with the Bavarian CSU, and Democratic Awakening (*Demokratischer Aufbruch:* DA), a 'social-liberal-ecological', intelligentsia-orientated grouping which, based similarly in Leipzig, had first 'emerged' in July 1989 and been founded formally on 16 December 1989 by the Rostock lawyer, Wolfgang Schnur (45), and the remarkable 'peace pastor', Rainer Eppelmann (47).

Although the East Berlin Round Table had earlier voted to oppose foreign participation in the March 1990 Volkskammer campaign, during February and March 1990, the West German CDU and CSU extended large-scale support to the Alliance for Germany. As a result, as New Forum's leader Bärbel Bohley was to lament, the elections were eventually 'hijacked'. Tens of thousands of leaflets and posters, bearing the slogan '*Zukunft beginnt zu Hause*', were printed in Düsseldorf and driven across the border for distribution and disco bands imported to enliven proceedings, while Chancellor Kohl himself addressed six major campaign rallies.

These were attended enthusiastically by a million people, including 300 000 at the last mass meeting held at Leipzig on 15 March. The Alliance resorted to 'negative campaigning' against its principal rival, the SPD (or, as it termed it, the 'PDSPD'), with the slogan 'No more socialist experiments' (*'Nie wieder Sozialismus'*) being employed frequently. More positively, however, it offered to the electorate the hope, indeed expectation, of a greatly improved material future, proposing that monetary union of the two Germanies 'within months' should be followed by the GDR's brisk accession to the Federal Republic in the form of new Länder, under the terms of Article 23 of the Basic Law.

This advocacy of 'fast-track' unification, combined with insinuations that West Germany's Chancellor Kohl would be able to negotiate much more effectively with an East Berlin Alliance, rather than an SPD-led administration, proved compelling for large numbers of East Germany's voters. As a consequence, and to the amazement of all parties and most outside observers, when the votes were finally counted after the Sunday 18 March poll, the Alliance for Germany was shown to have won a crushing victory. Described in some quarters as a vote of *'Deutschmark, Deutschmark über alles'*, in others as, essentially, a protest vote against socialism, it captured 48% of a poll in which the national turnout (*see* Table 23) was astonishingly high. In contrast, the SPD was able to muster just 22%, and the PDS a humbling 16%.

The Alliance polled most strongly in the rural, small-town and industrialized districts of the southern GDR, a region which had chronic pollution, health and housing problems. Remarkably, this conservative coalition drew the support of more than half, 58%, of the country's blue-collar workers, and in Karl Marx Stadt (Chemnitz) achieved a record, and poetic, 61% poll share. The SPD, in contrast, was able to capture a mere 17% share of the vote in Saxony and Thuringia, two of its Weimar era heartland Länder, and nationally, barely a fifth of the ballots cast by blue-collar workers. The Social Democrats performed best in East Berlin, where it secured a 35% share of the vote, in northern rural districts, 24%, and, somewhat surprisingly, among older electors. As a newly refounded party, its national effort was hampered by an organizational structure much inferior to that of the AFD, which had been able to use the inherited CDU 'bloc party' machine.

Despite its claims of having once constituted the vanguard of the working class, the PDS, as it was formally renamed on 4 February 1990, fared even worse than the SPD, though this poor performance

TABLE 23 THE MARCH 1990 EAST GERMAN ELECTION
(TURNOUT 93.4%)

Party	Votes ('000)	Share of Total Vote (%)	Seats
Alliance for Germany	5,525	48.1	193
(CDU)	(4,695)	(40.9)	(164)
(DSU)	(725)	(6.3)	(25)
(Democratic Awakening)	(105)	(0.9)	(4)
SPD	2,506	21.8	87
PDS	1,874	16.3	65
League of Free Democrats[1]	606	5.3	21
Pact '90[2]	333	2.9	12
Democratic Peasants' Party	251	2.2	9
Greens/Independent Women's Union	225	2.0	8
Others	155	1.3	5
TOTAL	11,475	100.0	400

[1] Comprising the Liberal Democratic Party, the East German Free Democratic Party and the German Forum Party.
[2] Comprising Democracy Now, New Forum and the Peace and Human Rights Initiative.

was by no means unexpected. Just 12% of blue-collar workers voted for the 'reformed communists'. Instead, it was forced to rely mainly on the support of white-collar workers, 19% of whom voted for the party in March 1990. They comprised, mainly, the still loyal and fearful remnants of the old privileged bureaucratic machine centred in East Berlin. In this city, the PDS's vote share reached 30%.

The PDS's list was headed by the popular Hans Modrow. However, fearing popular retribution if they took to the hustings too openly, the party's campaign was virtually invisible. In addition, the PDS was hamstrung by the internal chaos that had been engendered by a wave of mass resignations, reducing its membership to fewer than 700000. Among those who had chosen to leave was Wolfgang Berghofer, one of its deputy chairmen. Finally, the PDS was to do itself no favours by standing as the only significant party not approving of German reunification. Indeed, fighting to save as much of the status quo as possible and seeking to 'protect' the weak of East Germany from the threatened offensive of FRG capitalism, the PDS presented itself as a remarkably reactionary force.

Despite polling astonishingly well on 18 March, the Alliance for

Germany fell eight seats short of securing an absolute majority in the new Volkskammer. This was a direct consequence of the system of pure proportional representation that had been adopted. One obvious option lay open for it: the construction, as in Bonn, of a conservative-liberal coalition. Its potential partner in this compact would be the League of Free Democrats (*Bund freier Demokraten:* BFD), which, comprising the restructured Liberal Democratic Party, the German Forum Party (a breakaway splinter from New Forum) and the East German Free Democratic Party (established in November 1989), had secured just over 5% of the East German vote and had captured 21 Volkskammer seats. However, this conventional course was rejected by the Alliance's leader, Lothar de Maizière.[1] Instead, anxious to push through a programme of fundamental constitutional change so as to achieve reunification in as short a timespan as possible, he determined to construct a 'Grand Coalition' administration, which, embracing not only members of the Alliance and the League, but also of the SPD, would hold an overwhelming, and necessary, supra-two-thirds majority within the new parliament.

Actuated by a loathing of the right-wing DSU, which had engaged in a scurrilous election campaign, and with its attention distracted by an internal leadership crisis[2], the SPD at first rejected this offer of a share in power. Eventually, however, on 28 March 1990, its executive council agreed to commence negotiations on the possible formation of a 'Grand Coalition'. Within a fortnight, these talks had been successfully concluded and, on 12 April 1990, a new five-party (CDU, DSU, DA, BFD and SPD) government was sworn in. The first cabinet in the GDR's history not to contain a communist, it comprised 26 members. Four, Lothar de Maizière (CDU), Rainer Eppelmann (DA), Walter Romberg (SPD) and Kurt Wunsche (BFD), had been members of the outgoing cabinet. Twelve were drawn from the CDU, six from the SPD, which had been given, among others, the finance and foreign affairs portfolios, three from the BFD, two from the DSU, one from Democratic Awakening and two were independents. Three were pastors, Ebeling (economic co-operation), Eppelmann (disarmament and defence) and Markus Meckel (foreign affairs), the new SPD leader, and four were women.

Accorded a clear mandate from the people to press on and secure rapid reunification, this new, inexperienced administration was confronted with the formidable task of entering into and successfully concluding negotiations both with the Federal Republic and with the international allies and 'protectors' of the two Germanies. The countdown to reunion had begun. In the following section the mechanics by which this was eventually achieved are examined, attention focusing first on the 'internal track' and then on the external aspects of reunification.

The Road to Union: April–October 1990

The German-German Dimension: From GEMU to the Unification Treaty

The new Volkskammer, which assembled for its inaugural session on 5 April 1990, was, by East German standards, an unusually youthful body. Its membership's average age was 45, 97% being 'freshers'. Within days the new parliament passed a constitutional amendment to abolish the State Council and restore an elected state presidency, with its newly elected speaker, Sabine Bergmann-Pohl, assuming the vacant position of head of state in an interim capacity. However, real executive authority rested with the new Prime Minister, Lothar de Maizière. A reserved, mild-mannered, bearded and bespectacled former lawyer, a one-time professional viola player and Protestant lay official, de Maizière was a member of an old, well-connected Huguenot family which had been forced to flee to Germany from France. He had assumed the leadership of, first, the CDU and, then, the AFD out of a sense of duty rather than personal ambition. Now, he was to be very much thrown into the 'political deep end' as, from 12 April 1990, he had to get down to business and set about turning into substance the final two stages of the AFD-Kohl plan for rapid reunification. First, there was the negotiation of economic and monetary union and the building of interim 'confederative structures', and, second, the conclusion of a full political union with the FRG, under the terms of Article 23.

Originally, when Chancellor Kohl first unveiled his 10-point plan for confederation on 28 November 1989, many observers regarded the proposals to establish an economic and monetary union of the two Germanies (termed GEMU), in the intermediate second stage of the process of reunification, as effectively entailing the creation of a new *Zollverein* (customs union). Over time, with one currency and the free movement of goods and people, an equalization of the two German economies and societies would duly occur, paving the way, after a number of years, to full political union.

However, as the economic situation deteriorated sharply in East Germany, with the westward outflow of its people showing little sign of abating, GEMU was increasingly viewed as an emergency lifeline or bandage which would temporarily help to hold together a fast-crumbling GDR state while political reunification negotiations were being hurriedly conducted. This was necessary, it was argued, because only by presenting East Germans with the opportunity of earning a 'hard', convertible currency, the Deutschmark, at home could they be persuaded not to uproot and immediately leave, permanently or semi-permanently, for the Federal Republic. With the the westward exodus continuing at a rate of more than a thousand a week during March 1990 (*see* Figure 3), the swift introduction of GEMU was undoubtedly the new GDR administration's foremost priority. It was also of urgent importance to West Germany, which, under the growing strain of the refugee influx, had, on 20 March 1990, already begun to take steps to financially deter further immigration.

Already, during February and March 1990, discussions were underway between East and West German government and bank officials concerning economic and monetary union, though at this time it was not anticipated that the process would be completed before the end of 1992. After the conclusion of the 18 March 1990 Volkskammer election additional momentum was given to these negotiations, a full-scale debate beginning to rage over one particular issue, what should be the Ostmark-Deutschmark exchange rate?

At a 13 March rally held at Cottbus, near Dresden, during the Volkskammer campaign, Chancellor Kohl had given a public commitment that for 'small savers . . . when the change in currency comes it will be at one-to-one'. This was a clearly popular pledge within the GDR. However, it was strongly opposed by the West German Bundesbank which, taking a more objective view, calculated that, to reflect the real, 'comparative purchasing power', values of the respective currencies, an exchange rate of, at least, two Ostmarks to one Deutschmark should be used. Anything less, its president Karl-Otto Pöhl warned, would, by unduly swelling the money supply, have inflationary consequences for the Federal Republic, and thus force a subsequent hike of interest rates. In addition, it was cautioned that if applied to wages, a 1:1 conversion rate would make East German enterprises internationally uncompetitive. This was because their productivity rates were barely a third those of the West. As a concession, Pöhl said the Bundesbank would be willing to tolerate a 1:1 exchange rate for East German private savings up to a limit of 2000 Marks and to recommend that East German wages be increased by around 30% prior to GEMU.

The Bundesbank's views were leaked on 31 March 1990 and provoked a wave of protests outside the Volkskammer building in East Berlin during early April, banners being held aloft bearing the slogan: 'Without one for one, Germany will not be one'. Already East German workers were disgruntled at the rising level of inflation, eating into their pay packets, as subsidies were removed as part of the shift towards a free-market economy. Influenced by this strong feeling, Prime Minister de Maizière pressed firmly for an improvement of the exchange-rate terms when formal negotiations commenced with Bonn. He was to have some success and, on 18 May 1990, when the GEMU treaty was finally signed by the finance ministers of the two Germanies, it was agreed that conversion should be at parity for all East German wages, salaries and pensions and for the personal savings up to DM 2000 for children, DM 4000 for those aged between 15 and 59 years and up to DM 6000 for those over 60. All other savings, as well as state companies' debts and liabilities, were to be converted at a rate of 2:1. To secure this deal, considerable pressure had been exerted upon the Bundesbank by Chancellor Kohl, including the veiled threat of Bundestag legislation to overturn its independence.

GEMU did not, however, just entail monetary union, that is the creation of a unified currency area with the Deutschmark as the common currency and the Bundesbank as its central, or issuing, bank, and commercial union. It included the removal of border and price controls and extension of West German rates of VAT to the GDR. It also encompassed a 'social union' in which the labour laws and 'comprehensive system of social security' in force in the 'social market economy' (*soziale Marktwirtschaft*) of the FRG were extended to the GDR. At the same time, it meant a loss of some of the progressive 'social rights' that had recently been introduced, under the terms of a 7 March 1990 social charter, in East Germany. Among these were the right to work and the banning of lockouts by management. Indeed, on 10 May 1990 there were stoppages by tens of thousands of East German workers as a mark of protest against the loss of certain employment protections that GEMU occasioned. GEMU also involved 'environmental union', a specific article (number 16) of the 18 May treaty being concerned with protection of the environment. This was made a 'major objective' for both contracting parties, although when the GEMU draft treaty was subsequently debated in the Bundestag, the guarantees it offered were strongly criticized by both the Greens and SPD.

German economic and monetary union came into effect on 1 July 1990. It was accompanied by measures designed to speed up the transition to a market economy. These included the gradual privatization of 8000 state-owned industries under the supervision of a trustee agency, termed the *Treuhandanstalt*, established in March 1990, the elimination of subsidies, the encouragement of inward investment and German-German joint ventures, and an agreement that businesses nationalized in 1972 should be returned to their former owners. At the same time, as part of the 'confederative process', joint governmental commissions in such areas as economic co-operation, culture and posts and telecommunications were established.

As Figure 3 suggests, GEMU, combined with unilateral initiatives taken by West Germany to discourage further Ubersiedler migration, served its purpose in successfully checking the demographic outflow from East Germany. However, adjustment to the new monetary and commercial regime was to be painful. Between late June and late August 1990 the level of unemployment more than tripled within the GDR to 350000, or 4% of the workforce, as the country's overmanned and inefficient industries were forced to 'shed fat' to meet the challenge of a more competitive and profit-orientated environment. A further 10% of the labour force was employed on a short-time basis and it was predicted by West German research institutes that within a year the unemployment level in the East could reach as high as 1.4 million. The situation was exacerbated by a wave of strikes in the heavy industrial sector, where workers sought both pay rises and job-security guarantees. There were also huge demonstrations and street blockades by disgruntled farmers, who, from 1 August 1990, had become subject to European Community regulations and had thus had their state subsidies withdrawn. Other obstacles were the unwillingness of foreign entrepreneurs to commence investing within the GDR, because of uncertainty over both property rights and the political future, and the preference that was shown by East German consumers for western-produced goods, resulting in the bankruptcy of many eastern firms.

The continuing collapse of the East German economy as it became subject to the so-called 'shock therapy' of GEMU made the de Maizière government, which had already surrendered much of its effective sovereignty to Frankfurt and Bonn, anxious to bring forward the date of full political unification.

As early as 22 July 1990, a law was passed by the Volkskammer providing for the re-establishment of the five East German Länder which had been abolished in 1952. This opened the way for accession under the terms of Article 23 of the FRG's Basic Law. A month earlier, it had been agreed by the two German governments that an all-German election should be held on 2 December 1990. However, should East Germany's Länder accede to the Federal Republic before or immediately after this poll? This was to become an issue of intense debate within the East Berlin coalition during late July and early August 1990.

At first, scenting advantage for his DSU and DA allies, Prime Minister de Maizière advocated delayed accession, so that the 2 December 1990 election could be fought under the prevailing East German, liberal electoral arrangements. This course, which, embarrassingly was supported by the PDS, was strongly opposed by both the SPD and FDP. Indeed, on 24 July 1990, the FDP formally withdrew from the governing coalition as a mark of protest.[3] Then, in early August, as GEMU's repercussions were progressively felt, the Prime Minister suddenly changed tack and proposed that both the timing for reunification and for the all-German election should be brought forward to 14 October 1990, the date on which elections were set to be held in the GDR's reconstituted Länder. Support for this plan was forthcoming from Chancellor Kohl. However, the suggestion that the Bundestag should be dissolved prematurely was rejected outright by West Germany's SPD, who had a 'blocking' veto.

Eventually, a compromise was hammered out and agreed by the Volkskammer in the early hours of 23 August. Formal unification would take effect on 3 October 1990, under the terms of Article 23 of the Basic Law. However, all-German elections would be delayed until 2 December. In the interim, 144 delegated deputies from the Volkskammer would sit in the FRG Bundestag as 'observers'. Two hundred and 94 Volkskammer deputies voted in favour of this motion and only 62, all from the PDS, against. At last, the date for reunion had been agreed and its terms were set out in a State Treaty on Unification (*see* Chapter 3), which was signed by the two German governments on 31 August 1990. A German-German accord on reunification had been secured. All that was now required for the process to be made complete was international endorsement.

The External Dimension: From Two-Plus-Four to the Treaty of Final Settlement

With two like-minded governments in power in East Berlin and Bonn, both committed to a shared goal, the prospects of reaching swift German-German agreement on the economic and political details of reunification always seemed favourable. Much more formidable were the external hurdles to be surmounted before a new Germany could be born. In particular, three chief obstacles, psychological and practical, needed to be overcome. First, there were the fears instinctively aroused among neighbouring states by the proposition that a new Greater Germany (*Grossdeutschland*) should be re-established. Second, there were the dilemmas presented by the antagonistic strategic positions occupied by the two Germanies. One was a key member of NATO and the WEU and the other was a member of its sworn foe, the Warsaw Treaty Organization. Similarly, each belonged to a different economic community: the EC and Comecon. Third, there was the unique position of Berlin, still legally and physically occupied by the Four Powers (Britain, France, the USA and the USSR). So intractable did these impediments appear and so potentially destabilizing any attempt at their resolution, that the West German liberal weekly, *Die Zeit*, was to declare frankly: 'What is a dream for us [reunification] is a nightmare for most of our neighbours.'

During the closing months of 1989, when reunification emerged, at last, as a real possibility rather than mere ambition, the issue did, indeed, create initial apprehension throughout Europe and seemed likely to imperil international stability. This arose from a mixture of West Germany insensitivity, Chancellor Kohl failing to consult his Western allies over his 28 November 10-point plan, and early Soviet obduracy. Through the spring of 1990 discord continued, as the USSR and the Western Alliance engaged in a strategic poker game. Happily, however, as the summer advanced the mood changed to one of harmony and pragmatism. With extraordinary speed, each point of contention was successfully resolved and, in mid-September, a Treaty on the Final Settlement with respect to Germany was signed by the two German republics and the four powers, the so-called 'two-plus-four'. Reunification had finally secured international approbation, although there had been difficulties along the way.

The initial bone of contention concerned the borders of the new Germany: where should they be drawn? Chancellor Kohl's insistent use of the word 'reunification', rather than 'unification', disturbed the USSR and Poland in particular, since it could be interpreted as implying that Germany's long-term goal was a return to its 1937 borders, including 102 000 square kilometres of territory beyond the Oder-Neisse, rather than a simple amalgamation of the FRG and GDR. With an electoral eye on right-wing opinion within the Federal Republic, the Chancellor was, indeed, ambiguous in some of his public statements. However, on 8 November, on the eve of a six-day visit to Poland, which was interrupted by the breaching of the Berlin Wall, an official statement explicitly guaranteeing the inviolability of the Polish-German border was issued from Bonn. Two months later, on 17 January 1990, in a significant address to the French Institute on international relations, in Paris, this assurance was underlined by Kohl, who declared: 'I should like to say clearly: no responsible politician in the Federal Republic of Germany . . . is dreaming of a Germany on the 'pan-Germanic model'.' There was to be no Fourth Reich.

Briefly, early in March 1990, the 'Polish border controversy' was revivified by a controversial statement issued by Chancellor Kohl's office. In it, an attempt was made to link any future guarantee by the two German parliaments of the Oder-Neisse border with a Polish commitment to abide by a 1953 treaty waiving any claims for reparations from Germany, and also with the ratification of a new treaty establishing rights for the German community residing within Silesia. This provoked uproar in Poland and, because of FDP censure, within the Bonn coalition. Therefore, in mid-March, it was decided, so as to allay Warsaw's continuing concern, to invite Polish representatives to attend appropriate sessions of the 'two-plus-four' talks on Germany's future that had, by now, moved underway. In addition, between March and June 1990, the Bundestag and Volkskammer passed a series of 'declarations' and 'resolutions' according further formal recognition of the the permanence of the Oder-Neisse frontier. This reflected the overwhelming popular and party political consensus in the two states for the repudiation of revanchism. Only the far-right Republicans, who had been banned since 5 February 1990 from operating in the GDR, dissented. In mid-July 1990, at a ministerial-level session of the 'two-plus-four' talks, it was agreed that definitive confirmation of the Poland-Germany border should be accorded by the conclusion of a bilateral treaty soon after reunification was achieved. This commitment was fulfilled in Warsaw, on 14 November 1990.

In reality, such was the consensus within Germany, the 'border question' was a bogus issue, whose resolution was never genuinely in doubt. Far less assured was the outcome of negotiations between West Germany and the USSR, and between 'two-plus-four' countries, concerning the security aspects of the new Germany's future.

Publicly, the Federal Republic's Western allies had consistently voiced support for German reunification, so long as it occurred by peaceful means and through the democratically expressed wishes of its two peoples. In private, however, during the winter and early spring of 1989–90, its West European partners expressed unease about both the economic might that an enlarged German state would possess and the distraction from EC matters that might result. Along with the United States, they were also particularly anxious that there should be no 'decoupling' of the FRG from the Atlantic Alliance. They were determined that the new Germany, or at least its western portion, should remain within NATO.

The Soviet Union, with memories of its sufferings during the German-initiated 'Great Patriotic War' so deeply ingrained, had a much greater 'gut fear' of the re-establishment of a more powerful, and potentially more assertive, Greater Germany. Strategically also, it would, obviously, be greatly weakened if the GDR, a 'king-pin', buffer-state ally, was to leave the Warsaw Pact. For these reasons, throughout December 1989, the Soviet leader, Mikhail Gorbachev, consistently opposed any, as he termed it, 'artificial prodding and pushing' of the German Question. Its resolution, he believed, should be considered over a timespan of decades, not months or years. From the outset, however, the Soviet foreign minister, the reform-minded Eduard Shevardnadze, adopted a more realistic and flexible position. He was aware that, with the collapse of communism elsewhere in East-Central Europe, the Warsaw Pact had a limited future and the drive for German unity was developing an unstoppable head of steam. He, therefore, believed that the Soviet Union would be wise to reconcile itself to the inevitable, but, through negotiations, extract the most advantageous terms, economic and strategic, attainable. Despite misgivings within the Soviet military, Shevardnadze's pragmatic approach was sensibly pursued in seven months of hard-nosed bargaining during the spring and summer of 1990.

The Soviet Union's opening proposition, made with its permission by the East German premier Hans Modrow on 1 February 1990, was that a united Germany should be neutral and demilitarized. It was immediately 'strictly rejected' by Chancellor Kohl and also by the USSR's newly democratizing Czech, Polish and

Hungarian 'partners' within the splintering Warsaw Pact. They preferred to see a new Germany remaining 'anchored' within NATO. Nevertheless, the willingness of the Soviet Union to start 'trading' terms did occasion some misgivings within the West. This was because there had always been an unspoken fear that, anxious to secure swift unification and faced by the 'trump card' of the uncertain fate of the 380 000 Red Army troops still stationed within East Germany, the Federal Republic might be tempted to settle for an unacceptable 'halfway-house', compromise solution.

On 5 May 1990 in Bonn, at the inaugural session of the 'two-plus-four' powers' foreign ministers' conference, Eduard Shevardnadze unveiled a second Soviet plan. This envisaged the internal and external aspects of reunification being 'detached'. He suggested that, while speedy economic and political unification should be encouraged, the security status of the new Germany should be left to one side for resolution later, when the two opposed military alliances had been superseded by a new 'all European security system'. In the interim, extending perhaps to five years, the new Germany would remain a member of both NATO and the Warsaw Pact, Soviet troops would be stationed within its eastern Länder, and the Four Powers would continue to control Berlin. However, this revised plan also failed to find favour in Bonn. Viewing the conditions as an unacceptable infringement of German sovereignty, on 8 May 1990 Chancellor Kohl dismisssed the scheme as merely a 'poker move'. Indeed, throughout the period between February and June 1990, the West German government demonstrated, in its bilateral and multilateral talks with the Soviet Union, a firm resolution not to renounce its status as a full member of NATO. Public opinion was firmly behind it in this. The most it was willing to concede was that NATO forces should not be stationed within the new Germany's eastern Länder. This was a proposition which found particular favour with East Berlin's de Maizière government and, in Bonn, with foreign minister Genscher, who, in private, went so far as to contemplate the demilitarization of the entire Elbe-Oder zone.

Convinced that Bonn could be pushed no further and sweetened by a DM 5 billion government-guaranteed loan, provided on 11 June 1990 to help finance its growing balance of payments deficit, the Soviet Union finally reached an accord with Bonn on reunification at a Gorbachev-Kohl summit, held on 15–16 July at Stavropol, in the North Caucasus. The Soviet President accepted that the new, united Germany should be free to choose which military block it wished to belong to. In effect, its full membership of NATO had at last been sanctioned. However, it was stipulated that NATO structures could not be extended into the eastern Länder until all of the Red Army 'guest' force had been withdrawn. This pull-out would be accomplished by the end of 1994, with DM 12 billion of the cost of its upkeep and subsequent removal, retraining and rehousing in the Soviet Union to be borne by the FRG. Thereafter, German military units integrated into NATO's structures could then be deployed on former GDR territory, but without nuclear weapons. Additionally, it was agreed that the new German army should be reduced from its combined strength of 670 000 to 370 000 within four years, as part of a general contraction of military strength across Europe. Moreover, the *Bundeswehr* would continue to renounce the possession of nuclear, chemical and biological weapons. Finally, it was accepted that, before reunification, a Soviet-German 'Treaty of Good Neighbourliness, Partnership and Co-operation', covering security, economic, cultural and technological matters, would be negotiated. This treaty was concluded and signed on 13 September 1990.

Achieved partially through the allure of the Deutschmark, an accord on the new Germany's security status had been reached. It was approved formally by all the 'two-plus-four' powers in a Treaty of Final Settlement on Germany, signed in Moscow on 12 September 1990, and by the Bundestag and Volkskammer, eight days later. Two months later, on 17 November 1990, at the Paris meeting of the 35-member Conference on Security and Co-operation in Europe (CSCE), it was given its pan-European 'blessing'. The treaty's terms came into force on 1 October 1990 when, in New York, the 'four-powers' signed a declaration under which their residual rights and responsibilities regarding Berlin and the two Germanies were irrevocably suspended. This enabled the new federal Germany to begin life as a fully sovereign state.

Reunification is Achieved

At 0.00 hours on Wednesday 3 October 1990, designated by Chancellor Kohl as a 'day of joy', the black, red and gold flag of the new Federal Republic was raised outside the thronged, floodlighted Berlin Reichstag. Fireworks exploded overhead in a brilliant cascade and across the state the national anthem, pledging 'unity, justice and freedom' for the 'German fatherland', was joyfully sung. After 45 years of division, the German people now celebrated their nation's restored unity. Only in Berlin, headquarters of the former SED-regime, were the festivities marred by anti-reunion counter-demonstrations by a crowd numbering 10 000.

For its inaugural session, the new all-German Bundestag, expanded to 663 members to include 144 'observers' from the disbanded Volkskammer, was specially convened, symbolically, in the Reichstag. It voted five East Germans into the federal cabinet as new ministers without portfolio: Lothar de Maizière, Sabine Bergmann-Pohl, Gunther Krause (all CSU), Rainer Ortleb (FDP) and Hansjoachim Walther (DSU). Over the next few days, it formally ratified a succession of treaties, including the 'two-plus-four' Treaty on the Final Settlement.

On 14 October 1990, less than a fortnight after reunification had been achieved, elections were held in the five re-established eastern Länder. As in March 1990, the campaigns were dominated by 'political professionals' drafted in from across the Elbe. Indeed, 40% of the candidates of the two main parties, the CDU and SPD, were West Germans. Viewed in aggregate, the overall result, in terms of party vote shares, was broadly similar (*see* Table 24) to that of the preceding 18 March Volkskammer and the 6 May local and municipal contests.

TABLE 24   PARTY SUPPORT IN THE OCTOBER 1990 FIVE EASTERN LÄNDER ELECTIONS (OVERALL % SHARE OF THE VOTE)[1]

Party	Oct 1990 Länder Polls	May 1990[2] Polls	March 1990[3] Volkskammer Polls
CDU	43.6	34.4	42.7
SPD	25.2	21.3	20.8
PDS	11.6	14.6	15.2
Free Democrats	7.8	6.7	5.5
Greens/Alliance '90	6.7	2.4[4]	4.5
DSU	2.4	3.4	6.6
Others	2.7	17.2	4.7
(Turnout)	(70%)	(75%)	(94%)

[1] Elections were delayed in Berlin until 2 December 1990.
[2] Includes East Berlin results.
[3] Excludes East Berlin results.
[4] Figures for New Forum alone.

The Christian Democratic Union, as Table 24 shows, continued to poll strongly. It captured 44% of the overall vote and (*see* Appendixes B and C) emerged as the largest single party in four Länder. Indeed, in Saxony, where its list was headed by Kurt Biedenkopf, the former general secretary of the West German CDU (1973–7), the party secured a staggering 54% of the vote, enabling it to form a Land administration alone. Elsewhere, in Thuringia, Saxony-Anhalt and Mecklenburg-Western Pomerania, it entered into coalitions with the Free Democrats, who polled strongly, especially in Saxony-Anhalt (14%).

Building on earlier advances achieved in the May municipal contests, when they emerged as the largest force in East Berlin, Leipzig and Dresden, the Social Democrats also gained significant support in these eastern Länder contests. The party's strongest showing was in Brandenburg, where, with a list headed by the popular East Berlin lay Protestant leader and lawyer, Manfred Stolpe, they topped the poll with a 38% vote share. This enabled the SPD to form a coalition government with the Greens/Alliance '90 and the FDP.

The Greens/Alliance '90 also polled respectably, securing representation in the three Landtage, Saxony, Saxony-Anhalt and Thuringia, in which they presented joint lists. There were only two clear losers in October 1990: the PDS, on the far left, despite its campaigning jointly with a Left List (*Linke Liste*), and the DSU, on the right.

These October 1990 Länder elections were an important indicator of relative party standings within eastern Germany just seven weeks before the crucial all-German general election. In the next section, the run-up to and the outcome of this 2 December contest are examined, beginning, first, with an overview of the party-political situation in western Germany in the months preceding and immediately following reunification.

Reunification Completed: The All-German Elections of December 1990

The West German Context: Party Politics during 1990

At the start of October 1989, with a federal election only 14 months away, the political future of Chancellor Kohl and his CDU-CSU-FDP coalition seemed bleak. In municipal elections held in the

Republic's largest Land, North-Rhine-Westphalia, at the beginning of the month, the CDU's vote share plunged nearly five points to 37.5%. This was its worst result for 33 years. There was a continuing haemorrhage of support to the Republicans, who polled more than 7% in the major cities of Dortmund and Düsseldorf, thus securing council seats. The far-right party benefited from public discontent at unemployment and the housing shortages, exacerbated by the apparently ceaseless *Übersiedler* inflow, amounting to 184 000 during the first quarter of 1990. The CDU also trailed the SPD in national public opinion polls by more than five points. The SPD was newly united, well disciplined and had formulated a potentially popular policy programme. By his August–September 1989 manoeuvrings, Chancellor Kohl had secured his own immediate position as CDU leader. Outside, however, he was derided by political commentators as a bumbling, pedestrian failure, and a deeply unpopular 'spent force'. With the 'Realos' apparently back in control of the Greens and 'general talks' underway with the SPD, there was the increasing possibility that December 1990 could bring a new *Machtwechsel*: the formation of the first federal 'red-green' coalition.

Less than three months later, following East Germany's dramatic 'gentle revolution', the West German political landscape was transformed. In an Emnid poll, conducted in late December 1989, the CDU-CSU was shown to have regained its national primacy. Its support rating of 40% put it three points ahead of the SPD. The position of the union parties' coalition ally, the FDP, had also improved, to 9%. Meanwhile, the Republicans had fallen back to just 4%. One issue, reunification, had come to dominate the political agenda, presenting an historic opportunity to the ruling parties, which was boldly seized by Helmut Kohl. Establishing himself, during the spring and summer of 1990, as both 'champion' and 'architect' of reunification, and becoming, in 3 October 1990, the first Chancellor of a united Germany since Hitler, Kohl's public image was metamorphosed. Formerly decried as, at best, mediocre, the Kohl chancellorship was now presented as outstanding, comparable to that of Adenauer. Reunification had 'saved' Kohl.

However, although both the personal standing of Chancellor Kohl and the popularity of his CDU-CSU-FDP coalition were indisputably transformed during 1989–90, there was by no means a constant progression in their public-support levels within the Federal Republic. Instead, although, as the March and October 1990 Volkskammer and Länder elections clearly showed, Helmut

Kohl was enormously popular in East Germany, greeted with fervour at the campaign rallies he addressed, in West Germany he and his party endured spasmodic reversals in their fortunes. For many in the western Länder, at least until the early autumn of 1990, he remained the 'unloved Chancellor', who, with his gargantuan girth and provincial ways, was the continual butt of wounding jokes.

Indeed, in two of the three Länder elections held in West Germany during the first half of 1990 the CDU's vote share continued to decline: by 3.9% in the Saarland on 28 January and by 2.3% in Lower Saxony on 13 May. As a consequence, control of Lower Saxony was lost, after 14 years, to the SPD, who had formed a coalition with the Greens. In the process, the CDU-CSU's 23:18 seat majority in the Bundesrat was overturned. In local elections in Bavaria and Schleswig-Holstein, in late March, both the CSU and CDU similarly lost ground. Described by Chancellor Kohl as 'bitter' reverses, the results were ascribed to public concern about the pace and, especially, the economic consequences of reunification. However, in the North-Rhine-Westphalia, on 13 May, and Bavaria, on 14 October, Länder contests, support for the CDU and CSU held firm. This was because, by the early summer of 1990, the drift of support to the Republicans, which had been so worrying during 1989, had been checked. In the 25 March 1990 Bavarian council elections the Republicans secured a number of seats, but in October they fell narrowly short of the 5% hurdle in what was their home Land. Committed since their 13–14 January 1990 Rosenheim conference to securing the immediate reunification of Germany, militarily independent, with a capital in Berlin and the frontiers of 1937 restored, the Republicans polled poorly in the Saarland, Lower Saxony and North-Rhine-Westphalia Länder contests, capturing only 1.5–3.3% of the vote. They were, subsequently, riven by an internal factional dispute, resulting, between 25 May and 7 July, in Franz Schönhuber being persuaded to step down temporarily as party leader, under the duress of extremist neo-Nazis.

As an integral member of the Bonn coalition, the FDP also shared in the loss of centre-right support in Saarland in January 1990. Later, however, benefiting from the popularity and high profile of its tireless, conciliatory foreign minister, Hans-Dietrich Genscher, the party's fortunes steadily improved. In the two Länder elections held in May 1990 the FDP maintained its existing vote share and in October, in Bavaria, added 1.4%, thus securing re-entry to the Landtag. This was after an eight-year break.

Unlike the parties of the federal coalition, West Germany's Social Democrats polled encouragingly in the Länder and local elections of January–May 1990. In Saarland, on 28 January, led by prospective chancellor-candidate, Oskar Lafontaine, the party won a crushing victory, attaining an absolute majority of the votes cast and adding 5.2% to its 1985 result. In this Land, the campaign included a call for the curbing of the continued, uncontrolled immigration of Übersiedler and other ethnic Germans. Two months later, the SPD beat the CDU into second place for the first time ever in the 18 March local elections held in Schleswig-Holstein. A week later, they took control of several councils in Bavaria, including Munich, which, from late April 1990, was governed by a 'red-green' administration. However, the party's most significant success occurred on 13 May in Lower Saxony, since this victory gave it control of the Bundesrat.

However, despite these successes between January and May 1990 at Länder and local level, the SPD nationally became increasingly dispirited as 1990 progressed. Its hopes of regaining federal power in December progressively receded as it was thrown into a state of confusion about how best to respond to developments in East Germany and, in particular, to Chancellor Kohl's resolute drive for rapid, 'fast-track' reunification.

From the outset, when the 'gentle revolution' first broke in October–November 1989, the SPD found itself wrong-footed by events and consistently misread the popular mood. Right up to the autumn of 1989, it had been seeking to build a closer relationship with East Germany's SED, then, apparently, firmly in charge. When the Berlin Wall was breached and Helmut Kohl first declared publicly, on 10 November 1989, that he perceived a popular desire for reunification and would work to make it possible, the Chancellor's remarks were censured instantly by Walter Momper, SPD mayor of West Berlin. He charged the Chancellor with being 'out of touch with the current feelings of the people in this historic time'. Momper was wrong. It was the SPD which had become detached.

Willy Brandt, the party's former Chancellor, and still its honorary chairman, did his best to respond to the fundamental changes occurring in the GDR. Presenting himself as Ostpolitik's author and the 'father of unity', he made frequent visits to the east and began to advocate a gradual, but true, negotiated union of the two German states, rather than a hasty 'buy out' by the FRG. He argued that the process should begin with 'confederation' and this became the SPD's accepted policy line. The task of 'selling it' was given to Oskar

Lafontaine, who, on 19 March 1990, was officially confirmed as the SPD's chancellor-candidate. In his speeches, Lafontaine consistently emphasized and expressed concern about the cost and the stresses that the process of reunification would impose upon Germans, particularly West Germans. This approach, however, proved damaging since it generated resentment among East Germans who perceived the SPD as seeking to deny them the opportunity of rapid material advancement. Lafontaine similarly castigated the Chancellor's 'headlong rush' for union, calling for a slowing down of the process to a more measured, thoughtful pace. However, CDU supporters persuasively retorted that, with the East German economy fast collapsing and its government approaching bankruptcy, 'slow lane' union was no longer a practicable option.

Tarred as the 'foot-dragging' vessel of West German interests, the SPD was punished at the polls held in East Germany between March and October 1990, where it captured less than a quarter of the overall vote. The party's position in the 'eastern territory' was made worse by the evident personal unease exuded by Oskar Lafontaine whenever he attended campaign rallies beyond the Elbe, and also by the embarrassing conflict between the East and West German SPDs, during May–June 1990, over what should be their attitude to the GEMU treaty. The SPD's dismal standing in the east resulted, in mid-October 1990, after CDU victories in four of the latter Länder, in its losing its Bundesrat majority. It also, naturally, meant that its prospects of success in the 2 December all-German Bundestag contest had become even more remote.

Indeed, by mid-October 1990, with reunification achieved amid a wave of initial euphoria, national support for the SPD had plummeted to barely 33%, according to an Allensbach Institute public-opinion survey. Concurrently, in the Bavaria Land election, the party registered its worst ever performance, capturing a mere 26% share of the poll. Now enjoying a national support rating of more than 45%, the CDU-CSU seemed certain, in alliance with the FDP (9%), to achieve a resounding victory on 2 December. Indeed, privately, senior SPD officials had already resigned themselves to a further federal defeat. A few, however, did cling to the the hope that, perhaps subsequently, as the problems of integrating the eastern Länder mounted, an emergency, responsibility-sharing, federal 'grand coalition' with the CDU might be formed.

Preparations for 2 December: Party Mergers and Election Rules

Constituting the first poll of its kind, the all-German Bundestag election of 2 December 1990 was preceded by hectic preparations by the political parties, which hurriedly restructured themselves so as to be able to fight in both the new and the old Länder. It was also prefaced by an intense debate about the details of the electoral arrangements.

The restructuring of the two Germanies' leading political parties was effected in advance of formal political reunification, on 3 October 1990. The lead was taken by the Free Democrats, who, on 11 August, convened in Hanover, to agree on the merger of the East German BFD and West Germany's FDP into a new party, designated the 'FDP-Liberals'. In reality, however, it constituted a takeover. Otto Graf Lambsdorff, leader of the West German FDP, was elected the new party's chairman by an overwhelming margin. This occurred despite the fact that BFD membership was twice that of the western FDP. In compensation, additional deputy chairmenships were provided for the former leaders of the East German BFD and FDP. Amalgamation of the East and West German SPDs occurred six weeks later at a special congress held on 27–28 September. Hans-Jöchen Vogel became the merged party's chairman and Wolfgang Thierse, leader of the East German SPD since 9 June, a vice-chair. To provide places for easterners, the new federal party's presidium (executive) was enlarged from nine to 13 members. Three days later, at a congress held in Hamburg on 1 October, the CDU became the last of the two Germanies' major parties to combine. The terms were similar: Helmut Kohl was elected chairman of the merged party, Lothar de Maizière deputy chairman, Volker Rühe general-secretary, and three GDR politicians were brought into the expanded, 10-member presidium.

In what was a reverse of the typical arrangement, East Germany's PDS later effectively took over the Federal Republic's DKP Communist Party. The CSU, which had already established informal links with East Germany's DSU, and the Republicans now began to extend their direct interests into the eastern Länder, contesting, though without success, the Mecklenburg-Western Pomerania and Brandenburg Länder elections on 14 October. Finally, of all West Germany's significant parties which had siblings in East Germany, only the Greens chose not to seek formal merger in advance of the 2 December Bundestag poll. This decision could be explained by the re-ascendance of its pro-autonomy 'Fundi' wing, which had captured control of the party's rotating troika leadership at the 9–10 June 1990 Dortmund conference and had, in October 1989, persuaded the prominent 'Realo', Otto Schily, to defect to the SPD.

The dispute over the electoral regulations for 2 December arose, in similar vein to the contemporary altercation over reunification's precise timing, from inter-party manoeuvrings for advantage. An original attempt, during July 1990, by the CDU to have the two Germanies treated as separate-voting areas, in which the 5% cut-off 'rule' for representation would apply, was thwarted by the combined opposition of the SPD and FDP and, on 2 August 1990, agreement was reached by the East and West German governments that there should be a single voting area. However, as a concession to regionally based 'pygmy' parties, it was decided that the linking of lists to those of a major party should be permitted, for the purpose of calculation of the 5% rule, so long as the respective parties did not compete directly in any Land. This was dubbed the 'piggyback' procedure. To general surprise, on 29 September 1990, this electoral agreement was deemed inequitable and unconstitutional by the Federal Constitutional Court, which had been appealed to by the PDS, Republicans and Greens. While considered appropriate for future Bundestag contests, the Court ruled that application of the 5% 'rule' to one all-German voting area on 2 December 1990 would excessively disadvantage ex-GDR-based parties. The court said it allowed them insufficient time to extend their organizations into the western Länder and would have meant that, if unable to secure a 'piggy-back' partner, they would need to capture at least 23% of the eastern Länder vote to achieve federal representation. Therefore, for this one election, it was decided that, as had been originally contemplated in July, there should be two separate, eastern and western, voting areas in which the 5% hurdle applied.

At the Hustings: The One-Issue Campaign

During the early summer of 1990, public opinion polls suggested that, though pleased that reunification seemed at last to be at hand, other issues, most notably environmental protection, unemployment and safeguarding the strength of the *Deutschmark*, remained of paramount importance to individual prospective West German electors. Indeed, a *Der Spiegel* survey published in late May revealed that only 28% of *Wessis* believed that German unity should be a top priority and that more than 70% opposed making financial sacrifices to achieve the goal. However, from October 1990, with reunification accomplished, the popular mood began to change. Issues associated directly with reunification, in particular how integration of the eastern Länder could be successfully realized, began to dominate the political agenda and, in turn, the campaign for the 2 December Bundestag elections. Other significant concurrent concerns, notably the Gulf crisis and European union, became submerged. To an unusual degree, this became an election race centred around one real issue.

In the CDU campaign, which as usual was lavishly funded and highly professional, an unusually high profile was accorded to Helmut Kohl. In previous Bundestag elections, Chancellor Kohl's support rating had lagged behind that of the ruling coalition, and he had been an electoral liability, prone to make damaging verbal 'gaffes'. On this occasion, however, Kohl, with his recently acquired popularity as the 'unification Chancellor' and his increasingly astute, confident and statesman-like interventions on the world stage, had become a real asset. Now in his 60th year, he had, apparently, fully matured as a national leader. From June 1990 onwards he moved steadily ahead of his SPD rival, Oskar Lafontaine, as the party leader most popularly favoured to become the next Chancellor. Indeed, in October, the gap exceeded 20 points. A *Kanzlerbonus* seemed assured.

During October and November 1990, as in the 1983 and 1987 Bundestag races, the CDU advanced a positive message, with the fatuous slogan, 'Yes to Germany! - Yes to the future!', emblazoned across thousands of giant posters, depicting a smiling, genial Kohl and a special, feel-good, rock-and-roll anthem titled 'Touch the Future', played at rallies. The campaign material produced for the eastern and western Länder varied in the details of its language and policy emphases. This was because the party was aware that, for this election at least, there existed two distinct electorates, each with different problems, aspirations and levels of political sophistication. In the campaign directed at West German voters, particular stress was laid on the nation's economic achievements during recent months and years, annualized growth of 5.5% being registered during the third quarter of 1990. For eastern voters, emphasis was placed on the leadership strength of Helmut Kohl and his role as the region's 'great liberator'. There were also frequent, and well-received, patriotic references to 'our fatherland', attacks on 'socialist experiments' and promises of a prosperous future, the CDU presenting itself as the party best equipped to secure the region's swift economic and social reconstruction. Most crucially, to allay the anxieties of western Länder electors, the CDU pledged, at the same time, that East Germany's integration could be achieved successfully without the need to raise federal taxes. Instead, the cost of modernizing the east, the party's campaigners argued, could be funded through accelerated economic growth, through economies in defence spending, through the elimination of many subsidies, through the proceeds derived from privatization, through greater public borrowing and through increasing the rates of several minor duties, such as motorway tolls and carbon-dioxide emission imposts.

The CDU's 'no tax rise to pay for unity' pledge was castigated by the SPD opposition as deceitful and fraudulent. Throughout 1990, the SPD's chancellor-candidate, Oskar Lafontaine (47), had hammered home the message that reunification would entail massive cost to and considerable sacrifices by both German peoples. This, subsequently, became the party's simple, sobering theme during the Bundestag campaign. The governing coalition was accused of being unable, or unwilling, to do its sums. Lafontaine snidely asked his campaign audiences, 'Do you think Kohl knows how many zeros there are in a trillion?' In short, the CDU was depicted as 'offering [to the electorate] the German version of Reaganomics'.

The brash, charismatic Lafontaine was a much more accomplished and engaging orator than the often pedestrian Chancellor Kohl. He was to take to the hustings with typical relish during October and November 1990, believing that the large gap separating the governing coalition from the SPD in national opinion polls might still be closed. However, in this campaign his style was cramped by the intensive security that had become necessary as a result of an earlier attempt on his life, on 25 April 1990, in Cologne, by a publicity-seeking schizophrenic, Adelheid Streidel (42). The assault, with a butcher's knife produced from within a bouquet of flowers after Lafontaine had left the podium at a political rally, had severed a vein in his neck. It had enforced a week's hospitalization and meant that he had spent much of the early summer convalescing. During October and November 1990 he was forced to abandon 'meet-the-people' hand-shaking and autograph-signing forays and obliged to deliver his campaign addresses surrounded by a phalanx of bodyguards. In these speeches, as well as launching a succession of attacks on Chancellor Kohl's allegedly 'deceitful promises', and seeking to contrast himself as an honourable truth-teller, 'Honest

Oskar', Lafontaine attempted to shift the focus of debate towards 'SPD issues'. In particular, under the slogan, '*Der Neue Weg*' ('The New Way'), emphasis was given to the need to improve social justice and to increase environmental protection, founded on the novel principle of 'let the polluter pay'.

However, despite these valiant efforts, Lafontaine, who was described in some quarters as 'the wrong chancellor-candidate at the wrong time', proved unable to overcome the negative public image that he had acquired between May and October 1990. This was particularly the case among *Ossis*, by whom he was seen as the unenthusiastic 'Jeremiah of reunification'. Moreover, as a somewhat idiosyncratic and bluff 'loner', Lafontaine also alienated many within the SPD's traditional establishment. They included the still respected former Chancellor, Helmut Schmidt, a long-time adversary over defence strategy, who, in late November 1990, was quoted by a Dutch newspaper as having damagingly confided that Lafontaine would lose the election and 'deserves it too'.

The Election Result: An Expected Verdict

As almost universally anticipated, Schmidt was accurate in his prognosis. There were brief jitters in the CDU-CSU-FDP in late November, when a number of, what were later shown to be 'rogue', public opinion polls suggested that the SPD had begun to gain momentum and was rapidly closing a gap, with the coalition parties, which had been almost 20% at the campaign's outset. However, when the poll that really mattered took place, on Sunday 2 December 1990, and the counting got underway, it swiftly emerged from television computer predictions that the ruling federal coalition had been returned to power with a secure and substantially increased majority. At 8 pm, Oskar Lafontaine formally conceded defeat. When the counting was fully completed and seats allocated, this coalition victory was confirmed. As Table 25 shows, the CDU-CSU-FDP captured 54.8% of the all-German vote and 54.9% of the West German, compared to only 53.4% in January 1987. With 398 seats in the new 662-member federal assembly, they had a majority of 134, a Bundestag record. The attractions of peace, prosperity, in western Germany, newly attained unity and restored national confidence and pride had proved electorally compelling. But although the Bonn coalition's victory on 2 December 1990 was clearly comfortable, it was by no means a landslide triumph.

TABLE 25   THE DECEMBER 1990 FRG BUNDESTAG ELECTION (% SHARES OF ZWEITSTIMMEN VOTES)

Party	All Germany	(Western Germany)[1]	(Eastern Germany)[1]	Total Seats
CDU	36.7	(35.5)	(41.8)	268
CSU	7.1	(8.8)	(-)	51
FDP	11.0	(10.6)	(12.9)	79
(Governing Coalition)	(54.8)	(54.9)	(54.7)	(398)
SPD	33.5	(35.7)	(24.3)	239
Greens	3.9	(4.8)	(0.1)	0
Alliance '90/Greens	1.2	(-)	(6.0)	8[2]
PDS	2.4	(0.3)	(11.1)	17
Republicans	2.1	(2.3)	(1.3)	0
The Greys (die Grauen)[3]	0.8	(0.8)	(0.8)	0
Others[4]	1.3	(1.2)	(1.7)	0
TOTAL	100.0	(100.0)	(100.0)	662

[1] Western Germany includes West Berlin and Eastern Germany, East Berlin. Turnout in all Germany 77.8%, West Germany 78.6%, East Germany 74.5%.
[2] Two Greens and six citizens' movements deputies.
[3] Formed in July 1989 as a breakaway from the Greens to reflect the interests of older citizens, campaigning for better pensions and the abandonment of 'ageist' attitudes.
[4] The NPD captured 0.3% of the all-German vote, the DSU 0.2% (0.9% in eastern Germany) and the Ecological Democratic Party (ODP), 0.4%. (In all, 40 parties and 3696 candidates contested the election, with 24 parties and one alliance presenting a 'state list' in all or some of the 16 Länder).

Within western Germany, as Table 25 shows, the CDU-CSU together secured only the same vote share, 44.3%, as in the poor year of 1987. Indeed, while in Lower Saxony and North-Rhine-Westphalia (*see* Table 26) there had been some recovery in CDU support since the May 1990 Länder contests, in Bavaria the CSU lost ground quite significantly, both in comparison with January 1987 and, more recently, October 1990. One of the principal reasons for this disappointing CDU-CSU showing was that, unlike January 1987, they now faced competition on the far-right from the Republicans who, though falling well short of the expectations raised during 1989, drew away a third of a million conservative voters. Overall, the Republicans captured 2.1% of the all-German vote and 2.3% of the western German, including a 5% poll share in Bavaria.

TABLE 26   THE LÄNDER DISTRIBUTION OF BUNDESTAG (ZWEITSTIMMEN) VOTES IN 1990 (% SHARES OF VOTE)

Land	CDU^1	SPD	FDP	PDS	$Greens^2$	Republicans	Turnout (%)
EASTERN							
Berlin	39.3	30.5	9.3	9.7	7.2	2.4	(81.1)
Brandenburg	36.3	32.9	9.7	11.0	6.6	1.7	(74.0)
Mecklenburg-Western Pomerania	41.2	26.6	9.1	14.2	5.9	1.4	(71.0)
Saxony	49.5	18.2	12.4	9.0	5.9	1.2	(76.4)
Saxony-Anhalt	38.6	24.7	19.7	9.4	5.3	0.6	(72.4)
Thuringia	45.2	21.9	14.6	8.3	6.1	1.2	(76.4)
WESTERN							
Baden-Württemberg	46.5	29.1	12.3	0.3	5.7	3.2	(77.5)
Bavaria	51.9	26.7	8.7	0.2	4.6	5.0	(74.5)
Bremen	30.9	42.5	12.8	1.1	8.3	2.1	(76.6)
Hamburg	36.6	41.0	12.0	1.1	5.8	1.7	(78.3)
Hesse	41.3	38.0	10.9	0.4	5.6	2.1	(81.0)
Lower Saxony	44.3	38.4	10.3	0.3	4.5	1.0	(80.7)
North-Rhine-Westphalia	40.5	41.1	11.0	0.3	4.3	1.3	(78.7)
Rhineland-Palatinate	45.6	36.1	10.4	0.2	4.0	1.7	(81.8)
Saarland	38.1	51.2	6.0	0.2	2.3	0.9	(85.1)
Schleswig-Holstein	43.5	38.5	11.4	0.3	4.0	0.2	(78.6)

[1] CSU in Bavaria
[1] Alliance '90/Greens in the eastern Länder

The CDU, alone, was more successful in the eastern Länder, where it secured 41.8% of the vote. Nevertheless, its vote share here was below that of the combined performance of the CDU-CSU in western Germany and, perhaps more significantly, it was inferior to its showing in the March and October 1990 Volkskammer and Länder contests (*see* Table 24). This fall-back in support can be attributed to a growing sense of popular unease within the eastern Länder and to frustration with the deteriorating economic situation, almost a quarter of the population being either unemployed (0.5 million) or on short-time. Indicative of this changing popular temper were the series of job security and pay strikes which disrupted the *Deutsche Reichsbahn* rail network and eastern German steel production during late November 1990. Additionally, public opinion surveys revealed that that one in two *Ossis* were by now concerned about losing their jobs and were impatient with the slow progress made in raising their living standards. Reflecting this mounting sense of dejection, the electoral turnout on 2 December in the eastern Länder was, at only 74.5%, unusually low. As the fourth local or national poll within nine months, there was also evidence of 'voter fatigue'.

For one of the constituent parties within the Bonn coalition, the Free Democrats, the 2 December 1990 Bundestag election was, however, an undeniable success. For only the fourth time since 1949 and for the first since 1980, the liberals achieved a double-digit poll rating. They attracted 11% of the all-German vote, 10.6% of the western German and a most impressive 12.9% share of the eastern German. The newly merged party's vote was buoyed, in particular, by the 'Genscher effect': the popularity of its federal foreign minister. Indeed, in Halle in Saxony-Anhalt, Genscher's birthplace, the party captured, for the first time ever, an *Erstimme* (direct mandate) seat. The Free Democrats' success also derived from the cunning campaigning ploy they adopted, much to Chancellor Kohl's chagrin. With some ebullient members of the CDU-CSU anticipating, optimistically, that, for only the second time ever, the union parties might be able to secure an absolute majority of the federal vote and, thus, govern alone, the FDP called on electors to accord them their *Zweitstimmen* mandates, so as to ensure that a moderating voice was maintained around the cabinet table in Bonn.

For the opposition SPD, 2 December 1990 was something of a disaster, though by no means unexpected. The party secured barely a third of the all-German vote, including 24.3% of the vote in eastern Germany, where it faced competition on the left from the PDS and where its organization was in disarray, and 35.7% in western Germany. This western German showing was the party's worst since 1957, in the pre-Bad Godesberg era. The party's share of the vote fell, compared to January 1987, in every state within western Germany except Saarland, where, benefiting from the 'Lafontaine effect', it advanced by 7.7%. Indeed, in Lower Saxony and North-Rhine-Westphalia, where many blue-collar workers deserted it, the SPD's poll share was between six to nine points below its showing in the May 1990 *Landtage* contests. Confronted by Chancellor Kohl's 'unification juggernaut', the SPD failed to develop and project a positive message that would prove attractive to the electorate. Instead, its campaign was, in many ways, negative. In addition, with the Greens again in disarray, it lacked credibility as a potential government-in-waiting. There were, however, two tiny crumbs of comfort for it. Its 'new politics'-centred programme and comparatively youthful chancellor-candidate enabled it to poll strongly among young electors. It also achieved an, admittedly slight, advance, compared with March 1990, in the eastern Länder. However, SPD gloom on 2 December 1990 was exacerbated by the party's calamitous performance in the synchronous election held in the newly unified Land of Berlin. Damaged by the recent heavy-handed response of its administration in the west of the city to squatters' unrest, the SPD was trounced by the CDU, and captured only 30.5% of all the Berlin votes compare with the Christian Democrats' 40.3%. Later, however, a CDU-SPD 'grand coalition' was to be formed.

While the outcome of 2 December 1990 was depressing for the SPD, for the other 1987–90 opposition force within the Bundestag, the Greens, it was a humiliating débâcle. Faced by the counter-attraction of Oskar Lafontaine's 'eco-socialism' and by a CDU-CSU-FDP coalition now presenting the electorate with a much 'greener face', the, by now ageing and almost leaderless, environmentalist party lost substantial support in the western Länder and, as a result, for the first time since 1980, fell just short of the crucial 5% representation hurdle. This result came as a jolting surprise, since public opinion polls had suggested, during October and November 1990, that the Greens enjoyed between 7–9% support in all-Germany and that popular concern for environmental issues remained intense. However, as well as losing an estimated 600000 votes to Lafontaine's SPD, the party was clearly harmed by the hostile attitude it had exhibited during the summer and autumn of 1990 towards impending reunification. Indeed, its Bundestag deputies had actually voted against the GEMU treaty, castigating it as an 'Anschluss document'. The party also lost some crucial support to the *die Grauen* (the Greys), a new pensioners-orientated political organization. This newcomer had been formed, in July 1989, as a breakaway splinter from the Greens, drawing away 25000 members, including one Bundestag deputy, Trude Unruh (64). The Greens were able to maintain a Bundestag presence after December 1990 thanks to the success of the Alliance '90/Greens, civil rights/ecologist, electoral pact in the eastern Länder. Attracting a 6% share of the eastern vote, they secured eight Bundestag seats, two of them environmentalists. However, with formal linking of the two sibling bodies' lists, the Greens/Alliance '90 would, with a 5.1% combined federal vote share, have captured more than 30 Bundestag seats. The decision not to merge before 2 December had proved to be a grave tactical error.

Even more successful in the eastern Länder was the PDS. Despite its membership having contracted to 350 000, many of its eastern German assets having been expropriated and damage being inflicted by a succession of financial scandals, the 'reformed communists' managed to attract more than 11% of the eastern Länder vote. Securing 17 seats in the new all-German Bundestag, they had achieved what their leader termed, 'a victory of quality over quantity'. The party's campaign, headed by the engaging and eloquent Gregor Gysi, was refreshingly carefree and studded with humour. However, having proved able to attract only 0.3% of the western Länder vote, the PDS presence within the Bundestag seemed destined to be transient, since the the next federal contest will be fought within just one voting area. Moreover, even after the 2 December 1990, they had too few deputies to form an official Bundestag Fraktion.

Two concluding general observations emerge from reflections on the results of 2 December 1990.

The first is that, with such significant differences between the votes accorded to the parties of the Bonn coalition and the SPD opposition in the Bundestag and many Länder elections held only months apart, a distinction seemed increasingly apparent in German voters' minds about which of the major parties/voting blocs they wished to entrust with responsibility for national and local affairs. The CDU-CSU-FDP seemed to be viewed as likely to be the most competent federal administrators, while the SPD, in western Germany at least, was favoured for state and local administration. A similar, and even sharper, distinction has been established during recent decades in the United States, where 'caring' Democrats are invariably voted in at the congressional, state and municipal level, while 'frugal' Republicans have come to monopolize the presidency.

The second thought that emerges, with hindsight, is that the federal coalition was extremely fortunate in the timing of the 1990 Bundestag poll. Held soon after reunification, with its euphoria still lingering, but before the costs, both for East and West Germans, had begun to be truly appreciated, or were being masked by temporary job-sharing measures, it came at a high-tide point for the CDU-CSU-FDP's fortunes. Just months later, with problems of integration mounting, the mood changed sharply. Formerly the eastern Länder's popular 'liberator', Chancellor Kohl became the subject of jeers whenever he summoned the courage to cross the Elbe. So great and sudden was this popular reaction that increasingly prescient, if exaggerated, appeared to be the blunt words a CDU insider uttered on the very eve of the 1990 Bundestag poll: 'The elections on 2 December look like being the last ones we will win.' In Part Four, the reasons for this transformation in the public mood are examined.

Part Four

THE NEW GERMANY

Chapter 9

THE PROBLEMS OF INTEGRATION

The Kohl Third Term: Personnel and Policy Changes

Although returned on 2 December 1990 by the Federal Republic's voters for a third term, and for the first time by the all-German electorate, it was more than six weeks before, on 17 January 1991, Chancellor Kohl was formally elected Chancellor by the new Bundestag. On the following day the new federal cabinet was sworn in. During the intervening weeks there had been intensive negotiations between the three partners in the Bonn coalition, with haggling over the character and relative share of cabinet portfolios and also over the thrust and details of the government's new four-year programme.

The FDP was unusually conspicuous in this bargaining, having added 22 deputies to its Bundestag strength on 2 December 1990 and moved ahead of the CSU. It was naturally anxious to press for a strengthened executive position and the inclusion of its favoured policies in the agreed coalition programme.

Cabinet Changes

In its first goal, the FDP proved successful, being given five portfolios, including the nominally independent justice minister (*see* Table 27), in the federal cabinet. This represented an advance of one, the CSU correspondingly losing a seat. The most significant FDP promotion was that of Jürgen Möllemann (45), who now moved from education to head the economics ministry. He replaced the ineffectual and jaded Helmut Haussmann. An ambitious, self-regarding protégé of Hans-Dietrich Genscher, Möllemann was viewed as a possible future leader of the FDP. With reconstruction of the eastern Länder as the key priority of the new administration, he headed a strategic, high-profile ministry. The most notable CSU departure was the removal from the cabinet of Friedrich Zimmermann.

TABLE 27   THE KOHL ADMINISTRATION CABINET OF JANUARY 1991

Dr Helmut Kohl	CDU	Federal Chancellor
Hans-Dietrich Genscher	FDP	Vice-Chancellor & Foreign Affairs
Dr Gerhard Stoltenberg	CDU	Defence
Jürgen Möllemann[2]	FDP	Economic Affairs
Dr Theodor Waigel	CSU	Finance
Dr Wolfgang Schäuble	CDU	Interior
Rudolf Seiters	CDU	Head of the Chancellery
Klaus Kinkel[1]	Ind.	Justice
Dr Norbert Blüm	CDU	Labour
Ignaz Kiechle	CSU	Agriculture
Rainer Ortleb (E)[2]	FDP	Education
Dr Klaus Töpfer	CDU	Environment
Gunther Krause (E)[2]	CDU	Transport
Carl-Dieter Spranger[1]	CSU	Development Aid
Dr Christian Schwarz-Schilling	CDU	Posts & Telecommunications
Dr Heinz Riesenhuber	CDU	Research
Irmgard Adam-Schwätzer (f)[1]	FDP	Construction
Gerda Hasselfeldt (f)[2]	CSU	Health
Angela Merkel (f) (E)[1]	CDU	Women & Youth
Hannelore Rönsch (f)[1]	CDU	Family & the Aged

[1] New appointment.
[2] Altered responsibility.
(E) East German
(f) Female

Overall, however, the new 20-member federal cabinet differed little in its composition from its pre-election, and pre-reunification, forbear. Although four of its members switched portfolios, there were only five new faces. Four members were women. However, with the exception of Irmgard Adam-Schwätzer, they headed essentially secondary ministries, created through the break-up of the former department of women, youth, family affairs and health. Most striking of all, this first true all-German cabinet contained only three eastern German politicians and did not include Lothar de Maizière. The former GDR premier had been expected to be given a significant portfolio. However, accused on 10 December 1990 by the *Der Spiegel* magazine of having once been a Stasi informant, under a codename 'Czerny', he resigned as an interim minister without portfolio on 17 December 1990. Later, on 22 February 1991, he was exonerated by a government inquiry.

The Policy Programme

In the negotiations about the orientation of the new administration's policy programme, the liberal Free Democrats pressed for a commitment to two initiatives: first, an agreement that substantial cuts should be made in the defence budget, and, second, that the eastern Länder should be treated as a special, low tax zone, to encourage inward investment. They were only partially successful in securing their inclusion in the government's eventual, compromise programme. It was accepted that, to contain what, with the burden of the east's reconstruction and integration, had become a burgeoning federal budget deficit and also to adjust to the new post-Cold War world order, substantial defence economies should be made. It was also agreed that unemployment insurance contributions and telephone charges should be raised. However, rather than being treated entirely as a special low tax region, the eastern Länder were accorded in the CDU-CSU-FDP policy programme only piecemeal tax-break advantages. Companies operating there would not be required to pay the same local property and capital taxes as in the western Länder, investors would be allowed to write off against tax a half of all costs in a one year period, and the area's workers would be given higher income tax allowances.

The implementation of the new Kohl government's programme during the first half of 1991 is analysed later in this chapter. First, however, what of the new Germany that had been forged through reunification? How different was it from the former Federal Republic? What were its added strengths? What special problems did it face?

The New Germany: A Changed Federal Republic

The Changed Federal Republic in Snapshot Outline

The reunified new Germany was, as Table 28 shows, two-fifths bigger in its areal size than the former Federal Republic and comprised a population a quarter greater. This now made it clearly Western and Central Europe's most populous state, though not its most extensive, and will lead to its gaining additional seats, and thus extra bargaining power, in the European Parliament. Moreover, although the accession of the eastern Länder raised the FRG's GDP by less than one-eighth, it augmented its position as one of the world's economic giants. Accounting for 30% of EC output, it is undoubtedly the economic powerhouse of Europe. With a combined GDP of $1.3 trillion, it is the world's fourth greatest economy and, behind Japan, arguably the second strongest. With its increased demographic and economic weight, the new Germany, although its army will, by 1994, be smaller than that of the pre-reunification FRG, appears certain to become much more important and influential on the international stage. During 1990–1 there were already such indications. Chancellor Kohl and foreign minister Genscher were assiduously courted by President George Bush and state department secretary James Baker as the United States' pivotal European partner. At the same time, within Europe the new Germany played a leading role in the drive for a 'deepening', or federalization, of the European Community, something to which Kohl and Genscher are deeply committed. They also keenly promoted the economic and political reconstruction of Central and Eastern Europe's recently democratized states.

The obvious explanation for the new Germany's special interest in *Mitteleuropa* affairs is that, with its eastern border having shifted 200 kilometres beyond the Elbe and its capital now in Berlin, the FRG is a much more eastward-centred, and eastward-looking, state. Sharing frontiers with Czechoslovakia and Poland, it clearly has a direct interest in ensuring that Central Europe remains politically stable and economically viable. In particular, the FRG's leaders fear that if there is economic collapse in this neighbouring zone, it may precipitate a large-scale *Völkerwanderung*, resulting in the influx of millions of economic refugees into Western Europe, and particularly into the FRG. Already, during 1990–1 there were signs of this occurring, threatening to transform the Oder and Neisse rivers into Western Europe's 'Rio Grande'. For these reasons, on its re-election, the new Kohl administration pledged that it would

TABLE 28   THE NEW GERMANY: KEY STATISTICS

	West	East	United Germany
Area ('000 Sq Km)	249	108	357
Population (1988, Million)	61.7	16.7	78.4
Pop. Density per Sq Km	248	155	220
GDP (1988, US$ bn)	1,200	155	1,355
Per Capita GDP (1988, US$)	19,450	9,280	17,280
Employed (%)			
Males	61	55	60
Females	37	48	39
In Agriculture	5	12	7
In Industry	41	48	43
In Services	54	40	51
Life Expectancy (years, 1988)			
Males	71	69	70
Females	77	75	76
Pensioners as % of Population	15.2	13.2	14.8
Birth Rate (per 1,000)	10.4	13.4	11.0
Death Rate (per 1,000)	16.3	13.4	15.7
Marriage Rate (per 1,000)	6.3	8.3	6.7
Religion (% of population)			
Protestant	49	80	55
Roman Catholic	45	10	38
% of Households with			
Car	97	52	87
Deep Freezer	77	43	70
Automatic Washing Machine	76	10	62
Colour Television	94	52	85
Telephone	98	7	79

devote considerable political and economic resources towards aiding Middle Europe's reconstruction and would fight within EC councils to ensure that a new economic Iron Curtain, dividing East and West, is not allowed to be erected. This ambitious undertaking, termed the 'New Ostpolitik', has been supported by substantial private sector inward investment by German firms, often entailing joint partnership deals, within Eastern Europe, including the USSR. It has also been influenced by the fact that, with Soviet troops set to remain within its eastern Länder until the autumn of 1994, the Kohl administration clearly needs to maintain amicable relations with the USSR.

In its religious complexion, the new Germany, as the data in

Table 28 shows, is significantly more Protestant. As a consequence, it can be expected to be potentially more liberal in its social attitudes. Its age structure is also slightly younger. This is because the eastern Länder have proportionately fewer pensioners and, stimulated by the generous family allowances granted by the former SED-regime, a higher birth rate than the western. Reunification thus promises to lead to an infusion of new, younger blood into what, demographically, had become a sclerotic FRG. However, the large-scale east-west migrations that have taken place since 1989, involving approaching a million *Ossis*, have meant that this published demographic data is subject to revision.

The starkest divide between the eastern and western Länder of the new Federal Republic is socio-economic. As Table 28 reveals, prior to reunification GDR per capita incomes, and weekly wages, were less than half those in West Germany. They were more akin to those of contemporary southern Mediterranean Europe, for example Greece and Spain, or to West Germany during the late 1960s. Indeed, by 1989 the gulf had widened, to a third, and in many indicators of consumer goods' ownership, most notably cars, colour televisions, deep freezers and telephones (*see* Table 28), the divide between east and west was even greater. As well as spending, diet patterns also contrasted. Though, on reunification the two states became one politically, clearly, in economic matters, there still existed two Germanies. Significant differences were also apparent in the characteristics of the working population. In its gender employment pattern, the eastern zone, with its high female 'participation ratio', was somewhat more 'modern' than the western. However, in its occupational distribution it was much more backward. Large numbers continued to work in agriculture and old 'smokestack' industries, while comparatively few were engaged in the service sector. The outstanding task of the new Kohl administration would be to narrow this socio-economic divide.

Integrating the Eastern Länder: The Potential Difficulties

The most straightforward aspect of reunification has been institutional change in the political, administrative and socio-economic spheres. It has entailed the importation, amalgamation or extension of the spheres of activities of proven political institutions that were already operating successfully in the new FRG's western Länder. At the federal level, the eastern Länder have simply acceded to existing, though invariably enlarged, FRG structures: the Bundestag, Bundesrat, Federal Constitutional Court, Bundesbank and Bundeswehr. Likewise, political parties (*see* Chapter 8), trade unions[1] and the Protestant Church have either merged their eastern and western wings or there has been an enlargement of the sphere of activity for western German bodies. Similarly, western German judicial, police and penal structures have been established within the east, although a temporary exception has been in the contentious case of the abortion law. Here it has been decided that the comparatively liberal abortion regulations of the former GDR, which allow termination on request during the first three months of a pregnancy, should remain in force in the eastern Länder, and for Ossis only, for a two-year period. Thereafter, a new all-German abortion law will be framed and adopted.

Below, at the state and local levels of administration, new institutional structures, which are replicas of those already established in the western Länder, have been created. However, it has been decided to defer applying the *Finanzausgleich* system of horizontal (inter-Land) financial equalization. Instead, for a transitional period, the eastern Länder will receive direct grants in aid from the Bund to meet the costs of unification. In addition, they are entitled to a stipulated share of VAT receipts. However, when the Finanzausgleich system is eventually extended to the eastern Länder, dubbed because of their comparative poverty, the 'pfennigless five', the number of western states who are net contributors will undoubtedly rise.

However, although institutional change has been effected in a generally smooth, uncomplicated manner, the unavoidable human consequences have meant that the eastern Länder are not yet, nor may ever be, simple political extensions of the former FRG.

First, there has been the immediate inheritance of both personnel and ways of acting and thinking from the 40-year SED regime. As a consequence, there have naturally been large-scale dismissals of former SED-loyalist, nomenklatura personnel, particularly those connected to the Stasi. These have included administrators, police officers, university lecturers, particularly from the social sciences, teachers, judges, lawyers and senior managers. In an interim capacity, while new eastern Germans are being trained, they have often had to be replaced, at high cost, by imported *Wessis*. Concurrently, leading figures from the former SED regime have been gradually brought to justice, some Stasi files opened to those affected and claims for the compensation and rehabilitation of Stasi victims been gradually processed. However, so extensive were the tentacles of East Germany's former Communist Party and its security forces, that this process of 'destasification' and 'desocialization', affecting, for example, the educational syllabus and the teaching materials used, is bound to continue for a number of years. It is certain to cause distress and embarrassment as 'skeletons' from the old regime are progressively unearthed. For example, there have been widespread accusations that many West German politicians and civil servants were involved with the Stasi, including, during the early 1980s, possibly a member of staff in the Chancellor's office. Additionally, it is feared that Stasi cells (*Kameradenkreise*) will continue to operate underground in the new Germany, serving as a destabilizing force.[2]

Second, as already noted in Chapters 3 and 8, the popular attitudes and psychologies of the eastern Länder were clearly different from those in the western. There was, in short, a different political culture, one which was less party-rooted, more socially progressive and more volatile.

The gravest challenges presented to the new, enlarged Federal Republic were, however, economic and environmental, deriving, first, from the dismal legacy inherited in the eastern Länder and, second, from the need to transform what was a planned socialist 'command economy' into a capitalist, 'social market economy'.

Although the former 'showpiece' of the socialist bloc, the GDR economy bequeathed to the new FRG was, by West German standards, in an appalling condition. In an especially sorry state was eastern Germany's environment. Reliant for 70% of its primary energy needs on sulphur-laden brown coal, with many of its chemical plants running on ancient coal furnaces and with there being tremendous wastage in energy use, its Länder, most notoriously heavily industrialized Saxony and Thuringia, were blighted with perhaps the world's most polluted atmosphere. Certainly, East Germany's sulphur-dioxide emissions, which amounted annually to 240 kilograms per capita during the later 1980s, compared to less than 60 in the FRG, were the highest in Europe. This led, in turn, to high rates of lung cancer and, in the Leipzig-Karl Marx Stadt-Dresden zone, of *Waldstreben* (forest 'dieback'). Further north, in the new Land of Mecklenburg-Western Pomerania, though lightly industrialized, the Baltic coastline had been defiled by the continual dumping of industrial waste and there was the ever-present danger of a catastrophe at one of its accident-prone, Soviet-built nuclear power plants. Indeed, in January 1990, it was disclosed that, in 1976, the Greifswald nuclear power station had only narrowly averted a meltdown.

The infrastructure inherited from the GDR was in almost as backward a condition. This embraced its roads, railways, airports, telecommunications and its stock of housing, more than 40% of dwellings in Leipzig having been built before 1918. Its inadequacy meant that businesses operating within the eastern Länder found themselves at a comparative, international disadvantage.

However, as its essential lifeblood, it was the state of the eastern German economy that gave greatest cause for concern. Sustained formerly by hefty subsidies and, despite its large holding sizes (averaging 4600 hectares), the region's agricultural sector was much more labour intensive than its western German counterpart and notoriously inefficient. In the short term, as it faced European Community prices from the end of 1992, it would be forced to shed considerable manpower. Eastern Germany's industries, stocked with outdated technology and non-incentive-driven working practices, were similarly blighted by low levels of productivity, often less than a third of those of West Germany. Having never previously been required to operate in a truly competitive environment, their products were also of poor quality and unattractive design. As a result, when, in 1990, import controls were lifted and Ossi earnings and savings converted into hard currency, the shelves of its stores were filled with unsaleable goods produced by GDR firms, after consumers had voted 'West is best.' To compound its potential difficulties, East Germany's chemical industry, which contributed a tenth of its GDP and employed a third of a million workers, and its electronic undertakings were identical to those of West Germany, but their output greatly inferior. In short, there was no apparent complementarity.

With reunification, eastern Germany's industries needed to find new supply sources and markets for their products, much of which had formerly been sold to Comecon countries, and also to restructure so as to operate within a free-market environment. Initial estimates made by the East German government during the early summer of 1990 suggested that a fifth of the eastern Länder's 8000 state-owned, but soon to be privatized, companies would never be viable and would be forced to close. A further 50%, if granted interim credit guarantee support, could, it was believed, compete within the new Germany. The remaining 30%, it was expected, could successfully operate unaided. The associated job-shedding rationalization was projected to lead, towards the end of 1991, to an unemployment level of between 1.5–2 million, out of a total workforce of 8.6 million, representing a rate of 17–23%. However, as 1990–1 progressed, these initial forecasts were shown to be too sanguine. In February 1991 a confidential finance-ministry memo, leaked to *Der Spiegel* magazine, included an estimate that only a fifth of eastern Germany's 3.4 million manufacturing jobs would survive. By the late spring of 1991 even gloomier calculations were made by Western economists. These suggested that less than a tenth of eastern Germany's industrial workforce was employed in viable enterprises and that soon more than a third of the working population would be without jobs.

The Likely Cost and Timespan of Integration

Already at the close of the 1980s, before reunification, West Germany was ploughing DM 5 billion ($2.6 billion) annually into East Germany in the form of a variety of 'soft loans' and subsidies earmarked for the improvement of communications to West Berlin, to reduce pollution, and to the buy the freedom of political prisoners. During 1990, the 'Year of Reunification', this eastward resource drain had increased to more than $60 billion and it was estimated that during the rest of the decade between $600–775 billion would be spent on the eastern Länder's modernization and integration. Described as 'Project Germany', it can be seen as the 1990s inter-German equivalent of the Marshall Plan. An additional $8.3 billion (DM 15 billion) would be absorbed in connection with the 1990–4 Soviet troop withdrawal and DM 40 billion in export credits and subsidies to the USSR.

Of this 10 years' projected special expenditure, roughly a fifth, $140 billion, has been earmarked for cleaning up eastern Germany's environment, to bring it up to western German and European Community water and air pollution and safety standards.[3] The region's unsafe nuclear plants would need to be shut down immediately, production of, and reliance on, brown coal substantially reduced, new environmentally-friendly power stations constructed and anti-pollutant technology applied to existing plants, the electricity network linked into the western German grid, and greater efficiency in energy use encouraged. Infrastructure repairs and projects were expected to require a further $160 billion over this 10-year period, the re-equipping of factories with new plant and equipment, $155 billion, and the modernization of the telecommunications system, $20–30 billion, while unemployment payments were anticipated to amount to between $50–100 billion. However, as with the projections on the viability on the east's industry, these estimates were soon proved too optimistic. During

1991 alone, government payments to the eastern Länder were projected to exceed DM 120 billion, equivalent to 4% of the all-German GDP.

Much of this special government expenditure was financed by augmenting the size of the annual budget. During 1991, for example, DM 90 billion was funded in this way. It represented a quarter of the federal budget and was met substantially though increasing the size of the budget deficit, by borrowing. However, this had potentially adverse consequences for the all-German economy, leading to a weakening in the value of the *Deutschmark*, creating inflationary pressure and, in turn, countervailing increases in interest rates. An additional DM 115 billion of government spending on the integration of the eastern Länder between 1990 and 1994 was financed through the German Unity Fund. Established in May 1990, it was, like the budget deficit, also funded through federal and Länder government borrowing in the capital markets. Over time, however, when an improved infrastructure was in place and a market economy had been truly established, it was hoped that private investment would begin to bear the bulk of the cost of reconstructing and modernizing the east. An additional net $1.3 billion (1 billion ecus) per annum was to be provided, between 1991 and 1993, by the European Community for 'structural assistance'.

The official estimates made during the autumn of 1990 of the cost of rebuilding and integrating the eastern Länder suggested that the minimum timespan for this to be successfully completed would be 10 years. Some optimists, including Chancellor Kohl, believed that eastern German living standards could converge with western within as little as five years. However, the consensus, realistic view was articulated by Lothar de Maizière, in September 1990, after the last meeting of the GDR cabinet. He believed that it would take 'the equivalent of a single school generation [around 12 years]', before the two Germanies would become truly one, both economically and socially. More pessimistic observers believed, however, that, just as north-south and south-north divisions have persisted in contemporary Britain and Italy, within the new Germany there would always remain significant east-west structural and income-level differences.

In the following section attention is turned to the actual progress that was made in implementing this ambitious programme of modernization and integration during 1991 and at the problems, economic, social and political, that have been encountered in both the eastern and western Länder.

The Implementation of 'Project Germany' During 1991

Eastern Germany at the Start of 1991: The Strategy for Renewal

During the course of 1990, exposed to the 'cold shower' of western German and international competition and with tens of thousands of its skilled personnel continuing to migrate westwards, eastern Germany's GDP fell by a staggering 15%. By the year's end more than a quarter of its working population were either unemployed (0.7 million) or underemployed, on special, 'make work', part-time schemes. With subsidies removed, the prices of basic foodstuffs, fuel and public transport had increased sharply during the year, as, after a lag, had rents. Fears for job security mounted and living standards continued to be eroded, resulting in a rash of wildcat strikes during November and December 1990. Meanwhile, the region's new Länder and municipal governments faced a growing cash crisis.

Further deterioration of this socio-economic situation seemed certain during 1991, a year viewed as critical in the region's painful transition to a free, or social-market, economy. In the early summer many of the special job-sharing agreements that had done much to mask the true level of unemployment during the autumn and winter of 1990 were set to be phased out. In addition, while new FRG government-funded infrastructure projects would create some new employment, there would be extensive, labour-reducing rationalization in the industrial sector, as the eastern region's enterprises attempted to remain afloat in a competitive environment. In short, a further, 'ground clearing', supra-15% contraction in the zone's GDP was anticipated, nearly a half of its working population expected to be either unemployed (1.7 million) or on short-time (2 million) by the year's end. This slump threatened to be worse than that of the late Weimar era.

The newly re-elected Kohl administration had four immediate priorities for the eastern Länder during 1991: investment in improved infrastructure, the privatization of its remaining state-owned industries, the introduction of guaranteed apprenticeships for all school leavers and schemes to provide for the retraining of older workers, and the creation of a dependable legal and administrative environment, to make it attractive for inward investment by the private sector. To fund the huge outlays required to meet the demands of 'promotional investment' and the soaring social-security liabilities, finance minister Waigel anticipated, at the close of 1990, that the all-German public sector deficit would increase from its 1990 level of DM 117 billion to DM 140 billion. The latter figure would be equivalent to 5% of GNP, the highest proportion since 1975, half of this public borrowing being effected by the Bund and half by the Länder. However, the attainment of this level was dependent upon securing DM 35 billion of either cuts or revenue increases elsewhere in the government's programme. In particular, coal and agricultural subsidies were targeted for reduction, further privatizations within western Germany envisaged, and the level of unemployment contributions and telephone charges set to be raised.

The Progress Made towards Economic Integration during 1990–1

During the first 10 months of 1990 more than 226000 new private enterprises were registered in eastern Germany. A further 80000 had been formed by March 1991. Although many were admittedly small scale, including self-employed taxi-drivers and hot-dog stall owners for example, this was a positive sign that a new market economy was gradually being established from below. Also, towards the close of 1990, it was announced that three of western Germany's major automobile manufacturers, Volkswagen, Daimler-Benz and Opel, were intending, between 1991 and 1995, to invest at least DM 10 billion either in new plants or in expanding existing subsidiaries. They were seeking to take advantage of the region's comparatively low labour costs and its considerable 'pent-up' market demand. Indeed, for car and truck manufacturers, eastern Germany was regarded, in production and market terms, as a potential 'new Spain'. During the course of 1990–1 there was also considerable 'inward investment' in the eastern Länder by the electronics giant Siemens, and by western German banks, insurance conglomerates, retail chains, hoteliers, and media interests. This was because the service sector, like the automobile market which was comparatively underdeveloped by western German standards, seemed to present the greatest potential and the fewest impediments. They were to find, however, that the 'start-up' costs, entailing the modernization of acquired buildings, the retraining of staff, the computerization of offices etc, were much higher than had been anticipated.

These developments apart, the eastern Länder made an unpromising start during 1990–1 in their transition to a 'social market' economy. In March 1990 a trust body, termed the *Treuhandanstalt*, was established by the GDR government to oversee the restructuring and the privatization of 8000 state-owned industrial enterprises, which, at their height, had employed 6 million workers, as well as huge tracts of publicly-owned land. However, by the year's end only 400 firms had been successfully transferred to private hands, at a cost of DM 2.5 billion. A further 2175 companies were privitized during the first half of 1991 and it was anticipated that an additional 2000 would have followed this course by the end of 1991. These would include many enterprises in the energy-supply sector which were set to be taken over by western German utilities. However, the bulk of the remaining companies seemed certain to be wound up as unviable. Among them was the Dresden-based camera manufacturing company Pentacon, which, although formerly seen as one of the most successful and advanced manufacturing firms in the GDR, was liquidated in October 1990. Later, in March 1991, a tiny portion of the firm was saved by the western German company Beroflex. By April 1991 more than 330 other Treuhand enterprises, employing 80 000 people, had been closed, while four-fifths of the workforce at the high-tech firms Robotron and Carl Zeiss Jena had been dismissed.

In all, during 1990 around DM 3 billion was invested by western German manufacturing firms in the eastern Länder. For 1991, the expected total was DM 10 billion, a further DM 40 billion also being pumped in by service sector enterprises and public utilities, such as railways and telecommunications. However, although welcome, this investment failed to match the region's vast modernization and job-creation needs.

There were five chief reasons why western entrepreneurs proved unwilling to invest more directly in the eastern Länder and buy out its state-owned industrial companies. First, when their books were closely examined it was often found, as in the case of Pentacon, that they had formerly been heavily reliant on state subsidies. Deprived of these, they were uneconomic. Many of these former state enterprises were also burdened by huge debt acquired during the SED era. Second, the continuing uncertainty of ownership claims meant that western banks were sometimes unwilling to lend capital to western firms which sought to make acquisitions in the east. Third, this being particularly the case in the chemical industry, the existing plants were invariably considered too small and antiquated and there were fears that the new owners might, in future, be burdened by claims for compensation for past environmental damage. For these reasons, western investors preferred to start anew, building appropriately equipped factories on 'green field' sites and recruiting their own staff. Fourth, during the course of 1990–1, initially as a consequence of GEMU and then later of worker militancy and trade-union campaigns, eastern German industrial labour costs had begun to rise significantly, by more than 50%, but without corresponding efficiency improvements being achieved. As a result, eastern German productivity levels deteriorated further. Moreover, being part of a broader federation, the region was unable to follow the option that had been pursued by Poland, during its concurrent, 'big bang' shift to a market economy, that of currency devaluation, so as to make its goods more internationally competitive. Fifth, many of the larger western Germany companies considered that it was much more profitable for them to expand capacity within their existing western Länder plants so as to meet the enlarged market demand that was now provided by the east. In short the eastern Länder were treated as a new *Absatzmarkt*, simply a market for selling.

Matters were to be further compounded for the Treuhandanstalt by its understaffing and by the assassination, on 1 April 1991, of its executive head, Detlev Rohweddder (58), the former successful chief of Hoesch steel, by the Red Army Faction terrorist grouping.

The Reaction within Eastern and Western Germany

With the region's economy collapsing at a dramatic pace and its citizens suddenly confronted by a strange, psychologically confusing, new political and socio-legal order, including the loss of some former social benefits, it was not surprising that, as the spring and summer of 1991 progressed, popular tension and social disorder grew in the eastern Länder. With industrial production halved between July 1990 and April 1991, tens of thousands were thrown out of work each week, and a third of the workforce was either unemployed or on short-time by April 1991. There were no signs of living standards improving in the immediate future and there was mounting resentment at the downside of this 'crash course in capitalism'.

This disquiet expressed itself in the form of increasingly frequent lightning strikes and, from March 1991, the staging of major demonstrations against both the *Treuhandanstalt*, derided as the job-killing 'hatchet of capitalism', and the Kohl government. In December 1990, as the 'Chancellor of German Unity', Helmut Kohl had enjoyed a popularity rating of almost 50% in the eastern Länder, but by March 1991 it had plummeted to 26% and, a month later, an Infas poll revealed that more than four-fifths of easterners felt let down by the new federal government. Believing that the Chancellor had failed to uphold his electoral promise that the new, soon to be 'blossoming', eastern states 'would be no worse off after unity', 40% of those who had voted CDU on 2 December 1990 stated that they would not now do so. In Leipzig, birthplace of the 1989 'gentle revolution', an anti-government rally organized by IG Metall on 25 March 1991 drew 60000 protesters. They chanted slogans demanding jobs and better living conditions, and called for the resignation of Chancellor Kohl. These demonstrations spread to other cities and when, on 7 April 1991 in Erfurt, capital of Thuringia, Kohl made his first public, post-election appearance in the eastern region, he was jeered, pelted with eggs and rotten fruit, and subjected to chants of 'Liar!'

As well as this resentment, directed specifically against governmental personnel and institutions, there was increasing evidence of a growing, more generalized, hostility of Ossis towards western Germans and, within their region, to foreigners. In particular, they loathed the patronizing, and often ignorant, manner in which their richer, more cosmopolitan, Wessi cousins treated Ossis as drab, second-class citizens. They resented being viewed as idle and chronically state-dependent, constantly asking for handouts from the western Länder. As westerners gradually took over their industries, financial institutions, retail chains and even their newspapers, staffing many senior administrative and executive positions, and dominating the federal cabinet and Bundestag proceedings, they felt 'colonized' and exploited. In particular, they believed that more sympathy should be shown to their plight, since it had not been their choice to be left at the close of the Second World War on the wrong side of the, soon to be erected, Iron Curtain. The mental wall, termed *'Die Mauer im Kopf'*, which had grown up between the two German peoples since 1945, remained firmly in place.

The demonstrations in eastern Germany during the 'hot spring' of 1991 were almost always peaceful. There were, however, worrying signs that on its fringes the new Ossi society was becoming increasingly violent. In particular, there were recurrent outbreaks of hooliganism at football matches; new terrorist organizations had begun to emerge, most notably Thomas Munzer's Wild Pack, which firebombed a Berlin branch office of the *Treuhandanstalt*; and, most worrying of all, there were increasing signs of an, admittedly minority, revival of neo-Nazism among the young. This recrudescence of far-right extremism, the first signs of which were in Leipzig in February 1990, was derived, at a time of high unemployment, from popular xenophobia, especially directed against foreign workers. These included Poles, who had been granted visa-free entry into Western Europe from April 1991, Soviet Jews and the 90000 immigrant labourers 'imported' into East Germany by the SED regime from Vietnam, Angola and Mozambique. The perpetrators of this racial violence, which included the beating to death of, Jorge Gomondai, a Mozambiquan, in Dresden in February 1991, often escaped punishment. This was because a blind eye was turned by dispirited police officers, drawn from East Germany's former *Volkspolizei*. By June 1991, it was estimated that 30000 young East Germans were supporters and between 5000–15000, often conspicuous with their skinhead appearance, active on the neo-Nazi scene. They were members of such groups as National Resistance, German Alternative and the National People's Party. This drift of the young to the far right, with its offer of simple solutions to the region's economic ills and a spurious sense of racial superiority, reflected a breakdown in identity and self-confidence within the eastern Länder.

While the eastern German economy was disintegrating during 1990–1, the western was booming. GDP growth of 4.5% was registered during 1990 and this continued into the first half of 1991, with the motor-vehicle, consumer-goods and construction industries especially buoyant. Moreover, notwithstanding the incessant influx of tens of thousands of Ossis and other ethnic Germans, as well as 300000 Ossi commuters, the level of unemployment fell slightly in the western Länder. Against this favourable backcloth, it might have been expected that, during the first half of 1991, the Kohl administration would have retained its popularity in the west. However, this was not so.

On 20 January 1991, exactly seven weeks after the federal poll, the combined CDU-FDP vote share fell back, compared with 2 December 1990, by 4.6% in the Hesse Land election and support for the SPD and Greens advanced by 6%. As a consequence, a new 'red-green' *Landtag* coalition was formed. Three months later, on 21 April 1991, support for the CDU fell by more than six points in Helmut Kohl's home state of Rhineland-Palatinate. As a result, control of the Landtag was lost to the SPD, this time in coalition with the FDP, and the Social Democrats were now in government in 10 of the Federal Republic's 16 Länder and had also regained their Bundesrat majority. Nationally, the SPD had also moved ahead of the CDU-CSU, a public opinion poll published on 10 June 1991 according the party 39.5% of all-German support compared with the conservative unions' 38.5%. There were three main explanations of this sudden turnaround.

The first concerns the state of the western German economy as perceived at the individual level. Though it was still booming, surveys showing that business confidence remained high, there was tougher competition in the job and housing markets and, as the budget deficit grew and the first trade deficit for 10 years emerged, both interest/mortgage rates and inflation edged upwards. By May 1991 real interest rates had reached 6% and inflation was heading towards 4%. As family budgets were hit, there was a spate of strikes in western Germany's engineering industry, during May 1991, and, as interest rates still climbed, the rate of growth in the western Länder economy was predicted to slow down to around 2% during the rest of 1991–2. This growing sense of economic uncertainty was heightened, on 16 May 1991, by the surprise resignation of Karl-Otto Pöhl (60) as Bundesbank president.[4]

The second reason for this change was the western German voters' indignation in finding that that on 12 March 1991, barely three months after the Bundestag election, Chancellor Kohl had reneged on his campaign promise that taxes would not be increased to meet the burdens of reunification. Citing the unexpected cost, amounting to $7 billion, of German financial aid to the UN coalition fighting the Gulf War, and admitting that the full scale of 'Project Germany' had been underestimated, finance minister Waigel introduced a revised 1991 draft budget, in which government revenue during 1991 and 1992 was to be increased by DM 48 billion, this rise funded by the imposition, from July 1991, of a special one-year 7.5% income and corporation tax surcharge and an increase in tobacco and petrol taxes. The CDU's Rhineland-Palatinate defeat was directly attributable to the voter backlash engendered by this '*Steuerlüge*' ('great tax lie').

The third cause was the alienation of specific western German special-interest groups by the announcement by economy minister Möllemann, in July 1990, that state subsidies and tax breaks would be further reduced by DM 33 billion between 1991 and 1993. This arose from the government's concern to prevent total public borrowing from soaring to almost DM 200 billion. Farmers, shipbuilders and miners were specially targeted, plans being made to reduce the numbers employed in the western German coal industry by 70%, to 40000, by the year 2005.

The Kohl Administration's Response to its Mounting Difficulties

In late 1990 government officials had anticipated that the eastern German economy would move out of its 'tunnel' of decline by the middle of 1991 and, thereafter, begin to recover at an accelerating rate. However, this hoped-for revival failed to materialize and, as 1991 progressed, it was accepted that the eastern economy would continue to deteriorate into 1992. For this reason, the Kohl administration was forced to introduce a succession of additional public-spending packages. These were designed both to generate employment, by means of infrastructural and retraining projects, and to mitigate social distress. Thus, by the spring of 1991, eastern Germany's per capita GDP, which had fallen to a quarter of the western Länder level, was brought up to roughly a half through financial transfers. In addition, it was announced, on 8 March 1991, by labour minister Blüm, that the 'zero short-time' policy, whereby eastern employees whose labour was not in full demand were paid 70% of their salary to either stand idle on production lines or sit at home, rather than being made redundant, would be extended by a further six months, to the year's end.

In an effort to reclaim support for the CDU in the eastern Länder, where the party's opinion-poll rating had fallen to below 30%, Chancellor Kohl, from the spring of 1991, went out of his way to display a much closer personal interest in the region's development. As well as, at last, setting foot again in the region, he gave strong support to the campaign for Berlin to replace Bonn, the 'federal village', not just as the official capital of the new Germany, but also as the seat of the federal government and parliament. This crusade reached a successful conclusion when, on 20 June 1991, the Bundestag voted by 337 votes to 320 for a staggered transfer. It was estimated that the cost of this move might, over a 12-year timespan, amount to anything between DM 6–125 billion.

As the spring of 1991 progressed, Chancellor Kohl also sought to secure a measure of all-party consensus for the 'Project Germany' strategy. Encouraged by the promptings of President von Weizsäcker and Kurt Biedenkopf, the CDU minister-president of Saxony, who had forged alliances with SPD administrations in the eastern Länder to press jointly for increased federal aid, on 12 April 1991, Kohl met the SPD leader Hans-Jöchen Vogel for the first of a series of talks on the 'eastern crisis'. It was agreed immediately that joint commissions, including representatives from the governing coalition, the SPD and New Forum, should be established. In these deliberations, the opposition pressed for a switch to a more activist industrial and regional policy, in which emphasis would be placed on job creation rather than simple privatization. This apparent rapprochement between the CDU and the SPD was interpreted by some commentators as indicating that if the situation deteriorated further in the eastern Länder, an emergency federal 'grand coalition' administration might subsequently be formed.

However, in May 1991, this, always remote, possibility became even more unlikely after a rightward shift in the CDU's stance on such social issues as abortion and immigration. This change occurred after crisis talks with the CSU which had become increasingly restless within the ruling coalition and had threatened to depart and extend its organization into eastern Germany's southern Länder.

Eastern Germany's Future: A Second Wirtschaftswunder?

Despite its languishing in the deep trough of a depression during 1991, many analysts predicted that the eastern German economy would experience a strong upswing from the start of 1992 and that the medium-term future for the region was potentially promising. It had a well-educated and skilled labour-force, undergoing retraining, and a basic reservoir of the Teutonic virtues of diligence and frugality. Its factories were set to be equipped with modern, 'state-of-the-art' machinery, its infrastructure was to be upgraded, and it had been provided with a tried and tested administrative and legal framework. Thus, it was argued, once the process of 'ground clearing' had been completed between 1990 and 1992, a new *Wirtschaftswunder* would commence. Indeed, some economists optimistically predicted that annual GDP growth rates of 7% or more were likely between 1992 and the end of the century. There would be unfortunate victims, not least older workers whom it would be uneconomic to retrain, but, over time, the productivity and income levels of the two Germanies would progressively converge.

Others commentators were less sanguine. They feared that, in the short term at least, 40 years of communist rule had killed the flames of industry and enterprise and that it might be years before the basic German virtues could be rekindled. Furthermore, it was pointed out, even growth rates as high as 17% per annum during 1993–4, which were predicted in April 1991 by Dr Meinhard Miegel, director of the Institute for Economy and Society, would serve only to restore eastern German output to its 1989 level. Moreover, subsequent real growth, between 1994 and the year 2000, of at least 9% per annum would be needed if eastern living standards were to reach half the western German level, and an unprecedented, sustained 17% if they were to attain three-quarters. This was based on the assumption that annual real growth would average 1.7% in western Germany. Clearly, the *Wirtschaftswunder* would need to be even more spectacular than that in postwar West Germany if speedy convergence was to be secured.

Gazing Ahead: The New Germany's Party Political Future

Personally unpopular in both Germanies and with his CDU party trailing the opposition party in national opinion polls, Chancellor Kohl's political future, in mid-1991, seemed, yet again, in doubt. Kohl, himself, was determined to battle on. He had set his sights on surpassing Konrad Adenauer's record of 14 years as a modern German Chancellor. He was also anxious to play a key role in helping to secure a 'deepening' of the European Community and did not wish to retire before the integration of the eastern Länder had been successfully accomplished.

During 1991, while there was mounting unease within the CDU at his leadership, the Chancellor was fortunate in having few credible rivals. His two most prominent adversaries, Lothar Späth and the hugely popular Rita Süssmuth, were both damaged, to varying degrees, at the start of the year by scandals. Späth's alleged scandal, the most serious of the two, which he strongly denied, was that local companies had paid for a number of his family's vacations and, in return, had been favoured with state contracts. It forced his resignation as Baden-Württemberg minister-president on 13 January 1991. A month later, Rita Süssmuth's reputation, as Bundestag speaker, was tarnished by allegations that, infringing regulations, she had allowed her husband private use of her official car. This left three potential successors: Volker Rühe, the relatively young party general-secretary, Rudolf Seiters, the head of the chancellery, and Dr Wolfgang Schäuble, the interior minister. All three were, essentially, Kohl loyalists. However, Schäuble (48), who was confined to a wheelchair, after being shot twice on 12 October 1990 at an electoral rally in his home town of Oppenhau, Baden-Württemberg, by a deranged man, was rumoured to be Kohl's personal choice as 'crown prince'.

The immediate political and electoral future for the CDU seemed bleak. By the summer of 1991 it controlled only one of western Germany's 10 Länder, Baden-Württemberg, was finding it difficult to push controversial legislation through the Bundesrat, in which it was now in a 32–37-seat minority, and seemed set to endure an almost certain voter backlash in future elections in eastern Germany. In addition, as general-secretary Volker Rühe acknowledged in May 1991, the CDU faced an internal crisis of an ageing membership. It was reported in July 1991 in *Die Welt* that more than half the party's 670000 members were aged 50 or over, while fewer than 7% were under the age of 30. The CDU, hampered by a traditionalist, male-dominated image, was also finding it difficult to attract female members, in the western Länder at least.

In contrast, the opposition SPD was undergoing successful 'generational change' within its leadership councils and revamping its organizational structure.

In the immediate, disappointing aftermath of the 2 December 1990 Bundestag election, Oskar Lafontaine, despite entreaties to take on either the party's chairmanship or Bundestag floor leadership, announced that he intended to return to Saarland to concentrate on his work as minister-president. The exhausted Hans-Jöchen Vogel, who had been contemplating retirement, agreed to remain the SPD's parliamentary Fraktion leader. However, at the 28–31 May 1991 Bremen congress, he stepped down from the party's chairmanship. His successor, was Björn Engholm, the minister-president of Schleswig-Holstein. A youthful looking 51, the suave, determined Engholm, was viewed as a centre-left, 'Nordic social democrat' pragmatist, in the Brandt-Schmidt tradition.

Engholm took over a party, which, buoyed by its Länder contest successes during early 1991 and by its rising national opinion-poll rating, was increasingly confident about its future. Aligning itself with anti-government protesters, it was beginning to make real headway among the electorate of the eastern Länder, receiving almost 41% support there in August 1991 public-opinion polls. Also, having formed a coalition government with the liberals on 21 May 1991 in Rhineland-Palatinate, there were growing prospects that the FDP, infused with tens of thousands of new 'social liberal' easterner recruits, might, in the near future, leave the CDU-CSU-FDP federal coalition and seek a new alliance with the SPD. If it did, it would lead to a constitutional predicament, since neither the CDU-CSU nor the SPD-FDP alone held sufficient Bundestag seats to form a majority government. Instead, the PDS would be left holding the balance of power.

On the political fringe, the western Greens, though not polling as strongly as in the preceding Länder contests, achieved an increase in support over its 2 December 1990 level in the Hesse, Rhineland-Palatinate and Hamburg state polls of January–June 1991. Moreover, on each occasion the party retained its Landtag representation. Clearly the Greens, though suffering a temporary reverse nationally in December 1990, were set to continue as a significant minor party force. Indeed, in the Hesse Land contest, fought at the time of the Gulf conflict, the party benefited from a wave of anti-war feeling, and was successful enough to be able subsequently to form the junior partner in a new coalition government with the SPD.

After this Land election, Joschka Fischer, the Greens' 'Realo' leader in Hesse, called for a professionalization of the national party. This advice was later to be substantially heeded. At a turbulent congress held in Neumünster, Schleswig-Holstein, on 26–28 April 1991 it was agreed that the rotation of party posts should be abandoned. Two months later, on 8–9 June in Cologne, Heide Rühle was elected as party manager and the party's delegates voted in favour of seeking a coalition with the SPD after the next general election. This newly rediscovered realism was, unsurprisingly, condemned by 'Fundis' and, on 11–12 May 1991, 200 radical ecologists and feminists, under the lead of Jutta Ditfurth, formally broke away to establish the new Ecological Left/Alternative List grouping.

Meanwhile, on the far-right fringe, the Republicans continued to poll poorly in the western German Länder elections of January–June 1991. Its best performance was in Rhineland-Palatinate, where it secured 2% of the vote. Nevertheless, the Republicans' entry into eastern German electoral politics was awaited with some foreboding.

Part Five

ECONOMIC AND SOCIAL DEVELOPMENTS

Chapter 10

THE WEST GERMAN ECONOMY AND SOCIETY

The West German Economy to 1974: The 'Miracle Years'

In 1946 the West German economy lay in ruins. Its cities and factories had been bombed and destroyed and half its eastern territory had been lost to Poland and the GDR. Yet less than three decades later West Germany's industrial base had been fully rebuilt. The Federal Republic now ranked as the third major Western market economy (behind the US and Japan) and its citizens enjoyed a per capita income which was exceeded only by the United States, Scandinavia, Switzerland and the oil-rich principalities of the Middle East. The postwar regeneration of West Germany was so dramatic that the period between 1948 and 1974 has been termed one of 'economic miracle' (*Wirtschaftswunder*).

This economic recovery was achieved through hard, responsible labour by its educated, well-trained and expanding population and through high levels of industrial, research and development investment. The inflow of Marshall Aid and a high domestic saving ratio provided the funds: refugees from the dismembered Eastern sector and later workers from the Mediterranean lands and from agriculture provided the hands to man the new factories at competitive wage levels. These factories were equipped with up-to-date machinery and geared towards the expanding markets of postwar Europe –

machine tools, electrical goods, steel, automobiles, consumer durables and chemicals. Growth was export-led, with the European Community providing a wide integrated market on the FRG's doorstep and with the Korean war boosting demand during the 1950s. West Germany thus became heavily dependent on foreign trade, with manufactured goods exports accounting for 25% of its GNP (Gross National Product) by the 1980s and with large amounts of raw materials, energy products and foodstuffs flowing inwards to feed and fuel the expanding economy.

The CDU-FDP government presided over the West German economy during the early 'miracle years', providing a stable monetary and fiscal framework within which private companies could flourish while encouraging responsible co-operation from the trade union movement. From the mid-1960s state intervention in the economy, both direct and indirect, increased. In 1963 a five-man panel of economists, the Council of Experts, was established to report to the government each year on economic trends and between 1966 and 1969, at the time of the 'Grand Coalition', the SPD's economic expert, Karl Schiller, dabbled with Keynesian fiscal stimuli to pull West Germany out of the contemporary recession. In 1967 the role of government in steering and managing the economy was most clearly set out in the Stability and Growth Act. This called upon the government to seek to maintain a stable price level, full employment and a foreign trade equilibrium, fine-tuning the economy when necessary through the use of fiscal indicators.

Under the succeeding SPD-FDP administrations of Willy Brandt and Helmut Schmidt government intervention increased, as a unique corporate form of economic management was developed. To secure improved control over government spending, medium-term financial planning was now introduced, and to achieve closer co-ordination between federal and state policies and expenditure two bodies, the Financial Planning Council (*Finanzplanungsrat*) and the Counter-Cyclical Advisory Council (*Konjunkturrat*), were now established. The third innovation introduced by the SPD-FDP administration was the establishment of annual Concerted Action (*Konzertierte Aktion*) meetings which brought together leading figures from within industry, banking, the trade unions and governments to discuss general economic conditions and to agree upon guidelines for government spending, taxation and wage and price rises in the private sector. Under Helmut Schmidt, who maintained close personal relationships with prominent financiers and industrialists, this expert corporatist approach was taken furthest. Throughout this period government's direct involvement in the economy also increased as, with rising social and welfare spending, the state's share of GNP rose from 38% in 1969 to a peak of 51% in 1981, with 25% of the workforce now being employed in the public sector.

The growth performance of the West German postwar economy was impressive, as was the maturity of its interest group participants. Nevertheless the rate of economic growth, as in other Western economies, did decelerate over time. West German GNP, which increased at a rate of more than 6% per capita during the 1950s, and by 4% per capita during the 1960s (*see* Table 29), grew by barely 2.3% during the 1970s. This rate was still impressive compared to that registered by Britain or the United States, but it was well behind that recorded by Japan. The West German locomotive was clearly running out of steam.

TABLE 29   COMPARATIVE ANNUAL GROWTH RATES (%): 1950–73

	— REAL GROSS DOMESTIC PRODUCT (GDP) —					GDP per Man-Year
Country	1950–5	1955–60	1960–4	1964–9	1969–73	1951–73
Japan	7.1	9.0	11.7	10.9	9.3	7.9
Italy	6.3	5.4	5.5	5.6	4.1	5.5
West Germany	9.1	6.4	5.1	4.6	4.6	4.8
France	4.4	4.8	6.0	5.9	6.1	4.4
USA	4.2	2.4	4.4	4.3	3.4	2.3
UK	2.9	2.5	3.4	2.5	2.8	2.4

The quadrupling of world oil prices which followed both the Arab-Israeli war of 1973 and the Iranian revolution of 1979 was one important factor behind this sluggish economic performance. Indeed, these oil hikes were a turning point in West Germany's postwar economic history – marking the end of more than two decades of unparalleled economic growth fuelled by cheap, abundant oil and by expanding world trade, declining tariff barriers and stable exchange rates. They inaugurated an era of stagnant international trade, volatile exchange-rate movements, incipient protectionism and structural transformation, as the mature West German economy adjusted to the three challenges of more expensive fuel, new technologies and increased competition from the 'Newly Industrialized Countries' (NICs) of South-East Asia and ascendant Japan.

In this chapter the fortunes of the West German economy between 1974 and 1990 are first briefly sketched, before a number of the important broader trends are examined. At the close of the chapter the actions of politicians, employers and trade unions during the troubled 1980s are examined and an analysis of policy prescriptions and repercussions is provided.

The West Germany Economy: 1974–90

Recessionary Challenges: 1974–85

The 1973–4 oil price hike chipped away roughly 2% from West Germany's national income and precipitated a sharp recession between 1973 and 1975, before the economy learned to adjust to the changed circumstances of the post-OPEC world. The level of unemployment in West Germany shot up from barely a quarter of a million at the start of the 1970s to more than one million (4% of the working population) in 1974, inflation rose to a peak of 7% and the public-sector deficit increased from 0.7% of GNP in 1973 to 5.4% in 1975. Such was the severity of this short recession that West Germany's GNP actually declined by 2.5% in 1974. The country recovered quickly, however, aided at first by a budgetary and investment stimulus in 1975, before it set about quadrupling its exports of manufactured goods – machinery and consumer items – to the oil rich economies of the Middle East, thus restoring its trading balance with this region.

Recovery was clearly evident by 1977. Unemployment had fallen below the psychological barrier of one million, the public-sector deficit had been trimmed to 2.7% of GNP and inflation was kept down to below 3%. Economic growth was particularly sharp in 1975, with GNP increasing by 5.8%, before settling at 2% per annum during the following two years as the government maintained a careful budgetary stance. By 1978, however, there were fears that the FRG's recovery might stall – being choked at home by a tightening fiscal stance and by a spate of industrial disputes and being threatened abroad by vanishing markets and growing protectionism. In such circumstances, Chancellor Schmidt decided at the Bonn summit of June 1978 to risk large-scale reflation to the tune of DM 13 billion (equivalent to 1% of GNP) through the extension of tax concessions to industry and to consumers. The West German economy, which had been criticized during the early 1970s for maintaining a huge overseas trading surplus of more than $10

211

billion per annum, was now to act as the 'locomotive' to pull the world economy out of a threatened new recession. This reflation proved to be a startling short-term success, with West Germany's GNP increasing by 3.5% and 4% in 1978 and 1979, at the cost though of an increase in the inflation rate and growth in the budget deficit. It was a rare example of a home-demand, rather than export, based recovery in West Germany.

However, although the West German economy fared better than most of its European competitors during the 1970s, there were, by 1980, signs of a longer term decline in competitiveness, particularly vis-à-vis the NICs of South-East Asia and the thrusting power of Japan. One important factor behind this relative decline had been the rise in West German labour costs and the decline in the country's traditional passion for hard and extensive labour, evidenced by opinion poll data and by the extension in holiday periods and the shortening of the working week. By 1979 West Germany's labour costs per hour (including social security charges) amounted to DM 21 compared to a figure of DM 12 in Japan. Productivity increases had in the past paid for such wage increases, but by the 1970s West Germany was faced with fierce Far Eastern competitors devoted to the work ethic to an even greater degree, and which enjoyed lower average labour costs and rising rates of productivity. A second factor behind West Germany's competitive problems was the upvaluation of the traditionally undervalued *Deutsche Mark* which followed the establishment of, first, floating exchange rates in 1973 and, then, the European Monetary System (EMS) in 1979. A third factor, common to other West European nations, was the increasing level of government welfare spending between 1966 and 1980. This had begun to 'crowd out' private investment and had placed increased burdens on employers in terms of insurance contributions. In such circumstances, and with profits being squeezed at home, the growth rate for domestic West German industrial investment began to decline during the 1970s, while FRG investment abroad, particularly in the United States but also in developing nations, increased dramatically.

Matters came to a head between 1980 and 1985 with the second oil crisis and the slump in world trade. The West German economy was plunged into its deepest recession since the inter-war period. In 1979, as a result of the sudden rise in the cost of the country's oil import bill, it recorded its first trade deficit since 1965. This was followed by a sharp rise in the unemployment level, breaching the one million barrier in 1981 before climbing to an average of 2.3

million in the years between 1983 and 1985 (a rate equivalent to 9% of the working population – *see* Table 30). Inflation also edged upwards towards 5%, while interest rates moved up even higher. The severity of this recession was reflected by the fact that West Germany's GNP actually declined in two successive years between 1981 and 1982 and grew by only 1% in 1983. With stagnant world markets, the FRG found it impossible, before 1984, to export its way out of recession as had occurred between 1976 and 1979. It was not helped in this respect by the political and economic collapse during these years of a number of important new markets for its goods, for example, the debt-ridden states of Eastern Europe, and the troubled oil states of Nigeria, Iran and her Middle Eastern neighbours – countries which had taken almost 17% of West Germany's total exports in 1977. To make matters worse, competition also now intensified, both at home and abroad, from Japan and the NICs in a number of West Germany's traditional lines – for example, automobiles, machine tools and electrical goods. West Germany's traditional industries bore the brunt of the recession and the country was slow in pushing forward with the new 'high-tech' industries of the 1980s which were making headway in the United States and Japan.

TABLE 30   WEST GERMAN ECONOMIC INDICATORS: 1977–86

	1977 (%)	1978 (%)	1979 (%)	1980 (%)	1981 (%)	1982 (%)	1983 (%)	1984 (%)	1985 (%)
Industrial Prod.	+2.0	+3.5	+3.5	−5.0	0.0	−5.5	+1.9	+4.6	+3.8
Inflation	4.0	2.0	5.5	5.5	6.5	4.5	2.6	2.1	1.8
Wage Rises	6.0	5.5	5.0	7.5	5.0	4.0	3.1	3.1	1.9
MS Growth	10.0	13.5	5.5	3.5	−2.0	6.5	6.5	2.2	4.4
Unemployment	4.6	4.2	3.6	4.1	6.5	8.5	9.2	9.1	9.1
Trade Balance ($)	+16bn	+20bn	+15bn	+6bn	+10bn	+21bn	+18bn	+17bn	+24bn
DM Exchange Rate (*per dollar*)	2.2	1.8	1.7	1.9	2.3	2.4	2.7	3.1	2.5

The spread of protectionism throughout the world economy and the adoption of an unusually rigid fiscal policy by the CDU-CSU-FDP administration to maintain control over inflation and the budget deficit served to further exacerbate the situation during this transitional period. In such circumstances, recovery from the 1980–3 recession proved to be slow when compared to that from the troughs of 1966 and 1974, with unemployment continuing to rise as technological innovation economized on labour inputs in both the manufacturing and clerical sectors. From 1984, however, strong pump-primed demand in the United States coupled with a decline in the value of the Deutsche Mark gave an export boost to the West German economy. The country's rationalized and newly efficient firms made full use of this opportunity and exports boomed in 1984 and 1985, providing the basis for overall GNP growth of 2.6% and 2.4% respectively. This growth gained momentum and became more evenly balanced in 1986 as the sharp fall in OPEC oil prices gave a boost to world trade and as West German home demand was stimulated by tax cuts and rising real incomes. Real GNP growth of 2.5% was thus registered in 1986 and unemployment began to fall from a peak of 2.6 million at a rate of more than 200 000 per annum.

A 'Second Economic Miracle'?: 1986–90

By the autumn of 1986 the West German economy was in its healthiest condition for more than a decade. The inflation rate averaged barely 1.5% and reached negative figures during a number of months in 1986. The public sector deficit, which had stood at 4% of GNP in 1981–2, had been reduced to only 1.5% (one of the lowest levels in the industrialized world), overall public expenditure had been trimmed to 47.5% of GNP and interest rates had correspondingly fallen to only 8.5%. Industrial output, investment and productivity were booming and record trade surpluses were being recorded, as the country's new computer and office automation industries began to make their mark on world markets. The only adverse statistic for the CDU-CSU-FDP government was that for unemployment, which still exceeded 2.2 million.

This unemployment was largely structural in nature, being caused by technological change and demographic factors. The Kohl administration was, however, charged by the SPD opposition with exacerbating matters through its unduly rigid and doctrinaire fiscal stance. In addition, its economic strategy was viewed as socially divisive, unduly benefiting the rich and privileged at the expense of the poor, and, with the existence of more than 700 000 long-term unemployed unable to claim full social benefits, the government was seen as creating a 'new poverty' within the once affluent West German state. Overseas, competitor governments in Europe and America also criticized the Kohl administration's tight fiscal stance. They felt that West Germany, along with Japan, should pursue a more active role in helping to reflate the world economy and should reduce huge current-account surplus. Recognizing these criticisms, the Kohl government made some small adjustments to its policy approach after 1985. It assented to a staged DM 50 billion package of income and company tax cuts between 1986 and 1990, introduced a series of new retraining schemes and slightly loosened its monetary and budgetary corset. These measures were viewed as too limited by independent economic research institutes in West Germany, Europe and America, but the Kohl government remained determined to pursue a solid and steady growth path rather than risk a repeat of the 1978–9 abortive 'dash for growth'.

TABLE 31 WEST GERMAN ECONOMIC INDICATORS: 1986–90

	1986 (%)	1987 (%)	1988 (%)	1989 (%)	1990 (%)
Real GNP	+2.5	+1.8	+3.4	+4.0	+4.5
Industrial Prod.	2.2	2.0	4.2	5.4	5.7
Consumer Prices	−1.0	1.0	1.6	3.2	2.8
Wholesale Prices	−4.8	0.1	2.0	3.1	1.5
Wage Rises	4.2	3.5	3.4	4.0	6.1
Narrow Money Growth	9.0	7.5	10.6	5.3	6.9
Broad Money Growth	6.8	6.0	6.8	5.3	5.1
Unemployment Level	9.0	8.8	8.6	8.1	7.0
Trade Balance ($)	+53bn	+66bn	+73bn	+72bn	+64bn
Current Account ($)	+36bn	+44bn	+48bn	+52bn	+44bn
DM Exchange rate per ($) (at end of year)	1.9	1.6	1.8	1.7	1.5

During 1987 the pace of GNP growth slowed (*see* Table 31) to only 1.8%, a full percentage point below the OECD average. As a consequence, despite many thousand new jobs being created – 0.9 million between 1983 and 1988 – the unemployment level remained little changed. This arose from the increasing influx of women and young people into the labour market. However, this 'growth pause', which was most pronounced during the first half of 1987, preceding the 'Black Monday' Wall Street stockmarket crash in October which jolted policy-makers, proved to be short lived. During 1988, stimulated by a softening DM-dollar exchange rate, by a worldwide investment boom, by domestic tax cuts of DM 14 billion (equivalent to 0.7% of GNP) and by a special DM 21 billion three-year programme of 'soft loans' to muncipalities and medium and small firms, there was robust expansion in the market for West German manufactures both overseas, especially in Europe, and at home. Indeed, the trade surplus reached record levels, equivalent to around 4% of GNP, enabling the FRG to consolidate its position as the world's premier exporting nation. Concurrently, however, the budget deficit edged upwards to 2% of GNP.

During the course of 1989–90 the economic upturn gathered momentum. The growth rates recorded were the highest of the decade and approached 1960s levels, leading to Deutsche Bank economist Norbert Walter to declare in November 1989 that a 'second economic miracle' was underway. This boom was fuelled by strong domestic capital investment and consumer-goods demand – helped by further income-tax cuts amounting to DM 37 billion during 1990, as well as the burgeoning spending power of the maturing postwar baby-boom generation – and by soaring exports, especially to Eastern Europe and the European Community. Nevertheless, with hundreds of thousands of immigrants and refugees flooding into the Federal Republic during 1989–90, helping to keep wage costs down, the unemployment rate remained stubbornly high. Not until 1990 did it begin to edge significantly downwards, falling below 2 million.

Trends in the West German Economy and Society during the 1970s and 1980s

Energy Policy in the OPEC Era

For energy-deficient West Germany the rise in world oil prices from $2 a barrel in the early 1970s to $38 in 1981 was of particular consequence. The country's only indigenous natural sources of fuel were coal and hydro-electricity. More than half of its energy requirements were therefore imported – 50% being supplied by oil, 10% by gas – with key sectors, for example the large West German chemical industry, being unusually dependent upon Middle Eastern suppliers. During the nine years between 1973 and 1981, as a result of the OPEC measures, the country found its fuel costs increasing by 192%. The West German government was thus faced with an immediate problem of paying for its vital oil imports and with the longer term need to lessen its dependence upon imported oil.

The first difficulty was overcome between 1973 and 1979 by a spectacular expansion of West German manufactured exports to the Middle Eastern oil states. This, however, proved impossible to repeat between 1980 and 1985. The longer term problem of changing the FRG's energy balance proved to be even more intractable and has fuelled a significant political debate.

The West German government's energy programme from 1974 concentrated upon four areas: the encouragement of energy conservation, the revival of the declining coal industry, the expansion of the nuclear energy programme, and the importation of natural gas from Eastern Europe. Most success was gained in energy conservation and in gas diversification.

The West German coal industry had been in decline since the 1950s, with its manpower falling from almost 400000 to under 200000 by the later 1970s. Workers in the industry had retired or had been transferred to new expanding industries during the 'miracle years'. The industry still, however, remained substantial (the second largest in the West, producing 226 million tonnes per annum, its output only being exceeded by the United States) and relatively efficient, and it possessed reserves equivalent to more than 200 years' consumption. The government's enthusiasm for the coal industry was rekindled by the oil scare of 1973–4. Plans were now made, in common with other Western governments, to introduce new technology and to expand gross output, and experiments were entered into by the Rheinbraun group to examine the possibility of converting brown coal into synthetic petrol and fuel. Government subsidies paid to the coal industry were raised and the electricity industry became compelled to burn indigenous coal.

Plans were also made during the mid-1970s to press forward with West Germany's nuclear energy programme. Included in this programme was the introduction of the controversial fast breeder reactor. This programme envisaged the construction of more than 15 new nuclear power stations with the ultimate goal of producing 75000 MW of electricity (56% of projected power needs) by the end of the century from 60 stations. Chancellor Schmidt was a committed supporter of this programme, viewing nuclear power as a vital transitional 'bridge' which energy-deficient West Germany must draw upon before new alternative energy sources could later be substituted. In addition, the expansion of nuclear energy output was seen by Helmut Schmidt as crucial in lessening the country's dangerous dependence upon energy drawn from the unpredictable Middle East region.

The introduction of this extensive nuclear power programme brought, however, great opposition from the left wings of both the SPD and FDP and from the new Green movement. It proved difficult to implement, with projects being held up by court appeals, huge demonstrations and by worried state governments. Thus by 1980 only 14 nuclear power stations were in operation in West Germany – producing 9000 MW and providing a mere 3.3% of the nation's primary energy requirements and 14.5% of its electricity needs. Nine more stations were in the process of construction and a further two were held up in the courts. In the years between 1977 and 1981 only one new West German reactor came into service. In contrast, in neighbouring France, where environmentalist opposition was more muted, the number of operational nuclear power stations increased from 12 to 30 during the corresponding period, providing almost 38% of the country's electricity needs. The second oil price hike of 1979–80 gave increased urgency to the nuclear programme, which the new Kohl administration backed vigorously, but public opposition continued to prevent expansion at a more than crab-like rate. By 1986 West Germany boasted 19 operating reactors supplying 30% of electricity needs.[1]

The April 1986 Chernobyl nuclear accident in the Soviet Union – along with revelations, during 1986–7, of more minor mishaps and cases of contamination at nuclear complexes within the FRG, most notably at Hanau near Frankfurt – further increased public opposition to any further expansion of the nuclear programme. First, it prompted the North-Rhine-Westphalia SPD government to refuse to grant an operating licence to the Kalkar prototype fast-breeder nuclear reactor: a project which was formally abandoned in March 1991. Similarly, in 1988, it persuaded the new SPD administration in Schleswig-Holstein to cancel the operating licence of the recently opened Brokdorf reactor. The Kohl administration remained convinced of the vital importance of nuclear power in maintaining West Germany's economic pre-eminence. However, by 1989, with 40% of the country's electricity output being produced by the nuclear sector, a plateau had apparently been reached. No new stations were scheduled to be opened during the 1990s and it had been finally decided, in June 1989, to abandon plans to build a reprocessing plant at Wackersdorf in Bavaria.

The coal industry expansion programme similarly ran into opposition from environmentalists during the early 1980s, when it was discovered that the sulphur dioxide emissions from coal-fired power stations were creating acid rain which was destroying the fir forests of southern Germany at an alarming rate. (By 1986 50% of West Germany's forests and 80% of its fir trees were affected by this poisoning.) The government was forced to take action, and in February 1983 legislation was passed which required large power stations to fit filters and smaller stations to cut sulphur dioxide emissions sixfold within a decade. Even before this date, however, enthusiasm for the expansion of the coal industry had begun to wane as demand for fuel had failed to rise as had been projected. The deepening industrial recession and structural changes in the economy had led to a fall in demand from the traditional coal-burning industries, particularly steel, and this deficit had not been bridged by increased demand from the new 'sunrise' industries, which were low consumers of energy per value of output. In addition, substantial economies were being made during these years in domestic and industrial energy consumption – stimulated by the Schmidt administration's energy conservation packages of 1977 and 1979 – as conservation became a significant third plank in the country's energy programme. This conservation programme spawned a small industrial sector of its own, which attracted both small-scale entrepreneurs and even traditional heavy industry giants such as the Mannesmann corporation. Overall, between 1978 and 1990 West German coal consumption remained unchanged. However, employment in the industry fell to barely 130000. A further 30000 jobs were set to go by 1995, with annual output due to be reduced by 15 million tonnes.

The fourth element of the West German energy programme was the expansion of natural gas consumption and the diversification in its sources of supply. The German North Sea sector has proven, thus far, to be almost barren in gas or oil riches, but a long pipeline was established at Emden (Lower Saxony) by Ruhr-Gas to tap the large Norwegian Eldfisk field. This augmented existing supplies from the Dutch Groningen field. This was followed in 1982 by the signing of a major $15 billion pipeline deal between a Franco-German consortium and the Soviet government. The European consortium agreed to supply pipeline equipment on credit in return for a Russian undertaking to supply gas from its huge Urengoy field in Siberia without charge for 10 years and thereafter at an agreed rate. This 3000-mile pipeline was intended to supply 30% of West German gas requirements by 1990. Diversification in oil supply, away from the unstable Middle East, was also achieved during the early 1980s through importations from the British and Norwegian North Sea fields: by 1982 Britain had overtaken Saudi Arabia as West Germany's largest single oil supplier.

The period between 1974 and 1990 was thus one of considerable restructuring and change for West German energy consumption and supply. Total energy consumption rose by only 1.4% per annum between 1974 and 1982 compared to a rise of 4.4% per annum between 1960 and 1974. This former figure was well below the rate of industrial growth (2% per annum) and outlined the advances that had been made in fuel efficiency and consumption.

Changes in the mix of energy types consumed were not as marked as had once been anticipated – oil remaining the major fuel – but supply sources had become more diversified and the share taken by coal, nuclear power and gas had increased significantly. West Germany's energy base in 1990 was thus broader and more evenly balanced. The country still, however, remained overwhelmingly dependent upon external suppliers.

Population Movements and their Consequences

West Germany's population expanded from only 42 million in 1946 to 55.4 million in 1960, and continued to rise to a peak of 62.1 million in 1973. Such growth was caused at first by a rising birthrate during the 1950s 'miracle years' and by the influx of more than 10 million refugees from the divided east. It was boosted during the 1960s by the immigration of 2.6 million temporary foreign 'guest workers' (*Gastarbeiter*) from the Mediterranean region – Turkey, Yugoslavia, Italy, Greece and Spain – working in the coal mines, car factories, chemical works and public services, filling menial posts at low wages.

West Germany's population structure as it entered the 1970s was thus young (36% of the total being under the age of 25) and heterogenous, being composed of a mixture of refugees (22%), Gastarbeiter (4%), Catholics (45%) and Protestants (47%). During the preceding two decades there had been major changes in occupation and outlook, with the decline in the proportion of the workforce engaged in agriculture (forming 23% of the total in 1950: only 5% in 1980), a rise in the white-collar service sector (employing 21% in 1950: 45% in 1980), and a growth in secularism, as church attendance became less popular.

During the decade of stagnant growth and recession which followed the oil shock of 1973–4 there was an acceleration in the speed of change, particularly in the movement towards the service sector and the structural decline of traditional industries. There was also, however, an attempt to check and reverse the inflow of foreign Gastarbeiter as racial tensions mounted during this period of rising unemployment.

The Immigration Question – By 1973 2.6 million Gastarbeiter resided and worked in West Germany. During the 1960s and early 1970s they had been accepted as essential cogs in the successfully functioning FRG economy. However, with the onset of recession after 1973, they bore the brunt of criticism for the rising level of unemployment. Action was thus taken to halt the further inflow of Gastarbeiter in 1973, when a ban was imposed upon the recruitment of workers from outside the EC. This achieved its immediate goal – by 1984 the number of Gastarbeiter had been reduced to only 1.9 million. Immigrant workers continued, however, to enter West Germany by less direct routes.

The first and most direct channel of entry involved the wives and children of resident workers who were allowed to join their husbands. They established new families with birth rates well above the West German average and thus boosted the size of the immigrant community from within. The second channel of entry was less direct. It took the form of refugees entering the FRG in search of 'political asylum'. They were encouraged by West Germany's liberal entry laws which allowed refugees to remain in the country, work and claim welfare benefits while their cases were being dealt with by the courts – this could take, with appeals, up to four years. The number of such 'refugees' increased between 1972 and 1980 from 5300 per annum to 108000. Less than 10% of these claims were eventually accepted, but thousands of other 'economic refugees' gained temporary residence before final deportation. A third channel of entry was from Eastern Europe, particularly from Poland during the crisis years between 1979 and 1982 when more than 100000 were accepted into West Germany. The fourth channel remained always open – through the EC, for Italian and later Greek workers.

Through such direct and indirect means, the numbers of foreigners resident in West Germany continued to increase between 1974 and 1984 – rising from 4 million to 4.7 million (representing 7.6% of the total population). Popular antipathy to the immigrant community increased during this period, as immigrant workers took the blame for the Federal Republic's economic difficulties – even though unemployment rates were in fact far higher among the often unskilled and ill-educated sons and daughters of immigrant families. (In 1983 350000 of the 2 million unemployed were drawn from the immigrant community.) The large, poorly integrated Turkish community – which totalled 1.7 million in 1984 – with its distinctive Islamic lifestyle and its concentration in inner city ghettoes in West Berlin, Düsseldorf and Hamburg, bore the brunt of this hostility. Immigrants from Poland and Eastern Europe were more warmly accepted.

The SPD-FDP administration of Helmut Schmidt and interior minister Gerhart Baum (FDP) decided to take action to check infringements of the immigration rules in December 1980 by tightening up the regulations for political asylum. Under a new bill which was now introduced, would-be refugees needed to first obtain a visa before gaining entry to West Germany. During their first year of stay work permits would no longer be issued, welfare benefits would be paid in kind not cash, and the vetting and litigation procedures would be speeded up so that cases would be decided in months not years. These new regulations had immediate results – the number of applications for political asylum falling by more than 50% to only 49000 in 1981.[2] The Schmidt administration also tightened up the direct entry regulations in December 1980, when another bill limited the immigration of the dependants of settled Gastarbeiter and refugees to those below the age of 16.

During the early 1980s, as unemployment rose remorselessly above 2 million, public opinion hardened against the Gastarbeiter. Local citizens' action groups began to campaign for '*Ausländer raus*' ('foreigners out') and squatter riots erupted in West Berlin. This persuaded the new administration of Helmut Kohl to take firmer action to deal with the immigrant problem. The liberal-minded Gerhart Baum was thus replaced at the Interior Ministry by CSU right-winger Friedrich Zimmermann and in November 1983 a package of measures was introduced which included monetary inducements for the voluntary repatriation of unemployed foreign workers. This measure had some success, with more than 100000 having registered for repatriation by September 1984. An attempt was also made by the Foreign Ministry to persuade the Turkish government to agree to an annulment of articles of the 1970 EC 'associate membership' treaty, which, due to come into effect in 1986, would have allowed the free entry of Turkish citizens once again.

These measures by the CDU-CSU-FDP government served to place a temporary check upon the inflow of foreign workers, whose number had shrunk to only 1.6 million by 1987, and upon the growth rate of the immigrant community, and they assuaged political discontent during a period of economic recession. Foreign workers continued, however, to play a vital role in the functioning of key sectors of the West German economy and their proportionate size and contribution promised to increase further in future years as the West German birth rate continued to fall and its population stagnate.

The Declining Birthrate – West Germany's population peaked in 1973 at 62.1 million and subsequently declined slowly. By 1980 it had reached 61.4 million and – before the post-1985 influx from the East – it was projected to fall to 58 million in 1990 and to only 39 million in the year 2030.[3] Such population contraction was caused by a sharp drop in the FRG birth rate since the late 1960s to barely 10 per 1000 people – the lowest rate in the world. The primary factor behind this decreasing birth rate was the spread of the contraceptive pill during the 1970s. It was spurred on, however, by economic and social factors – for example, by the increased level of full-time female employment, particularly that of married women; the short hours of West German schooling; the high cost and scarcity of family housing; and the increasing material orientation of society. Belated additions to state family allowance payments failed to reverse this demographic trend.

West Germany's population decline promised to have serious medium-term consequences for the economy. The 'dependency ratio' (the ratio of retired persons per worker) seemed set to rise sharply from 0.46 in 1980 to 0.89 in 2030 and the cost of health services mount as the population aged. At the same time, however, savings were likely in education, as school rolls continued to fall. These prospective changes, as in other Western European countries, gave rise to a fierce debate on the future of the welfare state and balance of public spending. Population stagnation also presented serious problems for the West German army (*Bundeswehr*), half of whose manpower of 495 000 were young compulsory conscripts. The fall in the birth rate and rise in conscientious objection during the early 1980s 'peace years' persuaded the Kohl administration to pass unpopular legislation to lengthen the period of military service from 15 to 18 months after 1989. However, this planned increase was cancelled in 1989.

West Germany's declining birth rate did prove useful in one respect during the 1980s. It prevented the kind of rise in youth unemployment during the 1980–5 recession, which was experienced in neighbouring countries. The number of 16-year-olds in West Germany peaked in 1980 at 1.08 million and fell to only 630 000 in 1990. This, coupled with recruitment into the Bundeswehr and into three-year vocational training apprenticeships (for 90% of 16-year-old school leavers), kept youth unemployment during the mid-1980s at only 9% – a rate similar to the adult average and much below the supra 20% levels of Britain, France and Italy. This acted undoubtedly as a factor in calming social tensions during a difficult period. However, unemployment was a more serious problem for West Germans in their early twenties unable to secure a job after the end of their training contract. Indeed, by 1989, more than 40% of West Germany's unemployed were long term, having been out of work for more than 12 months.

Structural Change in the 1974–84 Recession

West Germany entered the 1970s with a strong manufacture-centred economy built around the steel, automobile, engineering, machine tools, chemical and electrical industries. Only Hong Kong and the GDR could exceed West Germany's figure of 46% for the proportion of the workforce engaged as manual workers: the European Community average was 39%. These core industries were unusually export orientated, with more than half of production being sent to foreign markets, the most important being the EC (which received 48% of West Germany's exports), other adjoining West European states (22%), North America (10%), Eastern Europe (6%) and the lesser developed countries (LDCs) of Africa, Asia and Latin America (13%). These industries were large and corporatist in organization, built around a specific managerial and technological ethos. However, by the close of the 1970s these industries and this form of organization were under dual attack from the aggressive, low-cost producers from the NICs and from the small-scale 'new technology' entrepreneurs from the United States and Japan. The traditional industrial base of the West German economy, with its emphasis upon capital goods, was seemingly becoming obsolete. Major restructuring and changes in outlook and organization were required as the 1980–4 recession bit deep. This involved both further investment at home to modernize and upgrade existing factories and the continued growth of the service sector, as well as increased investment and sub-contracting abroad in the NICs and LDCs to supply less complex inputs at low cost.

Coal and Steel

Rationalization and re-organization of the West German coal industry took place during the boom years of the 1950s and 1960s as the economy switched from coal to oil consumption. Miners were retrained and redeployed in newer industries under the umbrella of the state-created Economic Development Corporation. For the West German steel industry, restructuring was more painful and delayed. In 1980 West Germany's steel industry was still the largest in Europe (accounting for 31% of EC steel production and employing 200000 workers) and the fifth largest in the world, being centred around seven large private companies – the giant Thyssen and Krupp groups (*see* Table 32) based at Duisburg and Rheinhausen in the Rhine region; Hoesch, Kloeckner and Peine-Salzgitter from the Ruhr region; the smaller Arbed Saarstahl from the Saarland; and the diversified engineering corporation Mannesmann. The industry was highly efficient and had developed new product lines. It found itself, however, in difficulty from the mid-1970s as a result of increasing overproduction in the glutted European and world steel market, caused both by the expansion of steel production in the NICs of Asia and South America (in which countries production doubled between 1973–83), and by declining demand for steel within the developed world as new substitute materials were developed. The smaller companies of Arbed Saarstahl, Kloeckner, Hoesch and Peine-Salzgitter fared most badly during this period: the larger and more efficient Thyssen and Krupp upgraded, moving into special steels, and modernized production processes. They thus remained immune from the steel crisis until between 1981 and 1983.

TABLE 32   THE 20 LARGEST FIRMS IN THE FEDERAL REPUBLIC IN 1980

Rank	Name	Industry	Turnover 1980 (DM M)	Profit (Loss)	Employees
1	VEBA	Energy/Oil/Chemicals	39,970	+479	83,936
2	Volkswagen	Motors	33,288	302	257,930
3	Siemens	Electrical	31,960	487	344,000
4	Daimler-Benz	Motors	31,054	961	183,392
5	Hoechst	Chemicals	29,915	381	186,850
6	BASF	Chemicals	29,171	478	116,518
7	Bayer	Chemicals	28,825	331	181,639
8	Thyssen	Steel	27,128	144	152,089
9	RWE	Energy	18,262	489	68,007
10	Ruhrcoal	Coalmining	16,422	32	136,816
11	Gutehoffnungshütte	Machinery	15,417	121	86,018
12	Deutsche BP	Oil	15,201	13	4,340
13	AEG	Electrical	15,141	−278	145,200
14	Krupp	Steel/Machinery	13,919	38	85,706
15	Deutsche Shell	Oil	13,899	246	4,878
16	Esso	Oil	13,150	430	4,567
17	Mannesmann	Steel/Machinery	13,110	147	103,491
18	Bosch	Electrical	11,809	117	120,020
19	Preussag	Energy/Oil	9,412	89	21,283
20	Opel	Motors	9,224	+411	59,876

As problems mounted for Europe's steel industry the EC intervened in 1977 under Viscount Etienne Davignon, the commissioner for industry. A cartel of steel companies (Eurofer) was established to co-ordinate production and pricing, and surplus capacity was slowly reduced through plant closures in West Germany, France and Britain. This gentlemen's agreement based upon voluntary discipline broke down, however, in 1980, when the West German firms of Kloeckner and Thyssen began to slash their prices and step up production in a desperate attempt to maintain profitability during a period of sharply declining demand. These actions backfired, however, when Viscount Davignon, facing pressure from Italy, Britain and France, took increased powers into his hands in October 1980 and tightened the Commission's control over the European steel industry. Production quotas were now set for each company, price levels were fixed (at higher levels) and cuts in capacity were determined from Brussels, with the sanction of heavy fines for firms which breached these limits. These measures resulted in a reduction in West German steel firms' output and capacity by almost 40% between 1974 and 1982.

Further reductions were carried out between 1983 and 1985 as the recession deepened. These combined measures meant that between 1974 and 1985 total West German steel output fell from 50 million tonnes per annum to only 35 million tonnes. Efforts were made by the government throughout this period to encourage modernization and rationalization through the merger of individual companies and government grants, amounting to DM 3 billion between 1983 and 1985 (the majority of which went to Arbed Saarstahl, which was taken over by the North-Rhine-Westphalia government in 1985), were provided in an effort to smooth this transition. Following such drastic surgery – which involved the loss of more than 20 000 jobs between 1983 and 1985 alone – FRG steel firms began to turn the corner of profitability in 1984.[4] Production of special steels was stepped up and companies diversified in an attempt to move into more profitable areas. The most spectacular diversification occurred at Mannesmann, which moved completely out of steel during the early 1970s, transferring into engineering and electronics, and at Thyssen, steel accounted for 56% of its sales in 1974 but only 33% in 1985 and 27% in 1988. At Krupp, steel accounted for 20% of group sales in 1987 compared to 27% in 1980.

Despite such re-organization and rationalization, the short- and long-term future for the West German steel industry remained disturbing. In 1987 the leading steel producers, most seriously

Thyssen, fell into the red once again. In response, a package of further drastic labour-shedding – 40 000 out of 140 000 jobs by 1990 – was announced, despite output subsequently rising to 40 million tonnes during 1989. It included plans to close Krupp's huge Rheinhausen works. The industry's problems stemmed from continuing overcapacity in a glutted and subsidized world steel market and from the progressive decline of traditional steel-consuming heavy industries. Two such industries were the shipbuilding industry and the automobile industry.

Shipbuilding

In the shipbuilding industry West Germany met with competition from Japan as early as the 1950s. While West Germany's share of the world market for new shipping decreased from 17% in 1956 to 7% in 1968, Japan's share increased from 24% to 49%: a share which it still held in 1980. Advanced high-productivity manufacturing techniques and the growth in the merchant fleet of South-East Asia were the two factors which explained this movement. The West German shipbuilding industry – centred in the old northern Hanseatic cities of Bremen, Hamburg and Kiel and employing 71 000 in 1975 – faced with a declining market share, was forced to redirect production towards new lines, such as container ships, roll-on ferries, gas transporters, oil rigs and power station boilers. Much of this diversification was successful. This did not, however, prevent the industry from being seriously damaged by the 1973–4 and 1979–80 oil price hikes and the ensuing economic recession which reduced the volume of world trade at a time when new shipping and container capacity was being developed in the NICs. The world shipbuilding order book slumped between 1974 and 1978 from 129 million gross registered tons (grt) to a miserly 28 million grt, and the portion captured by West Germany fell from 7.35 million to barely 0.5 million grt. Major yard closures became necessary, with in Hamburg the workforce being more than halved from 35 000 to 15 000. This naturally had a deleterious 'knock-on' effect on the troubled steel industry of the Ruhr and Lower Saxony.

The Automobile Industry

The expansion of the West German car industry – based around the huge Volkswagen-Audi corporation (the fifth major car producer in the world, producing 1.9 million vehicles in 1988), Ford, Opel (a

General Motors' subsidiary), Daimler-Benz (also Europe's major, and most profitable, lorry producer), BMW and Porsche – created thousands of new jobs during the boom years of the 1950s and 1960s. By 1974 the industry was the third largest in the world (producing 3.6 million vehicles and standing behind the US and Japan). It employed almost 600000 workers and was the second-largest export sector (behind mechanical engineering) in the West German economy, with its output enjoying an enviable reputation for quality, fuel efficiency, engine power and reliability. By comparative European standards the West German motor industry was strong and profitable as it entered the 1974–84 recession. During the recession, however, demand for new vehicles stagnated in West Germany at a level of 2.1–2.2 million cars per annum. At the same time, German car producers faced sharpening competition from Japanese producers both at home – the Japanese share rising from only 2% in 1977 to 12% in 1980 and 15% in 1988 in what remains an unusually open market – and abroad in the lucrative American and overseas market, to which more than 50% of West German motor industry production was orientated. The Japanese firms offered attractive, streamlined low-cost models, with the inducements of substantial discounts and special extras.

The European and American car markets were glutted by the early 1980s with an overcapacity of almost 25%. Prices and profit margins were slashed in response, as the motor industry entered a cannibalistic crisis period between 1980 and 1984, from which West German car firms were not immune. The most seriously affected West German concerns were the American subsidiaries Ford and Opel, whose operations were limited to Western Europe. They recorded substantial losses between 1980–3 and were forced to close down plants, with the consequent destruction of 16000 jobs. The indigenous firms of Volkswagen, Daimler-Benz and BMW proved less willing to shed labour. Volkswagen, the mass lower- and middle-market producer, which recorded its first losses during the energy crisis of 1974–5, fell even further into the red in 1982 and 1983. In response, Volkswagen stepped up its export efforts in lower-wage overseas and underdeveloped markets – entering into agreements to open new plants in East Germany, Spain and China, to add to its extensive activities in the United States and Brazil – and it began to learn from Japanese production techniques and marketing ploys, adding new features to these export models. Its fuel-efficient Golf model proved to be particularly successful. BMW and Daimler-Benz, with a secure hold over the high-quality upper-range market, were less seriously affected by the recession, but they sought greater security by diversifying into middle-range and fuel-efficient diesel models and into other industries.

West Germany's car firms began to emerge out of the worst of the recession by 1984 and with a boom in exports to the United States – helped by the weak Deutsche Mark – they began recording improving profit returns, with balance sheets now in the black. Their fortunes further improved in 1985 and 1986 as home demand picked up. West German firms, with the exception of Ford Werke, proved themselves able to cope with NIC competition, the switch to lead-free petrol and the catalytic converter, and the rise in labour costs which followed the damaging 1984 IG Metall strike. Thus by 1985 West German car production had increased to over 3.8 million vehicles and, although substantial investment had been made in automation, the labour force began to expand once more, reaching a level of 700 000. However, despite breaching the 4 million vehicle units per annum barrier, a new wave of labour-shedding rationalization was instituted from 1988.

Engineering, Electronics and Chemicals

West Germany's major industry, mechanical engineering and machine tools, employing more than one million workers and producing 18% of the country's exports, passed more comfortably through the 1974–84 recession. It faced increasing competition from the Japanese in the lower range of mass-produced machine tools, but retained its lead in higher quality, custom-built machinery. During the years between 1974 and 1980 a boom in exports to the Middle East oil countries helped maintain the profitability of Germany's leading engineering firms – GHH, Krupp, Thyssen, Deutsche Babcock and Mannesmann – enabling them to dip into their accumulated reserves to ride out the sharp 1980–3 recession. Upgrading and diversification away from seamless steam tubes and into electronics, aerospace, information systems and environmental protection equipment enabled Mannesmann to record net profits throughout this troubled decade. West Germany's chemical and electronics industries suffered more severely.

The electronics industry met with particularly fierce competition from Japan and the NICs in audio and visual lines and from Dutch and Italian firms in consumer durable lines. In 1970 foreign penetration of the FRG market had reached only 14%, by 1980 it had risen to 32%. In certain lines, such as the manufacture of black and white televisions, West German firms were forced to concede defeat and cease competing with lower-cost overseas suppliers. Siemens (Europe's largest electronics company) and Grundig managed to maintain profitability, though at a reduced level and with reductions in manpower levels, and engaged in tie-up deals with the Dutch giant Philips in the expanding video recorder, office automation and micro-chip sector.[5] AEG-Telefunken, however, after recording successive losses from 1973 onwards, was forced into the hands of the official receiver (*Vergleich*) in September 1982. The prime factor behind this decline was the loss made in the competitive consumer electronics sector. This was compounded by AEG's unfortunate involvement in the Siberian pipeline and a number of nuclear power station projects. After 1983 AEG hobbled along as a slimmed-down concern, supported by government credits and asset sales. Its television and hi-fi manufacturing wing Telefunken was sold to the French Thomson group and 49% of AEG's stake in its word-processing subsidiary, Olympia Werke, was temporarily sold to a banking consortium. By 1985, however, shorn of its loss-making consumer durables division, AEG had recovered. It had paid off a substantial portion of its debts, recaptured its stake in Olympia and was recording healthy profits as a leaner and more specialized concern.

In the chemical industry West Germany, with three (BASF, Bayer and Hoechst) of the world's top four companies, was the world's second-largest chemical producer, holding an 18% share of the global market. This industry was, however, undermined by the oil price hikes of the 1970s – which sharply increased raw material input costs – and by the severe contraction in demand for chemicals during the 1980–4 recession. The profits of the country's chemical firms were more than halved between 1980–2, as factories were forced to work at two-thirds capacity and to sell products at artificially low prices. The largest losses were in the petrochemicals, bulk chemicals and plastics divisions, where competition was growing from new producers in the oil-rich countries of the Middle East. This particularly affected BASF. Bayer and Hoechst, involved to a greater degree in pharmaceuticals, paints, agricultural chemicals and speciality plastics, were better able to ride out the recession. The closure of a number of unprofitable ventures (such as polyethylene and pvc) and an upgrading into specialist markets restored the profitability of West Germany's chemical giants in 1984 to pre-1980 levels. However, future prospects in the traditional 'heavy chemical' divisions remained bleak for West Germany's oil deficient companies, which needed to continue to upgrade and diversify. As part of such a strategy, in 1987 Hoechst acquired Celanese, a broadly-based American chemical plant, transforming itself at a stroke into the world's leading chemical conglomerate.

Restructuring and Merger Mania

West Germany's traditional industries, while fitter and stronger than many of their European rivals, were clearly severely affected by the 1974–84 economic recession and by the heightened competition from low-cost producers in Japan and the NICs. Firms were forced to rethink their production methods and market strategy and to slim down their workforce and modernize their plant. This sometimes involved moving the production of component items to lesser developed, low wage countries, adding further to the loss of jobs in West German factories. Indeed, during the course of the 1980s West German direct investment abroad doubled. The broad balance and base of the West German economy, with its nucleus of engineering, steel, electrical and chemical industries, remained in place in 1990, but it had contracted in size and had been forced to change and upgrade product mixes. Government involvement in the economy had increased during the early 1980s with the granting of subsidies – although still low by comparative standards – to ailing concerns in the shipbuilding, steel and electrical industries. Overall, manufacturing's share of the workforce had declined, while that of services had increased.[6]

A more dramatic restructuring of the West German economy, with the growth of new 'high-tech' industries, was also becoming apparent by 1990. West Germany's electrical, engineering, automobile, steel and chemical giants began to expand into the new spheres of aerospace, microtechnology, automation and biotechnology as a rash of mergers took place from 1985 in readiness for the post-1992 challenge of a Single European Market. The most prominent of which were Daimler-Benz's take-over of AEG and Dornier (both in 1985), MTU and MBB, as it diversified into the aerospace, arms and electrical sectors, becoming in the process the FRG's largest industrial company, and Siemens' joint acquisition (with GEC) of Plessey in 1989. The smaller firms of Olympia and Nixdorf (which, having run into financial difficulties, merged with Siemens in 1990) were also making a significant impact in the office machines and computer markets.

West Germany still remained far behind Japan and California in

231

these new high-tech and high-growth sectors – its share of world high-technology output falling from 26% in 1972 to 17% in 1987 – and appeared to need to remodel its organizational approach if the gap was to be fully bridged. It needed to foster an industrial culture geared towards invention as well as innovation and to encourage small-scale entrepreneurs and 'intrapreneurs'. Greater state research investment and pan-industrial and pan-national co-operation was also required in a number of costly, pathbreaking fields: the technical tie-ups between Siemens and SGS-Thomson, IBM and Philips in memory-chip research and development and between Daimler-Benz and Mitsubishi in aerospace and electronics being promising examples of this. Such developments were, however, concentrated in the southern states and served to accentuate regional divisions as West German industry underwent progressive movement away from its traditional centres in the north.

Regional Changes: The Movement South

Regional differences in income and unemployment levels remained low in West Germany when compared, for example, with the north-south divides evident in contemporary Italy or the United Kingdom. Traditionally the richest regions in the republic were the industrial Länder of North-Rhine-Westphalia[7] and Hesse, in which states was situated the Rhine-Ruhr colliery and steel mill belt. It was here, and in portions of the more northerly Länder, where the FRG's primary industries were located, being positioned at the centre of the vast European market, well served by waterway and land transportation networks – the East-West *Hellweg* and the northward-flowing Rhine river. With the decline, however, of traditional industries during the 1974–84 recession, the northern Länder became depressed, recording unemployment rates in excess of 10% in 1984. By contrast, during the same period, the attractive, weakly unionized,[8] southern Länder of Baden-Württemberg and Bavaria became new centres of industrial growth, drawing in migrants from the north and exhibiting unemployment rates of under 6%. The West German economy was moving southwards.

During the 1950s, Baden-Württemberg and Bavaria remained poor and relatively backward, small-farmer, agricultural states containing only a few industrial nuclei in Karlsruhe, Stuttgart and Munich. These two states, however, topped the Länder growth league from the mid-1960s, catching up, during the 1980s, and passing many of the northern Länder in terms of income per capita. In Bavaria, utilizing cheap labour drawn from local agriculture and Gastarbeiter brought in from Yugoslavia, modern electrical goods, electronics, aerospace and arms industries were set up, as well as the up-market motor manufacturing firm of BMW. In Baden-Württemberg, which inherited a decaying textile industry, the quality car and truck giant Mercedes-Benz and the sports car manufacturer Porsche were established, in addition to investment goods industries manned by industrious local Swabians. These two southern Länder did not inherit the weight of older and declining traditional industries which dragged down the northern states. The heavier industries which they did possess, for example the car manufacturers BMW and Mercedes-Benz and the engineers GHH, continued to expand and take on additional labour during the 1970s recession. It was, however, flexible smaller and medium-sized firms (*Mittelstände*) and modern 'high-tech' concerns which proved to be the dynamic engine of growth in Baden-Württemberg and Bavaria from the mid-1970s.[9] The cluster of universities, industrial and defence research establishments around Munich and Stuttgart helped create a small '*Silzium Tal*' bustling with workshops producing data-processing, micro-electronics and computer equipment. Munich, the home of Siemens, the aircraft firm Messerschmitt-Bölkow-Blohm, the silicon producer Wacker Chimie and the US companies Texas Instruments and Digital Equipment, developed into an important 'growth pole'. The CDU and CSU state leaders, Lothar Späth and Franz-Josef Strauss, favouring a mixture of deregulationary free-enterprise and interventionist state tax concession and infrastructural support, in terms of research facilities and communications, aided this growth process.[10] The completion of the Rhine-Main-Danube canal, opening up full waterborne communications between Rotterdam and the Black Sea through Regensburg in Bavaria, helped add further impetus to industrial growth in southern Germany.

By contrast the older industrial was been forced, painfully, to restructure itself during these years of recession. In these Länder were located the declining shipbuilding industry, the problem car firms Ford and Opel, the stagnant (labour-contracting) coal industry and the troubled steel mills which had played a vital role in West German economic growth during the 'miracle years'. The cities of Bremen, Hamburg and isolated West Berlin (dependent in 1987 on central government for handouts of DM 12 billion per annum – equivalent to half its budget total) and the Saarland were particularly seriously affected (*see* Table 33).

**TABLE 33   THE NORTH-SOUTH DIVIDE IN WEST GERMANY
DURING THE 1980s**

Land	(1986) Unemployment Rate (%)	(1984) GNP per Capita (DM.046000)	(1986) Receipts (+) From or Payments (−) to Länder Compensation Fund (DM million)	(1970–87) Real GDP Increase (%)
North				
Schleswig-Holstein	10.3	25.8	+ 616	47
Hamburg	12.9	44.1	− 199	33
Bremen	15.7	30.6	+ 446	28
Lower Saxony	11.1	25.2	+ 856	41
North-Rhine-Westphalia	10.8	28.4	— —	32
Centre				
Saarland	13.2	24.3	+ 382	42
Hesse	6.6	29.9	− 783	55
Rhineland-Palatinate	7.9	26.2	+ 379	48
South				
Bavaria	5.9	27.8	+ 48	65
Baden-Württemberg	4.9	30.9	−1746	50
National Average	8.6	28.7	—	45

Within the old Rhine-Ruhr industrial belt there were sub-regional
shifts with production moving away from the Ruhr interior (Essen
and Dortmund) towards the Rhineland cities which were served by
cheap water communications. This formed part of a longer-term
process of decline for the east-central FRG, which was cut off after
1945 by partition from traditional markets and supply sources to the
east. Within the Rhineland, Düsseldorf emerged as a nuclei for
modern and often Japanese-owned new industries, being the site for
300 of the 450 Japanese firms established in West Germany by the
mid-1980s and housing a local Japanese community amounting to
more than 6000. In Hamburg and Bremen, production diversified
away from maritime industries with, for example, the establishment
of an MBB aerospace works and a huge 250000 cars-a-year
Daimler-Benz factory (employing 10000) in Bremen in 1984, and in
West Berlin a high-tech renaissance was in evidence by 1986. Inside
the decaying inner cities, however, considerable social problems
and tensions emerged, including racial conflicts directed against the
large Gastarbeiter communities and squatter conflicts over housing
shortages.

The movement south in the West German economy created new

problems of fairly apportioning regional development aid as redistribution formulas were too slowly adjusted to the new conditions and as conservative alliances in the Bundesrat blocked changes in the regulations. The Ruhr, in particular, remained unfairly treated until the Constitutional Court ruled in June 1986 that changes should be effected in the *Finanzausgleich* (finance equalization) tax system. Depression in the north and growth in the south produced, in addition, diverging trends in national politics. This was highlighted by the 1985 Länder elections in the Saarland and North-Rhine-Westphalia, which resulted in resounding victories for the SPD advocating firm interventionist policies to support ailing industries and to improve the infrastructure of these northern states. Such policies contrasted with the deregulationary policies favoured by the popular Späth and, until his death in 1988, Strauss in the CDU-CSU-controlled south.

Policy Differences and the Breakdown of Economic Consensus

The divergent policy prescriptions offered by the SPD and by the CDU-CSU-FDP coalition in the March 1983 election campaign illustrated the breakdown in the consensus which had embraced approaches to the West German economy since the mid-1960s. The SPD and CDU had never offered identical programmes during the years between 1966 and 1982, but differences had been only slight. Both parties favoured, after the 'total state' experience of the Nazi era, leaving the economy to the operation of free-market forces and to competitive private companies, while the government and Bundesbank pursued tight fiscal and monetary policies to provide a stable environment with low inflation and a secure currency. Thus by comparative European standards the West German economy was notable for its 'open' nature, for the limited extent of state participation in and support given to the industrial sector, and for its semi-privatized welfare system. The SPD and CDU differed by degrees in their enthusiasm for fiscal dabbling, selective intervention and welfare support – the SPD favouring greater intervention to iron out inequalities and injustices: the CDU preferring to leave matters to the marketplace – with the FDP playing a significant role in bridging the differences and pushing the SPD, when in power, closer than it would have chosen towards a traditional liberal economic stance.

The budgets of the years between 1974 and 1985 showed a constant concern to maintain fiscal rectitude and low budgetary deficits. Only in 1975 and 1978 was a reflationary demand boost sanctioned. Chancellor Schmidt, in close personal contact with leading industrialists and financiers and with the controller of the Bundesbank, played a prominent role in this economic strategy. Hans Apel, Hans Matthöfer and Manfred Lahnstein from the SPD headed the Finance Ministry and Hans Friderichs and Otto Lambsdorff from the FDP controlled the important Economics Ministry, ensuring that coalition policy did not sway too far from a 'hands-off', free-market course.

The Neo-Liberal Wende of 1982

After 1982, however, significant differences emerged between the two parties over approaches to the economy. The SPD now came to favour introducing a sizeable job creation package to deal with the economic crisis, financed, if necessary, through tax increases and through a larger budget deficit. In addition, the SPD, drawing its support from West Germany's ailing industrial regions, accepted the need to extend temporary aid to the country's troubled, traditional industries to give them the opportunity to modernize and re-organize their production processes. The CDU, CSU and FDP, by contrast, remained committed to controlling and reducing the budget deficit through tight fiscal and monetary control and they remained hostile to the idea of state subsidies for troubled industries. More radical elements within these parties, including the economics ministers, Lambsdorff and Bangemann, and finance minister Stoltenberg, favoured de-regulating and freeing the economy even further – through taxation reform, privatization, the setting of targets for the reduction of government spending, and the abolition of restrictive controls on enterprise.

The implementation of this new 'neo-liberal' strategy, or economic *Wende* (change of course), proved at first to be slow and halting. Between 1983 and 1985 significant cuts in welfare spending were made and rent controls were eased, but only part of one company, the energy conglomerate VEBA AG, had been sold to the private sector, while political pressures forced the grant of substantial subsidies to the ailing coal, steel and shipbuilding industries.[11] It gained momentum, however, in 1986 with the unveiling of a major schedule of privatization – involving the sale of the remaining federal government stake in VEBA, Salzgitter (steel) and Volkswagen, and part of its stake in VIAG, Prakla-Seismos and IVG – the introduction of tax cuts, the reduction in industrial subsidies, the splitting and opening up to competition of the Bundespost (a vast banking, telecommunications and postal organization) and the reform of the labour law. This Reaganite-Thatcherite 'supply-side' programme was further extended following the CDU-CSU-FDP coalition's re-election in 1987, endangering the consensual basis of the West German 'social market economy'.[12] Concurrently, the Bundesbank also promoted a liberalization of the nation's capital market, encouraging growth of the Frankfurt stock exchange, company flotations and bank diversification, for example into insurance.

The Demise of Concerted Action

A second and more serious fissure emerged after 1978 in the co-operative 'Concerted Action' consensus which had been built up between West Germany's government (federal and Land), trade unions and industrial and financial groups. 'Concerted Action' set out the need for all major groupings which exercised economic responsibility to work together in the formulation and execution of economic policy – meeting annually to set guidelines for wages, prices and economic growth. This depended upon the supply of reliable information to the participants, from which they could make informed and sensible judgments; upon a consensus existing for the policies being pursued; and upon each side, particularly the trade unions, being able to deliver their promises. The first prerequisite, trustworthy economic information, was supplied regularly by West Germany's five leading economic research institutes and by the Council of Economic Advisers; the second, political consensus, by the lack of class differentiation in the postwar Federal Republic. The last requirement, the ability of trade unions to adhere to broad agreements, derived from the structure of the labour movement in West Germany. There existed one major supra-union body, the DGB (*Deutscher Gewerkschaftsbund*) (the West German equivalent of the TUC, though more powerful), which, in 1988, incorporated 7.8 million members connected with 16 member unions, including IG Metall with its 2.6 million members involved in a broad range of industries.[13] West German trade-union concentration contrasted with the diffuse British craft unions. It was thus possible in West Germany for union leaders to enforce discipline and ensure that bargains were honoured. This was most evident between 1966 and 1978, with union bosses delivering productivity increases and industrial peace, their members gaining in return a share of the economic prosperity built up during these growth years, and an increasing voice in company affairs with the spread of 'industrial co-determination' (*Mitbestimmung* – workers' participation).

This consensus began to break down, however, with the onset of recession and the end of the era of full employment. The unions, after a brief surge in wages during the mid-1970s, were called increasingly to bear the brunt of austerity measures and to accept declining shares of the national cake during the years between 1976–9. Employers, meanwhile, seeking to push ahead with the introduction of new labour-saving technology and shed excess manpower, objected to union attempts to block this process through the influence they exerted under the 'co-determination' system.

'Co-determination' was a form of industrial partnership which provided for almost equal representation of shareholders and workers on companies' supervisory boards – the balance was tilted narrowly in the employer's favour since the chairperson with a casting vote was nominated by the shareholders and one employee representative had to be drawn from senior management. It was applied to the coal and steel industry in 1951 (where full parity existed with a neutral chairperson) and was extended to all firms with workforces in excess of 2000 between 1976 and 1978.[14] Some companies attempted to get round the regulations by changing their corporate status or breaking down their operations into smaller units. However, the West German employers' federation (BDA – *Bundesvereinigung der Deutschen Arbeitgeberverände*) decided to challenge this new law in the Federal Constitutional Court on the grounds that it violated the constitutional guarantee of the right to own and freely use property. The Constitutional Court subsequently ruled (in March 1979) that the new law was legitimate, but that co-determination should go no further. The employers' action had served in the meantime, however, to worsen an already deteriorating industrial relations climate and persuaded the unions to withdraw from the tripartite 'concerted action' committee in July 1977 – attending only informally in subsequent years.

A spate of strikes during 1978 – involving the engineering and steelworkers' union, IG Metall, and the militant printing workers' union, IG Druck und Papier – further soured relations. The management responded by resorting to 'lock-outs', increasing the numbers of workers affected to thus stretch union resources. These tactics proved largely successful and almost bankrupted IG Druck, who after calling out 2000 workers in five newspaper plants had finally to support 32000 workers in 500 firms throughout the country as a result of management lock-outs. IG Metall and IG Druck challenged the use of this strike-breaking weapon, taking their case to the Federal Labour Court in Kassel. The court ruled, however, in June 1980 that 'lock-outs' were legitimate, although they should bear a 'reasonable relationship' to the extent of the strike, involving a similar number to those on official strike.

The 1978 engineering strike, like earlier disputes in 1976, revolved around the traditional issue of pay. In contrast, the printing and steel strikes of 1978 centred upon the introduction of new technology and its threat to job security. This was to become a key issue for the West German labour movement during the following 12 years, with IG Metall at the forefront of this new struggle.

The Fight for a 35-Hour Week

IG Metall, concerned at the rapid contraction of the workforce in the steel industry as firms rationalized and modernized, began to press for the introduction of a 35-hour working week and the inclusion of an extra time shift as a means of stabilizing employment. This was rejected by the steel employers in 1978 who argued that it would cost the troubled industry the equivalent of a 20% pay rise and disastrously reduce its international competitiveness. The most they would offer was six weeks annual paid holiday. This was rejected by IG Metall who called out 37000 workers in selected motor industry supply plants in North-Rhine-Westphalia. The steel management responded with 'lock-outs' and a bitter six-week dispute – the first in the steel industry since the war – was entered into between November 1978 and January 1979, involving almost 100000 workers in the Rhine-Ruhr belt. IG Metall held out for their 35-hour week demand until the very last moment, but were finally forced to capitulate, achieving few concessions from management – only a modest pay increase and an extension of paid leave and holidays. This bitterly disappointed the union rank-and-file, who only narrowly approved the settlement when it went to an end of strike ballot.

The position of West Germany's employers hardened following their victory in the steel dispute. They pressured IG Metall into signing an agreement which fixed their standard week at 40 hours until the end of 1983 (with six weeks paid holidays in return) and the Federation of German Employers (BDA) drew up a 'taboo catalogue' binding all employers not to concede working weeks below this limit. The unions responded in turn by vowing to adopt a firmer stance in future disputes. They failed, however, to carry this threat through. In the 1979 and 1980 pay rounds IG Metall and the public services union (OTV), after engaging in token stoppages, backed down from major industrial action and accepted wage increases close to the inflation mark.[15] This set an upper standard and forced smaller unions to accept cuts in real wages throughout the period between 1979 and 1983.

The West German union movement thus faced, as in other West European countries, a difficult five years after 1979 as its membership and political influence diminished during a recession period.[16] From the winter of 1983, however, with the IG Metall 40-hour week agreement due for expiry and with engineering firms returning to profitability, the ground was prepared for a resumption of the fight for a shortened 35-hour week. This struggle promised to be prolonged and bitter as a result of the accession to power of the sterner CDU-CSU-FDP government and the movement up the union ranks of a younger and more radical generation of leaders, for example Franz Steinkühler, IG Metall's deputy leader. The Federal Chancellor, Helmut Kohl, and his popular labour minister, Norbert Blüm (a former Opel factory worker who was on the moderate 'labour wing' of the CDU), at first attempted in December 1983 to head off a dispute by introducing, as compensation, a state-assisted scheme for early retirement at the age of 59 (instead of at between 63 and 65). However, IG Metall rejected this proposal and, with the support of the DGB and the post, printing, banking and railway unions, continued to press for its 35-hour week. It gained the support of the SPD, whose chairman Willy Brandt firmly backed the principle of the shorter week at a major rally in February 1984. This brought to an end the postwar tradition of party neutralism during industrial disputes and turned the 35-hour week into a highly charged ideological issue.

The IG Metall union engaged in 69 regional and two national negotiating meetings during March and April 1985 in an attempt to reach a compromise solution. It was willing to seek ways of phasing in a movement towards the 35-hour week. But the *Gesamtmetall* employers' federation, backed by the CDU government, took an uncompromising stand, sticking firmly to the principle of a 40-hour week to maintain West German industry's competitiveness. IG Metall was thus forced, after winning the necessary 75% majority in ballots, to take strike action in May 1984. It had prepared in advance for the strike, having built up a strike fund of DM 500 million, and it concentrated on a number of target strikes against prosperous employers in specific regions – against Daimler-Benz and Porsche in Baden-Württemberg; against Siemens in Frankfurt; and against Opel, engineering firms and car component manufacturers in Hesse – instead of calling a crippling, national strike. Further support was provided by the print union IG Druck, which engaged in sporadic strike activity between April and July.

The engineering-metalworkers' strike, however, became lengthier, costlier and more extensive than IG Metall had envisaged as a result of the firm stance adopted by management and the government. Employers retaliated to the union's selective strikes with 'lock-outs' and lay offs once again. In the past, under the previous SPD administration, such laid-off workers had been awarded unemployment pay by the Federal Labour Institute – a tripartite body, comprising management, unions and government, in which the government held the deciding vote. In 1984, however, the CDU-CSU-FDP government sided with management and vetoed the payment of short-term unemployment benefits to workers made idle by the effects of strikes elsewhere. This decision burdened IG Metall with unexpected additional liabilities and stretched the union's funds, which were already being rapidly reduced by the burden of official strike play (set at a level 70% of normal pay). The strike dragged on for seven weeks and eventually involved 1.5 million workers and thus ranked as West Germany's most serious postwar industrial dispute – resulting in the loss of DM 10 billion in production (equivalent to 0.5% of GDP), including 380000 motor vehicles. The dispute ended at the close of June 1984 with a compromise solution – management agreeing to introduce, without loss of pay, a 38.5-hour working week (38 hours in the steel industry) from April 1985.

This represented a partial victory for IG Metall and an important step towards the 35-hour week at the cost though of an embittering of worker-management relations.[17] Employers managed to get round the new 38.5-hour working week regulations by introducing more flexible working patterns and increased overtime, minimizing the overall employment impact of the reform. In addition, however, they persuaded the federal government to push through in March 1986 a reform of the National Labour Code to prevent the payment of unemployment benefit to workers indirectly laid off during disputes who later benefited from strike settlements. This measure, aimed at preventing 'striking on the cheap', enraged the unions, who had briefly resumed tripartite 'concerted action' negotiations in September 1985. The DGB pronounced the labour minister, Norbert Blüm, to be a 'class traitor' and took the unprecedented step of refusing to allow Chancellor Kohl to address its quadrennial congress in 1986. Protest strikes against the government's new policies were carried out in October and December 1985 and February–March 1986 by the union movement which accused the federal government of seeking a 'permanent conflict' with the forces of labour.

In comparative terms, West Germany's labour movement negotiated the testing economic and political waters of the 1980s in a remarkably successful fashion. As the economy picked up and as determined efforts were made to recruit the growing number of female, particularly service sector and part-time, workers, union membership rolls began to edge up slightly from 1985 and the country's high overall unionization level of supra-40% was maintained. Apart from general economic factors, a key reason for this comparative success – in Britain the level of workforce unionization fell dramatically from 54% to 40% between 1979 and 1989 – was the continued moderation and responsibility of the trade-union leadership, particularly the so-called 'Gang of Five' unions involved in the chemicals, foodstuffs, mining, construction and textiles industries. This meant that unions remained more acceptable to management and retained the public's respect. As evidence of this restraint, between 1980 and 1987 wages and incomes remained steady in real terms, while the number of working days lost in 1985 was only 35 000. The latter compared to 6 million in Britain.

Public confidence in the FRG's union movement was somewhat dented by scandals in 1986 and 1989 respectively, concerning the DGB's involvement with the *Neue Heimat* housing syndicate and the retail branch of the co-operative movement. However, it remained sufficiently influential between 1987 and 1990 to secure further advances for its membership. In the engineering and motor industry, in April 1987 IG Metall secured an agreement from management for a further staggered reduction in the length of the working week from 38.5 hours to 37 hours by 1989, along with a 13% rise in the hourly wage rate. Ten months later, employers similarly conceded a phased three-year contraction of the working week from 38 to 36.5 hours in the steel industry and from 40 to 38.5 hours for public-sector employees. Then, finally, in May 1990, following the launching of a spate of wildcat strikes involving a quarter of a million workers, the goal of a 35-hour week was secured by IG Metall. The engineering employers Gesamtmetall, at last, assented to introduce such a working week from October 1995 and a similar undertaking was made by the printing industry, following pressure exerted by the new union IG Medien. In 1987–8 protests by steel and other unions in the Ruhr region against the proposed closure of the Krupp and Mannesmann steel plants at Rheinhausen were also partially successful in securing a temporary reprieve and in persuading Chancellor Kohl, in February 1988, to announce a DM 500 million five-year package of regional aid, much of which was earmarked for the Ruhr. This was interpreted as evidence that a consensus approach had by no means been abandoned by Bonn.

Part Six

EXTERNAL RELATIONS BEFORE REUNIFICATION

Chapter 11

FOREIGN POLICY UNDER SCHMIDT AND KOHL

The Foreign Policy Interests of the Federal Republic

Two key issues have dominated the Federal Republic's foreign policy during the postwar decades – the 'German question' and the functioning of the international economy.

The 'German Question'

With the defeat of Hitler and the sequestration of almost one half of the country by Poland and the GDR after 1945 all hopes of the creation of a *Grossdeutschland* uniting the scattered Germanic tribes of Central Europe appeared to have finally been lost. The Soviet Union, United States and the FRG's Western European neighbours sought to maintain the two Germanies as weakened and divided nations in the interests of future peace in Europe. Within West Germany, however, the goal of reunification was sustained by the existence of a substantial refugee and 'expellee' community and by the demands of the Basic Law. The 'German question' became the pre-eminent issue in German foreign affairs, with reunification in 'peace and freedom' the foremost goal.

During the 1950s and early 1960s opinions differed as to the best route to take in pursuance of this goal. Konrad Adenauer, seeking to first rehabilitate the country and gain acceptance by the Western alliance, and concerned with the danger of the spread of communism, supported the United States in its hard-line policy against the Soviet Union, seeking to eventually negotiate German reunification from a position of strength. This policy involved joining NATO (1955), accepting re-armament and refusing to formally recognize the illegitimate puppet regimes of Eastern Europe (the Hallstein Doctrine). The SPD, however, criticized this stance as being essentially flawed, driving the two halves of Germany further and further apart. The erection of the Berlin Wall in August 1961 and America's subsequent meek acceptance gave support to this interpretation and prompted a re-assessment of German foreign policy during the early 1960s.

The views of both the SPD and the CDU began now to converge as a new 'policy of movement' (*Bewegungspolitik*) was devised during the mid-1960s, involving a thawing in relations (diplomatic and trading) with the Eastern bloc nations, excluding East Germany. This policy, however, ran into opposition from the Soviet Union, which viewed it, in the wake of the 1968 Czech crisis, as being essentially divisive, destabilizing Eastern Europe. A more radical re-appraisal of the 'German question' was thus called for and was carried out by the SPD and FDP.

They recognized that, after more than twenty years, major changes had occurred within Eastern Europe and that the possibility of rapid and peaceful German reunification was now remote. In such circumstances, it was argued that a realistic attempt should be made to harmonize and normalize relations with West Germany's eastern neighbours and to improve conditions for Germans living in the GDR, opening up the borders for the movement of families and friends. In the short run, it was felt that this increased contact and co-operation would prevent a further drifting apart of the two Germanies. In the long run, it was hoped that such 'change through rapprochement' would bring a convergence between the economic and social systems of the two countries, so that political barriers would eventually wither away. Willy Brandt, Egon Bahr and the FDP leader, Walter Scheel, were the key figures behind the formulation of this new conciliatory *Ostpolitik*. It fitted in with the more general climate of detente which was extending between the USSR under Leonid Brezhnev and the United States under President Richard Nixon, and with the decline in popular concern for German reunification as a new and distinctive West German 'free-market' nationality developed in contradistinction to the communist evolution of the GDR.

The establishment of full diplomatic relations with Romania in 1967, in contravention of the Hallstein Doctrine, marked the first step in this new Ostpolitik. Even more significant departures were made following the coming to power of the new SPD-FDP coalition. Thus, in 1970, treaties were entered into normalizing relations with the Soviet Union and Poland, recognizing the Oder-Neisse line; in 1971 the Four Power Berlin Agreement secured access to West Berlin; and in September 1972 a 'Basic Treaty' was signed with East Germany, recognizing the GDR's frontiers and separate existence. This came close to giving full recognition, but stopped short of acknowledging a separate East German nationality (permanent missions were stationed in Bonn and East Berlin instead of ambassadors). The CDU remained critical that too much had been conceded and too little gained, but it did not block the new treaties in the Bundesrat. It was left to the CSU, led by Franz-Josef Strauss, to fight the legality of the treaties in the Federal Constitutional Court in 1973, but without success. Ostpolitik – the opening up of human and commercial frontiers between the East and West – had become the new consensus in the Federal Republic's foreign policy.

Economic Factors in the Federal Republic's Foreign Policy

The FRG economy is outward looking, depending heavily upon foreign trade. It imports raw mineral and energy inputs and foodstuffs, and exports manufactures to the value of almost 30% of its GNP. Successive administrations have thus been anxious to maintain friendly and peaceful international relations and to push for liberalization in tariff policies. West Germany's entry into the European Coal and Steel Community (1952) and the European Economic Community (1957) were clear and successful indications of this desire. Although remaining a net contributor to the EC budget – to the value of 1.8 billion ecu in 1981 – the FRG gained tremendous commercial and political advantages from its member-ship – the EC providing both the largest single market for its manufactured goods and a platform for the German voice in international affairs. Eastern Europe and the Middle East became other areas of economic and political importance for the Federal Republic from the 1960s.

As it became rehabilitated into the international community, signalled by its acceptance into the United Nations in 1973, and as its economic power continued to expand during the 1960s, so the Federal Republic began to play a more important role on the world stage. Lacking the colonial responsibilities of Britain or France, its direct global interests remained limited. But at world economic summits, instituted in 1975 by Giscard d'Estaing, the West German voice, as the third largest economy in the West and enjoying large trading surpluses to the value of more than $10 billion per annum (1967–78), was listened to with respect and its influence upon policy prescriptions progressively increased.

West German Foreign Policy: 1976–90

Ostpolitik after the Fall of Brandt

Some of the initial optimism and enthusiasm surrounding the new Ostpolitik had waned by the mid-1970s, with the realization that there were clear limits to Eastern concessions. Links between West Berlin and West Germany were improved, but the Berlin Wall remained and severe restrictions were still placed upon movement from the GDR to the Federal Republic, as East Germany, while grateful for finally obtaining international recognition and while seeking to raise living standards through expanded trade, sought also to protect its embryonic social and political system from undermining by the West.[1] Thus, under Helmut Schmidt and the FDP foreign minister, Hans-Dietrich Genscher, Ostpolitik detente was carried out with greater caution and scepticism. Progress continued, however, to be made – new supplementary treaties were signed with East Germany and Poland in 1975 and 1976: the treaty with Poland providing for the resettlement of 120 000 German nationals living in Poland wishing to move to the Federal Republic in return for a 'transfer fee'.

It was, however, in the economic sphere where advancement and co-operation went furthest. Aided by substantial West German concessions (for example, the 'swing' overdraft facility, the 1978 Traffic Agreement and the 1979 Long Term Trading Agreement) inter-German trade increased substantially, expanding at an annual rate of 14% between 1969 and 1976. Increased market and investment outlets were created for West German manufacturers, particularly during the mid-1970s, with Comecon's share of West Germany's exports rising from 5½% in 1970 to 9% in 1975. Aided by its geographical position, West Germany became the single largest external trading partner for Eastern Europe. However, the major beneficiaries of this 'economic detente' were the East Germans, who granted a number of limited humanitarian concessions in return for large financial subsidies and a welcome improvement in their domestic living standards.

The pursuit of conciliatory Ostpolitik and economic detente during the early and mid-1970s did not, however, signal any weakening in West Germany's commitment to the United States and the NATO alliance. The FRG firmly supported the United States in its plans for a neutron bomb, later shelved by President Carter in 1978, and was a prime instigator behind the NATO nuclear weapons 'modernization programme' of November 1979. This was because Chancellor Schmidt viewed the maintenance of a credible balance of deterrence as essential both to guarantee the security of West Germany and West Berlin and to maintain pressure on the Soviet Union to make genuine concessions in human rights and armament levels.

US-Soviet relations had been comparatively amicable during the 1970s, allowing room for the West Germans to develop their own form of Ostpolitik detente with the Eastern bloc. After 1980, however, American attitudes hardened once more following the Soviet invasion of Afghanistan, in December 1979, the troubles in Poland and the accession to the presidency of the Republican, Ronald Reagan, in January 1981. This new 'Cold War' atmosphere developed during a period of gathering world recession which, with mounting Comecon debts and narrowing export markets, caused a sharp contraction in East-West trade. (The Comecon bloc's share of West Germany's exports declined to only 6% in 1981.) Both factors meant that the maintenance of Ostpolitik detente became increasingly difficult during the years between 1980–5.

In 1980 President Carter and the US administration called for economic sanctions against both Iran, which was holding American citizens hostage at the US embassy in Teheran, and the Soviet Union, following its invasion of Afghanistan. Chancellor Schmidt, who disdained President Carter as a naive and unpredictable amateur in international affairs, and foreign minister Genscher eventually supported the United States in these actions, restricting high-technology sales to the Soviet Union and boycotting the forthcoming Moscow Olympics, but this was only after considerable dithering and delay. The West German government aimed to maintain bridges between East and West and prevent a full return to 'Cold War' isolationism and militarism. Thus, while supporting the United States in its sanctions and boycotts and while strengthening

NATO's Turkish ally with a substantial aid package, Schmidt and Genscher continued to meet the Soviet leader, Leonid Brezhnev, in July 1980, entering into a 25-year agreement on economic co-operation, and arranged large-scale measures of economic support to prop up the tottering Polish regime of Edward Gierek. Inter-German contacts were also maintained. Although at the height of the Polish crisis in August 1980 the planned meeting between Helmut Schmidt and the East German leader, Erich Honecker, was cancelled and in October 1980, five days before the Bundestag elections, the compulsory exchange limit for West German visitors to the GDR was drastically raised from DM 13 to DM 25 a day, deterring entry, top level talks were resumed fourteen months later. Little was achieved, but Ostpolitik, though stagnating, was kept alive, with both sides, the East Germans for economic reasons, the West Germans for political reasons, anxious to maintain the dialogue during a troubled period for superpower relations.

Between 1982 and 1984, US-Soviet relations reached their lowest point since the Cuban missiles crisis of 1961, as the date (December 1983) for the stationing of NATO's new medium-range nuclear missiles in Western Europe approached, martial law was declared in Poland (December 1981) and Soviet troops remained stationed in Afghanistan. The uncompromising stance adopted by President Reagan towards Soviet actions imperilled the whole structure of detente and Ostpolitik and placed the West German government in a difficult position during these years. While remaining loyal, despite considerable internal party opposition, to the Pershing-II deployment decision, Helmut Schmidt and Hans-Dietrich Genscher began to take a partly independent line and failed to acquiesce in a number of crucial American demands.

The first and most serious German-American rift occurred over reactions to martial law in Poland. The Reagan administration pressed for stern sanctions against both the Soviet Union and the new Polish regime under General Jaruzelski. The Schmidt government, however, while suspending official aid to Poland, accepted the temporary imposition of martial law by the Polish army as a necessary evil to pre-empt direct Russian intervention. It therefore refused to join the US in its wide range of economic sanctions and continued to participate in the huge Siberian pipeline project.[2] The US suspected that pecuniary motives, at a time of economic recession, swayed the German decision. Relations between America and Bonn were further strained by the Schmidt government's failure, as a result of fiscal constraints, to fully keep up with its 1979

NATO pledge to increase its military budget by 3% per annum in 'real terms' during the first half of the 1980s.

These actions coincided with a wave of anti-American demonstrations by the German peace movement and assassinations of NATO military personnel by terrorist organizations. Coupled with Soviet talk concerning the 'divisibility of detente', they precipitated American fears that West Germany was being slowly decoupled from the NATO alliance and becoming neutralized or 'Finlandized'. However, although a number of voices, for example, the Greens and Herbert Wehner of the SPD, inside Germany did dream of a neutral Federal Republic on good terms with its Eastern neighbours, majority opinion in West Germany remained firmly committed to the NATO alliance and the United States. It sought only to add a European voice to the East-West dialogue and avoid a blinkered, doctrinaire approach to these issues.

The rift between Washington and Bonn was only temporary. It was healed by the decision of European legislatures, including the Bundestag, to accept the deployment of Cruise and Pershing-II missiles during the winter of 1983, and by the accession of a new CDU-CSU-FDP administration which was more Atlanticist in its outlook, with its defence minister, Manfred Wörner, playing an active role in NATO's modernization planning. Relations with both the East and West did not fully, however, return to their mid-1970s condition.

The Kohl administration, with Genscher remaining as foreign minister, sought to maintain Ostpolitik (Helmut Kohl visiting the Soviet leader, Yuri Andropov, in Moscow in June 1983) and a neighbourly relationship with East Germany to prove to the electorate that the SPD did not have a monopoly over solutions to the 'German question'. There was a short-term deterioration in relations with the Eastern bloc during 1983, culminating in the retaliatory deployment of short-range SS-22 nuclear missiles in East Germany and Czechoslovakia, as the Soviet Union sought to put pressure on the Kohl government to shelve NATO modernization plans. However, from the spring of 1984 both the East Germans, reacting to a power vacuum in Moscow following the death of Andropov and to its own desire for Western finance to meet its growing debt liabilities, and the Kohl government made steps towards a rapprochement, creating a small island of micro-detente in a troubled world of superpower conflict.

Thus, in June 1984 Bonn arranged, through the unlikely envoy of Franz-Josef Strauss, a large DM 1 billion loan to East Germany. In return, the East German government eased a number of its inter-German travel restrictions, exempting visitors below the age of 15 from compulsory exchange requirements and allowing a record number of East Germans (44 000) to leave the country to resettle in the Federal Republic during 1984, and handed control of the S-Bahn railway to West Berlin. Moscow later stepped in to pull East Germany into line and persuaded Erich Honecker to call off his much publicized and historic first official visit to West Germany in September 1984. A resumption in top-level contacts between West Germany and East European governments, including the Soviet Union, Poland and East Germany, during the winter of 1984 suggested that relations with the East were beginning to thaw once more. However, the eruption of the Tiedge spy scandal (August 1985) and the coming to power of the new Gorbachev administration in the Soviet Union, which was keen initially to re-establish firm control over its East European partners, dampened these hopes during 1985–6.

Relations with East Germany particularly deteriorated during the summer and autumn of 1986 as a result of West German concern over the mounting influx of Third World 'economic refugees' through the 'Berlin hole' and East Germany's anger at Chancellor Kohl's critical remarks on human rights within its borders.[3] In addition, during 1985–6 the new Soviet leadership targeted the opposition SPD as a potential future ally in its drive to remove American nuclear weapons from Western Europe and destabilize the NATO alliance, and thus sought to boost the SPD's prospects of gaining federal power in the January 1987 Bundestag election by giving it preferential treatment. A string of SPD officials, including party chairman Willy Brandt (September 1985), were thus invited to East Germany for top-level talks during 1985–6 and chemical weapons and nuclear-free zone agreements were negotiated by the neighbouring socialist parties of Germany. This strategy failed, however, in securing the SPD's election to power in January 1987. With the CDU-CSU-FDP Kohl administration set to govern for a further four-year term and foreign minister Hans-Dietrich Genscher anxious to promote a new 'second phase of detente', an improvement in relations with the Soviet Union and East Germany seemed likely to occur between 1987 and 1990, as each side adjusted to the new realities of power.

West Germany's relations with its American ally improved more perceptibly and steadily during the Kohl administration. However, the West German government did display alarm at a number of the more adventurist initiatives of President Reagan, particularly his policy in Lebanon and Libya, and was divided over the American 'Star Wars' programme. Such doubts served to push the West German government closer to its French allies within the European Community, and raised interest in the development of a more concerted and co-ordinated EC foreign and defence policy programme as a counterweight to the rival superpowers.

The Federal Republic in Europe and the Developing World

The European Community provided, in addition to a huge open market on the Federal Republic's doorstep, a respectable route back to the international stage, although only during recent years has the voice of the EC acquired strength and unity. All the major political parties in the FRG have, since 1959, been committed to the European ideal and this has been backed up by the government financially underwriting each new step in the Community's programme of development. It was not, however, until the early 1970s, based around the close co-operation of France and West Germany, that major advances were made in achieving greater economic and governmental co-ordination and a political voice was successfully added to what had hitherto existed merely as a customs union and agricultural support service.

Under Helmut Schmidt and the French President, Valéry Giscard d'Estaing, whose careers as national ministers and later leaders coincided between 1972 and 1981, the traditional hostility of France and Germany, which had still smouldered on during the Brandt-Pompidou era, at last gave way. A close rapprochement developed, born out of the mutual respect and affection of the two new leaders and out of a growing identity of interests.

The Federal Republic, though possessing the largest and most powerful economy in Europe, remained wary, as a consequence of its past history, of playing a direct and overt role on the international stage. Having renounced the development of its own nuclear force and the stationing of German forces outside its frontiers, it lacked, in addition, the military might to perform such a role. However, Helmut Schmidt, the new West German Chancellor, was very much an internationalist with a broad vision and a desire to leave his imprint on world politics. The FRG thus sought to work with and through the French government, led by an equally ambitious and confident leader, to achieve a number of its international aims. Contacts between the two countries' leaders, by telephone and bilateral summits, were frequent and economic policies converged, as

Giscard d'Estaing, impressed with the postwar West German 'economic miracle', sought to transpose the 'German model' into a French setting. In the European Community, the establishment of tri-annual 'European Council', co-ordinating meetings and an elected European Parliament, and the creation of the European Monetary System (EMS) in 1979, set up to insulate European currencies against fluctuations in the US dollar, were significant policy developments in which the German input was immense, although much of the credit was allowed to pass to the French government. Outside Europe, the Federal Republic worked with and through France to foster stability and peace in mineral-rich Africa and the Middle East.

With the fall of first Giscard d'Estaing in June 1981 and then Helmut Schmidt in October 1982, to be replaced respectively by the socialist leader, François Mitterrand, and by the CDU leader, Helmut Kohl, the future of the firm Paris-Bonn axis was placed in question. France's new leader sought out alternative allies in Britain and Italy, while his reflationary domestic policies threatened to undermine the new EMS. The overtures to Britain and Italy failed, however, to elicit a reciprocal response, while Mitterrand's economic policy was soon subject to a deflationary U-turn. The Franco-German *entente cordiale* thus remained firmly in place during the years between 1983 and 1986, the major difference being that under the insular Helmut Kohl, the initiative for reform passed increasingly towards France.

The most important such initiative was François Mitterrand's drive for a more united and independent European defence strategy, with close co-operation between the French army and the Bundeswehr and the development of the Eureka programme as an alternative or supplementary to US 'Star Wars' research, representing first steps in this direction. This was partly stimulated by French anxiety concerning a possible dangerous drift towards Central European neutralism, which they saw developing in neighbouring Germany.

The West Germans under Helmut Kohl and Hans-Dietrich Genscher, in contrast, placed particular emphasis on more rapid moves towards closer economic and political union within the Community and towards expediting the 1985 EC entry of Spain and Portugal, smoothing over financial disputes between France and its Mediterranean neighbours through pecuniary subsidies. The strength of the West German farm lobby, particularly within the FDP, CDU and CSU, and friendship with France prevented the

Federal Republic, however, from pushing firmly for reform of the costly Common Agricultural Policy (CAP). Thus, as in Eastern Europe, the FRG had to pay a significant economic price for diplomatic advances gained under the European and French umbrella.

Outside of Europe, the Federal Republic's direct actions remained limited to economic affairs, gaining, through its sheer economic weight, a seat at Western summits, which, as Helmut Schmidt demonstrated in 1978, could be used in a most effective and dramatic manner. The FRG's interest in other areas was to promote stability and ease tensions between the superpower blocs. Such a concern reflected the twin economic and political imperatives for a country so heavily dependent on external trade and until 1990 with its old capital Berlin cut in half and standing inside a hostile region, dependent upon the goodwill of its Eastern neighbour and the security provided by its Western allies.

Foreign Policy Developments between 1987 and 1990

As anticipated, the Kohl adminstration's second term was characterized, after an initial hesitation, by a warming of relations with the Eastern bloc. The long-postponed Honecker visit eventually took place and the level of human and commercial contacts between the two Germanies increased significantly (*see* Chapters 6 and 7). Much more dramatic, however, was the closening of links between Bonn and Moscow. Following ice-breaking visits by President von Weizsäcker, in July 1987, and Franz-Josef Strauss, in December 1987, Chancellor Kohl visited Moscow, in October 1988, and President Gorbachev Bonn, in June 1989. It became clear that Gorbachev was committed to forging a new, amicable relationship with the West and with effecting genuine and substantial reductions in the levels of nuclear and conventional weapons within Europe. As the proponent of this 'new detente', the Soviet leader was accorded such an enthusiastic reception by the western German public in June 1989 that the term 'Gorbymania' was coined by the popular press. Eventually, the Gorbachev initiative was to lead to intermediate-range nuclear forces being removed from western and eastern German soil and provide the conditions in which reunification could be achieved. In return, the Soviet Union received from the FRG billions of Deutschmarks of financial aid and 'soft loan' credit. These developments are discussed in Chapters 6–9.

Between 1987 and 1990 the Kohl administration, while developing closer contacts with Eastern Europe, also continued to work for closer military co-operation with France and, despite initial Länder misgivings, a 'deepening' of the economic and political integration of the European Community. In January 1988 the French and FRG governments established a joint, consultative Council for Defence and Security and joint, cabinet-level committees on financial and economic policy, telecommunications and education. In addition, a 3500-member Franco-German joint military brigade was later formed. Standing outside the structure of NATO, it was stationed near Stuttgart. At the same time, Chancellor Kohl and foreign minister Genscher, both committed 'integrationists', supported moves towards monetary union within the EC, entailing the establishment of a single currency and independent European central bank from the mid-1990s. They had already enthusiastically promoted the 1986 Single European Act, which provided for the creation of a single European market for the movement of goods, services, capital and labour by 1992, along with a 'social charter' of minimum workers' rights.

APPENDIX A

The Länder (States) of the Federal Republic of Germany in August 1991

Land	Area (Sq Km)	(1989) Population ('000)	Capital	Land Government	Bundesrat Seats
EASTERN GERMANY					
Berlin	883	3,410[1]	Berlin	CDU-SPD	4
Brandenburg	29,059	2,641	Potsdam	SPD-FDP-Alliance '90	4
Mecklenburg-Western Pomerania	23,838	1,964	Schwerin	CDU-FDP	4
Saxony	18,337	4,901	Dresden	CDU	4
Saxony-Anhalt	20,445	2,965	Magdeburg	CDU-FDP	4
Thuringia	16,251	2,684	Erfurt	CDU-FDP	4
	(108,813)	(18,565)			(24)
WESTERN GERMANY					
Baden-Württemberg	35,751	9,618	Stuttgart	CDU	6
Bavaria	70,553	11,221	Munich	CSU	6
Bremen	404	674	Bremen	SPD	3
Hamburg	755	1,626	Hamburg	SPD	3
Hesse	21,144	5,660	Wiesbaden	SPD-Greens	4
Lower Saxony	47,439	7,284	Hanover	SPD-Greens	6
North-Rhine-Westphalia	34,068	17,104	Düsseldorf	SPD	6
Rhineland-Palatinate	19,848	3,702	Mainz	SPD-FDP	4
Saarland	2,569	1,065	Saarbrücken	SPD	3
Schleswig-Holstein	15,728	2,595	Kiel	SPD	4
	(248,259)	(60,549)			(45)
ALL GERMANY	(357,072)	(79,114)	Berlin	DU-CSU-FDP	(69)

[1] East Berlin 1.279 million; West Berlin, 2.131 million.

APPENDIX B

Länder Election Results: 1974–91 (% of vote)

	CDU	SPD	FDP	*Greens*
Baden-Württemberg				
1976	56.7	33.3	7.8	—
1980	53.4	32.5	8.3	5.3
1984	51.9	32.4	7.2	8.0
1988[1]	49.1	32.0	5.9	7.9
CDU Controlled				
Bavaria (*CSU*)				
1974	62.1	30.2	5.2	—
1978	59.1	31.4	6.2	1.8
1982	58.3	31.9	3.5	4.6
1986[2]	55.8	27.5	3.8	7.5
1990[3]	54.9	26.0	5.2	6.4
CDU Controlled				
Berlin				
1990[4]	40.3	30.5	7.1	5.0
CSU-SPD Controlled				
Brandenburg				
1990[5]	29.4	38.3	6.6	2.8
SPD-FDP-Alliance '90 Controlled				
Bremen				
1975	33.8	48.7	13.0	—
1979	31.9	49.4	10.8	5.1
1983	33.1	51.3	4.6	5.4[6]
1987[7]	23.4	50.5	10.0	10.2
1991[7]	30.7	38.8	9.5	11.4
SPD/Greens Controlled				
Hamburg				
1974	40.6	44.9	10.9	—
1978	37.6	51.5	4.8	4.5
1982a	43.2	42.8	4.8	7.7
1982b	38.6	51.3	2.6	6.8
1986	41.9	41.8	4.8	10.4
1987	40.5	45.0	6.5	7.0
1991	35.1	48.0	5.4	7.2
SPD Controlled				

	CDU	SPD	FDP	Greens
Hesse				
1974	40.3	48.5	10.2	—
1978	46.0	44.3	6.6	—
1982	45.6	42.8	3.1	8.0
1983	39.4	46.2	7.6	5.9
1987	42.1	40.2	7.8	9.4
1991[7]	40.2	40.8	7.4	8.8
	SPD-Greens Controlled			
Lower Saxony				
1974	48.8	43.1	7.0	—
1978	48.7	42.2	4.2	3.9
1982	50.7	36.5	5.9	6.5
1986	44.3	42.1	6.0	7.1
1990[8]	42.0	44.2	6.0	5.5
	SPD-Greens Controlled			
Mecklenburg-Western Pomerania				
1990[9]	38.3	27.0	5.5	4.2
	CDU-FDP Controlled			
North-Rhine-Westphalia				
1975	47.1	45.1	6.7	—
1980	43.2	48.4	4.9	3.0
1985	36.5	52.1	6.0	4.6
1990[10]	36.7	50.0	5.8	5.0
	SPD Controlled			
Rhineland-Palatinate				
1975	53.9	38.5	5.6	—
1979	50.1	42.3	6.4	—
1983	51.9	39.6	3.5	4.5
1987	45.1	38.8	7.3	5.9
1991	38.7	44.8	6.9	5.9
	SPD-FDP Controlled			
Saarland				
1975	49.1	41.8	7.4	—
1980	44.0	45.4	6.9	2.9
1985	37.3	49.2	10.0	2.5
1990[11]	33.4	54.4	5.6	2.7
	SPD Controlled			
Saxony				
1990[12]	53.8	19.1	5.3	5.6
	CDU Controlled			
Saxony-Anhalt				
1990[13]	39.0	26.0	13.5	5.3
	CDU-FDP Controlled			

	CDU	SPD	FDP	Greens
Schleswig-Holstein				
1975	50.4	40.1	7.1	—
1979	48.3	41.7	5.8	2.4
1983[14]	49.0	43.7	2.2	3.6
1987[14]	42.6	45.2	5.2	3.9
1988[14]	33.3	54.8	4.4	2.9
	SPD Controlled			
Thuringia				
1990[15]	45.4	22.8	9.3	6.5
	CDU-FDP Controlled			
West Berlin				
1975	44.0	42.7	7.2	—
1979	44.4	42.6	8.1	—
1981	47.9	38.4	5.6	7.2
1985	46.4	32.4	8.5	10.6
1989[16]	37.8	37.3	3.9	11.8
	CDU-FDP Controlled			

[1] The NPD and Republicans secured a combined 3.1% of the vote.

[2] The Republicans captured 3% of the vote.

[3] The Republicans captured 4.9% of the vote and the Ecological Democratic Party (ODP) 1.7%.

[4] The PDS captured 9.2% of the vote, Alliance '90 4.4% and the Republicans 3.1%.

[5] The PDS captured 13.4% of the vote, Alliance '90 6.4% and the Republicans 1.2%.

[6] The Bremen Green list also won 2.4%.

[7] In 1987 the DVU captured 3.4% of the vote and one seat, and, in 1991, 6.2% and six seats.

[8] The Republicans captured 1.7% of the vote.

[9] The Republicans captured 1.5% of the vote.

[10] The PDS captured 15.7% of the vote, New Forum 2.9%, Alliance '90 2.2% and the CSU 1.1%.

[11] The Republicans captured 1.8% of the vote.

[12] The Republicans captured 3.3% of the vote.

[13] The PDS captured 10.2% of the vote and the DSU 3.6%.

[14] The PDS captured 12.0% of the vote and the DSU 1.7%.

[15] The South Schleswig Electoral Union (SSU), representing the Danish-speaking minority, captured one seat in 1983, 1987 and 1988 based on a 1.3–1.7% vote share. It was exempt from the 5% requirement for representation in the Landtag.

[16] The PDS captured 9.7% of the vote and the DSU 3.3%.

[17] The Republicans captured 7.5% of the vote and 11 seats.

EUROPEAN PARLIAMENT ELECTIONS
(% of Vote)

	CDU-CSU	SPD	FDP	Greens	Turnout
1979	49.2	40.8	6.0	3.2	(66%)
1984	46.0	37.4	4.8	8.2	(57%)
1989[1]	37.8	37.3	5.6	8.4	(62%)

[1] The Republicans secured 7.1% of the vote.

APPENDIX C

Contemporary Länder Parliaments and Minister-Presidents

Baden-Württemberg Landtag
(Seats after March 1988 election)

CDU	SPD	Greens	FDP
66	42	7	10

Minister-President: Erwin Teufel (CDU) since January 1991

Bavaria Landtag
(Seats after October 1990 election)

CSU	SPD	Greens	FDP
127	58	12	7

Minister-President: Dr Max Streibl (CSU) since October 1988

Berlin Senate (Bürgerschaft)
(Seats after December 1990 election)

CDU	SPD	PDS	FDP	AL[1]	Alliance '90
100	76	23	18	12	11

[1] Alternative List (Greens)

Minister-President: Eberhard Diepgen (CDU) since January 1991

Brandenburg Landtag
(Seats after October 1990 election)

CDU	SPD	PDS	FDP	Alliance '90
27	36	13	6	6

Minister-President: Manfred Stolpe (SPD) since October 1990

Bremen Senate (Bürgerschaft)
(Seats after September 1987 election)

CDU	SPD	Greens	FDP	DVU[1]
25	54	10	10	1

[1] German People's Union

Mayor (Bürgermeister): Klaus Wedemeier (SPD) since September 1985

Hamburg Senate (Bürgerschaft)
(Seats after June 1991 election)

CDU	SPD	Greens	FDP
44	61	9	7

Mayor (Bürgermeister): Dr Henning Voscherau (SPD) since June 1988

Hesse Landtag
(Seats after January 1991 election)

CDU	SPD	Greens	FDP
46	46	10	8

Minister-President: Hans Eichel (SPD) since January 1991

Lower Saxony Landtag
(Seats after May 1990 election)

CDU	SPD	Greens	FDP
67	71	8	9

Minister-President: Gerhard Schröder (SPD) since June 1990

Mecklenburg-Western Pomerania Landtag
(Seats after October 1990 election)

CDU	SPD	PDS	FDP
29	21	12	4

Minister-President: Alfred Gomolka (CDU) since October 1990

North-Rhine-Westphalia Landtag
(Seats after May 1990 election)

CDU	SPD	Greens	FDP
89	122	12	14

Minister-President: Johannes Rau (SPD) since September 1978

Rhineland-Palatinate Landtag
(Seats after April 1991 election)

CDU	SPD	Greens	FDP
40	47	7	7

Minister-President: Rudolf Scharping (SPD) since May 1991

Saarland Landtag
(Seats after January 1990 election)

CDU	SPD	FDP
18	30	3

Minister-President: Oskar Lafontaine (SPD) since March 1985

Saxony Landtag
(Seats after October 1990 election)

CDU	SPD	PDS	FDP	Alliance '90/Greens
92	32	17	9	10

Minister-President: Kurt Biedenkopf (CDU) since October 1990

Saxony-Anhalt Landtag
(Seats after October 1990 election)

CDU	SPD	PDS	FDP	Greens/New Forum
48	27	12	14	5

Minister-President: Gerd Gies (CDU) since October 1990

Schleswig-Holstein Landtag
(Seats after May 1988 election)

CDU	SPD	SSW[1]
27	46	1

[1]Südschleswigscher Wählerverband

Minister-President: Björn Engholm (SPD) since May 1988

Thuringia Landtag
(Seats after October 1990 election)

CDU	SPD	PDS	FDP	Greens/New Forum Democracy Now
44	21	9	9	6

Minister-President: Josef Duchac (CDU) since October 1990

The Positions of the Parties in the FRG's 16 Landtage in October 1991

Party	Seats	Number of Landtage under Full Control	Number of Landtage under Shared Control	Bundesrat Seats
CDU-CSU	896	3	4	32
SPD	777	4	6	37
FDP	135	—	5	—
Greens	99	—	3	—
Alliance '90	27[1]	—	1	—
PDS	86	—	—	—
Others	7	—	—	—
TOTAL	2,027	7	9	69

[1] Includes seats shared with Greens in Saxony Landtag.

APPENDIX D

The Constitutional Position of West Berlin until October 1990

West Berlin, although classed in the Basic Law, under the designation 'Greater Berlin', as a Land of the Federal Republic, remained subject to the supreme authority of the three Allied powers of the United States, Britain and France in accordance with postwar agreements. This ambiguous status was confirmed by the September 1971 Four Power Agreement in which the three Allied nations agreed that West Berlin was not a constituent part of the FRG, while the Soviet Union confirmed the Allied troika's governing rights. It was brought to an end by the Four Power Declaration of October 1990.

Under the Land's August 1950 constitution, West Berlin had a single chamber, popularly elected 133-member legislature, the House of Representatives (*Abgeordnetenhaus*). The House elected a 10–16 member executive, termed the Senate, and a Governing Mayor (*Regierender Bürgermeister*) to run the city's affairs. In addition, it appointed four delegates to the Federal Bundesrat and 22 'honorary delegates' to the Bundestag who were debarred from voting in plenary sessions. The latter delegates were selected on a proportionate basis so as to accurately reflect the balance of party strength within the House.

APPENDIX E

The FRG's Political Parties: Membership and Organization

PARTY MEMBERSHIP: 1950–88

	('000)					
	1950	*1960*	*1970*	*1980*	*1985*	*1988*
SPD	683	650	780	980	930	920
CDU	265	270	300	696	736	668
CSU	85	—	93	175	186	190
FDP	80	—	56	85	70	65
Greens	—	—	—	18	40	39
DKP	—	—	22	45	49	48
NPD	—	—	—	10	15	15
Republicans	—	—	—	—	4	25

Social Democratic Party (SPD)
(Sozialdemokratische Partei Deutschlands)

Date of Formation: 1875

Chairperson: Björn Engholm (since 1991)
Deputy Chairpersons: Johannes Rau (since 1982), Oskar Lafontaine (since 1987) Herta Däubler-Gmelin (since 1988), Wolfgang Thierse (since 1990)
Bundestag Leader: Dr Hans-Jöchen Vogel (since 1983)

Organizational Structure
The SPD is the most centralized and tightly organized of the major parties in the FRG. The party congress is held every two years and elects a policy-making 42-member National Executive Committee. The Executive Committee is dominated by an inner 13-member Presidium which includes the party's chairman, deputy chairpersons and Bundestag Fraktion leader. Executive Committees similarly function at the Länder level, often displaying considerable autonomy from the federal party headquarters. The party also possesses influential 'youth' (Jusos) and trade union wings and maintains the Friedrich Ebert Foundation as a research/educational organization.

Party Finance
Total income in 1984, DM 210 million, of which 34% was derived from the state in reimbursement for its campaign expenses, 50% from membership fees, 8% from the parliamentary party and 8% came from donations.

Free Democratic Party (FDP)
(Freie Demokratische Partei Deutschlands)

Date of Formation: 1948

Chairman: Dr Otto Graf Lambsdorff (since 1988)
Bundestag Leader: Wolfgang Mischnick
Secretary-General: Cornelia Schmalz-Jacobsen

Organizational Structure
A 400-member federal FDP Congress meets annually and elects a national committee and federal executive, headed by the party chairman, at two-yearly intervals. Länder FDP organizations retain, however, considerable independence. The Friedrich Naumann Foundation is the party; research/educational organization.

Party Finance
Total income in 1984, DM 30 million: 37% from the state, 28% from membership fees, 5% from the parliamentary party, 30% from donations.

Christian Democratic Union (CDU)
(Christlich-Demokratische Union)

Date of Formation: 1945

Chairman: Dr Helmut Kohl (since 1973)
Bundestag Leader: Friedrich Böhl
Secretary-General: Volker Rühe (since 1989)

Organizational Structure
The party, having been formed as a 'Union' of regional conservative groupings, is necessarily decentralized in structure. Biannual congresses are held in each Land to elect executive committees which select Bundestag candidates and frame local policies. A national Congress of 800 delegates chosen by Länder officials meets annually to elect, for a two-year term, a 60-member Executive Committee headed by the party Chairman and a 10-member Presidium. The party also possesses important youth and business wings and maintains the Konrad Adenauer Foundation as a research/educational organization.

Party Finance
Total income in 1984, DM 218 million; 37% from the state, 43% from membership fees, 7% from the parliamentary party, 13% from donations.

Christian Social Union (CSU)
(*Christlich-Soziale Union*)

Date of Formation: 1946

Chairman: Dr Theo Waigel (since 1988)
Secretary-General: Erwin Huber (since 1988)

Organizational Structure
The party, which is based in Bavaria, forms a joint Bundestag Fraktion with the CDU and supports a commonly agreed chancellor-candidate in federal Bundestag elections. Traditionally, the chairman has dominated party policy making, although there exist 2900 local associations which retain considerable autonomy. The Hans Seidel Foundation is the party research/ educational organization.

Party Finance
Total income in 1984, DM 43 million: 32% from the state, 34% from membership fees, 5% from the parliamentary party, 29% from donations.

Green Party
(*Die Grünen*)

Date of Formation: 1980

National Spokespersons: Ludger Volmer, Christine Weiske (since 1991).
Party Manager: Heide Rühle (since 1991).

Organizational Structure
The party, having been formed by bringing together a group of regionally based environmental pressure groups, is unusually decentralized in structure. National congresses are, however, held annually to elect a National Executive Committee which is composed of representatives from all Länder. The party has a unique collective form of national and parliamentary leadership and, until 1991, regularly rotated leadership functions. In addition, the party's statutes require that women be equally represented at all executive levels.

Party Finance
Total income in 1984, DM 43 million: 58% from the state, 9% from membership fees, 20% from the parliamentary party, 13% from donations.

Party of Democratic Socialism (PDS)
(Partei des Demokratischen Sozialismus)

Date of Formation: 1989

Chairman: Gregor Gysi (since 1989)

German National Party (NPD)
(Nationaldemokratische Partei Deutschlands)

Date of Formation: 1964

Chairman: Martin Mussgnug

Party Finance
In 1980 53% of party funds were derived from donations and 33% from membership fees.

Republican Party
(Republikaner Partei)

Date of Formation: 1983

Chairman: Franz Schönhuber (since 1983)

APPENDIX F

Extra-Parliamentary Activity: Extremism and Terrorism

The postwar FRG, concerned to prevent a possible recrudescence of Nazism, has been most vigilant in its efforts to curb political extremism. Radical 'anti-constitutional' parties have been banned and their members have been debarred from public service.[1] However, despite these measures there have been periodic revivals of extremist activity, particularly during periods of cyclical depression. In addition, a new problem of political terrorism emerged during the 1970s among radical far-left groups who remained critical of what they saw as the controlled oppression of the contemporary bourgeois political system and who rejected the use of the ballot box and instead concentrated on direct, destabilizing action.

This left-wing terrorist activity peaked during the 1970s and was centred around the alienated middle-class Baader-Meinhof gang. The leaders of this group were captured and imprisoned in June 1972 and eventually committed suicide in their cells in May 1976 and October 1977. However, splinter groups – for example, the Red Army Faction *(Rote Armee Fraktion)*, the June 2nd Movement and the West Berlin and Düsseldorf-centred Revolutionary Cells – continued the spate of hijacks, kidnappings and murders which reached a chilling crescendo in 1977 with the triple assassinations of the federal prosecutor, Siegfried Buback (April 1977), the banker, Jürgen Ponto (July 1977), and the president of the employers' association, Hanns-Martin Schleyer (October 1977), and the hijacking of a Lufthansa airliner at Mogadishu (October 1977). During the following five years terrorist activities subsided both as a result of the successful efforts of the police and newly established GSG-9 *(Grenzschutzgruppe 9)* anti-terrorist unit in capturing a large proportion of the most wanted terrorists and as a result of a diversion of potential new recruits into alternative channels – for example, into the peaceful Green movement. However, since 1983 terrorism has begun to revive once more, though at a reduced level compared to the mid-1970s. American and NATO military officials, rather than politicians or industrialists, became the new targets for kidnappings and bomb threats in these new campaigns which were sometimes carried out in collaboration with the French terrorist organization *Action Directe*, the Italian *Red Brigades*, the Spanish *Grapo*, the Irish Republican Army and varied Arab-based groups. These incidents moved towards another peak in 1985–7 with the assassinations of the arms-industry executive, Ernst Zimmermann (February 1985), Siemens executive Karl-Heinz Beckurts (July 1986), and the senior civil servant, Gerold von Braunmuhl (October 1986) and the destructive bombings of the US Rhine-Main air base (August 1985) and West Berlin La Belle discothèque (April 1986). Inside the prisons, captured terrorists also engaged in periodic hunger strikes in an attempt to gain preferential conditions.

Outside these narrow terrorist cells, a broader-based and non-violent protest movement emerged on the left and among the young during the 1980s in the form of the huge, anti-nuclear, peace and environmental demonstrations which were organized by the new Green Party. More violent were the squatter riots which erupted in West Berlin and Nuremberg during the spring of 1981 and the anti-police disturbances in Frankfurt in September 1985, which followed the death of Günter Sare (36), who had been knocked over by a water-canon vehicle during a protest against an NPD neo-Nazi party meeting. Terrorist, anarchist (*Autonomen*) and extremist factions attempted to attach themselves to the fringes of these movements, becoming most prominent in the violent anti-nuclear demonstrations of June 1986.

The left-wing terrorist organizations remained, however, insignificant in terms of the numbers involved – the revived Red Army Faction possessing only 25 hard-core activists in 1986 and an estimated 1000 'sympathizers'. It was right-wing extremist organizations which presented the greater danger during the early 1980s. These groups thrived during economic recessions, as the brief rise of the NPD between 1966 and 1969 had previously demonstrated.[2] The years between 1980 and 1985 were the most depressed since the inter-war period, with unemployment rising to more than two million and with the issue of *Gastarbeiter* (foreign workers) producing a xenophobia which could be manipulated by the extreme right. There was thus a small revival in the activities of neo-fascist groups during these years – the most striking of which was their planting of a bomb at the Munich beer festival on 26 September 1980, killing 13 people and injuring more than 200.

However, the far right remained disorganized – there existing in 1981 more than 83 fascist groups with a combined membership of 20000 and 22 fanatical 'action groups' with less than 1000 members. The largest single organization was the NPD with a membership of 15000. The NPD failed, however, to make significant advances in the federal elections of October 1980 and March 1983, capturing barely 0.2% of the national vote. (This represented support from only 70000–90000 voters in total.) The tough immigration stance adopted by the Kohl administration and, in particular, by interior minister Friedrich Zimmermann, helped, to some extent, to take the sting out of such right-wing extremism between 1982 and 1985. Only from 1986–7, with the emergence of the newly formed far-right Republican Party[3] in Bavaria, which captured 3% of the vote in the Land election of October 1986, and with the tripling in support (to 0.6%) for the NPD in the Bundestag election of January 1987, did the extremist parties show signs of gaining ground.

In general, however, support for extremism remained remarkably limited during the troubled early 1980s. It was rather the more pacific radical groups – the Greens and anti-nuclear organizations – which attracted support and which were tolerated by the political authorities. This was an indication of the growing political maturity of the FRG political system. It also, however, reflected the capacity of the West German economy to cope more successfully than neighbouring countries with the difficulties presented by the economic changes of this period.

As is noted in Chapter 6, from the late 1980s far-right extremist parties, most notably the Republicans, NPD and German People's Union, have enjoyed their most significant revival in support since the mid-1960s. This has been a consequence of the competition in the jobs and housing markets presented by the influx of hundreds of thousands of ethnic German, Übersiedler and Asylanten immigrants. Even more disturbing has been the development of neo-Nazism and racism in the depressed eastern Länder of the new united Germany.

Additionally, western German terrorist organizations, such as the Red Army Faction, have attempted to win a new base of support within the discontented eastern Länder through the assassination of prominent 'capitalists', most brutally Detlev Rohwedder, head of the Treuhandanstalt and the so-called 'manager of German unity', in April 1991. It is feared that they may have received support in these activities from an underground network of former Stasi agents. This is because, since the collapse of the SED regime, it has emerged that East Germany's security service had, for decades, provided support, including training and shelter, for western German and Middle Eastern terrorist organizations. For example, the Stasi has been linked to the 1986 La Belle disco bombing and the Red Army Faction's November 1989 assassination near Frankfurt of Alfred Herrhausen (59), chairman of Deutsche Bank, the FRG's largest financial institution. During 1990–1 a succession of 'most wanted' western German terrorists who had been living in exile in the GDR under new identities were arrested and brought to trial. They have included Susanne Albrecht (39), who, in June 1991, was sentenced to 12 years' imprisonment in connection with the 1977 murder of Jürgen Ponto, a family friend. The FRG police estimates that the Red Army Faction now comprises a hard core of between 15 and 20 'third-generation' activists and has around 300 collaborators and sympathizers.

NOTES

Part One

CHAPTER 2

[1] Bavaria was alone among Länder parliaments in May 1949 in voting against the Basic Law.

[2] The Presidents selected were usually moderate, elderly, centrist figures, whose ability to influence the national debate on policy issues varied with their individual personalities and national standing. The present President, Richard Von Weizsäcker, has been one of the most active and respected Presidents, delivering, in May 1985, on the 40th anniversary of the ending of the Second World War, what became recognized as one of the great speeches of postwar Germany, cautioning his fellow countrymen not to be complacent or forgetful about the nation's past and to guard against a revival in crude nationalist sentiment.

[3] This excluded the 22 'honorary deputies' from West Berlin who lacked a federal vote (*see* Appendix D). The term 'at least' is employed because 'overhang' (*Überhangmandate*) seats were added when a party won more constituency (*Erststimmen*) seats in a Land than was indicated by its list vote. In such circumstances, which resulted from the uneven geographical distribution of a party's support within a Land, the party was entitled to retain all its Erststimmen seats and the Bundestag was accordingly increased in size. (At the 1980 West German election there was one Überhangmandat seat, in 1983 two and in 1987 one.)

[4] Elections could only be called mid-term or more than several months before they were officially due in exceptional circumstances when a deadlock of power emerged in the Bundestag and the President was forced to grant a dissolution. In normal circumstances, however, West German governments, in contrast to British ones, were obliged to see out their full term and were unable to set their own date for opportune early elections.

[5] Of West German legislation, 60% stemmed from the government (three-quarters of such bills becoming law) and a third from the Bundestag (18% becoming law).

[6] Parties were required to form official groups or caucuses termed *Fraktionen* (sing. *Fraktion*) within the Bundestag, with the number of committee chairs and seats to which they were entitled to depending on their Fraktion size.

271

[7] Cabinet ministers in West Germany did not need to be Bundestag deputies, although, usually nearly all were. This enabled a number of technocrat experts, for example Manfred Lahnstein, who was finance minister in the Schmidt government of 1982, to be inducted into the ministerial team. The cabinets themselves were, however, less collegial than their British counterparts, possessing only a weakly developed sub-network of co-ordinative, policy-framing committees. Instead, many key policy decisions were taken at informal gatherings of the coalition party leaders.

[8] The Länder legislatures were all single-chamber bodies with the exception of bicameral Bavaria. In the city states of Bremen, Hamburg and West Berlin, the elected chief executive officer was termed a *Bürgermeister* (mayor) rather than minister-president.

[9] In 1987, the Länder governments employed 1.5 million workers and the lower tier county (*Kreise*) and municipal (*Gemeinden*) authorities 1.0 million. In comparison, the federal government employed 313000 workers. For this reason, federal ministries in West Germany were smaller and less powerful bodies than British central ministries.

[10] West Berlin sent four non-voting delegates to the Bundesrat.

[11] There were more than 30 amendments to the Basic Law between 1949 and 1989. The most important, which were introduced between 1954 and 1956 and 1966 and 1969, were concerned with the new federal armed forces and defining the extent of emergency powers.

[12] A 50% Bundestag countervailing vote was required for bills rejected by a simple majority in the Bundesrat; a 66% vote for bills rejected by a two-thirds majority in the upper house. In addition, if the opposition parties gained a two-thirds majority of seats within the Bundesrat they were entitled to veto **all** legislation passed on from the Bundestag, leaving the federal governing party/coalition needing to muster regular 66% majorities of its own in the lower house to see through its legislation.

[13] Between 1972 and 1980 the Bundesrat successfully vetoed 20 laws (2% of the total) and delayed 72 (8%).

[14] In West Germany, unlike in Britain or the United States, civil servants were not debarred from holding legislative office. Instead, he/she was granted six weeks' paid leave while fighting a campaign and, if elected, was allowed a leave of absence during the term of office. Selection of half the Bundestag through the list system also facilitated the election of skilled bureaucrats who may have lacked the political wiles to have succeeded through a direct hustings route. By the mid-1970s, surveys showed that around 44% of Bundestag deputies were former public employees and 25% were officials of interest groups. In the 1983–7 Bundestag one-third of the deputies were civil servants and a seventh either party or interest-group employees.

CHAPTER 3

[1] The Bundesbank, as a consequence of the establishment of central banks in the BGTD, gained five additional Länder bank-chairmen members on its central council.

[2]   The CSU also found itself attracted by the opportunities of spreading its message into the eastern Länder, establishing informal links with the German Social Union (DSU), a right-wing party which had been formed in the GDR in January 1990 by pastor Hans-Wilhelm Ebeling. It provided electoral support to the DSU, but not being a federal party itself, no formal all-German merger was effected.

Part Two

CHAPTER 4

[1]   Strauss, born in Munich in 1915, had served for 30 years in the Bundestag between 1949 and 1978, holding the offices of minister without portfolio (1953–5), minister of nuclear energy (1955–6) and minister of defence (1956–62) in the administrations of Konrad Adenauer. His federal career suffered a severe setback, however, in 1962 when he was forced to resign as defence minister following the 'Spiegel affair' in which he sanctioned illegal police raids of the *Der Spiegel* newspaper offices in Hamburg and Bonn as a result of its publication of critical reports on West Germany's defence policy. Strauss returned to federal administration between 1966 and 1969, serving as finance minister in Kiesinger's 'Grand Coalition' government. From the 1960s, however, he concentrated increasingly on Bavarian issues, having become chairman of the CSU in 1961.

[2]   These conservative ecologists formed a new, but unsuccessful, grouping, the Ecological Democratic Party in 1981.

[3]   In Baden-Württemberg the Greens, in addition, benefited from the traditional rivalry and enmity between the population of Baden who resisted dominance by the Swabians of Württemberg.

[4]   The Party Law, which operated at both the federal and state level, reimbursed parties for a proportion of their election expenses on a scale determined by the number of votes achieved.

[5]   Coppik and Hansen were subsequently excluded from the SPD's Bundestag *Fraktion* by the party's disciplinary committee in July 1981 and January 1982 respectively and became independents. This prompted the two rebels, following a public meeting attended by 1200 at Recklinghausen (North-Rhine-Westphalia), to form a new left-wing party called the Democratic Socialist Forum (*Forum Demokratische Socialisten*).

[6]   In June 1982 the CDU (including its three votes from Saarland) had a 26–15 majority in the Bundesrat. A victory in Hesse would have tipped the balance over the required 28, to 30–11.

CHAPTER 5

[1] Vogel, born in Göttingen in February 1926 and educated as a lawyer at Munich University, had been appointed SPD Land chairman in Bavaria in 1972 and had been mayor of Munich between 1960 and 1972. Between 1975 and 1981 he had served in the Schmidt cabinet as federal justice minister, before being sent to West Berlin to replace Dietrich Stobbe as mayor in January 1981 with the brief to 'clean-up' and overhaul the unpopular local party machine. Vogel was the first Catholic and southern-based leader of the postwar SPD. (His younger brother Bernhard Vogel was CDU minister-president of Rhineland-Palatinate between 1976 and 1988.)

[2] Opinion polls during the campaign showed that 56% of the population regarded unemployment and 32% the deployment of nuclear weapons as the key electoral issues. Defence was, however, the decisive polarizing 'hinge issue', with SPD supporters – unlike CDU – being evenly split on their attitude towards deployment of Cruise and Pershing-II.

[3] In the large state of North-Rhine-Westphalia, for example, the CDU's vote climbed from 40.6% of the total to 45.8%, pushing the SPD into second position.

[4] In March 1983, by contrast, Helmut Kohl, benefiting from the 'Chancellor bonus' that came from incumbency in the Federal Republic, led his SPD challenger, Hans-Jöchen Vogel, by a respective 44% to 37% approval rating.

[5] Helmut Kohl, born in April 1930 into a Roman Catholic family based in Ludwigshafen (Rhineland-Palatinate), studied law and history at Frankfurt and Heidelberg Universities and worked initially in the chemical industry. A former leader of the CDU's youth wing, in 1959 he was elected to the Rhineland-Palatinate Landtag. He became state minister-president in 1969 and contended for the CDU's Chancellor candidature in 1970.

[6] The November 1979 NATO decision envisaged the stationing of 464 Cruise and 108 Pershing-II ground-launched medium-range nuclear missiles in West Germany from the winter of 1983 as part of a major arms modernization programme. West Germany alone was to deploy Pershing-II missiles which, being able to reach the Soviet Union in 15 minutes compared to the two hours taken by the Cruise, represented a unique threat to the USSR.

[7] The new Republican Party, although describing itself as a 'conservative-liberal party', aligned itself towards the far right of the political spectrum, supporting lower taxes for businesses, compulsory military service and the use of plebiscites.

[8] Raised to DM 5 from 1984.

[9] Unlike the British Labour Party, the SPD does not receive trade-union contributions, such donations being debarred by law.

[10] Under the terms of this new 1984 party law, donations up to 5% of a private person's income or 0.002% of a firm's turnover were tax deductible. This regulation was amended in July 1986.

[11]   Barzel was replaced as Bundestag president in November 1984 by Kohl's close aide Philipp Jenninger, with Wolfgang Schäuble, the former CDU-CSU Bundestag floor leader, being inducted as the new head of the Chancellery and 18th member of the federal cabinet.

[12]   In May 1985 the SPD held 18 votes in the Bundesrat (from North-Rhine-Westphalia, Hesse, Hamburg, Bremen and Saarland), the CDU 18 and the CSU 5.

[13]   Axel Springer, the press magnate who controlled 25% of West Germany's national daily newspaper circulation and who was strongly supportive of the CDU, the free-market economy, the peaceful reunification of Germany and reconciliation with Israel, and who fervently opposed communism and *Ostpolitik*, died on 22 September 1985 at the age of 73.

[14]   The CSU leader, Franz-Josef Strauss, and SDP former leader, Willy Brandt, were also accused of receiving funds from the Flick corporation during this trial.

[15]   The FDP supported sanctions against South Africa and were wary of participation in the 'Star Wars' (space-based anti-ballistic missile system) project. The CSU took a directly contrary line.

[16]   At the 23–25 May Hanover conference motions were carried calling for a 'review' of the need for and safety of nuclear reprocessing at the Wackersdorf plant being built in Bavaria (a project strongly supported by Franz-Josef Strauss); a review of the fast-breeder reactor project at Kalkar (North-Rhine-Westphalia) near the Dutch border; and a freeze on the building of new nuclear power plants until the causes of the Chernobyl accident had been fully assessed.

[17]   The division between *Realos* and *Fundis* has been not just generational, but also regional, with urban branches, such as Hamburg and West Berlin, being notoriously radical. They seek to construct 'alternative coalitions', including feminists, squatters, homosexuals, peace activists, environmentalists, single-parents and the disabled, and propound Marxist-tinged economic programmes, while rural branches, for example Baden-Württemberg, have been more conservative in their approach to economic and social issues.

[18]   They had threatened to sit as independents if they had been forced to rotate their seats. This would have reduced the Greens to only 23 official deputies – insufficient under the West German constitution to qualify as a Bundestag *Fraktion*. They would thus have lost the right to sit on committees and to draw office and campaign funds from the state. Later, in 1986, Bastion rejoined the Greens.

[19]   The Greens, in addition, were given the post of state secretary for women's affairs in Hesse.

[20]   The Hanover conference did, however, bring one victory for the party's 'Realos', with the abandonment of the mid-term Bundestag deputy 'rotation principle'.

[21]   The SPD's disastrous performance in the West Berlin election of March 1985 – picking up only 32% of the poll in a traditional party stronghold – can be attributed to

factional divisions within the local party, its unpopularity as a result of a series of corruption scandals and the successful administrative records of the CDU mayors Richard Von Weizsäcker (who left to become federal president in May 1984) and Eberhard Diepgen.

[22]   Rau, born at Wuppertal in January 1931, first worked as a salesman for a church publishing company and emerged as an early supporter of the pacifist, SPD-convert, Gustav Heinemann. He was elected into the North-Rhine-Westphalia *Landtag* in 1958 and served as mayor of Wuppertal (1970–8) and Land minister for science and research during the 1970s, before rising to become minister-president of North-Rhine-Westphalia in September 1978. In the state elections of both May 1980 and May 1985 Rau succeeded in successively increasing the SPD's share of the Land vote.

[23]   In the summer of 1985 Egon Bahr sighed a draft treaty with the East German Communist Party banning chemical weapons from German soil as an initial step in this new strategy and in October 1986 the two German socialist parties jointly called for the creation of a 94-mile-wide demilitarized nuclear-free zone either side of their respective borders.

CHAPTER 6

[1]   In a separate, but partly related case, the Federal Constitutional Court also finally ruled on changes to the party finance law in July 1986, allowing for individuals or companies to make tax-free political contributions of up to DM 100000 per annum.

[2]   This new, 19th, federal ministry (termed the ministry of the environment, nature conservancy and reactor safety), which was headed by Walter Wallmann (53), the popular mayor of Frankfurt and Land chairman of the CDU in Hesse, took powers away from Friedrich Zimmermann's hard-nosed interior ministry. In October 1986, following rigorous safety checks, the new ministry sanctioned the opening of the Brokdorf pressurized water reactor in Schleswig-Holstein.

[3]   Neue Heimat, which was owned by the DGB's industrial holding company BGAG (*Beteiligungsgesellschaft für Gemeinwirtschaft*), had been formed in 1954 to provide cheap rented housing for the poor and underprivileged. In return for agreeing to invest 96% of its profits in housing, it had been given generous tax concessions and by 1980 owned 330000 homes and controlled an additional 240000. Since 1980, however, the company had fallen prey to unwise property speculations.

[4]   In 1982 the SPD vote in Hamburg had, however, been unduly inflated by contemporary sympathy for deposed Chancellor and 'local hero', Helmut Schmidt.

[5]   In the 1987 election 15.5% of 18–24-year-olds voted for the Greens, 38.1% for the SPD, 37.5% for the CDU-CSU and 8.3% for the FDP.

[6]   In the Green Party women not only formed a high proportion of its elected deputies but also held many of the key executive and policy-making posts. For example, two of the most prominent, powerful and popular figures on the Greens' national executive committee, Petra Kelly and Jutta Ditfurth, were women, while

four of its new six-member Bundestag leadership (including *Fraktion* leader Hannegret Hönes) were also female.

[7]   Strauss, during the coalition negotiations, was offered by Kohl the choice of the finance, interior or defence ministries along with the rank of deputy-chancellor but declined them, deciding to concentrate on his work as minister-president of Bavaria.

[8]   One of the party's leading figures, Dr Otto Lambsdorff (60), seemed likely to later be brought back into the cabinet after being finally cleared by the Bonn court of the charge of accepting bribes from the Flick corporation on 16 February 1987. Lambsdorff was, however, fined DM 180000 (£67000) for tax evasion on gifts he had accepted on behalf of the FDP. Hans Friderichs was fined DM 61500 (£23000) and Eberhard von Brauchitsch given a two-year suspended prison sentence and fined DM 550000 (£204000) for similar tax evasion.

[9]   In particular, they called for a ban to be imposed on marchers who masked their faces. This demand gained strength after *Chaoten* (masked extremists) shot dead two policemen during an environmentalist protest march at Frankfurt airport on 2 November 1987.

[10]   In the January 1987 federal election a majority of voters aged between 18 and 45 years had supported either the SPD or Greens.

[11]   Mathiopoulos, despite impressive academic qualifications, was criticized for not being a member of the SPD and as having previously applied for a post under the CDU minister Heinz Riesenhuber and for currently being engaged to marry a CDU member. She resigned from her post along with Brandt in March 1987.

[12]   The term 'new left' was used to denote a new group of, usually university-educated, white-collar professionals within the party who had adopted a radical stance on the 'post-materialist' issues of nuclear power, the environment and defence and who supported an individualist and libertarian approach to economic and social issues. They differed markedly in both background and outlook from the blue-collar, centrist party workers of the 1960s and early 1970s who supported a firm defence policy and placed major stress on jobs and social welfare.

[13]   Lambsdorff was opposed in this Wiesbaden congress election contest by Frau Irmgard Adam-Schwätzer (46), a former FDP secretary-general and foreign office junior minister, who captured 187 votes to the Count's 211. Frau Adam-Schwätzer was supported by younger, more radical elements within the party who were sympathetic towards the possibility of forming a future federal coalition with the SPD.

Part Three

CHAPTER 7

[1]   Indeed, it was subsequently suggested that a written order from SED leader Honecker to 'shoot if necessary' was ignored by the security supremo Egon Krenz, after receiving an urgent message from Moscow.

2   Mittag, who was subsequently to be blamed by Krenz for gross mismanagement of party and state affairs during these crucial summer months, was expelled from the SED on 23 November 1989, while Herrmann was discharged from its Central Committee on 8 November.

3   Honecker, who had undergone surgery on a malignant kidney tumour on 10 January 1990 and was recuperating in a Church-run home for the handicapped, was placed under house arrest. His health deteriorating, he was transferred to a Soviet military hospital in April 1990. Both he and Mielke were to face charges of treason.

4   Krenz was subsequently expelled from the Communist Party on 21 January 1990. Three months later, he was to have published an exculpatory account of the events of 1989, bearing the title *Wenn Mauern fallen* ('When Walls Fall').

CHAPTER 8

1   De Maizière had replaced Wolfgang Schnur as the leading candidate on the Alliance for Germany's election list in March 1990 after Schnur's reputation had been tarnished by allegations that he had worked for the Stasi for 20 years. Initially, Schnur denied the charges, but on 14 March admitted their truth and resigned as leader of Democratic Awakening. He was the first significant Stasi-linked political victim, though it was suggested that as many as 10% of the new Volkskammer, including Lothar de Maizière, had, at one time, been Stasi informants.

2   This crisis resulted from allegations, subsequently shown to be untrue, that the party's chairman, Ibrahim Böhme, had formerly been a Stasi informant. Though cleared of the charges, Böhme was persuaded to resign and on 1 April 1990 was succeeded by his sombre deputy, pastor Markus Meckel.

3   The SPD also subsequently withdrew from the coalition on 19–20 August 1990. This followed Prime Minister de Maizière's dismissal of Walter Romberg (SPD) as finance minister, who was accused of ineffective leadership and mismanagement.

Part Four

CHAPTER 9

1   East Germany's SED-subservient FDGB trade-union confederation was dissolved in 1990 and its 20 constituent unions subsequently joined the western German DGB. Leading West German trade unions, such as IG Metall, also established new branches in the eastern Länder from the spring of 1990 onwards. This was a prelude to subsequent merger which was effected in 1991, swelling the union's membership by 1 million to 3.6 million. The unionization level in eastern Germany was 90%.

2   The first former SED Politburo member to go on trial after reunification was Harry Tisch. He was found guilty in June 1991 of 'multiple fraud against socialist property' and given a 19-month prison sentence. Having already spent a year in pre-trial custody, he was set free on parole. Earlier, on 13 March 1991, the former SED leader Erich Honecker, along with his wife Margot, was secretly flown to

Moscow by the USSR military, ostensibly for medical treatment. The FRG government seeks his return to Germany to face trial on charges of manslaughter, in connection with the Berlin Wall escapees 'shoot-to-kill' policy.

[3] EC standards for water and air pollution will apply to eastern Germany from 1996, but compliance with its nuclear-safety rules became mandatory at once. Indeed, the eastern Länder were granted temporary exemption from about a fifth of EC rules until the end of 1992. These included regulations on state aid to industries.

[4] Pöhl ostensibly resigned in mid-term for family reasons. However, as a member of the SPD, he had been increasingly at odds with the Kohl administration since the GEMU controversy. His interim replacement was Helmut Schlesinger (66), the bank's vice-president and a renowned inflation fighter. Hans Tietmeyer (59), a former adviser to Chancellor Kohl, became the new vice-president and was set to take over from Schlesinger in 1993.

Part Five
CHAPTER 10

[1] In France, by contrast, 40 nuclear reactors were in operation in 1986, supplying 65% of the country's electricity requirements.

[2] Applications for political asylum, many coming through the 'Berlin hole', rose sharply again, however, in 1985 and 1986 to a level of almost 75000 per annum. They fell back in 1987 (to 57379), but then shot up to 103076 in 1988. This led to further calls for a tightening of the asylum regulations. Thus in March 1989 a visa requirement was introduced for visitors from Yugoslavia (29000 of whom had sought asylum in 1988) and the rights of non-visa-holding Turkish citizens to stop over were ended.

[3] In fact, the 1987 census, the first to be held in the FRG since 1970, revealed a population of 61 million, of whom 4.1 million (6.8%) were non-Germans.

[4] Federal subsidies to the West Germany steel industry ceased in 1986.

[5] Grundig became subject to management by Philips from 1982, after the latter had built up a 31.5% stake in the company.

[6] The manufacturing sector's share of West German output fell from 39% of GNP in 1967 to 33% in 1987 and of employment from 36% to 32% During the same period, the service sector's share of output rose from 45% of GNP to 56%, while agriculture's fell from 4% to 2%.

[7] In 1950 North-Rhine-Westphalia accounted for 42% of West Germany's GDP, in 1986 only 29%.

[8] In the 1980s the unionization level stood at 25% in Bavaria compared to 40% in North-Rhine-Westphalia and 50% in Saarland.

[9] Since the early 1980s, there has been a revival in the vitality of small companies in the FRG, with a net addition of 50000 new 'start-ups' being registered annually.

[10] In Bavaria Franz-Josef Strauss helped build up the aerospace industry, his state government promoting the European Airbus project and taking (along with the Bremen and Hamburg city-states) the lion's share of a 52% stake in MBB.

[11] Privatization plans for Lufthansa airlines also had to be shelved as a result of the strong opposition of Franz-Josef Strauss, although the federal government did subsequently reduce the extent of its holding from 80% to 50%.

[12] Between 1984 and 1990 the federal government raised DM 10 billion from its privatization sales and handed out DM 50 billion net in income tax relief, reducing the top rate from 56% to 53% and the bottom rate from 22% to 19%. It was less successful in reducing subsidies – paid principally to farmers, coalminers and railway workers – which (federal and regional) rose from 1.8% of GNP in 1982 to 2.2% in 1988. Overall, however, government spending did fall as a proportion of GNP during the 1980s, with, indeed, West Germany being the only OECD country to reduce spending on social security as a share of GNP during this decade.

[13] In 1989, 42% of West German workers belonged to trade unions compared to 40% in Britain and 15–17% in France and the United States. Outside the DGB were 1.3 million trade unionists in the clerical (CAG) and civil servants (DB) labour federations.

[14] In companies with fewer than 2000 employees the unions were entitled to only a third of the seats on the supervisory board.

[15] IG Metall and the OTV put in claims of 9–10% in 1979, but settled for 6.5%, coupled with a lengthening of holiday allowances. In 1980 IG Metall initially demanded an 8% pay rise, but was forced to accept one of only 3.2%.

[16] Membership of the DGB fell from 7.9 million in 1981 to 7.6 million in 1985; 22% of its members were female.

[17] This action, coupled with the promotion of the more militant Franz Steinkühler to full leadership of IG Metall in October 1986, threatened to place in jeopardy West Germany's postwar tradition of peaceful social and industrial co-existence.

Part Six

CHAPTER 11

[1] The FRG-GDR Traffic Treaty of 1972 allowed for the free movement of West German citizens to East Germany to visit relatives and for tourism, subject to compulsory daily currency exchange limits. It only, however, allowed East German pensioners (men over the age of 65, women over the age of 60) to visit West Germany and West Berlin. Thus during the 1970s around 8 million West Germans visited East Germany each year, while only 1.3 million East Germans moved in the opposite direction.

[2]   France and Britain, who also had engineering firms participating in this project, similarly refused to accede to pressure from the United States, forcing President Reagan to eventually back down.

[3]   In consequence of this deterioration in relations, only 25 000 East Germans were allowed to leave and resettle in West Germany during 1985 and only 20 000 during 1986.

APPENDIX F

[1]   Recently, however, there have been signs of a wish to relax these *Berufsverbot* (professional ban) job-vetting rules (which were originally introduced in January 1972), with the Lafontaine Saarland government, for example, having ended the political vetting of public employees and FRG courts proving less willing to uphold dismissals on political grounds.

[2]   The NPD (*Nationaldemokratische Partei Deutschlands* – National Democratic Party) had been formed in November 1964 out of a merger of the DRP (*Deutsche Reichs Partei*) and GDP (*Gesamtdeutsche Partei*). Between November 1966 and April 1968 it gained representation in the majority of Länder, capturing 9.8% of the vote in Baden-Württemberg, and enjoyed considerable support from lower-middle-class groups, small towns and rural areas during a period when agriculture was depressed and there was considerable public alienation and antipathy towards the newly formed 'Grand Coalition'. The party's vote fell, however, to 4.3% in the September 1969 federal election and, since it failed to enter the Bundestag, its support rapidly drained away at the CDU and CSU during the 1970s. In September 1972 the NPD captured only 0.6% of the national vote and by this date the 'flash party' had lost representation in all the Landtage.

[3]   The Republican Party, which included former CSU deputies was, by 1986, led by Franz Schönhuber, a former Nazi Waffen-SS officer, and claimed an initial membership of 4000 (80% of whom were in Bavaria). It opposed trade unions, membership of the EC and sought to repatriate immigrants.

ABBREVIATIONS, GLOSSARY OF GERMAN TERMS AND ADDITIONAL BIOGRAPHICAL INFORMATION

Abgrenzung – East German policy of 'ideological delimitation' instituted by Erich Honecker.

Adenauer, Konrad (1876–1967) – Chancellor 1949–63 and dominating figure in West German politics and the CDU during the first postwar decade. Born into a lower middle-class Cologne family, he trained as a lawyer and served as a 'Centre Party' mayor of Cologne (1917–33) during the Weimar period. He gained a reputation as a firm opponent of Nazism during the 1930s.

AFD – Alliance for Germany. Conservative coalition which contested the March 1990 Volkskammer elections.

AIDS – Acquired Immune Deficiency Syndrome.

APO (Ausserparlamentarische Opposition) – The controlling body behind the student protest movement of the mid and late 1960s.

Asylanten – Non-ethnic German immigrants seeking asylum in the FRG.

Aussiedler – Ethnic German immigrants from Eastern Europe, excluding GDR, to the Federal Republic.

BDA (Bundesvereinigung der Deutschen Arbeitgeberverbände) – Confederation of German Employers' Associations: President Dr Klaus Murmann. The BDA is particularly concerned with social questions and industrial relations issues affecting employers.

BDI (Bundesvereinigung der Deutschen Industrie) – Confederation of British Industry. The BDI is closely linked to the BDA and concentrates on economic issues of concern to industrialists.

Beamte (pl. –n) – Career civil-servant with special privileges and responsibilities.

Berufsverbot ('Professional Ban') – Job-vetting rules for public service introduced in 1972 to exclude members of anti-constitutional groupings.

BFD – League of Free Democrats of East Germany.

BFV (Bundesamt für Verfassungsschutz: Office for the Protection of the Constitution) – Internal counter-intelligence agency.

BGTD – Beigetretne Teile Deutschlands ('Newly Adhered Parts of Germany'). The eastern German Länder.

BHE (Block der Heimatvertriebenen und Entrechteten: 'League of those expelled from their homeland and deprived of their rights') – Expellees Party formed in 1950. It gradually lost support to and was absorbed by the CDU during the 1950s.

BMW – Bayerische Motoren Werke: Munich-based quality car manufacturer.

BND (Bundesnachrichtendienst) – Federal Counter-Intelligence Service. Concerned with foreign espionage.

Brandt, Willy (1913–   ) – Born Herbert Ernst Karl Frahm, the illegitimate son of a Lübeck shopgirl, he joined the SPD at the age of 16 in 1929 and became an active opponent of Nazism. During the Third Reich era he was forced into exile in Norway, where he changed his name and became a resistance leader. He returned to Germany after the war and based himself in West Berlin, becoming its mayor in 1957 and holding office during the 1958 airlift and 1961 Berlin Wall crisis. Brandt was appointed chairman of the SPD in 1964 (holding the post till 1987) and served as foreign minister during the 1966–9 'Grand Coalition' and as Chancellor between 1969–72, establishing the reputation as the architect of Ospolitik.

Bund (pl. –e) – Federation. Receiving all the revenue from petrol and spirit duties, plus stipulated shares of income tax (42.5%), corporation tax (50%) and VAT (65%), the Bund is responsible for 38% of public spending.

Bundesbank – Germany's central bank. Based in Frankfurt, the country's financial capital, it was established in 1957 and has control of monetary policy. It has the duty of maintaining price stability and defending the value of the currency. Its president and board of directors are appointed by the federal government for secure eight-year terms and policy is framed by a central council, which also includes the presidents of the central banks of the Länder. The Bundesbank is considered to be one of the world's most independent central banks, the federal government having only the authority to ask for decisions to be postponed for two weeks.

Bundesrat – Upper chamber of federal parliament composed of 69 representatives drawn from Länder governments.

Bundestag – Lower, popularly elected, chamber of federal parliament (Diet). It is composed of 662 deputies and meets in plenary session about 60 times a year.

Bundesverfassungsgericht – Federal Constitutional Court. An independent 16-member constitutional watchdog.

Bundesversammlung – Federal convention composed of Bundestag deputies and an equal number of Landtage representatives which is specially convened to elect the Federal President.

Bundeswehr – Federal German army.

Bürgerinitiative (pl. –n) – Citizens' Initiative Group (Local Pressure Group).

Bürgermeister – City mayor.

Bürgerschaft – City parliament.

CAP – Common Agriculture Policy of the EC, involving a system of price subsidies to maintain agricultural production.

CDU – Christian Democratic Union.

Comecon – Council for Mutual Economic Assistance. Eastern bloc economic organization established in 1949.

CSCE – Conference on Security and Co-operation in Europe. A 35-member grouping, including the United States and Soviet Union, which met in Helsinki in 1975 and Paris in November 1990 to reach agreement on co-operation in security, human rights, economics, science and technology.

CSU – Christian Social Union.

DA – Democratic Awakening.

DBD – Democratic Peasants' Party of (East) Germany.

Democratic Centralism – Disciplined obedience to decisions taking by superior party agencies. The governing principle of Leninist communism.

Deutsche Mark – (West) German currency unit. In 1976 there were 2.52 DM per US $, in 1980, 1.82, and in 1991, 1.5.

DFB – Democratic Women's League of (East) Germany.

DGB (Deutsche Gewerkschaftsbund) – FRG trade union confederation: total membership 7.8 million (1989), President Heinz-Werner Meyer.

DKP – (West) German Communist Party (since 1968).

DP (Deutsche Partei) – German Party. A conservative party drawing strong support from Protestants in Lower Saxony and Bremen during the 1950s. It was gradually absorbed by the CDU.

DSU – German Social Union.

DVU – German People's Union.

EC – European (Economic) Community. Formed following March 1957 Treaty of Rome.

ECU – European Currency Unit, based on the composite value of different EC currencies. In 1991 there were two Deutschmarks per ECU.

EMS – European Monetary System of fixed exchange rates. Established in 1979.

Erhard, Ludwig (1897–1977) – Chancellor 1963–6 and finance minister 1949–63, he was the architect of the postwar West German 'economic miracle'. The son of a North Bavarian

Catholic farmer turned haberdasher and a Protestant mother, he was brought up as a Protestant and, after studying economics at Nuremberg's Handelshochschule, worked in the Institute of Market Research during the interwar period. His career was held back during the 1930s by his refusal to join the local Nazi party, but took off during the 1945–9 American occupation era when he was placed in charge of financial planning for the Frankfurt economic council. He resigned as Chancellor in 1966 when his party and coalition colleagues refused to support his proposal to increase taxes at a time of economic difficulty.

Erststimme (pl. –n) – First vote cast in FRG elections which is used to elect constituency members on a first-past-the-post basis.

FDGB – Confederation of Free German (GDR) Trade Unions.

FDJ – Free (East) German Youth Movement.

FDP – Free Democratic Party.

Finanzausgleich – System of horizontally adjusting the vertical tax shares given to each state to take account of population and social needs.

Finanzplanungsrat – Financial Planning Council, which helps co-ordinate economic activity at the federal and Länder level.

First Reich – AD 769–911 Carolingian Empire.

Fourth Reich – Term sometimes used to describe the postwar West German Federal Republic.

Fraktion (pl. –en) – Party caucus of a size equivalent to at least 5% of the Bundestag's membership on which basis committee seats and chairs are assigned.

FRG – Federal Republic of Germany (West Germany).

Fundi – Fundamentalist member of the Greens' movement.

FWG – Independent Electors' Associations.

GAL – Green Alternative List. Lists put up by environmentalists in a number of Länder.

Gastarbeiter – Foreign workers brought into the FRG from southern Europe during the 1950s and 1960s 'miracle years'.

GAZ (Grüne Aktion Zukunft) – Moderate environmentalist party led by Herbert Gruhl and based in Baden-Württemberg.

G7 – Group of seven leading industrial nations: Britain, Canada, France, Germany, Italy, Japan and the United States.

GDP – Gross domestic product. Measure of the total domestic output of a nation. Includes exports, but not imports.

GDR – German Democratic Republic (East Germany).

Gemeinde (pl. –n) – Municipality. Receiving all the revenue from property and local business taxes, plus a 15% share of income tax, gemeinden, along with kreise, are responsible for a quarter of total public spending.

GEMU – German Economic and Monetary Union. Achieved on 1 July 1990.

Genscher, Hans-Dietrich (1927–   ) – Born in Halle, formerly in East Germany, Genscher settled in the Federal Republic in 1952 and became a leading member of the FDP. He was elected a Bundestag deputy in 1960 and served as federal interior minister between 1969 and 1974, before being appointed Vice-Chancellor and foreign minister in 1974: posts he has held ever since. Genscher was chairman of the FDP between 1974 and 1985 and remains an influential party strategist. A committed supporter of Ostpolitik detente, he was a key architect of reunification.

Glasnost – 'Public openness'. Movement for greater frankness in the Soviet media encouraged by Mikhail Gorbachev from 1986 onwards.

GNP – Gross national product. Total value of the final goods and services produced in the economy, including income from abroad minus income earned by foreign investors.

Grundgesetz – The 1949 'Basic Law' constitution of the Federal Republic.

Guillaume, Günter – A former East German Army officer, Guillaume came to the Federal Republic in 1956 as a 'refugee', joined the SPD (1957) and worked his way up to become a close aide to Willy Brandt in the Federal Chancellery, handling secret and sensitive documents. His unmasking as an East German spy in April 1974 forced the resignation of Willy Brandt as Chancellor in May 1974.

Heinemann, Gustav (1899–1976) – President of the Federal Republic 1969–74. Originally a member of the CDU and minister of the interior in the first Adenauer cabinet of 1949, he resigned, being a pacifist, over the question of West German rearmament in 1950 and formed his own neutralist party, before later joining the SPD. He served as justice minister in the 1966–9 'Grand Coalition'.

Honecker, Erich (1912–   ) – Leader of the ruling SED in East Germany between 1971 and 1989. Having been born in the Saarland in West Germany, he was a supporter of Ostpolitik.

INF – Intermediate-range nuclear forces.

Judos – Young Democrat section of FDP.

Junker – Large, estate-owning landlord during Second Reich era.

Jusos – Young Socialist section of the SPD.

Kaiser – German Emperor during the Second Reich.

Kanalarbeiter ('Channel Worker') – Member of moderate grouping, loyal to the leadership, within the SPD.

Kiesinger, Kurt (1904–88) – Chancellor of the Federal Republic 1966–9. He was born near Stuttgart and was brought up as a Catholic (his father was a Protestant and his mother a Catholic). He trained as a lawyer and was a member, although not active, of the Nazi Party between 1933–45. After the war he joined the newly formed CDU and served as minister-president of his native Baden-Württemberg between 1958–66. He was a member of the Bundestag between 1949–58 and 1969–80, aligning himself to the liberal wing of the CDU.

Konjunkturrat – Counter-cyclical advisory council for economic development.

Konzertierte Aktion ('Concerted Action') – System of tripartite discussions between government, business and trade union leaders which sought, during the 1970s, to establish a framework within which wage bargaining and industrial investment decisions could be rationally made.

KPD – German Communist Party (1918–56). It was formed from the USPD.

Kreis (pl. –e) – County.

Land (pl. Länder) – Constituent state of the Federal Republic. Receiving all the revenue from car and capital taxes, plus a stipulated share of income tax (42.5%), corporation tax (50%) and VAT (35%), the Länder are responsible for 37% of public spending.

Landtag (pl. –e) – State assembly.

LDC – Lesser developed country.

LDPD – Liberal Democratic Party of (East) Germany.

Leverkusen Circle – Leftist trade union and Jusos grouping within the SPD.

Machtwechsel – Changeover in political power.

MBB – Messerschmitt-Bölkow-Blohm. The FRG's largest aerospace company. In 1990 it was acquired by Daimler-Benz and merged with Dornier to form Deutsche Aerospace.

MDB – Mitglied des Bundestages (Member of the Bundestag).

Mitbestimmung – Industrial co-determination, involving the co-option of workers' leaders on to boards of management.

Mittelstand (pl. –stände) – Small and medium-sized, niche firms. Highly flexible and often family-owned, much of the success of the postwar FRG economy has been attributed to such enterprises. In

1989 a half of the FRG's GDP was derived from and two-thirds of its workforce were employed in companies with up to 500 workers apiece.

MTU – Motoren-und-Turbinen-Union. Aerospace firm which is now part of the Daimler-Benz conglomerate.

NATO – North Atlantic Treaty Organization. The grouping of West European nations with the United States and Canada in April 1949 to work together to safeguard the security of Europe. West Germany joined the organization in 1955.

NDPD – National Democratic Party of (East) Germany.

Neutralos – Centrist faction within the Greens.

NICS – Newly Industrialized Countries (particularly of SE Asia).

Nomenklatura – System of vetted appointments to leading administrative, military and managerial positions within communist states.

Nordlichter ('Northern light') – Term given to liberal, often Protestant, members of CDU based in northern Germany.

NPD – National Party of Germany (since 1964).

OECD – Organization for Economic Co-operation and Development. Paris-based grouping which comprises the 24 leading Western nations, including Japan, Australia and New Zealand from the southern hemisphere.

OPEC – Organization of Petroleum Exporting Countries.

Ossi – East German.

Ostpolitik ('Eastern policy') – Policy of improving relations with Eastern Europe launched by Brandt in 1966.

OTV – Gewerkschaft Öffentliche Dienste, Transport und Verkehr. FRG public services and transport workers' union. Membership 1.2 million in 1988.

Parteiengesetz – 1967 Party Law regulating the position of parties and providing for partial state financing.

Parteienstaat ('Party State') – Term used to describe the FRG political system as a result of the privileged position given to political parties.

PDS – Party of Democratic Socialism. Successor to SED.

Perestroika – 'Economic restructuring'. Slogan used by the USSR leader Mikhail Gorbachev to describe his economic modernization programme.

PLO – Palestine Liberation Organization.

PR – Proportional Representation.

Realo – Pragmatic member of the Greens' movement.

Reichstag – Elected federal parliamentary assembly during Second Reich and Weimar (1919–33) periods.

Schiller, Karl (1911–   ) – A former, though non-active, member of the Nazi Party during the 1930s, he became an economics professor at Hamburg University after the war and served as a successful SPD minister of finance between 1966 and 1972. He resigned in June 1972 as a result of policy differences with Chancellor Brandt.

Second Reich – 1871–1919 German Empire period.

SED – East German Communist Party, (1946–89).

Soziale Marktwirtschaft ('Social Market Economy') – Postwar system of capitalist/Christian Socialist form of economic management in the Federal Republic.

Spartakus Revolution – January 1919 uprising in Berlin by the extreme left USPD which was crushed by moderate members of the SPD and military forces.

SPD – Social Democratic Party.

SRP (Sozialistische Reichspartei) – Far-right Socialist Reich Party, led by Major Remer (who had helped to foil a plot against Hitler in 1933). It was banned in 1952.

Staatssekretar (pl. –e) – Chief civil-servant at the head of a ministry.

Stasi – East German ministry for state security.

Third Reich – 1933–45 Nazi (National Socialist) period.

Treuhandanstalt – Trust agency established in March 1990 to oversee the restructuring and privatization of eastern Germany's 8000 state-owned industries.

Übersiedler – East German immigrants to western Germany.

Überhangmandat (pl. –e) – Additional seat gained by a party winning more seats in a Land in constituency contests than was indicated by its overall List vote.

USPD (Unabhängige Socialdemokratische Partei Deutschlands) – Far-left breakaway grouping from SPD in 1917 which was the forerunner of the KPD.

USSR – Soviet Union.

Vermittlungsausschuss – Joint conciliation committee of Bundesrat (one from each Land) and Bundestag representatives established to iron out differences over legislation.

Volkskammer – East German parliament (1949–90).

Volkspartei (pl. –en) – A 'catch all' party drawing support from a wide range of social groupings.

Warsaw Pact – Eastern bloc defence organization established in 1955 and disbanded in 1991.

Wehner, Herbert (1906–90) – Born in Dresden, he joined the German Communist Party in 1927 and was forced into exile during the Nazi era. On his return to Germany in 1946, he joined the SPD in Hamburg and became party manager during the late 1950s. During the 1966–9 'Grand Coalition' he served as minister for inter-German affairs, emerging as a strong advocate of Ostpolitik detente, and between 1969–83 acted as the SPD's Bundestag Fraktion leader and as an influential party technician.

Wehrmacht – German Army during the Third Reich.

Wende – Political, economic and social turning point.

Wessi – West German.

WEU – Western European Union. A consultative forum for West European defence issues, established in 1955.

Zollverein – German free-trading union established during the Second Reich.

Zweitstimme (pl. –n) – Second vote at elections which is used to determine the number of seats a party will receive in each Land

BIBLIOGRAPHY

GENERAL GERMAN POLITICS

K.L. Baker, R.J. Dalton & K. Hildebrandt (eds)—*Germany Transformed: Political Culture and the New Politics* (Cambridge, Mass.: Harvard University Press, 1981)

K. von Beyme—*The Political System of the Federal Republic of Germany* (Aldershot: Gower, 1983)

K. von Beyme & M. Schmidt (eds)—*Policy and Politics in the Federal Republic of Germany* (Aldershot: Gower, 1985)

C. Burdick, H.A. Jacobsen & W. Kudzus (eds)—*Contemporary Germany: Politics and Culture* (Epping: Bowker, 1984)

D. Childs & J. Johnson—*West Germany: Politics and Society* (London: Croom Helm, 1981)

D.P. Conradt—*The German Polity* (New York: Longman, 4th edn, 1986)

L. Edinger—*West German Politics* (New York: Columbia University Press, 1986)

N. Johnson—*State and Government in the Federal Republic of Germany: The Executive at Work* (Oxford: Pergamon, 2nd edn, 1983)

P. Katzenstein—*Policy and Politics in West Germany: The Growth of a Semi-sovereign State* (Philadelphia: Temple University Press, 1987)

R.F. Nyrop (ed)—*Federal Republic of Germany: A Country Study* (Washington DC: The American University, 1982)

W.E. Paterson & G Smith (eds)—*The West German Model: Perspectives on a Stable State* (London: Cass, 1981)

W.E. Paterson & D. Southern—*Governing Germany* (Oxford: Basil Blackwell, 1991)

G. Smith & H. Doring (eds)—*Party Government and Political Culture in Western Germany* (London: Macmillan, 1982)

G. Smith—*Democracy in Western Germany: Parties and Politics in the Federal Republic* (Aldershot: Gower, 3rd edn, 1986)

THE FEDERAL SYSTEM

P.M. Blair—*Federalism and Judicial Review in West Germany* (Oxford: Clarendon Press, 1981)

WEST GERMAN POLITICAL PARTIES

General

T. Burkett & S. Padgett—*Parties and Elections in West Germany: The Search for a New Stability* (London: C Hurst, 1986)

291

E. Kolinsky—*Parties, Opposition and Society in West Germany* (London: Croom Helm, 1984)

The Christian Democrats

G. Pridham—*Christian Democracy in Western Germany* (London: Croom Helm, 1977)

The Social Democrats

G. Braunthal—*The West German Social Democrats, 1969–1982: Profile of a Party in Power* (Boulder, Col.: Westview Press, 1983)

W. Graf—*The German Left since 1945* (Cambridge: Oleander Press, 1976)

S. Miller & H. Potthoff—*History of the German Social Democratic Party from 1848 to the Present* (Leamington Spa: Berg, 1986)

The Green Movement

R. Bahro—*From Red to Green* (London: Verso Books, 1984)

W. Hulsberg—*The German Greens: A Social and Political Profile* (London: Verso, 1988)

P. Kelly—*Fighting for Hope* (London: Chatto & Windus, 1984)

E. Kolinsky (ed)—*The West German Greens: Policy Making and Party* (Oxford: Berg, 1989)

E. Papadakis—*The Green Movement in West Germany* (London: Croom Helm, 1984)

ELECTIONS

K.H. Cerny (ed)—*Germany at the Polls: The Bundestag Election of 1976* (Washington DC: American Enterprise Institute, 1978)

M. Kaase & K. von Beyme (eds)—*Elections and Parties: Socio-political Change in the West German Federal Election of 1976* (London: Sage, 1978)

EXTRA-PARLIAMENTARY ACTION AND TERRORISM

S. Aust—*The Baader-Meinhof Group* (London: The Bodley Head, 1987)

R. Burns & W. van der Will—*Protest and Democracy in West Germany: Extra-Parliamentary Opposition and the Democratic Agenda* (London: Macmillan, 1988)

WEST GERMAN POLITICAL HISTORY

General

M. Balfour—*West Germany: A Contemporary History* (London: Croom Helm, 1982)

V.R. Berghahn—*Modern Germany* (Cambridge: Cambridge University Press, 2nd edn, 1987)

E. Hartrich—*The Fourth and Richest Reich* (London: Macmillan, 1980)

T. Prittie—*The Velvet Chancellors* (London: Frederick Muller, 1979)

The Pre-Schmidt Era

W. Brandt—*People and Politics: The Years 1960–75* (London: Collins, 1978)

M. Donhoff—*Foe into Friend: The Makers of the New Germany, from Konrad Adenauer to Helmut Schmidt* (London: Weidenfeld & Nicolson, 1982)

A. Grosser—*Germany in Our Time: A Political History of the Post-War Years* (Harmondsworth: Penguin, 1974)

The Schmidt Era

J. Carr—*Helmut Schmidt: Helmsman of Germany* (London: Weidenfeld & Nicolson, 1985)

H. Schmidt—*Men and Powers* (London: Jonathan Cape, 1990)

The Kohl Era

P. Merkl (ed)—*The Federal Republic of Germany at Forty* (Cambridge: Cambridge University Press, 1989)

G. Smith, W.E. Paterson & P.H. Merkl (eds)—*Developments in West German Politics* (Basingstoke: Macmillan, 1989)

P. Wallach & G. Romoser (eds)—*West German Politics in the Mid-Eighties* (New York: Praeger, 1985)

R. von Weizsäcker—*A Voice for Germany* (London: Weidenfeld & Nicolson, 1987)

EAST GERMAN POLITICS AND HISTORY

D. Childs (ed)—*Honecker's Germany* (London: Allen & Unwin, 1985)

D. Childs—*The GDR: Moscow's German Ally* (London: Unwin Hyman, 2nd edn, 1988)

D. Childs, T.A. Baylis & M. Rueschemeyer (eds)—*East Germany in Comparative Perspective* (London: Routledge, 1989)

A.W. McCardle & A.B. Boenau (eds)—*East Germany: A New German Nation under Socialism?* (New York: University Press of America, 1984)

M. McCauley—*The German Democratic Republic since 1945* (London: Macmillan, 1983)

C.B. Scharf—*Politics and Change in East Germany: An Evaluation of Socialist Democracy* (Boulder, Col.: Westview Press, 1984)

M. Simmons—*The Unloved Country* (London: Abacus, 1989)

R. Woods—*Opposition in the GDR under Honecker, 1971–85* (Basingstoke: Macmillan, 1986)

GERMAN UNIFICATION

J.F. Dunn—*A New Germany in a New Europe* (London: HMSO, 1991)

M. Frankland—*The Patriots' Revolution* (London: Sinclair Stevenson, 1991)

N. Hawkes (ed)—*Tearing Down the Curtain: The People's Revolution in Eastern Europe* (London: Hodder & Stoughton, 1990)

D. Marsh—*The New Germany* (London: Century, 1990)

The Times Guide to Eastern Europe (London: The Times, 1990)

THE GERMAN ECONOMY AND SOCIETY

General

J. Ardagh—*Germany and the Germans* (London: Hamish Hamilton, 1987)

D. Childs—*East Germany to the 1990s: Can it Resist Glasnost?* (London: Economist Intelligence Unit Special Report No. 1118, 1988)

P. Katzenstein (ed)—*Industry and Politics in West Germany* (Ithaca: Cornell University Press, 1989)

E. Kolinsky—*Women in West Germany: Life, Work and Politics* (Oxford: Berg, 1989)

J. Leaman—*The Political Economy of West Germany, 1945–85* (Basingstoke: Macmillan, 1988)

A. Markovits (ed)—*The Political Economy of West Germany* (New York: Praeger, 1982)

R.C. Rist—*Guestworkers in Germany: The Prospects for Pluralism* (New York: Praeger, 1978)

The Trade Unions

V. Berghahn & D Karsten—*Industrial Relations in West Germany* (Oxford: Berg, 1987)

A.S. Markovits—*The Politics of West German Trade Unions* (Cambridge: Cambridge University Press, 1986)

FOREIGN POLICY

S. Bulmer & W. Paterson—*West Germany and the European Community* (London: Unwin Hyman, 1987)

C. Clemens—*Reluctant Realists: The CDU/CSU's Adaptation of West German Ostpolitik* (Durham, NC: Duke University Press, 1989)

W.E. Griffiths—*The Ostpolitik of the Federal Republic of Germany* (Cambridge, Mass: MIT Press, 1978)

W.L. Kohl & G. Basevi (eds)—*West Germany: A European and Global Power* (Lexington: Gower, 1981)

A.J. McAdams—*East Germany and Detente: Building Authority after the Wall* (Cambridge: Cambridge University Press, 1985)

E. Moreton (ed)—*Germany Between East and West* (Cambridge: Cambridge University Press, 1986)

E. Schulz et al—*GDR Foreign Policy* (New York: ME Sharpe Inc., 1982)

H. Simonian—*The Privileged Partnership: Franco-German Relations in the European Community, 1969–1984* (Oxford: Clarendon, 1985)

A. Stent—*From Embargo to Ostpolitik: The Political Economy of West German-Soviet Relations, 1955–1980* (Cambridge: Cambridge University Press, 1982)

S.F. Szabo—*The Changing Politics of German Security* (London: Pinter, 1990)

CHRONOLOGY OF RECENT EVENTS: 1976–91

1976—Oct, Bundestag elections, CDU-CSU, led by Helmut Kohl, gain 48.6% of vote, but SPD-FDP stay in power. Nov, Strauss's CSU temporarily break with CDU.

1977—Genesis of Green Party. Jan, Carter new US President. Sept, FRG terrorist outrages peak with kidnap of Schleyer and Lufthansa hijack: firm Schmidt emerges as the 'hero of Mogadishu'.

1978—July, Bonn summit, Schmidt launches DM 13 billion reflation package. Nov, six-week steel strike in FRG for 35-hour week.

1979—Jan, EMS begins operation. March, Three Mile Island nuclear power station accident in the USA. July, Strauss adopted as CDU-CSU chancellor-candidate. Oct, Greens gain first seats in a Landtag (Bremen). Nov, Iran-Iraq war leads to oil price hike. Dec, Soviet Union invade Afghanistan.

1980—Polish crisis. Oct, SPD-FDP coalition led by Helmut Schmidt and Hans-Dietrich Genscher win Bundestag election, CDU-CSU vote falls to 44.5%. Dec, new immigration controls in FRG.

1981—Jan, Reagan new US President. May, Mitterrand new French President. SPD lose in West Berlin stronghold. Dec, Chancellor Schmidt meets Erich Honecker in the GDR; martial law is declared in Poland. Unemployment soars to 1.7 million in FRG.

1982—Sept, Lambsdorff 'memorandum'. Oct, Kohl (CDU) with FDP support topples Schmidt and becomes FRG Chancellor. Schmidt resigns as SPD leader to be replaced by Hans-Jöchen Vogel.

1983—March, CDU-CSU-FDP win Bundestag election. Greens win 27 seats. Oct, peace demonstrations in FRG. Nov, SPD conference opposes Pershing deployment, but Bundestag votes in favour. Kiessling and Flick scandals. New FRG immigrant repatriation scheme.

1984—May, seven-week IGMetall strike leads to 38½-hour week in FRG; Von Weizsäcker elected federal president. June, FDP fail to win seats in Euro-election; Greens win 8% of vote. Lambsdorff (FDP), and in Oct., Barzel (CDU) resign over 'Flick affair'.

1985—Feb, Bangemann becomes FDP leader. March, Greens 'rotate' Bundestag deputies; accession to power of Mikhail Gorbachev in Soviet Union. May, SPD, led by Johannes Rau, gain huge victory in North-Rhine-Westphalia. Sept, Tiedge spy scandal. Dec, Greens-SPD coalition formed in Hesse.

1986—Unemployment begins to fall below 2.3 million in FRG. April, Chernobyl nuclear disaster in the Soviet Union; Erich Honecker is re-elected SED general-secretary by 11th Congress. May, Kohl cleared of perjury. June, CDU retain control of Lower Saxony. Aug, Rau elected chancellor-candidate for the SPD. Sept, Neue Heimat affair. Oct/Nov, setback for SPD in Bavaria and Hamburg election: significant advances by the Greens, helped by Rhine river chemical disaster.

1987–Jan, CDU-CSU-FDP coalition re-elected to power in Bundestag election: CDU-CSU and SPD vote falls, FDP and Greens gain substantial support. Feb, Flick trial ends: Lambsdorff cleared of bribery. March, new Kohl cabinet sworn in and tax-reforming legislation programme proposed; resignation of Willy Brandt as SPD chairman. April, CDU-FDP defeat SPD in Hesse Land election. May, first census for 15 years is held in FRG; SPD-FDP (in August) and CDU-FDP coalition governments are formed after elections in Hamburg and Rhineland-Palatinate; the Fundis strengthen their hold over the Greens' national executive at the Duisburg congress. June, Hans-Jöchen Vogel is elected SPD chairman. Aug, Rudolf Hess dies in Spandau prison. Sept. CDU vote falls sharply in Bremen and Schleswig-Holstein Länder elections; Schleswig-Holstein minister-president Barschel resigns as a result of 'Waterkantgate' scandal; the GDR leader Erich Honecker visits West Germany officially for the first time. Oct, federal tax-reform package is agreed; 'Black Monday' Wall Street crash. Dec, day of protest against proposed closure of Rheinhausen steelworks; US and USSR sign INF treaty in Washington.

1988—May, SPD is swept to power in Schleswig-Holstein. June, tax reform bill is passed by Bundestag; USSR leader Gorbachev accepts the concept of 'socialist pluralist democracy'. Aug, SPD government in Schleswig-Holstein refuses to allow Brokdorf nuclear plant to re-open. Sept, at its Münster congress, the SPD agrees to establish fixed minimum quotas for party posts and assembly representation. Oct, death of Franz-Josef Strauss, who is replaced by Dr Theodor Waigel as CSU chairman; Count Otto Graf Lambsdorff is elected the new leader of the FDP. Dec, the Greens' Fundi-dominated national executive is forced to resign as a result of financial irregularities.

1989—Jan, CDU-FDP coalition is defeated in West Berlin election: far-right Republicans secure 7.5% of the vote. Feb, USSR withdraws its forces from Afghanistan; Hungary's communists accept the need for a multi-party democracy. March, the Fundis are marginalized at the Greens' Duisburg congress; an SPD-Alternative List 'red-green' coalition is formed in West Berlin; NPD poll strongly in Frankfurt. April, major FRG cabinet reshuffle and policy concessions. May, Hungary removes its barbed-wire border fence with Austria, prompting an outflow of East German refugees; protests in GDR over rigged municipal elections. 3–4 June, massive pro-democracy movement is crushed in Tiananmen Square, Beijing (China). July, Gorbachev propounds new 'Sinatra Doctrine'. 24 Aug, Tadeusz Mazowiecki is elected Prime Minister in Poland, becoming the first non-communist Prime Minister in the Soviet bloc. Aug–Sept, GDR leader Honecker is hospitalized; 4 Sept, weekly protest marches commence in Leipzig. 9 Sept, New Forum is formed. 11 Sept, Hungary allows East Germans to cross into Austria without visa restrictions. 3 Oct, GDR stops travel to Czechoslovakia. 6–7 Oct, Mikhail Gorbachev, visiting East Berlin on GDR's 40th anniversary, urges reform. 9 Oct, police decline to stop major pro-democracy demonstrations in Leipzig. 18 Oct, Honecker resigns as the GDR's Communist Party leader and head of state, being replaced by protégé Egon Krenz. 1 Nov, GDR travel restrictions to Czechoslovakia are lifted. 7–8 Nov, GDR government and ruling party Politburo resign, 'reform communist' Hans Modrow takes over as Prime Minister. 9 Nov, Berlin Wall is re-opened. 10 Nov, 'Action programme' of fundamental reform is unveiled by the GDR Communist Party's Central Committee. 10 Nov–11 Dec, communist hegemony overthrown in Bulgaria. 17 Nov–10 Dec, 'Velvet Revolution' in Czechoslovakia. 28 Nov, Chancellor Kohl unveils three-stage plan for 'German confederation'. 1 Dec, Volkskammer abolishes the SED's constitutionally guaranteed role. 3 Dec, following Communist Party corruption revelations, the SED Politburo and Central Committee resign en masse. 6 Dec, Krenz steps down as GDR head of state. 7 Dec, commencement of Round Table talks in GDR. 8–9 Dec, Gregor Gysi is elected leader of the restyled SED-PDS. 18–20 Dec, West Germany's SPD adopts the new 'Berlin Programme'. 21–25 Dec, Ceausescu regime is overthrown in Romania.

1990—Jan, Stasi headquarters in East Berlin is ransacked by protesters. Feb, government of national responsibility formed in GDR, headed by Modrow. March, the Treuhandanstalt is established to oversee the privatization of eastern Germany's state-owned enterprises; the CDU-dominated Alliance for Germany wins a surprising victory in the GDR's first free general election; Oskar Lafontaine is confirmed as the SPD's chancellor-candidate for the December FRG election. April, 'Grand Coalition' government formed in East Germany, with Lothar de Maizière Prime Minister; Lafontaine is badly wounded following an assassination attempt. May, 'two-plus-four' talks commence in Bonn; GEMU treaty signed by the two Germanies; the SPD, in coalition with the Greens, secure control in Lower Saxony following a Land election. June, Fundis regain control of the Greens' executive. July, economic and monetary union is introduced; Gorbachev and Kohl reach agreement, at Stavropol, that a new, united Germany should be free to join whichever security block it wishes. Aug, the SPD leave de Maizière's coalition government; a Unification Treaty is signed by the two Germanies. Sept, the 'two-plus-four' powers sign the Treaty on the Final Settlement with respect to Germany. Oct, reunification is achieved; the CDU polls strongly in elections for the restored eastern Länder; interior minister Schäuble is paralysed after an assassination attempt. Nov, German reunification is 'blessed' by the CSCE in Paris; Dec, The CDU-CSU-FDP coalition is returned with an increased majority after the first all-German general election; Lothar de Maizière resigns from the cabinet after Stasi-linked accusations.

1991—Jan, Kohl cabinet sworn in; new 'red-green' coalition formed in Hesse after Land election; Lothar Späth resigns as Baden-Württemberg minister-president. March, anti-Kohl demonstrations in eastern Germany, as a third of the region's workforce are either unemployed or on short-time; western German voters are angered by the Kohl administration reneging on its election pledge that taxes would not be raised. April, Detlev Rohwedder, head of the Treuhandanstalt, is assassinated by the Red Army Faction; CDU defeated in Rhineland-Palatinate Land election and a new SPD-FDP coalition is formed, giving the SPD a majority in the Bundesrat; the Greens' congress votes to abandon the rotation of party posts. May, Björn Engholm is elected SPD chairman; Karl Otto Pöhl resigns as Bundesbank president. July, major cuts in state subsidies for miners and farmers announced; CDU polls poorly in Hamburg Land election; Aug, attempted conservative coup to oust Mikhail Gorbachev is foiled, leading to the effective collapse of Soviet communism; the remains of Frederick the Great are reburied in Postdam. Sept, Lothar de Maizière resigns from all his CDU posts and retires from politics; swing to far right in Bremen Land election.

INDEX

Index

National Gathering (*Nationale Sammlung*), 13
National Resistance, 201
National Zeitung, 93
NATO, 15, 17, 42, 48, 49, 50, 51, 57, 59, 60, 63, 66, 78, 79, 80, 92, 106, 163, 165, 166, 167, 245, 248, 249, 250, 251, 255
Nazism, 3, 4, 12–13, 19, 39, 86, 93, 99, 100, 103, 121, 126, 150, 200–1, 235
Nemeth, Miklos, 133
Neue Heimat (New Home) affair, 83, 242
'New Economic System', 120–1
New Forum (*Neues Forum*), 137, 142, 148, 151, 152, 153, 154, 204
NICs, 210, 212, 213, 224, 225, 227, 229, 231
Nigeria, 213
Nixdorf, 231
Nixon, Richard, 245
Nolte, Ernst, 100
nomenklatura system, 23, 118, 191
Norway, 219
nuclear power, 47, 49, 50, 64, 74, 78, 80, 81–2, 84, 192, 194, 217–18
nuclear weapons, 48, 65, 92, 105, 248, 249, 250, 254
Nyers, Rezso, 133

O
OECD, 215
oil price hikes, 41, 48, 123, 210, 211, 212, 216, 227, 230
Ollenhauer, Erich, 16
Olympia Werke, 230, 231
OPEC, 36, 123, 211, 214, 217
Opel, 197, 227, 228, 233, 240, 241
Ortleb, Rainer, 168
Ossi, 27, 134, 135, 178, 180, 190, 191, 193, 200, 201
Ost, Friedhelm, 106
Ostpolitik, 15, 18, 34, 36, 43, 52, 53, 72, 73, 80, 85, 86, 89, 124, 147, 172, 189, 245–6, 247–51
OTV, 110, 240

P
Palestine Liberation Organization (PLO), 41
Parteiengesetz (Party Law), 49, 67
Parteienstaat, 12
party finance, 49, 66–8
Party of Democratic Socialism (PDS), 29, 155–6, 162, 183, 207
peace movement, 49, 65, 74, 136, 250
Pentacon, 198
Peoples' Party (*Volkspartei*), 15
perestroika, 127

Pershing missiles, 49, 52, 59, 65, 74, 78, 80, 92, 249, 250
Pfeiffer, Reiner, 94
Pflugbeil, Sebastian, 151
Philips, 230, 232
Plessey, 231
Pöhl, Karl-Otto, 159–60, 202
Pohl, Wolfgang, 144
Poland, 128, 129, 130, 135, 137, 164, 165, 188, 208, 221, 244, 246, 247, 248, 249, 251
Polish United Workers' (Communist) Party, 128
Political Unification Treaty, 32
Pompidou, Georges, 252
Porsche, 228, 233, 241
Portugal, 253
Potsdam Accord, the, 115
Pozsgay, Imre, 133
Prakla-Seismos, 237
Pravda, 59
privatization, 193, 196, 204, 236–7
Protestant Church, 122, 136, 189, 191
public sector deficit, 197, 202, 211, 214

R
Rau, Johannes
  and the 'red-green' coalition', 108
  as chancellor-candidate, 82–3, 84
  background, 80
  popularity of, 81
Reagan, Ronald, 59, 124, 237, 248, 249, 251
Realpolitik, 40
Red Army, 116, 129, 131, 166, 167
Red Army Faction, 41, 199
refugees, political and economic, 188, 221–2, 251
Reich, Jens, 137
Reiche, Steffen, 153
Republican Party, 97, 98, 102, 103, 164, 171, 175, 179, 207
religious complexion of FRG, 189–90, 220
reunification of Germany, 25–6, 158–69, 244–6
Rheinbraun, 217
Rhine-Ruhr region, 225, 227, 232, 234, 235, 239, 243
Robotron, 198
Rohwedder, Detlev, 199
Romania, 132, 245
Romberg, Walter, 157
Round Table meetings, 150, 154
Rühe, Volker, 29, 107, 174, 205, 206
Ruhfus, Jorgen, 40
Ruhle, Heide, 207

S
Salzgitter, Peine, 225, 236

307

Index